CENTURY TRAVELLERS

CAMEROON
WITH
EGBERT

Dervla Murphy

ARROW BOOKS

Century Travellers

Published by Arrow Books Limited
20 Vauxhall Bridge Road, London SW1V 2SA

An imprint of Random Century Group

London Melbourne Sydney Auckland Johannesburg
and agencies throughout the world

First published in 1989 by John Murray (Publishers) Ltd
Arrow edition 1990
10 9 8 7 6 5 4 3

Front cover illustration: Paul Wright

Printed and bound in Great Britain by
The Guernsey Press Co Ltd
Guernsey, C.I.

ISBN 0 09 972800 1

Contents

Illustrations

For permission to reproduce the above illustrations, the author and publisher would like to thank John Fox (Plates 1–9 and 11–14) and Jaqueline Fox (Plate 10).

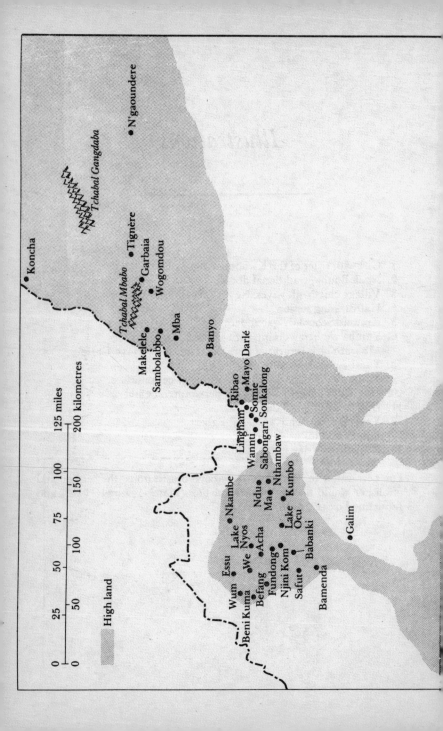

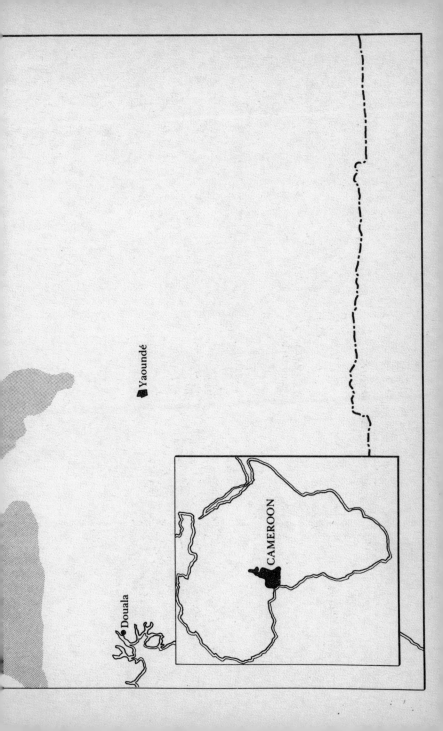

Yaoundé

Douala

CAMEROON

For Jane and David Hughes, who inspired our Cameroonian journey, and for Joy and John Parkinson, and Jacqueline and John Fox, without whom we would not have survived it.

Introduction

CHANCE WAS RESPONSIBLE for our going to Cameroon. During the autumn of 1985 an Anglo-Pakistani couple, based in Kano, invited me to Northern Nigeria. When I hesitated, explaining my dread of West African heat, they assured me that after the rains it would be cool enough – and fertile enough – to trek from Kano to Lake Chad with a pack-horse.

Soon after, a *Sunday Times* interviewer asked me 'Where would you like to go next?' I was then in the middle of writing a book and uninterested in forward-planning. But, when questioned, that Nigerian trek popped out of my unconscious and was in due course announced to the world – or as much of it as reads the *Sunday Times*.

Months later came a letter from Cameroon, its envelope half-obscured by enormous, vivid bird-stamps. It was a delightful echo from the past; thirteen years previously we had stayed with the writers, Jane and David Hughes, in their Coorg (South India) home. Since 1982 they had been based in Cameroon; a friend had sent them that *Sunday Times* interview; they felt sure Cameroon would be much more my scene than Nigeria and urged me to use their Bamenda home as my base while I negotiated for a sound Fulani stallion. I was still immersed in my book but the enthusiasm with which the Hughes described Cameroon penetrated all my defences against distraction. Gratefully I replied, 'See you in March.'

It was then my intention to trek alone. In June 1986 Rachel had left school and migrated to India, to spend six months of her 'in-between' year teaching English to Tibetans and travelling solo. On her return she planned to earn some money in Paris before going up to university, but on hearing of my Cameroonian plan she quickly wrote back asking if she could come too. Like many another foot-loose adolescent, she found the prospect of returning to the First World disconcerting –

something to be postponed for as long as possible. This felt like good news to me. For fifteen years we had been travelling together – most recently, in 1986, to the United States – and in an odd way we seemed to have become a team, despite natural changes in the quality of our relationship.

The tall young Cameroonian in the Holland Park embassy was slender and impassive and spoke no English. He stood behind a small uncluttered desk in a long, sparsely furnished room and scrutinised our passports and return tickets to Douala. Then he gave me six forms to fill in and requested £18; our visas, he said, would be ready for collection in forty-eight hours.

In a much smaller room across the hall three plump ladies sat at huge desks piled with documents and overshadowed by giant filing-cabinets. They all spoke English but were rendered inarticulate by the notion of two white women wandering through the bush with a pack-horse. The senior lady admitted, 'We have no tourist information.' A younger lady suggested, without much conviction, that the nearby Cameroonian Trade Office might be able 'to advise'.

The Trade Office occupied another enormous building but only two staff were visible, a timid hall porter and a Trade Attaché who provided a 'Factsheet' and took umbrage when asked about Cameroon's varieties of malaria. 'Every country has malaria' he snapped. 'But in our country there is malaria only in the cities, where flies breed on garbage. In the bush there is *no* malaria!'

In the tube I read my Factsheet, dated 1 March 1986. It seemed on the whole a lucid document, designed to help businessmen, though I couldn't quite understand why 'Prior Ministry of Finance approval is required for loans contracted abroad by public or private physical or moral person habitually residing in the country.'

The Republic of Cameroon, lying in the Gulf of Guinea, has an area of 183,000 square miles and an estimated population (June 1983) of 9.6 million, of whom 53 per cent were then under twenty years of age. (By March 1987 an estimated 60 per cent were under sixteen.) The 1984–5 per capita income was $820 and the rate of inflation 10 per cent. This means that Cameroon is the second richest, by far, of the Central African states. Only Congo is ahead, with $1,230. Burundi ($240) and Zaire ($170) are more 'normal'. All these are World Bank figures and perhaps not very meaningful if you live in Central Africa.

For the past ten years oil has been Cameroon's most valuable product. Her other main products are coffee, cocoa, bananas, palm kernels, cotton, rubber, wood, aluminium and tobacco. In 1984 her exports to Great Britain were worth £132.5 million, including £122 million worth of oil. Her imports from Britain, worth £23.3 million, included beverages, chemicals, specialised machinery and road vehicles.

Cameroon's official languages are French and English; some three hundred African languages are spoken throughout her territory. Religiously, the population is about equally divided between Islam, Christianity and Traditional – i.e., what used to be known as 'pagan' in less semantically sensitive times. The form of government is officially defined as 'Unitary State, Presidential régime, monocameral assembly'. Unofficially, Cameroon is generally recognised as a benevolent (most of the time) dictatorship. The country is divided into ten provinces, forty-one divisions and numerous sub-divisions. It has a 200-mile coast-line on the Gulf of Guinea and the local time is GMT plus one.

Our visa'd passports were handed to me precisely forty-eight hours later, but the visas were valid for only thirty days. I protested that I had applied (and paid) for ninety-day visas, the maximum allowed to tourists. The young man shrugged and turned away; he either couldn't understand or couldn't be bothered. I continued to protest and he continued to ignore me. When I sought support from the three ladies across the hall their leader insisted that tourists could see all they needed to see of Cameroon in thirty days. I counted ten before explaining, slowly and calmly, that a thirty-day visa is useless to a travel writer. I asked to see the First Secretary but the ladies chorused that that was not possible. I repeated, through clenched teeth, that I *must* see the First Secretary, at which point the hall door banged and the senior lady yelled, 'BOSCO, we need you!'

A tubby, middle-aged gentleman of indeterminate status joined us and listened impatiently to my complaint. 'You have no problem,' he assured me. 'Your visas are very good. Don't be in a hurry! You must wait . . .' He ushered me back to the large room and commanded, 'Sit!' as though I were an unruly dog. The young man regarded me with faint disdain, before locking his desk and departing. Bosco then sat heavily on the edge of the frail desk and rang a friend to whom he talked animatedly, at great length, in one of Cameroon's three hundred languages. Seemingly his friend was a wit; he roared and rocked with laughter until the desk crackled ominously.

Embassies are foreign territory, both legally and emotionally – places where visitors feel suspended between the contrasting worlds of home and away. Immediate reactions tend to be conditioned by 'home standards', yet already one is striving mentally to adapt to 'away standards'. My own reactions to this hiatus were classic. It threatened to wreck our plans for the rest of the day and early next morning we were to fly from Heathrow. At first I roved restlessly up and down the hallway and around the big room, thinking racist thoughts. Then the Cameroonian vibes got through and quite suddenly I unwound – OK,

3

our plans were being wrecked, but so what? They could be remade, or simply forgotten ... As Bosco rang another friend I settled down by a wide window, overlooking an agreeably undisciplined garden, and resumed my rereading of Mary Kingsley's *Travels in West Africa*. I had got to page 330, where she observes, 'The cannibalism of the Fans, although a prevalent habit, is no danger, I think, to white people, except as regards the bother it gives one in preventing one's black companions from getting eaten.'

An hour later Bosco – who meanwhile had been entertaining the ladies – peered around the door. 'Soon,' he said, 'you will see our Big Man.' I tried to make grateful noises.

Twenty minutes later Bosco reappeared. 'Now,' he said, 'you will see our Big Man.' He beckoned me to follow him upstairs.

In the First Secretary's small office I got my first whiff of what we came to know and love as the real Cameroon. Mr Deng was tall and burly, exuberant and amiable. He received me with a vast smile and an enthusiastic, lingering handshake. Our visa application forms were still lying on his desk and I pointed to my unambiguous request, in CAPITAL LETTERS, for ninety-day visas. Mr Deng chuckled and slapped the forms dismissively. 'You have no problem, these are not important! In every town your visas can be renewed. When you go to the Immigration Officer he will immediately renew – we don't make difficulties for tourists, you must feel no worries!'

Déjà vu assailed me. This was a re-run of arguments in the embassies of Pakistan, Ethiopia, Mexico, Peru, Madagascar ... The refusal to grant adequate visas, the assurances that renewal was easy within the country, the expiry of visas a fortnight's walk from the nearest town, the danger of being arrested for overstaying, the much more alarming risk of being expelled from the country half-way through a trek ... Making no attempt to conceal what has by now become a visa neurosis, I explained to Mr Deng that we were not tourists but *travellers*, that our route would take us far, far away from Immigration Offices. For good measure I added a graphic description of our arrest by Peru's Political Police and our expulsion from that country.

Mr Deng's face puckered with concern. 'No, no! It is not possible that you can be arrested in Cameroon! Your visas expire, you get a bush-taxi to the next town – there is no problem.'

'Except,' I said, 'our horse. I know bush-taxis can carry most things, but not horses. Also, we may not be anywhere near a motor-road when the visas expire.'

'Your *horse?*' said Mr Deng. 'You are both riding on one horse? That is cruel!'

'We are walking,' I reassured him. 'The horse will be carrying our gear, only.'

Mr Deng drew a deep breath, held it, then exhaled, 'Won-der-ful! Won-der-ful! You are *walking* through my country? From where to where are you going?'

We moved to stand before a faded wall-map hanging above a decrepit sofa. I felt reluctant to admit that as yet we had only a vague notion of where we were going. Tentatively my forefinger wandered from Bamenda to Wum, Banyo and points north, keeping to the coolish highlands. '*Wonderful!*' repeated Mr Deng. 'You white people have courage, no Cameroonian women will make this journey. Even men will be afraid, beyond their own land.'

'Afraid of what?' I asked.

Mr Deng turned away, avoiding my gaze. 'There are many things to fear. Storms, floods, lions, tigers, maybe volcanoes, maybe finding no food or shelter as it gets dark – *so many* dangers!'

I refrained from pointing out that the area in question is lion-less and that there are no tigers in Africa. It would have seemed impolite to instruct Mr Deng about the fauna of his own country. Then suddenly he cheered up. 'You must stay always near villages, then you will be safe. Everywhere people will help you, giving meals and shelter and showing you the path. Nowhere need you fear *people* – in the bush we have no criminals, no bandits, no bad men. But Douala – be careful in Douala, very careful. All big port cities have *so many* bad men!'

This was refreshing; the embassy staffs of most countries, when confronted by trekkers, at once predict bandit-trouble, though their predictions rarely come true. There was something won-der-fully sooth-ing about Mr Deng, despite his inexplicable resolve not to issue ninety-day visas. He made me feel that even if we were arrested in Cameroon it wouldn't much matter. My neurosis receded, I pocketed our passports and we parted amiably.

At 11.40 p.m. on 16 March I finished my book on race relations in Britain and early next morning – an auspicious date for Irishwomen to begin a journey – we shouldered our rucksacks and took the tube to Heathrow. I was then rather below par: exhausted, distressed and bewildered after an intense two-and-a-half-year involvement in Bri-tain's confused and confusing inner-city-cum-race-relations scene. As our Aeroflot plane took off I felt a sense of liberation; it seemed safe to assume that Cameroon was free of 'race relations' in the fraught, quasi-political British interpretation of that term.

During an eight-hour wait at Moscow for the Tripoli-Douala-Braz-zaville flight, *glasnost* was startlingly apparent. Far fewer armed soldiers than usual were patrolling the airport and the very young passport officer was of a new breed. His predecessors habitually scowled at arriving capitalist pigs but this youth smiled shyly at me and winked flirtatiously at Rachel – a superficial change, perhaps, but it *felt* quite significant. Later I had a long discussion about the future of mankind with a comely young woman wearing a natty Intourist uniform. She denounced not only NATO and US foreign policy but Soviet bureaucracy, lethargy, corruption and drunkenness. Such an encounter would have been unthinkable on any of our previous stop-overs.

When the bar closed at a puritanically early hour – a spin-off of *perestroika*? – we were fed massively at Aeroflot's expense. Then we wandered down to that vast area of green tiles and uncomfortable shiny seats where passengers condemned to small-hours departures droop silently. Or the Whites do – not so the Blacks. Their ebullience, at midnight, was enviable. The men in our group were pin-stripe-suited young lawyers, handsome and confident, returning to Douala or Brazzaville from an international conference in Stockholm. Mostly they were very black and very tall and their vivacious wives wore African robes with Gallic panache. They spoke French among themselves, while excitedly discussing the inevitable crates of hi-tech goodies piled beside their gold-embossed leather suitcases. Each couple seemed to have at least three small children, happy bundles of energy who romped tirelessly.

We had another two hours to wait. Rachel escaped into Elizabeth Bowen's short stories and I looked around for an interesting companion. Mrs G. T. Jackson, travelling alone with the *Guardian* in her hand-luggage, beamed when I sat beside her. 'You have a beautiful daughter!' she said, which got us off to a good start.

Mrs Jackson's two thick sweaters, under a tweed overcoat, made her seem fubsy but as a young woman she must have been quite beautiful. She came from a village near Maroua in the far north of Cameroon, close to Lake Chad. Although her Muslim family had disapproved of her marrying an Englishman she was forgiven after father's death. 'Now', she explained, 'I go home every other year. I love to see my own people and I need *heat*! For three months I store it up in my body to get me through those terrible, *terrible* English winters!'

Mrs Jackson knew nothing about West Cameroon or even Adamawa, where the population is largely Muslim. 'For us those areas are like another country – Cameroonians do not travel within Cameroon unless they have to, for their jobs.' She did not however think our trekking plans remarkable. 'The English are like that,' she observed. 'My husband when he worked in Nigeria was always away in the bush, camping and riding.' On hearing that we are not English she nodded thoughtfully. 'It's good you have this feeling about being Irish. Our government has to work so hard to make Cameroonians *feel* Cameroonian ... Why should we? What is Cameroon? It is a European invention, like all African countries!'

6

'But at least,' I said, 'it's been more successful than the neighbouring "inventions" – Nigeria, Chad, the Central African Republic, Congo, Gabon, Equatorial Guinea. Why? Are Cameroon's tribes in some way different?'

Mrs Jackson thought hard, running her fingers through tight grey curls. Then she asked, 'Have you noticed how little is known about the history of our area?'

I had noticed; London's libraries and bookshops had yielded no *History of Cameroon*, only histories of West Africa containing brief references to Cameroon. As a Cameroon Airways booklet states: 'In the 5th century B.C. Hanno, a Carthaginian, explored the Gulf of Guinea and discovered an active volcano which he christened the "Chariot of the Gods". From that period onwards and for twenty centuries, events related to this country remain hazy.'

'No history makes Europeans uneasy,' my companion went on. 'They feel they can't understand people today if they can't study their past. But maybe it's easier to keep a new state peaceful without history shadows lying over it? I often read about your country in the newspapers and watch television programmes – and maybe you have too much history? Our population is about one-third Muslim, one-third Christian of many different denominations, one-third pagan. If we were as history-conscious as you we could have a lot of tension. My Muslim ancestors invaded a few centuries ago, enslaved thousands, took over tribal lands and ruled many pagans until the Europeans came. But most Cameroonians don't know this. They've no written native languages and no interest in their own past, apart from keeping in touch with family ancestors. Of course there's some suspicion and jealousy and animosity between the religions, especially Christians and Muslims. The pagans are quite primitive and keep in the background. But we never have serious trouble about the awful things we did to one another centuries ago and there are advantages in having no big swollen sense of being a *nation*. Around Maroua we're now sheltering and feeding a quarter of a million refugees from Chad that the world has never heard of! It's not a rich area but my neighbours accept those refugees without resentment. They don't think of them as *foreigners*, just as frightened hungry people who had to run away. International boundaries don't mean much to our villagers – even now they can't really understand them. Maybe it's a mistake to try to make a *Cameroonian* identity ... But you asked if our tribes are in some way *different*. I don't know about that, I only know our *leaders* have been very different – how would we be now if we'd had at the top mad devils like Idi Amin and Nguema and Sekou Touré and Bokassa? To name but a few! You must have heard we've been lucky in our two Presidents. And this is all-important in Africa, where the *people* are helpless. That's the first lesson of our

7

experiences since Independence. In Cameroon less than a thousand men form our ruling class and no one else has any real power – or any hope of ever achieving it.'

Clearly Mrs Jackson did not devote all her time to housework. When challenged, she admitted to being a lecturer in political sociology and we discussed some of the obstacles she has to overcome at a British university.

'My students don't like to hear the truth about Africa. They don't want to know that in most African countries the villagers are *materially* worse off now, after a generation of "Independence", than they ever were in colonial times. This is partly because of neo-colonialism, but that only works so well because there are so many corrupt Black rulers. Our first President, Ahmadou Ahidjo, didn't encourage multinationals to exploit the country more than they were doing already. He was a wise man, a Muslim from the north who managed our resources well for twenty-two years. And he was quite honest. People say he only embezzled a few million French francs, which most Cameroonians think is a fair reward for a lot of hard work. He wasted no time pretending to run a democracy. But even though he was an absolute dictator, in practice, he couldn't control corruption. And it got worse during his last decade in power. When he suddenly retired in '82 he appointed our second President, Paul Biya, a Christian from the south, who'd been working with him for years. He's said to be very honest. Certainly he's been running a major anti-corruption campaign – but is it doing any good? He's also encouraging more foreign investment, from the United States, Canada, Europe, Japan, China. And because Cameroon is so stable big corporations are keen to invest. But there's a trap there. Maybe our stability is tied in with a lack of foreign investment, so far. Big corporations bring big opportunities for *massive* corruption, which could lead to new political factions with conflicting interests. Some think Biya isn't as far-seeing as Ahidjo. There's *less* corruption in Cameroon than in most Black countries, but still it thrives. When most people don't think it's wrong, how can anyone clean it up? The best you can do is what Ahidjo did: limit the opportunities.'

By the time our flight was called, at 2.30 a.m., Mrs Jackson had taught me more than any 'Factsheet' could.

There was a certain piquancy about our stopping at Tripoli on the way to Cameroon. In the fifth century BC Hanno, the Carthaginian navigator and would-be coloniser, sailed from Tripoli with sixty ships and thousands of men and women to begin his voyage to the Bight of Benin. Extraordinary courage was required to sail through unknown waters around an unknown coast. But, according to the Greek translation of Hanno's *Periplus,* West Africa's humans and animals so unnerved the brave Carthaginians that they soon abandoned their colonial ambitions and for the next 2,000 years no one else dared follow in their wake.

Yet West Africa was not, as many imagine, completely cut off from the rest of the world before the arrival of the fifteenth-century Portuguese. Herodotus reports that a regular Tripoli-Kawar-Chad trade route had been established by the fifth century BC. And this trans-Saharan so-called 'salt trade' flourished until the turn of the nineteenth century, forming a link between the Mediterranean world and what is now northern Cameroon. In Roman times gold, ivory, carbuncles and ostrich feathers were exported from the areas around Lake Chad in exchange for salt. But the most important export, then and for another 2,000 years, was slaves – about 10,000 a year when the trade was at its most flourishing. Young men had to walk in leg-irons, chained together by the neck; girls and women walked free. Not all survived the three-month desert crossing and the route was littered with skeletons. At Fezzan the survivors were held for a time in a prison compound while being fattened for the Tripoli market. People still argue passionately, though rather pointlessly, about which was the crueller: the trans-Saharan or trans-Atlantic slave-trade. Probably the former, in terms of suffering *en route*, but at least those who made it to Tripoli were not condemned to a lifetime's misery on plantations. As 'luxury goods', they could be reasonably sure of considerate owners in Albania, Cyprus, Turkey or Tunisia.

When the Portuguese first entered the Wouri estuary – the Cameroons River – they found the water swarming with prawns and named it Rio dos Camaroes: River of Prawns. In due course this became the Spanish Camerones, the English Cameroons, the German Kamerun, and finally the French Cameroun.

Douala's past is as murky as the waters of its estuary, from which unreckoned thousands were transported to the New World on British ships. From the fifteenth century Europeans favoured the estuary as a trading-post; it not only provided a cosy harbour but offered valuable direct water-links with the interior. European traders preferred to remain on the coast, buying slaves from local middlemen like the Douala merchants. These Cameroonian Chiefs were cannier than their neighbours up and down the Slave Coast. They refused to allow Europeans to build forts, arguing that their own control of trade – and even of their followers – would be endangered by the presence of organised European communities. Dealing therefore took place aboard vessels permanently anchored in the estuary. At first, and for a long time, barter was used: beads, cloth, alcohol, guns and gunpowder in exchange for slaves, ivory, palm oil and palm kernels. Thus armed, the slave-raiders of the interior became much more efficient. Trade prospered and for centuries the coastal Cameroonians remained firmly in control. Europeans were allowed to operate only as individuals who, being dependent on local goodwill, had no choice but to provide lavish credit while also paying duty on their human merchandise. In exchange, the Chiefs built sturdy prison compounds where slaves were stored while awaiting shipment.

By the mid-nineteenth century Douala was made up of the affluent towns of trading Chiefs: Hickory Town, Bell Town, George Town, Akwa Town. MacGregor Laird described the last in his diary:

> In the morning we went ashore to visit King Akwa. After viewing his house, which was of two stories with a gallery surrounding it outside, we walked through the town, which in order and beauty far exceeded anything I had yet seen in Africa ... The principal street is about a quarter of a mile in length, about forty yards wide, perfectly straight, and the houses being of the same plan give a regular and handsome appearance.

As competition between European traders increased, following the abolition of the slave-trade and the development of European industry, the Africans demanded and received more and more credit. This out-of-control situation contributed significantly to the German take-over. By 1884 the powerful commercial house of Woermann had allowed the Douala Chiefs so much credit that the Germans would have been hard hit by a French or British annexation.

Europe's colonisation of West Africa was inspired less by imperialistic territorial lust than by nervous jealousy about 'spheres of influence'; the present-day echo is Soviet and American interference in (or provocation of) Third World conflicts. Britain was notably reluctant to get involved in the administration of any part of the White Man's Grave. British soldiers were being sent from India to 'pacify' and 'relocate' East African tribes – and to slaughter them if they refused to be displaced from their salubrious highlands to make way for White settlers. But West Africa was so uninviting that in 1881 the Douala Chiefs felt it necessary to dictate letters to Queen Victoria and Gladstone, probably at the instigation of British traders and missionaries, begging for annexation. The best known of these does sound suspiciously like a trader-inspired concoction:

> Dear Madam,
> We your servants have join together and thoughts it better to write you a nice loving letter which will tell you all about our wishes. We wish to have your laws in our towns. We want to have every fashion altered, also we will do according to your Consul's word. Plenty wars here in our country. Plenty murder and idol worshippers, perhaps

these lines of our writing will look to you as an idle tale. We have spoken to the English Consul plenty times about an English government here. We never have answer from you so we wish to write you ourselves. When we heard about Calabar River that they have all English laws in their towns, and how they put away all their superstitions, oh, we shall be very glad to be like Calabar, now.

Had the French not been moving towards Douala from several points – annexing territory, setting up factories and imposing tariffs to protect French goods – the British might have ignored the pleas of Kings Bell and Akwa. As it was, Edward Hewett, newly appointed Consul of Calabar, was dispatched in April 1884 to sign treaties with the Douala Chiefs. But he was too late. Sailing into the estuary, he saw the German flag flying over Douala. While the Brits had been fretting about those devious Froggies, yet hesitating to take action, the unconsidered Krauts had moved in. Dr Nachtigal, the personal representative of two German commercial houses – Woermann and Jantzen und Thormahlen – had been instructed to 'treat with the natives' and explain Germany's wish to annex their territories. He had also been authorised by Bismarck to sign treaties and ordered to claim for the Emperor of Germany all the land his employers had already acquired, or planned to acquire, in what was soon to become Kamerun.

By then the meddling and squabbling of European traders and missionaries had reduced coastal Cameroon to chaos. So the Douala Chiefs, despairing of a British take-over, reluctantly put their marks to a treaty with Dr Nachtigal. A Nigerian historian, Onwuka Dike, has pointed out that 'the petty kings of the Cameroons were perhaps unable to distinguish between informal control and outright annexation'. They soon learned the difference, when the Germans cynically broke the 1884 treaty by seizing the Douala Chiefs' cultivated land, which they held, by tradition, on behalf of their followers. Mini-rebellions then became frequent and Douala's English missionaries, who loathed the German occupation, were suspected of inciting their flocks to violence.

By 1885 Kamerun had been created – its borders agreed on by Britain, France and Germany – as one of Germany's African colonies. (The others were Togoland, South-west Africa – now Namibia – and Tanganyika.) Sir Clavel MacDonald has described the invention of the 'border' between two hypothetical 'nations', Nigeria and Cameroon: 'In those days we just took a pencil and a ruler and we put it down at Old Calabar and drew that line up to Yola ...'

The German Zintgraff became the first White to explore inland from Douala. He found a society which accepted occasional human sacrifices, frequent poison-ordeals and regular slave-raids as part of normal village life. Yet no attempt was made to bring South-west Cameroon under

11

German control until 1901; there are still people alive who remember how that area was compelled to adjust to European mores.

When the Germans set about establishing their administration they were assisted in Adamawa, and points north, by those Fulani rulers who a few generations previously had reduced the indigenous population to semi-serfdom. The Germans had no time for the anarchy, as it seemed to them, of the multitudinous village 'governments' of the south. But they admired the Fulanis' efficiency and interfered as little as possible with the sixty or so Muslim Lamidats, an 'indirect rule' policy later adopted by the British in West Africa.

Although Fulanis began to move into Northern Cameroon in the sixteenth and seventeenth centuries, few settled in the South-west until the turn of the twentieth century. Their origins are disputed but for at least seven hundred years they and their herds have been gradually wandering further west across that vast area – some 3,000 miles wide – between Dakar and the Gabon. Despite their more or less Caucasoid appearance they speak a purely West African language, belonging to the Niger-Congo group – which much mystifies the experts. The majority remained pagan until the eighteenth century, though many of their Bantu neighbours were converted to Islam long before. By 1800 most had been converted, after a fashion, and were ready to take part in Uthman don Fodio's Jihad, declared in 1804. Before this they had co-existed peacefully with the settled Bantu farmers; during those uncrowded centuries pastoral and agricultural communities were often symbiotic.

In 1902 the Germans built a military station, durable but dour-looking, on the edge of the escarpment overlooking the Bamenda Plateau. This area interested them only as a source of manpower for their coastal plantations, the linchpin of their whole Cameroonian enterprise. High poll-taxes forced men to leave their villages to earn cash, a favourite ploy of all colonial governments. Prisoners were taken from the gaols and made to do plantation jobs; anyone caught resisting the German take-over of the interior was punished by exile to the plantations; peace treaties with defeated Chiefs insisted on their regularly providing hundreds of workers. Many did not survive the long journey from the cool malaria-free plateau. And resistance to unfamiliar coastal diseases was lowered by fear of the unknown and by loneliness for home, family and friends. The plantation death-rate soon became an ugly scandal. Herded into filthy, overcrowded, humid living-quarters, the half-starved labourers died at the rate of 30 to 50 per cent per annum.

In many parts of Cameroon colonialism irreparably shattered traditional social structures. For centuries, elaborate long-distance trading missions had been organised by numerous Chiefdoms, large and small.

But the colonial demands on the labour-force, not only as cultivators and carriers but also as construction workers, were of another order. The forced migration of thousands of men, and the recruitment of women and children to load-carry, caused the disintegration of scores of local cultures. At one time, on the 150 miles of track from the port of Kribi to Yaoundé, 85,000 men, women and children were employed in the transport of goods – a figure not including Hausa merchants' slaves. Often the starving carriers had to raid villages for food and huge areas were reduced to chronic civil disorder. Other demoralising factors were the spread of hard liquor and venereal diseases, epidemics of smallpox and measles, the bribing of Chiefs with guns and gunpowder, the unavoidable neglect of farming and the loss of local handicraft skills.

In October 1915 a British force drove the Germans out of Bamenda. On 1 January 1916 the first British Senior Divisional Officer, Mr G. S. Podevin, arrived from Calabar and at once summoned the region's Chiefs to a palaver. When those who had been allies of the Germans refused to come a military patrol was ordered to burn their villages. Yet Podevin was less inhumane than his German predecessors; before his death in the 1918 influenza epidemic he had reorganised the native courts and eliminated the worst excesses associated with plantation recruitment.

Under the League of Nations the Cameroons became Mandated Territories, five-sixths going to France and one-sixth to Britain. The French ignored the rules and behaved like colonists, allowing French settlers to buy land and exploit resources. The British allowed the Germans to buy back cheaply, in 1924, all their pre-war plantations – confiscated in 1916. By 1936, 300,000 British Cameroonian acres were owned by Germans and less than 20,000 by the British. Three times as many Germans as British were resident in the country, most of the plantation produce was shipped to Germany and half the territory's imports came from there. Because the British administration ensured that working conditions were tolerable, the plantations attracted many migrants from French Cameroon – men eager to avoid forced labour on construction projects.

The French were intent on developing their Mandated Territory, by fair means or foul. Hospitals, schools, administrative buildings, hotels, churches, office-blocks, telegraphic services and shopping-arcades proliferated; roads and railways were maintained or extended. Meanwhile British Cameroon regressed; apparently Britain regarded its mandate as a genuine White Man's Burden, to be shouldered uncomplainingly but unenthusiastically. From 1922 to 1939 the Government of Nigeria had to spend more, annually, on Cameroon than it received in revenue from the area, a position that need never have arisen had

Britain taken over the confiscated plantations in 1920.

The 1920s were a difficult decade for the British administrators. In April 1922 they had officially adopted the Indirect Rule policy, which meant ignoring pretty well every 'native excess' apart from poison-ordeals and human sacrifices. (All the members of the Bagham Chief's court were hanged for having been professionally involved in a human sacrifice, which seems not quite cricket. Presumably the executed men were following some immemorial tradition and acting according to their consciences. But it did prevent – or at least prevent the discovery of – further human sacrifices in the Grassfields.) Indirect Rule enraged the missionaries of various nationalities and denominations, and their more fanatical converts. The latter argued that the Administration – manned, they assumed, by God-fearing Englishmen – should prevent Chiefs from practising polygamy, from using their followers' womenfolk as goods to be exchanged in the market and from enslaving girls as concubines and boys as palace 'pages'. They also refused to pay their taxes to the Chiefs – an integral part of Indirect Rule – and demanded to be allowed to pay them instead to the Missions. This the grievously embarrassed Administration could not allow; nor could it do anything about 'human rights' without first abandoning Indirect Rule.

Egged on by their European mentors, many converts (especially Roman Catholics) became quite paranoid in their opposition to 'the old ways'. No doubt some missionaries enjoyed being the new 'Supreme Authority', to whom the converts submitted as unreservedly as once they had to their 'natural' leaders. Originally those leaders had been well disposed towards missionaries. But when the converts rejected all traditional customs and standards of behaviour, and refused to contribute their share of public work – being too busy building churches, schools and houses for priests – they were, naturally enough, regarded as subversives and severely ill-treated by the Chiefs and their followers. And things became even more fraught when it was discovered that in several areas Chiefly wives, who had been encouraged to run away from home to study Christian doctrine, were also studying the Christian male anatomy.

It is doubtful if there were many genuine Christians among that generation of converts; both their behaviour and the speed with which they were absorbed into various Churches suggest a limited under-standing of the new religion. Yet one can see the inevitability of this grim phase in Cameroon's colonial experience. The missionaries believed it to be their duty to oppose the Chiefs' disregard for 'human rights' and some reckoned that it made sense to use converts to oppose them, thus avoiding direct Black versus White confrontations. Nowadays, when the value of many elements within 'paganism' is widely recognised, the Chiefs might have been challenged more imaginatively and sympathetically. But in the 1920s and '30s Christian/pagan antagonism was raw, crude and implacable.

Between 1938 and 1945 the unlikely alliance between Cameroon's Chiefs and the men from Whitehall was gradually replaced by a new policy based on the recruitment into the Native Authority administration of mission-educated public servants. As Bill Freund has noted in *The Making of Contemporary Africa*:

> Conquest brought a quickening tempo to mission activities and in some areas mass conversions by the 1920s. Some of this may be comprehended as part of a desire by Africans to succeed in, and be accepted as part of, the new régime. In all the colonies where schools were common the missionaries completely dominated the new formal education and insisted on conversion as part of the price of schooling. So an ardent Christian faith became a part of the cultural baggage of many African accumulators. Missions were often of great significance in the acceptance of new commodities, commerce and crops and the source of technical and artisanal skills. They were *par excellence* the vehicle for capitalist values in much of the continent.

1

To Bamenda: Looking for the Other Four Feet

WE TOUCHED DOWN at noon, precisely, and dragged our stiff, over-fed bodies through what felt like a substance – Douala's humid midday heat. In the small uncrowded Arrivals Area Rachel muttered, 'There's a bureaucrat to every passenger!' Anxiously we waited by the conveyor-belt: was our irreplaceable gear in Douala or Ulan Bator? Beside us stood Rosa, a young Italian linguist specialising in Pidgin and embarking on three months' research in Anglophone Cameroon. She was being met by a compatriot, a road-building engineer, and had generously offered us a lift into Douala. When her suit-cases appeared she promised to wait for us at the entrance.

Dreadful things can happen to rucksacks on aeroplanes and at Heathrow we had packed ours in a tough orange survival-bag, together with bit and bridle, riding-hat and picket. The picket had been specially designed and made for this trek by a young welder friend who knows a lot about horses – but not enough, as we were to discover, about Africa. It was a formidable object: two feet long, heavy and thick, with a wide loop on top, a four-inch half-bar and foot-long swivel-chain two-thirds of the way down and a very sharp point. To anyone unfamiliar with pickets (99 per cent of most modern populations) it must have looked like a weapon bought in some kinky Martial Arts shop.

Our sack was the last item to be disgorged. As we marched out to the Customs area – Murphy Junior wearing a hard hat and a bridle round her neck, Murphy Senior grasping the picket – a frisson of alarm went through the assembled bureaucrats and jostling porters. We might have been arrested then and there – instead of much later – but for Rosa's friend. Bernard had taken the precaution of bringing with him a senior police officer who quickly surmounted, on our behalf, the numerous hurdles of a Third World airport. Yet even a police escort did not deter one customs officer – while our protector was coping with 'health' – from attempting to appropriate a tin of mini-cigars.

'For me!' he exclaimed gleefully, delving into my hand-luggage and grabbing a tin.

'*Not* for you!' I contradicted with a wave of the picket.

'I am joking!' he gasped, dropping the tin and backing away. I began to see that this picket might have secondary uses.

Some four-letter words are peculiarly graphic. When a city has been described as a 'dump' the speaker need say no more. At once we can visualise the place, on whichever continent it may be, and so I had vivid preconceptions about Douala. Those few who know it speak ill of it. I cannot recall a single person, Cameroonian or otherwise, who did not denigrate its climate, architecture, insects, morals, entertainments, prices and unrelieved dullness. Clearly no one would *choose* to live at sea-level on the Bight of Benin, yet for me there was an intense excitement about this arrival in Douala, my first point of contact with Black Africa. (I don't count a 1967 trek through northern Ethiopia, with its distinctive history and Coptic culture, or a 1983 journey through Madagascar, which is not purely *African*.)

All was rampantly green by the road from the airport: trees, shrubs, vines, grasses and crops seemed aglow despite an overcast sky – an eager greenery that invades and softens the city streets. The traffic seemed sparse, the few pedestrians sluggish – it was siesta time – and both roads and pavements were scarred with the standard man-trap holes. Behind expensive bars, restaurants and shops, catering for Douala's large expatriate colony, we glimpsed pullulating street-markets, rowdy shebeens and collapsing or collapsed lean-tos. Just as some ugly people can be attractive, so is Cameroon's biggest city – which has a population of less than half a million. Tales of murders, muggings, pickpocketings and car-thefts are common, yet one's antennae pick up no threats. Most of the inhabitants are recent arrivals from all over Cameroon, optimists who imagine that fortunes can be made where industry burgeons, and the atmosphere is more rural than urban.

Rosa had booked into the Catholic Mission city-centre guest house. Otherwise the choice was between (tower-block) Tourist Hotels, where bed-minus-breakfast costs £40 to £60 a night, and Unclassified Hotels – otherwise known as 'Africa hotels' – at £4 a night. In the latter, asserted Bernard, our property, our virtue and even our lives would be gravely endangered. So we left our gear in his flat and accompanied Rosa to the Mission, five minutes' walk away.

Missionaries have been busy in Douala for more than a century and we found a substantial but characterless three-storey colonial building half-surrounding a bare dusty compound. Beside a broken-down truck, full of medical supplies, a young Dutch priest was being semi-hysterical.

Someone at the docks, where the vehicle was held up for five weeks, had removed a vital part. What to *do*? The priest was a newcomer to Africa and had moral scruples about giving bribes ...

In a tiled hallway languid goldfish drifted through the clear water of an ornamental pond fed from a coolly-splashing mini-fountain. A row of wall-cabinets, facing the door, contained specimens (happily deceased) of Cameroon's more spectacular creepy-crawlies. I averted my eyes from the palm-spider – very common, the size of a tea-plate and the only living creature for which Gerald Durrell can feel no affection.

A surly German priest in 'Reception' could find no record of Rosa's booking. Sister Veronica might know something about it but wasn't around. When would she be around? No one knew. But all bookings must be confirmed before 5 p.m. We tried to confirm them with Father Surly but only Sister Veronica could handle bookings.

Back in the hallway Rosa wondered, 'Do Europeans become *mentally* African after they've been here for years?' As she had an appointment with a potential landlady we volunteered to wait for Sister Veronica and sat on a wide verandah overlooking a swimming-pool fringed with hibiscus, dwarf palms and poinsettia.

This was the Mission bar; a tall money-in-the-slot refrigerator dispensed beer and soft drinks (same price) to those who struck it with sufficient violence on both sides simultaneously. Here we had our first bottle of excellent Cameroonian beer – the first of how many hundreds?

During the next two hours a cross-section of expatriates wandered in, sat around for a while and wandered out. There were pairs of nuns coming from or returning to the bush, and emaciated young lay-missionaries who looked as though their guts and blood were permanently parasite-infested, and elderly priests with weather-withered skins, yellowish eyes and nicotine-stained fingers. Dermatologically, even the youngest looked as though they had already spent too long in West Africa. Then there was a French colonial antique – part of the establishment – very short-bodied and long-armed, with a tangled white beard, spindly bow legs and a gross belly hanging over knee-length khaki shorts. Otherwise he wore only pink plastic flip-flops and a limp straw sombrero. His lips were set in a demi-snarl, revealing jaggedly broken teeth, and he was forever busy: refilling the refrigerator, testing the water in the pool, hurrying in and out of storerooms, fiddling with air-conditioning machines.

Father Surly came to the refrigerator for a beer but ignored us; he had a bushy blond beard and hard pale eyes. On that verandah no one ever smiled and conversation was restricted to occasional murmured comments. Even the few servants who drifted to and fro were – most unusually for Cameroonians – dour and silent.

We received quite a few openly hostile glances. 'I suppose they think we're spongers' remarked Rachel, 'and you can't blame them.' She told me then about a scandalous guidebook, available in English and German, which advises 'over-landers' on how to travel through West Africa *without spending any money*. Such travellers were beginning to infest Cameroon when political chaos in the surrounding countries put a stop to their predatory gallop.

At 4.30 I went map-hunting, leaving Rachel to cope with the evanescent Sister Veronica. In London, where we had been able to get only United States Air Force aeronautical charts – hardly ideal for trekkers though better than nothing – a young man, then writing a guidebook to West Africa, had misinformed us that detailed maps were available only in Yaoundé. In fact we could have bought them from the Topographical Institute at 36 rue Joffre, ten minutes walk from the Mission; it was consistent with our whole Cameroonian experience that we made this discovery only on our return to Douala, when we were about to fly home. However, it wasn't for lack of assistance that I failed to find even an oil-company road-map; two men and a woman went out of their way to lead me to stationery-cum-bookshops.

I then began to notice a difference between the *évolué* and the 'normal' Cameroonian – a difference not apparent in Anglo-Cameroon where the colonial power had no grand design for the mass-production of Black Englishmen. Douala's affluent 'Black Frenchmen' (and women) were perceptibly less friendly than the majority. They also looked less happy, as though they saw being sophisticated and Frenchified as incompatible with spontaneous *bonhomie*. A superficial French influence is apparent in all Franco-Cameroon's small towns – themselves French or German creations – but only during our brief visits to Douala and the capital, Yaoundé, did we encounter this disconcertingly haughty middle class.

The late afternoon heat was just tolerable; I sweated steadily, but not to saturation point, as I walked down the crowded Avenue Poincaré. Long limousines were parked on the pavements, forcing pedestrians to disrupt the traffic and risk their lives by walking on the streets. Watching for tourists, I saw only expatriates: one can't confuse the two. France is notorious for retaining an economic grip on ex-colonies (unless, as in Madagascar, neo-colonialism is actively combatted) and independent Cameroon has many more French residents than colonial Cameroon ever had.

At street junctions cheerful men stood by tiny cigarette stalls selling American brands at negotiable prices. Outside smart European-type delicatessens cheerful women stood by tiny vegetable stalls hoping to sell a few avocados, or misshapen blotchy tomatoes, or minute purple onions. The larger wayside greengrocery stalls, some twenty yards long, were piled with local and European fruits and vegetables including, absurdly, imported Golden Delicious apples. Douala's big stores stock everything, at a price. Given the money (as expatriates are, or they wouldn't be in Cameroon) one could live as well here as in Paris. Yet the rich-poor contrast is much less distressing than in Bombay or Lima.

One's first day in a new country is largely a sensory experience: body-contact between the stranger and a myriad unfamiliar sights, sounds and smells. These have an acute – oddly animal – importance while the traveller's mind is uncluttered by personal knowledge or acquired opinions. There is nothing to puzzle over, analyse, dissect; one is merely a passive, though excited, receiver of impressions. Also one's psychic pores are open wide, absorbing messages – their significance not yet understood – from a whole new cultural-spiritual environment. That first day rarely deceives. And having escaped from Douala's rather tiresome West End, I felt certain that I was going to enjoy Cameroon and the Cameroonians.

In a large side-street bar beer cost 120 CFA (about 25p – 100 Cameroonian francs is equivalent to about 22p) a half-litre, as compared to 1,200 CFA (about £2.50) in the Akwa Palace. I had to shout my order above three different tunes simultaneously emanating from battered juke-boxes. The place was so crowded – mainly with young men and women – that I took my drink outside; a row of blue plastic beer crates had been placed on the pavement for the overflow. A young man from Bamenda, now working for the Port Authority, at once joined me, shook hands and asked, 'You are missionary?' (This, I thought, spoke well for the present generation of missionaries; I doubt if many of their predecessors were found in bars.)

When I explained myself – not an easy task – the young man looked worried. 'This journey is too difficult! You must not walk, you will be tired! In Cameroon we have plenty bush-taxis – you must use them!'

'But,' I said, 'we like to get away from motor-roads, into the bush.'

The young man leant forward, almost toppling off his crate, and grasped my elbow. 'In the bush people are *savages*! You will not like them. They have no toilets, no beds, no water, no bread, no shops, no light from electricity ... They eat only fufu – you know fufu? It is not nice!' (Fufu is a tasteless but sustaining maize-flour dumpling.)

I assured him that almost any food is nice at the end of a day's trekking and stood up to go.

'Where is your daughter?' asked the young man. 'I would like to meet her, please bring her here now. She is married?'

'No,' I replied, 'she's only eighteen.'

'*Eighteen!*' exclaimed the young man. 'Why are you waiting? Does she like Cameroonian husband? Can we meet now?'

'Not now,' I said, 'because early tomorrow we go to Bamenda. But perhaps – who knows? – another time . . .'

Returning to the Mission, I relished not being one of a dominant, and too often domineering, White majority. Recently I had been living in a British city where many Afro-Caribbeans were tortured by a sense of inferiority or embittered by White refusals to accept them as equals. Now it felt good to be among Blacks who could unselfconsciously regard me as a potential mother-in-law.

Sister Veronica was still missing so Bernard invited us all to spend the night at his construction company's flat, where three bedrooms lay empty. But we hesitated to impose on him until Sister Veronica, materialising out of the dusk, revealed that a three-bed room would cost us 4,500 CFA (£10) *each*.

At 5 a.m. Douala's wide colonial streets were dark, silent and very hot. After walking a mile or so, we were sweat-soaked. According to Bernard's houseboy, Bamenda bush-taxis left at dawn from the railway station. He was however mistaken and someone advised us to take a shared taxi to another 'motopark' four miles away. We shared with two thin men, three fat women and five squirming children.

As the sun rose we stood bewildered among scores of buses and bush-taxis. Hearing us ask for the Bamenda rank, a kind young man in a dark lounge suit explained that one could get to Bamenda *only* from outside the Cameroon Hotel, several miles away.

We shared the next taxi with an adolescent soldier, stationed in Bamenda, who was pertinaciously curious. 'Why must you *walk* in the *bush*? This is strange! What is your *reason*? Does your government pay for this work? Have you walked in other places?'

I explained that I walk in many places and then write books about them.

'Aha!' said the soldier. 'So it has become a habit!'

The Cameroon Hotel looked very 'Unclassified'. Beside it a strip of wasteland – the motopark – was crowded and cheerfully chaotic. A smart white minibus, labelled 'Bamenda' on the windscreen, would leave when full and already half the seats were booked. Its ticket-seller-cum-driver (tall, obese, grey-haired) treated all women with hectoring contempt. When I had handed over our fares – 4,000 CFA (almost £9) each – he demanded our passports, then disappeared with them. At once a little knot of tension tied itself inside me: every traveller's gut-reaction to being even momentarily out of sight of vital documents. Nobody had warned us that all bush-taxi passengers must hand over identity cards or passports when buying tickets; the details are entered on a list which drivers have to show at frequent police check-points. Evidently my anxiety was obvious; a slim young man, with tribal incisions on his cheek-bones, stepped forward to shake my hand. 'You

have no problem,' he soothed, 'because this is the custom. Your passports will safely come back with your tickets.' Which they did – fifty
minutes later.

Cameroon's public transport is well organised. Notices stating the
official fare (so many CFA per kilometre) are displayed in every vehicle
and even foreigners are not overcharged. But undercharging can
happen when passengers know the driver and all uniformed servants
of the State travel free in the best (front) seats. Baggage charges vary.
On that minibus we paid 1,000 CFA (£2.25) for both rucksacks. Had
they travelled free we would have been given no receipt.

Rachel returned disgruntled from a breakfast-hunt. 'No *chai-khanas*
here,' she complained. But moments later a mobile *chai-khana* (tea-
house) appeared – a ragged, barefooted man carrying two buckets.
One contained opaque water, the other a huge kettle and several mugs.

'You can't get hepatitis twice,' Rachel reminded me. (That was
our viral souvenir from Madagascar.) We chose to ignore the other
possibilities in the bucket and when two mugs had been rinsed out and
vigorously shaken they were filled with aromatic clove tea, scalding hot
and heavily sugared.

Then a baker's barrow arrived, wheeled by a stocky youth shouting
his wares in Pidgin. To us his prices seemed alarmingly high but soon
every tiny fist in sight was clutching a sticky bun or doughnut. We
splurged on two baguettes and I produced out of a sock six triangles of
hoarded Aeroflot soft cream cheese.

'Why,' demanded Rachel, 'is our breakfast in a *sock*?'

'Because,' I explained, 'I've been carrying it carefully all morning as
hand-luggage. It might have been squashed in a rucksack.'

'You get madder by the minute,' said Rachel.

Our water-bottles had not been filled, since between us we were
shouldering a horse's load of gear, and already we felt dehydrated.
Opposite the motopark stretched a line of ramshackle lock-up stalls
but, unusually, there was no bar in sight. Shelves of expensive bottled
drinking water promised relief until I noticed something suspicious; the
labels looked soiled, as did the liquid. Turning away, I noticed a small
boy lifting off his head a crate of full bottles which he shelved before
disappearing with a crate of empties. I followed him. Around a nearby
corner he was filling the empties from a wayside tank of murky water,
then skilfully replacing the metal caps.

Even in that smallish motostop crowd the variety of types made our
crude European image of Black Africans – 'primitives' about whom
one may loftily generalise – seem at once laughable and offensive.
Observing the different features, skin-shades, body-structures, hair-
styles, languages, garments, gestures, jewellery, miens and tribal markings, I felt almost intimidated by this diversity. Technologically Black

Africa may be primitive, but already I was sensing more complexities and subtleties than ever an outsider could cope with. Clearly nobody could even begin to understand Cameroon in three months – or, perhaps, three decades. Before travelling in Asia it is possible to establish some rapport with the countries to be visited through translations of their literature – a preparation one can't make for Africa. Perhaps this is why Cameroon seemed to me immeasurably more mysterious than the 'Mysterious East'.

At last loading began. An agile young man leaped onto the minibus roof and received from his muscular colleague six sacks of maize, two enormous woven baskets of rice, ten jerry-cans of palm oil, three rolls of raffia matting, four gigantic aluminium cauldrons serving as suit-cases, eight crates of empty bottles, countless plastic hold-alls, several amorphous bundles – and two rucksacks.

Those passengers who had been sitting on a low wall, coping with innumerable offspring, now stood up expectantly – detaching infants from nipples and toddlers from severely mauled sticky buns. But our hour had not yet come. We were, it transpired, waiting for two wealthy Fulani merchants, dignified and handsome in freshly-ironed pale blue robes, who arrived by taxi at 7.45 a.m. and at once occupied the roomy seats beside the driver. No hanging about with the proles for *them*!

When we were given the signal to pack in I found myself in the centre seat of the middle row, ill-placed to observe the landscape. On my right, a puny, heavily-pregnant girl alternately slept and crocheted baby-clothes. On my left, a tall, svelte young woman was being witty in French about the problem of what to do with her very long legs. As we were about to start two elderly steatopygous women, with bosoms to match, slid back the door and squeezed aboard, breathing heavily. Extra seats materialised in the narrow aisle and we all politely tried to make our persons and hand-luggage more compact.

Compared to Malagasy motor journeys this six-hour drive seemed sybaritic; the new velvet-smooth road was of an excellence rarely found in Britain and never in Ireland. For two hours we remained in the low humid zone, where occasional rubber plantations interrupted miles of dense jungle. Near the villages women and girls hacked rhythmically at the soft red earth – bent low, using short-handled, broad-bladed hoes. Some grannies (probably no older than myself) had grievously curved spines and moved stiffly. Many men sat around talking and drinking and laughing.

In this comparatively Westernised region most dwellings were breeze-block-built, tin-roofed, shoddy and surrounded by a squalid abundance of 'consumerist' litter. It seemed that no one took any pride in their homes or gardens, that here were people suffering from incurable culture-shock Although modern building materials are chosen for convenience or swank, the Cameroonians remain uninterested in using them creatively, or even sensibly.

The road began to climb near the base of Mount Koupe, which seemed higher than its 6,000 feet after so much flatness. Beyond and above many forested foothills we entered Cameroon's most densely populated province, an area so fertile that it can support more than one hundred inhabitants per square kilometre – as compared to *one* per kilometre in the Tchabal Mbabo. Now the air felt blessedly cool and in the near distance, heaving along the horizon, were the sort of chunky mountains that over-stimulate my adrenalin.

Abruptly Bamenda appeared, sprawling across a red-dust plain 1,000 feet below the edge of an unexpected escarpment. It is a fast-growing town of some 70,000 inhabitants, its buildings mainly one-storeyed, its streets mainly rough, its people – we soon discovered – mainly warm-hearted and welcoming.

From the motopark a taxi took us to a grotty ex-colonial office block where we hoped to find David Hughes in the MIDENO headquarters. Already we looked like vagrants and MIDENO's well-groomed receptionist viewed us with distaste verging on horror. David was not expecting us on any particular day, owing to the vagaries of Cameroon's postal service, so I sent up a chit: 'Rachel and Dervla have arrived'. The receptionist looked affronted when we were immediately summoned to her Big Man's office.

The Hughes introduced us not only to a reliable horse-dealer but also to Western Cameroon's history and customs. Unlike many expatriates, they lived not merely in Cameroon but with it: concerned about its problems, affectionately studying its traditions, camping all over the Grassfields (see map on p. *viii*), while making friends and influencing people, agriculturally, as best they could. They were too experienced to be starry-eyed, too sympathetic to be impatient. Without our four days as their pampered guests and eager pupils, the social nuances of Cameroonian rural life would have greatly perplexed us.

Jane's letters had mentioned Doi, a rich young Fulani from whom the Hughes had bought their own horses four years ago, and to whom they had sadly sold them back a few days previously, their departure from Cameroon being imminent. At 7 a.m. on a cool clear morning (all golden light and blue shadows) we set off for Doi's compound in Jane's jeep, climbing steeply on a rough red track below a rugged ridge with 'bite marks' along its crest – volcanic craters containing sacred lakes. Everyone, recognising the jeep, greeted Jane. And at one point a messenger bearing a letter for David came leaping down a precipice from the local Fon's invisible hilltop palace.

This Fon had served twenty-five years in the Cameroonian army and recently retired, on a meagre sergeant-major's pension, having been selected as ruler after his father's death. When we met him next day at a Bamenda Hash Harriers' meet (he was a keen cross-country runner), I observed him overcoming two awkwardnesses with aristocratic aplomb. Fons may not shake hands with anyone, ever – a confusing rule for strangers, who will at once have learned that vigorous handshaking is among Cameroon's most important courtesies, neglected only by boors. At the meet were two newly-arrived expatriates' relatives, a frail elderly French lady and a rather solemn little German boy. When the French-woman offered her hand the Fon bowed graciously, gently grasped her forearm with both hands and greeted her so charmingly that she could not possibly have resented (or even noticed) her hand being ignored. Again, when the little boy shyly extended his hand he found himself, to his evident delight, being hugged and kissed instead of formally greeted.

Doi's isolated compound occupied one of the province's highest points, an 8,500-foot flat ridge-top overlooking some hundred miles of Grassfields. We were startled to see a shiny red saloon parked amidst the thatched huts and even more startled by the news that Doi was still abed, having just returned from a four-day visit to an international agricultural show in Paris. He was, Jane explained, an atypical Fulani. One of his stepmothers was an Englishwoman who had retired to England on being widowed and with whom he still kept fondly in touch – even visiting her, occasionally, in Surrey.

Yet in most respects this was a classic Fulani family. Doi's senior wife (the senior of two: doubtless two more will follow) was tall, lissom, poised – but shy of strangers, for she rarely left the compound. We shook hands, then saw little more of her. She was busy around the kitchen-hut, cooking breakfast for Doi, his adult brothers, an aged uncle and sundry 'followers'.

In the men's living-room we watched them eating mountains of rice, with fried plantain and giant omelettes, while we drank Bournvita imported from Nigeria. The small, dark room was furnished with grubby easy chairs, an unstable sofa and a low table. Several garments and a kerosene lantern hung from nails in the mud wall and an Islamic calendar depicted Mecca. The only other decoration was an enormous wall-chart, new from Paris, illustrating the various parasites – many times enlarged – that infest farm animals all over the world.

It is a Fulani characteristic to live simply, eating and dressing well but never squandering money on unnecessary possessions. Most other Cameroonians, if they could afford to fly to Paris for a long weekend, would live in an ostentatious villa, garishly furnished and equipped with a plethora of electrical gadgets – mainly ornamental, because of power shortages. And of course their womenfolk would lead easier lives, not cooking on charcoal between three stones and washing-up in the nearest stream.

While Jane gossiped with Doi, no one else spoke. The purpose of our visit was generally known but not mentioned until a small boy had cleared away the dishes and a slightly larger boy had handed around ewer, basin and towel.

Then Doi stood up, adjusted his robe with a few fluent flicks and assured me, 'I will have news in a day or two. It's hard to find the horse you need but I will search and search – though I am a very busy man. Because you are Jane's friend I'll find you a good horse – the best! Don't have any worry.'

No one, at that stage, was sordid enough to mention money. Doi said he could also provide a saddle, saddle-blanket and bridle; he looked faintly disappointed on hearing that we had brought our own head-collar and bridle.

On the way home Jane told us that horses are comparative new-comers to the Grassfields. They were first seen during the 1820s when a band of Ba'ni from the north raided the Bamenda Plateau. The mounted invaders – wearing pantaloons and flowing gowns, making martial music on flutes and armpit drums, attacking with bows and arrows – terrorised the peaceable Grassfields tribes who fled into the roughest mountains where no horse could follow. Ironically, while the Ba'ni were wreaking havoc in the Grassfields the Fulani were doing likewise in the Ba'ni homelands.

At Jane's bank she introduced me to one of the staff, then wisely abandoned us; many British-orderly queues stretched away into the middle distance. Because I was twice directed to join an irrelevant queue it took two and a quarter hours to change our French franc travellers' cheques.

One thousand pounds in Cameroonian francs is dauntingly bulky. The temptation was to assume the bank clerk had got it right and make way for the next customer. But I told myself to have sense and stood firmly at his glass-enclosed cubby-hole where he could watch my every move as I counted and counted and counted pile after pile after pile of ragged, smelly notes. Out of the corner of my eye I observed his increasing tension. He was prepared for my challenge and without argument handed over what could so easily have been his 'com-mission' – the equivalent of £50.

Carefully, I packed the notes into two deep double-zipped side pockets of my trekking-slacks. 'You *are* a strange shape!' commented Rachel, surveying my hips. I wasn't worried about my silhouette but being so well worth robbing did make me feel a trifle uneasy.

In an earth-floored off-licence (as bars are oddly known in Anglophone Cameroon) we were welcomed by half-a-dozen men of varying ages and types. As we drank our beer – the only alcohol sold in most off-licences – a group of giggling small girls with babies on backs crowded excitedly around the unglazed window just behind us. This surprised me, since Bamenda has a few score expatriate residents; but perhaps not many expatriates drink in off-licences.

Most of the passers-by looked clean, well fed and well dressed. Only a few were barefooted. The majority carried head-loads: anything from a lone tin of Ovaltine to a colossal bale of cloth. Many women, even young women, were grossly overweight, though one never sees fat pre-puberty girls. Obesity is a sign of beauty – something to be worked (eaten) for – and also of prosperity.

The locals think of Bamenda not as a town but as a series of villages, known as 'quarters'. These straggle along the base of the escarpment, extending up the lower slopes where the gradient permits, and each has its quarterchief – a title I at first found slightly disconcerting. The mud-brick, tin-roofed dwellings vary in size but most are surrounded by flowering shrubs, banana plants and mango trees. Short-haired dwarf goats are tethered on patches of scrub. (The rich eat goat-meat; beef is for the hoi polloi and mutton is rare.) Plump dogs lie on shady verandahs beneath laden washing-lines and don't bark at White strangers. Men lounge around listening to compound-blasters. Women carry loads to and from the market, pound maize for fufu, sit in doorways making children's clothes on antique sewing machines, dig or weed in little gardens, fetch water from distant standpipes and firewood from the rapidly dwindling forest far away over the top of the escarpment.

In pre-colonial days the men of this region warred and slave-raided occasionally, hunted regularly and spent much time repairing or building thatched huts and maintaining local tracks and footbridges. They also smelted a massive amount of iron and made a variety of tools which they traded over long distances, bartering them for goods unavailable in their own area. These occupations have long since been eliminated, while the women's daily chores remain no less demanding – if not more so, since many men can now afford only one wife.

Yet the poorest men still work hard. In Bamenda one sees them descending from the blue mountains high above the escarpment, balancing formidable loads of firewood on their heads. Children, too, carry huge loads, their little neck muscles bulging under the strain. One morning I met a barefooted, sweat-soaked father and son hurrying down the rough path. On the steepest stretch the little fellow, aged perhaps seven or eight, slipped and fell, scattering his load over the inaccessible cliff. At once he burst into tears, his chubby face piteously puckered, his eyes fixed despairingly on those precious branches which had cost so much labour to collect and bring thus far. Carefully then

28

his father laid down his long load – not an easy manoeuvre on a narrow path – and knelt to take his son in his arms and cuddle him and stroke his hair.

That Friday evening everyone rejoiced because there was a violent thunderstorm with torrential rain – the first rain for months. Cameroon's 'little rains' are supposed to start on 15 March and people begin to worry if they are even a few days late. The electricity promptly went off for several hours and we dined by lamplight.

Next morning Jane drove us down to the market to buy equipment. She had presented us with a plastic bucket, a kettle and a saucepan; so we needed only two mugs, two bowls, twenty yards of leading/tethering rope and two sacks (old-fashioned gunny-bags, not fragile nylon jobs) to act as pannier-bags. Cameroon's First World cost of living had caused me to scrap a grandiose plan to buy real saddle-bags, or have them made.

The market was crowded, vociferous, colourful, friendly. A maze of rough alleyways, muddy after the rain, ran between ramshackle stalls selling everything from French toothpaste and Taiwan T-shirts to Nigerian plastic floor mats, red-brown palm oil in dirty five-gallon tins, bananas, avocados, groundnuts, plastic shoes, strange spices, bundles of tree bark, miniscule tins of Italian tomato purée, piles of rice and maize flour, bloody mounds of freshly slaughtered beef, pungent dried fish, boxes of lump sugar, brilliant bales of cotton, ox-tails in buckets of slimy water, giant Chinese thermos flasks, local and American cigarettes, bunches of a green vegetable (or weed) with which we were to become very familiar, and sardines from Peru, which we bought for sentimental rather than gastronomic reasons.

A personable young Nigerian merchant sold us blue nylon rope, measuring the metres fingertip-to-elbow. Cameroon, he said, is a much happier country than Nigeria. 'It is safer, too. Here we have very, *very* little crime. In Nigeria's towns life has become too dangerous – so I left!'

Jute sacks were harder to find; but at last I noticed a few neatly folded by the entrance to a cramped, windowless hut. An ancient Fulani squatted in one corner, rocking to and fro and mumbling prayers. He had a hawk nose and trembling hands and tried to persuade me that I didn't need two empty sacks, that I couldn't *possibly* need them. Then he sold both for 1,100 CFA (about £2.50).

That afternoon's multiracial meet of Bamenda's Hash Harriers was a memorable occasion. David, who imported this bizarre offshoot of the Raj to Cameroon, was retiring as 'Grand Hash Master' and after a strenuous two-hour cross-country race his boozy farewell party began at sunset on a high mountainside. Midway through these revels Doi arrived with the good news that a sound horse would be available for our inspection early on Monday morning.

Next day, after Sunday lunch, I explored the hills behind the Hughes's bungalow. The sun appeared only occasionally, between low banks of dove-grey cloud, and along the highest ridges small wisps of vapour drifted one after another in single file like ghostly presences. A narrow red track looped up and down between new hoed fields, well tended banana-groves, stands of palm-trees, stretches of scrubland (not useless, but lying fallow) and patches of forest. In every direction billowing smoke marked fields being 'fire-weeded' in preparation for sowing. Such fires often run wild and on a slope near the Hughes's a young eucalyptus plantation was wastefully aflame.

All the traffic was pedestrian. Everyone smiled and made welcoming noises; most adults shook hands. Those schooled in colonial times usually speak better English than their juniors – many of whom speak none, only Pidgin, and a tribal language.

At one hairpin bend I paused to listen. From several large compounds, set well back from the track, came sounds of merriment: laughter, song, playful teasing, teenage tittering. When the juvenile population noticed me they swarmed forwards, clad in little or nothing, delirious with excitement – shouting greetings, waving, running away in mock alarm when I approached, turning somersaults in the dust to entertain me, dancing and singing on the roadside ditches. The traveller in Cameroon doesn't need to be told that 60 per cent of the population is under sixteen.

Viewed ecologically, the Africans' procreative recklessness chills the blood – how long before there is a Cameroonian Famine Appeal? Viewed otherwise, these happy, loved and loving children seem a moving affirmation of the Black appreciation of *life*, as a gift to be enjoyed. A positive sense of enjoyment often emanates from a Black crowd – a group of fieldworkers, a market throng, a family gathering – even if the individuals concerned are not engaged in any obviously enjoyable activity.

Those positive energies are invigorating, though they have inspired no great technological or artistic achievements. But in our society only a few are involved in 'great achievements' – from some of which millions benefit without understanding them, while the individual feels increasingly insignificant in an impersonal world controlled by a greedy oligarchy. In contrast, most rural Africans have significant personal duties and how these are performed can be observed – and praised or blamed – by all.

These reflections were interrupted by Aziki, an English Literature student home for the Easter holidays from Yaoundé University. As we walked together he explained sadly, 'For us from this side Yaoundé is difficult. Too many Francophones think studying English is time-wasting. And they have too much control of our university, like we're only second-class citizens. Jane Austen is my favourite English writer – you know about her? Her books are not complicated. They are about village people, so if you come from a village you understand them – though English villages are rich and ours are poor.'

Aziki already knew that I was staying with the Hughes; in Bamenda White visitors are uncommon enough to arouse curiosity. He pleaded, 'Could you not make your friend change his mind? You know how it will be when Mr Hughes leaves? MIDENO will fall to bits! It will be inefficient, corrupt, with jobs only for followers of Big Men. Then in a few years the government must call for another Englishman to put it right. I know how it is because my brother works there and now is sad because the policy is "Cameroonians should run everything!" But MIDENO is not African. It's a European *idea* so it needs a European to keep it organised, to make decisions. We know how a thing like MIDENO should be run, we're not stupid. But we're too much afraid of responsibility. We push problems from office to office until all files are lost and nothing is done. You can't lose your job if you make no decision, only if you make the *wrong* decision!'

Aziki's outburst (the first of many such) recalled the standard colonialists' blanket condemnation: 'Africa has no tradition of service or integrity'. He had however used a key phrase: 'It's a European *idea*'. For centuries, throughout Western Cameroon, a stable farming-and-trading society depended for its prosperity on a complex and highly developed tradition of 'service and integrity'. But it was too inflexible to withstand the impact of Fulani invaders, never mind the imposition of Western *ideas*.

At sunset we called on close friends of the Hughes, Joy and John Parkinson, to whom the Murphy Expedition, with all its hypothetical future woes/problems/diseases/crises, was being bequeathed. Little did they – or we – then realise what that introduction augured.

Later we spread our enormous USAF charts on the Hughes's dining-table and sought guidance.

'Those sheets would be just fine,' said David, 'if you were touring by light aircraft. But I can't see too many footpaths marked. And half the place-names are figments of the Pentagon's imagination. The locals won't know where you're talking about – they use utterly different names.'

On the Hughes's map we plotted a bush-path route from Bamenda to N'gaoundere, via the remote and wondrously beautiful Mbabo mountains. Our first week or so would be spent crossing the highlands of Western Cameroon – 'the Grassfields' – which made global news in August 1986 when Lake Nyos, a crater lake, exploded one evening killing hundreds of people and thousands of cattle. The shadow cast over many Cameroonians by this natural yet mysterious disaster was perceptible from the day of our arrival, though most seemed not to want to discuss it. No one said anything about the subjects being in any way taboo, yet it did have a strong taboo *feel*. The trauma had been particularly severe for the Grassfields folk, whose small territory is studded with some three dozen volcanic lakes. In August 1984 a gas release from Lake Manoun, sixty miles south of Lake Nyos, had killed thirty-seven people as they walked home from their fields at sunset. That tragedy, almost certainly provoked by a landslide, received little publicity at the time but was uneasily noted around Nyos, where odd happenings had been observed within the previous decade or so. Most experts believe that only five or six of the Grassfields crater lakes are potential killers. However, few locals are aware of this and the Nyos catastrophe, following on Manoun, has inevitably caused them to fear that their nearest lake will be the next to explode.

The Hughes guaranteed that our bush-path route would keep us at an agreeably high altitude, apart from one unavoidable hot plain, at 1,500 feet, between Ntem and Somie. Beyond the sparsely inhabited Tchabal Mbabo, we planned to explore the virtually uninhabited Tchabal Gangdaba before turning east towards N'gaoundere. This important Muslim town lies as far north as the climate would permit us to trek; beyond its escarpment Cameroon slopes steeply towards the hot lands south of Lake Chad. And, as Jane remarked, a Fulani Lamidat would be a good sales-point for our horse.

2

Enter Egbert

HIS NAME, DOI said, was Mbodeyoo.

'We'll call him Egbert,' decided Rachel.

'Why?' I demanded. 'Why *Egbert*?'

'Because he *is* an Egbert,' replied Rachel enigmatically.

Looking at him more closely, I saw what she meant. 'But,' I reminded her, 'we haven't bought him yet.'

Mbodeyoo was politely co-operative as we examined his feet and teeth.

'Five years old,' said Doi.

'Surely *at least* eight!' said I, pretending to be more knowledgeable than I am.

'He was *born* here!' said Doi, a trifle huffily. 'He was born here in 1982.'

As Rachel led Mbodeyoo around the compound I stood watching with Doi and his two full brothers; most of the younger males in the background were half-brothers by various stepmothers. Jane was absent, dealing with removal men. David's driver had dropped us off at the compound and we would return to Bamenda with Doi.

Mbodeyoo moved nicely and was quick to respond to directions. A glossy bay with four white socks and a slightly Roman nose, he stood about fourteen hands and to our eyes was oddly shaped. From the rear Fulani horses look more like tall bony cows than anything equine; from the front they seem pathetically narrow chested. But Jane had told us not to be put off by their eccentric contours or lean and hungry looks. They are notable for speed and stamina – and indeed Mbodeyoo was a compact mass of muscle. We didn't, that morning, think him particularly handsome; but when we had compared him with many other Fulani horses we realised that he was, by local standards, an Adonis. His golf-ball-sized congenital hernia didn't in fact worry me though I judged it expedient to feign alarm. When I prodded this protuberance Mbodeyoo looked around wearing a faintly surprised expression. '*Not* good!' I exclaimed, frowning.

'His father had it too,' said Doi. 'Other horses in this area have it. It makes no trouble.' He nodded then towards an adolescent brother who flowed onto Mbodeyoo in one beautiful sinuous movement and went galloping away across the grassland beyond the compound. When he returned I nodded to Rachel who mounted less sinuously and cantered off into the distance, looking comfortable.

'He's my best horse,' said Doi, as we watched them.

By this stage I was having trouble concealing the fact that I had fallen madly in love with Mbodeyoo/Egbert. 'He seems quite steady,' I conceded.

'He is good to ride and good to carry,' observed Doi. 'He is strong and gentle.'

That sounded like a professional horse-coper's spiel; but it proved to be true.

When Doi and I withdrew to the palaver-room, followed by the full brothers, Rachel remained on the verandah with the half-brothers.

'I think 200,000 is a nice price,' said Doi. 'It is a special price only for you, because you are Jane's good friend – and she is *my* good friend!'

I looked amused at this little joke and suggested that 100,000 (about £220) would be a much nicer price. Doi laughed at my little joke and protested that even for Jane's good friend he couldn't *give away* his best horse.

Five minutes later we had settled on 130,000, for which Doi would also provide a brand new saddle-blanket and an extremely decrepit dual-purpose saddle.

'But,' I stipulated, 'you must have the saddle repaired *today*.' When Doi had agreed I counted out 130 one-thousand CFA notes and shouted to Rachel, 'He's *Egbert* now!'

Doi tucked the money away in a pouch beneath his gown. Then he said, 'In the market you must buy very strong antibiotics for your horse. If you don't know how, I can give injections today and tomorrow.'

This startled me. 'What's wrong?' I asked sharply. 'Why does he need antibiotics?'

Doi smiled reassuringly. 'Nothing is wrong – yet. But if the road cuts him, or thorns poison him, or ticks give him fever, then it's better he has big doses of antibiotics *now*, to be ready. You are taking him to hot places he doesn't know, then if he's ill there's no town, no vet, no medicine – and he dies!'

It was impossible to make Doi understand that antibiotics are not a prophylactic but a cure, that to give them unnecessarily is not only useless but counter-productive. Involuntarily I glanced at the parasite poster from Paris and felt mingled exasperation and despair. Doi was no ignorant villager but a literate young man fluent in English, French, Pidgin and several African languages – a cattle-breeder interested enough in animal husbandry to fly to a Paris show. Yet to him, as to millions all over the Third World, antibiotics are, quite simply, White Man's Magic. Everyone has heard about their swift, mysterious power and many have experienced it. So if you can afford to give your horse this magic protection why not do so *before* exposing him to various hazards? Plainly Doi regarded my adamant refusal to have Egbert injected as just one more symptom of White parsimony.

We had been advised not to bring our gear to the compound as that might have suggested a willingness to buy *any* horse. Now it was arranged that when Doi had completed his day's Bamenda business he would collect us, plus gear, and we would sleep in his guest-hut.

On the way down I asked what 'extras' Egbert liked when working hard.

'Nothing!' said Doi. 'You give him only grass – for a horse grass is the natural food. He has never eaten anything but grass.'

This was a too-familiar misapprehension. I explained how experience has taught us that horses, mules and ponies do need 'extras' when carrying a load twenty or twenty-five miles a day in hilly country for months on end.

Doi refused to be persuaded. 'You give him salt to lick, then he needs only grass.' His mind was on more important matters, like our Deed of Sale. 'Now at once,' he went on, 'you get this form in triplicate. Three copies, you understand? And a 300 CFA fiscal stamp.'

'Which form?' I asked apprehensively, recalling our bureaucratic travail when mule-buying in Peru.

'A simple form,' said Doi, 'a Deed of Sale. David knows, he'll type for you three copies. It proves you own this horse when people steal him – I mean *if* they do! I keep one copy, the police keep one. When you sell the horse you must show your copy to the buyer – otherwise he says you have stolen this horse. And remember you get only *one* fiscal stamp, not three for 100 CFA each – that is important.'

'I'll remember,' I promised meekly. Mine not to reason why ...

Not far from Bamenda we swung off the main track and jolted into a village centre. The arrival of Whites provoked shouts of glee from dozens of pickins who raced after the car.

'Here we may find a policeman,' said Doi.

'But,' I objected, 'don't we need the forms and the stamp first?'

Doi smiled. 'You don't understand! Here the policeman may be able to open the post office to find a stamp.'

'But,' I persisted obtusely, 'wouldn't it be easier to find in the main post office?'

Doi laughed aloud. 'You *still* don't understand! To find this stamp can take a long, long time. It is scarce. Many people use it. Most post offices don't have it when you need it.'

I registered a big logic gap somewhere in all this but remained silent.

We stopped under an avocado tree outside a mud hut with 'PO' scrawled in white chalk on its padlocked but flimsy door. When Doi yelled imperiously a very young policeman came loping out of a nearby off-licence and greeted him deferentially. The post-master had gone to his fields but the policeman knew for certain it wasn't worth his entering the post office through the window. He knew there were no fiscal stamps inside because the day before his uncle had sold twenty-two goats as he was not feeling well and was moving to live with his eldest daughter in Yaoundé where it would be troublesome to keep goats and anyway too expensive to transport them there ... But had we tried the post office at Bafut?

'We're not going anywhere near Bafut,' I said. 'We're going to Bamenda.'

The policeman sighed and passed a hand across his eyes and declaimed, 'It is too hard to live!'

Twenty minutes later we were in David's office. He briskly typed out the Deed of Sale in triplicate, then again put his driver at our disposal: 'Roger will know where to get those damn stamps.' He also provided an elaborate To Whom It May Concern 'Attestation', sealed and stamped like a medieval treaty, for use in emergencies. We read it and were bemused. 'What does it *mean*?' I asked.

'You're not supposed to know,' replied David. '*No one* is supposed to know. And because no one will admit they don't know, you'll go on your way unmolested. That's putting gobbledegook to a constructive use.'

We gazed at him respectfully; four decades of hard labour in the underdeveloped vineyard endow a man with much practical wisdom. He then gave us a chit for the Chief Immigration Officer, whom he had already telephoned with a request that our visas should be extended to those ninety days for which we had already paid. Roger took us to the Immigration Office circuitously, via three post offices from the last of which he emerged triumphantly waving The Stamp.

Bamenda's Immigration Office is an attractive old bungalow embowered in a mini-jungle of scarlet and blue shrubs. We waited for ten minutes in the cool, twilit hallway, sitting beside three jittery Nigerian youths who never took their eyes off the door of the Big Man's office. I could smell their nervous sweat and wondered yet again why Black body odour is so much less disagreeable (to us) than White ditto. When we were summoned I hung back, pointing out that the Nigerians had arrived first. But we had a chit from Mr Hughes ...

The CIO was an engaging character, chubby and bouncy with a twinkle in his eye and what can only be described as an affectionate handshake. He spoke fluent English yet once the civilities had been completed communication broke down irretrievably. *Why* did we consider a one-month visa inadequate for a three-month trek? Smiling down at our passports he observed – 'This is good, you have visas from London! You are English ladies?'

I closed one passport to show him the green cover with EIRE writ plain. He gazed at it blankly, then repeated, 'These are *good* London visas! When you wish to leave Cameroon you come to me again and I will give you exit visas.'

I made a final effort, leaning across the desk and drawing a finger under the 'ONE MONTH' carefully written in capital letters on each visa.

The CIO nodded and said, 'If you wish to remain three months in our country these are good visas for three months. It is fine that you wish to remain so long in our country – we are proud and happy! It is not necessary for me to do anything more.'

'Count ten!' murmured Rachel.

I did so, then asked, 'What if we come to a police check-point and they see our visas are long out of date?'

The CIO twinkled and chuckled. 'No problem! You tell them I say your visas are good!'

'But by then we'll be in Adamawa!' I protested. 'In another province they won't know anything about *you* – they won't even speak *English*!'

'Then you tell them you are coming here to me for your exit visa,' said the CIO.

'I think we'd better go,' advised Rachel quietly. 'This is becoming unproductive.'

We had arranged to meet Doi 'sometime after three' outside an uncle's hardware shop in the Fulani sector of Bamenda's scruffy commercial centre. Pending his arrival camp-chairs were unfolded on the dusty roadside and beers ordered. Over-amplified African pop assaulted our ears painfully; we were to discover that even in small Cameroonian towns merchants incessantly compete to produce the highest decibel level.

Again we studied our inadequate maps, attempting to plan the morrow's route in detail. Soon a small friendly crowd had gathered round us and one tall Fulani youth, with a long narrow face and intense eyes, knelt beside me to point out the best trekking-path to Lake Ocu. We didn't then realise how unusual he was; many weeks were to pass before we met another Cameroonian who could map-read.

'You must go *this* way,' said our adviser, 'because it is fine high Fulani country. And you will see how some bad men from Yaoundé – very rich men, maybe government ministers – have fenced off all our best grazing land. They want to make a new European-type ranch with imported breeds. You will have trouble getting in, they don't want people to see what is happening. It is not legal, they are not paying for the land – it is like when the Germans and French came and took land in times past. But you *can* get in, people will tell you where to find a man with a key . . .'

Later I sought more information about these 'bad men from Yaoundé', but neither Doi nor anyone else was prepared to discuss this 'little local difficulty' with an outsider.

I had hoped we might get back to the compound in time to consolidate our relationship with Egbert before loading him at dawn and severing him from home and family. But it seemed this was a high-pressure day for Doi the Tycoon. At intervals we saw him in the near distance, haggling, discussing, arguing, explaining, laughing, quarrelling, examining the contents of crates and sacks, ordering loads to be stored in uncle's shop, or put in his or another car-boot, or transported elsewhere on a non-Fulani head.

We were beginning to get the 'feel' of this social scene. Relations between Fulanis and non-Fulanis appear to be – and on the whole are – excellent. Yet in many areas Fulanis are the people with most wealth, authority and self-confidence. Hitherto they have not thought a modern academic education important for their sons. But that attitude is now beginning to change and in twenty years' time relations may be less good if a disproportionate number of Fulanis have qualified for Top Jobs.

We wondered how much of Doi's time was being spent on business matters and how much on ritualistic exchanges of courtesies, followed by long, light-hearted gossips.

'Here you probably can't separate the two,' observed Rachel. And after a moment she added, 'Awful to think of those beautiful young wives confined to the compound while Doi does all the living-it-up . . .'

In that market-place the role of the few visible Fulani women seemed subservient, though Cameroon's Muslim women do not of course wear the veil or maintain purdah. In contrast, non-Fulani women – or at least those who participate in commercial activities – usually give the impression of being very much in command of their particular situations.

For two hours we watched the ebb and flow of that colourful, noisy crowd and I pondered an African paradox: the coexistence of exuberance and laid-backness. Often an individual's bursts of physical exertion or animated sociability were followed by interludes of wandering vaguely about, or just sitting and being. This capacity to work hard and then to relax, forgetting time, seems a whole world away from our regimented life-style – so many hours work, then off to play. It may well provide a healthier framework for human endeavour but it must also partly explain why most Africans cannot successfully run Western organisations – political, commercial or industrial.

Doi joined us briefly at 4.45 and looked evasive when questioned about saddle repairs.

'It will be seen to,' he said, and disappeared. Of course it never was seen to: the saddler had been in his fields all day.

An hour later we left Bamenda after a few false starts caused by uncertainty about who wanted, or expected, to travel with us. Doi insisted on Rachel's sitting in front; he very obviously felt that she would make an excellent third wife. The two full brothers sat with me in the back, each clutching a huge angular parcel. We soon stopped to buy delicious kebabs, then paused again outside a prosperous-looking compound to pick up an 'uncle and aunt' – presumably courtesy titles since they weren't Fulanis. Both were enormously bulky, as was their luggage; so Rachel escaped into the back seat, causing me to suffer at every jolt from too close contact with the angular parcels. When the elderly couple's bundles had been tightly packed over and around them, Doi's driving ability was much impaired.

The sunset sky was sullen when we bumped into the compound. Then, from beneath swollen blue-black clouds, a stream of red-gold light poured briefly across the Bamenda Plateau, very far below.

A wiry elderly man offered to help carry our gear to the guest hut. He wore what looked like baggy white pyjamas under a threadbare tweed jacket (surely ex-David). This was Danieli, Doi's chief cattle-herd and for the past three years Egbert's *de facto* owner. He had a kind, creased face and looked at me searchingly, anxiously, as we shook hands. I walked with him through the dusk to where Egbert had been tethered for the night on sparse grass, tied short to a fence. At the end of the dry season I hesitated to suggest using our picket and rope to widen his range; but Danieli indicated that later he would change him. Although he spoke only Foulfouldé we seemed to communicate effortlessly and he was openly upset about this abrupt ending to a three-year partnership. He watched closely while I greeted Egbert and our burgeoning rapport evidently consoled him. The quality of his relationship with his herding-partner must have partly accounted for Egbert's excellence as a trekking-partner; he was a horse who had never known ill-treatment.

We supped, inevitably, with the men. I longed for an evening in the women's quarter but that would have been to downgrade the White guests. This was our first encounter with fufu and jammu-jammu, the staple diet in Western Cameroon. Fufu is a tasteless but sustaining maize-flour dumpling, served in a communal enamel dish. Jammu-jammu is a thick slimy stew of spiced spinach-like leaves; it comes in a smaller dish and if a family is rich includes a few cubes of meat. Having scooped out a ball of fufu with the fingers, one dips it in the jammu-jammu. Spoons were provided for us but we soon discarded them as unsuitable implements for the business in hand. Then came cups of Ovaltine, another mark of affluence. Although Cameroon produces much coffee and some tea, neither has become popular with the inhabitants. And cocoa, one of the country's main cashcrops, seems to be unknown as a beverage.

We ate by the light of a hurricane-lamp, placed in the centre of the low table. As our shadows moved erratically on the walls Doi's small son, already plainly conscious of his privileged status, played with them quietly but intently.

'He has made this game for himself,' said Doi proudly. 'He tries to guess which way they'll move next.'

Bamenda was then seething with rumours about every household in Cameroon soon having US-supplied satellite television. It was however hard to imagine electricity-cum-television ever reaching this remote compound – unless Doi himself were to install a generator. I hoped he never would. Television does not encourage children to make games for themselves.

Doi looked puzzled when I asked whether Cameroon's Muslims are Sunni or Shi'a. Even he, a much-travelled Fulani, had never heard of the historic split. Blessed is Islam where no sects are known! And the Cameroonian government, it seems, is conscious of this blessing and takes care to stamp out any spark of Islamic fundamentalism or sectarianism that may chance to alight on Cameroonian soil.

And so to bed, in a three-roomed rectangular mud hut on the edge of the compound. Our room had rough-hewn rafters, a tiny unglazed shuttered window and two narrow but comfortable iron beds with clean cotton sheets, soft homespun blankets and intricately embroidered pillowcases. The storerooms on either side were not rat-free.

At dawn (5.40 a.m.) I looked around the compound for signs of activity. There were none; March mornings seem cold to the locals and all, who can, stay abed while things are hotting up. After a night of heavy rain the pale blue sky was cloudless, the air cool and fresh. As the sun appeared above the nearby rock-summit I heard the unrhythmic tattoo of many cattle hoofs and a handsome roan herd came trotting swiftly past the compound, followed by two agile young women – one was Doi's junior wife – holding long skirts above brawny knees and waving sticks and yelling directions.

Egbert had had no previous dealings with Whites so it seemed a good idea to groom him then, while the two of us could be on our own, by way of establishing a closer relationship before the first loading. He turned his head, pricked his ears and stood steady as I slowly approached. After some leisurely conversation and fondling I began to groom his back and he shuddered with delight. For half-an-hour I worked, neglecting no inch; even his furry little hernia was burnished. Then I stood back and admired him; unsuspected red-gold glints had come up and in the slanting sunlight he shone like a new-minted copper. At that felicitous moment Danieli appeared and registered astonished admiration. The Fulanis, however much they may love their horses, don't waste time grooming them unless they are putting on a display for their Lamido.

By now the sun was warm. Smoke and the smell of frying came from the kitchen hut. Little boys were carrying bundles of firewood, little girls plastic buckets of water. Doi's junior wife was hurrying off to a nearby stream with a stack of dirty pots on her head and two half-brothers were loading sacks into the car-boot. Doi himself stood on the verandah brushing his teeth while complacently surveying his domestic kingdom. He might well feel proud of it. In significant contrast to Bamenda's squalor, this rural compound, like all the others on our route, was immaculate. Not so much as a stray leaf or twig or wisp of straw was allowed to untidy it. Even the latrine in a far corner – a deep hole in the ground, covered by a flat stone and encircled by a raffia screen – was spotlessly clean and completely odourless.

For our morning ablutions a shyly smiling small girl carried to the guest-hut a wide tin basin in which stood a full bucket of hot water. The child's arms were so short that I had to lift this load off her head. We had assured Doi that cold water would suffice; but he was not going to lower his standards at our behest.

Breakfast was a meal to remember: high hills of rice, tender chunks of braised meat, herb-flavoured omelettes, fried plantains (ripe and unripe), baguettes thickly spread with avocado and many mugs of Bournvita. Danieli – who had come to help load Egbert – was served last, but otherwise treated as family in the best Islamic-democratic tradition. During the meal our bit and bridle were handed round and much admired; so coveted are such European items that we could probably have exchanged them for Egbert.

The equipment and saddling technique of Doi and Co. severely taxed my native fatalism. Never in all my years of travelling with pack-animals have I seen such an unpromising combination of odds and bobs or such rashly ingenious adaptations. Yet the main item, from Egbert's point of view, was sound; whatever other misfortunes might befall us, he wouldn't develop sores while wearing his brand-new, red and green thickly-padded saddle-blanket. But the unmended wooden saddle was a potential disaster area. Its underside sheeps-wool padding seemed most unlikely to last the course, its crude iron hoops might or might not support our load, its stirrup 'leathers' were strips of nylon sacking and the stirrups themselves looked like relics from the Early Iron Age.

We couldn't even guess what the girth might have been in its previous incarnation; my main worry was the fearsome complexity of the method used to secure it. A reliable girth is the single most important requirement for carefree trekking with a pack-animal: so I appointed Rachel Expedition Saddler and watched admiringly while she mastered the intricacies of Danieli's technique. This demanded not only uncommon skill with knots but considerable physical strength – and those gifts had to be synchronised with split-second timing. The application of immense force was essential at a certain moment in the construction of a knot; otherwise all was lost and the whole process had to begin again. At her third attempt Rachel mastered this mind-boggling art – Danieli was a good teacher – and ever after she securely saddled Egbert at least twice a day as though she too had been born in a Fulani compound.

Then there was the little matter of a crupper. Doi pooh-poohed the need for any such refinement but Danieli was on our side. When another strip of nylon sacking had been produced I insisted that its use would soon cause a tail sore.

Silence. Hard thinking.

A small boy fetched an old sock which Doi dextrously bound to the centre of the 'crupper' with a strand of tough grass plucked from nearby. Sceptically I watched, foreseeing disintegration in the near future. I had a lot to learn; Cameroonian improvisations are the fruits of long experience and that crupper was to prove the least of our worries.

Now it was my turn to display some expertise. Danieli tested our sacks and conveyed approval of the weight distribution. Egbert continued to stand statue-still while the sacks were held up and I roped them to the saddle's central hoop – with real rope, brought from London. Our five-litre water-bottle was tied to one of the smaller front hoops and our two-litre bottle plus the heavy picket to the other. Two multi-coloured raffia shoulder-bags, bought nine years previously in Morelia market in Mexico, were draped over the pommel to hold maps, camera, salt, rain-capes and food for the road. When Egbert's bright blue bucket, the smoke-blackened kettle and pot and our purple mugs had been tied on at various strategic places, with strong boot-laces, the ensemble looked decidedly tinkerish. But it seemed secure enough and Egbert showed no sign of disapproval.

By 8.40 a.m. we had completed our handshaking marathon and were off. Rachel led Egbert, I followed behind to watch the load just in case . . .

'This time a week ago,' I recalled, 'we were arriving at Heathrow.

It's astounding that within seven days we've got the show on the road.'

'Thanks to Jane and David,' said Rachel.

3

The Forbidden Ranch

CERTAIN INTERLUDES SEEM quite separate from the rest of one's life. They have the simple perfection of a Tang lyric, a Chopin *étude*, an Inuit carving. And they do not drift away, becoming blurred by time; mysteriously they continue to give sustenance. For me that first day of our trek was one such interlude. I experienced pure happiness – something quite different from the everyday underlying contentment which is my fortunate lot.

Following Rachel and Egbert down the red-earth track from Doi's compound, life seemed wondrously simple. The sun shone warm, the breeze blew cool, Mount Ocu beckoned. My daughter had become a congenial adult, our horse was charming and amenable, the Big Bad World (including my latest troublesome typescript) could be forgotten. Time was meaningless; it didn't matter when we reached where – or, indeed, if we ever reached it. Should there be no habitation in sight, our tent would go up at sunset. Should we feel like lingering for a few days here or there, or turning east instead of west, why not? Uncomplicated months stretched ahead, or so I then imagined. Hundreds of miles of glorious unknown territory also stretched ahead, populated by warm-hearted people not condemned to hopeless poverty. With difficulty I overcame an impulse to skip, instead of walking.

From Doi's compound there was nowhere to go but down. Below that bare, over-grazed mountain we crossed an alleged main road which becomes virtually impassable during the big rains (October to December). Here a bush-taxi gave us our baptism of dust; from that moment, until our return to Bamenda, we and all our possessions were permanently ochre-tinged. Egbert loftily ignored the swaying, hooting vehicle and its yelling, waving passengers.

Our narrow path to the Forbidden Ranch led down a grassy slope, scattered with rotund yellow-blossomed bushes and a variety of trees, most of them unidentifiable since we had been unable to find any guidebooks to the flora and fauna of Cameroon. On the valley floor, beyond several neat compounds, a tiny mud church, filled with roughly made wooden benches, stood isolated amidst dense bush. Here we met two young men, carrying machetes and balancing tall piles of prayer-books on their heads. They stared at us, transfixed, then fled into the bush.

All around, contrasting colours glowed and shimmered under a deep blue sky: richly red new-dug fields, glossy banana and plantain groves, mighty mango trees, coppices of young burgundy-tinted eucalyptus, flowering bushes – red, white, orange – long tawny grass on the slopes, short bright green grass by the streams.

Each turn of the path revealed a new combination of topography and vegetation. As Rachel observed, there is a miniature quality about this corner of Cameroon. She of course was looking at it with the eyes of one recently returned from trekking in the Himalayas, but I could see her point – though Cameroon's mountains don't feel miniature while one is ascending or descending.

At noon clouds piled up in the west. We lunched on a high ridge under a solitary, towering, gnarled tree; its visible root system extended for many yards and housed many ants. The grass was meagre and tough yet not despised by Egbert who rolled ecstatically when the load came off. Picketing him, I discovered that a picket well suited to damp Ireland is less suited to Africa at the end of the dry season. Meanwhile Rachel had been discovering that Cameroon's large black ants, though omnipresent and hyperactive, do not bite unless molested. (Driver ants are another and later story.)

The rain came as we reloaded: gentle steady rain, not a tropical downpour. The landscape ahead differed dramatically from the shallow fertile valleys behind us. Tall clumps of rough grass covered an expanse of apparently uninhabited hills, broken by frequent outcrops of volcanic rock. As we descended towards a tree-filled cleft the rain became a chilling deluge, driven by a strong cold wind.

'This is no one's idea of trekking in West Africa,' commented Rachel. Then she wondered, 'Are we on the right track?' – because the cleft presented an Egbert-barrier.

The foot-bridge over a tumultuous mountain stream consisted of two wobbly eucalyptus poles; I didn't much fancy it myself. We sought an animal ford, but there was none. Then I examined more closely the banks beside the bridge. Both looked negotiable by an agile horse and the water was only about six feet wide and two feet deep. A ford could be created by the clearing of some vegetation – an easy task, if one had a machete, though with bare hands it took fifteen rather painful minutes. And after all that Egbert refused to approach the noisy torrent.

Had we continued patiently to persuade him he would certainly have crossed; later he took on many more alarming obstacles. But we were then ignorant of his prowess and reluctant to nip a beautiful friendship in the bud by being too insistent.

The sun returned as we climbed a steep grassy hill. Then a broader path appeared; it proved to be the right one and led to a two-hut Fulani compound where a strong-featured woman – high cheek-bones, slightly hooked nose, square chin – slowly approached and formally greeted us. She refused however to shake hands with me; virtuous Muslim wives don't shake hands with men and 90 per cent of rural Cameroonians mistook my gender. Evidently she assumed us to be connected with the Forbidden Ranch. Pointing through a pathless tangle of tall trees she said, 'Fence! Fence!'

As we continued, somewhat hesitantly, two little girls came running after us, doubtless instructed by Mamma. They were enchanting, with the sort of gracious good manners and dignified friendliness that we were coming to recognise as Fulani traits. The elder insisted on leading Egbert, the younger took the empty bucket from me and placed it on her head. (I had been carrying it since the handle broke.)

Beyond the trees we crossed an unpleasant acrid-smelling area of burnt scrub, descended to a swift shallow river – the girls observed our white feet with interest – and ascended a jungly slope to a wide, brilliantly green plateau encircled by forest. Here our guides pointed to a large Fulani compound of thatched huts, then smiled goodbye and raced away.

Outside the compound three men in long robes and embroidered pill-box hats were talking animatedly. As we approached they fell silent and stared at us with, I sensed, some unease. If we were being associated with The Fence we could scarcely expect warm welcomes hereabouts. They were however civil, though distant. One indicated an almost invisible pathlet on the green turf and said, 'Go to gate.' Then abruptly they all turned away.

On the edge of that plateau we suddenly found ourselves directly overlooking a volcanic crater, some two miles in circumference, with a smooth pale green floor fringed by dense forest. Here we rested, eating bananas while peering – awestruck – over the 500-foot crater wall. Several tree tops were swaying far below and we heard for the first time those half-eerie, half-comic monkey calls which were to become so familiar.

Continuing through woodland grievously vandalised by fire – hundreds of fine trees had been destroyed – we were impressed by Egbert's jumping, without encouragement, four mighty obstructing trunks. Then a rider emerged from the shadows ahead, followed by an unsaddled horse. 'It's Danieli!' exclaimed Rachel. 'Egbert must know this path well!' When we paused to shake hands Danieli congratulated us on the load's being still in place.

Next came the day's toughest climb. Strangely rutted volcanic soil made for exhausting walking up a brutal gradient closely covered with small grey scratchy bushes. Near the top we heard a distant shout; Danieli was urging his sweat-flecked horse up the slope to give us the name of 'the man with the key'. When Rachel had written it down phonetically he cantered away and we stood watching. To me the partnership of a Fulani and his horse is more beautiful than any ballet. Danieli rode downhill with one arm outstretched for balance, his wide blue sleeve flowing in the breeze. At the edge of the burnt wood he paused, looked up at us, pirouetted his horse in farewell and disappeared beneath the trees.

'They're such *kind* people!' said Rachel. 'But it's one thing to have this man's name – how do we find him?'

Below that crest lay many miles of rough pasture and woodland – a jumble of long ridges set at eccentric angles to one another and divided by shallow valleys. No compounds were visible but soon we heard maize being pounded and around the next corner saw yet another beautiful young woman in an unfenced two-hut compound. Like most Fulanis she spoke no English or French but was an excellent sign-linguist. The Fence was over *that* way, the gate was down *that* way, the man with the key lived up *that* way. We were moving off when she signalled us to wait, hurried to cover her maize from marauding hens, adjusted her baby-blanket (the huge infant was sound asleep) and beckoned us to follow her. She too insisted on leading Egbert and carrying the bucket.

For a mile or so we were guided across scrubby grassland, liberally fertilised by old cow-pats and horse droppings. In all this area there was no trace of a path. Then the barbed-wire fence appeared – an odious sight, some eight feet high and constructed with non-local thoroughness. To defy it without a wire-cutter would be impossible. Our guide pointed to a spot on a distant hillside and made a key-turning movement. Staring hard, we could see a compound; then my binoculars revealed scores of cattle nearby. But this compound was on the far side of The Fence, from which we deduced that the as yet invisible gate was not person-proof but that Egbert would have to wait while one of us fetched the key.

When our friend left us only forty minutes of daylight remained. To Rachel's eyes the key compound looked easily accessible before sunset; to my older and (in this case) wiser eyes it didn't. From where we stood, on a level with it, it seemed close enough; but much of the intervening terrain was down and up.

'Let's find a camp-site,' said I, in the no-nonsense voice so often used before my daughter became an adult. (Such habits are not easily dropped.) Rachel obviously had her heart – or stomach – fixed on compound fufu; yet she gave in gracefully, perhaps also out of habit.

Soon a level woodland glade offered ample grazing, ample firewood and soft ground for the picket. We dithered about putting up the tent; the sky was indecisive, mostly clear but with cloud around the edges. Recalling the previous night's downpour, we chose to play for dryness rather than comfort. The tent was a veteran of our Andean campaign, a high-altitude one-(wo)man job weighing three pounds including poles. In Peru Rachel had of course been less than half her adult size, but we had parsimoniously decided that our old friend would be tolerable for a trek during which we did not expect to camp every night.

Our fire caused a mild personality clash. The wood, being surface-wet, was slow to light – with damp grass as a starter – and Rachel impatiently accused me of 'wasting matches on a doomed enterprise'. I however was trebly motivated: by hunger for dehydrated vegetable stew, by a romantic addiction to camp-fires and by pride in my ability to light one under adverse conditions. Sure enough, a tiny glow at last appeared and after much skilful blowing became a tiny flame – and moments later a dance of many big flames.

Complacently I settled the saucepan on three logs (there were no adequate stones around) and opened the stew packet. As we supped a gusty wind blew smoke into our faces wherever we sat. Between coughs Rachel wiped her watering eyes and said, 'Some people know about camp-stoves – very light and cheap.'

When the wind dropped after dark we piled on more wood and discussed our dash dilemma. (In Cameroon 'dash' is used loosely to mean a rewarding tip as well as a softening-up bribe.) Should we have dashed Danieli when he followed us? Should we have dashed our guides, in either or both cases? I thought not; money is a dangerous substance that quickly corrodes human relationships unless handled with care. The modern practice of parents (or other relatives) paying young children for help in everyday tasks is to me abhorrent. And everyone knows what the economics of mass tourism have done to human relationships world-wide. Clearly the two little girls, who so rapidly left us, expected no tip. They might have been gratified to receive one; but then, in the unlikely event of other Whites straying past their compound, would the prospect of dash have insidiously tainted the atmosphere? It is reviving, for us denizens of an evilly materialistic society, to be among people who offer help simply because they have generous hearts.

Rachel didn't entirely agree with me. Some temperaments find it harder to receive than to give and she had been quite upset when our guide with the heavy baby left her urgent chore (pounding maize for the evening meal) and walked far from her compound to show us The Fence. I admired this scrupulousness about not being a nuisance, not taking advantage of people's good nature. Yet it would have been inappropriate (quite apart from my personal inhibition) to dash that dignified young woman with money. But should we have given her one of our standard cheap 'travellers' gifts' – a lipstick, or gaudy hair-slide, or card of safety-pins? That ploy uncomfortably recalls European traders bartering almost worthless (to them) coloured beads for gold, ivory and slaves. Yet those beads were not worthless to the Africans; many are still in use as admired and envied necklaces. So is it wrong to allow White hang-ups to deprive Black villagers of baubles they would prize? Before 'settling in' to Cameroon, I took this and related questions seriously. But such soul-searching about inter-racial attitudes or motives soon came to seem superfluous. One couldn't go far wrong by spontaneously responding to the differing expectations and per-sonalities of individual villagers.

Although dashing one's host is a clear-cut obligation, the manner of fulfilling it may be far from clear-cut. In rural Cameroon, and I believe elsewhere in West Africa, a sponger could live well, indefinitely, by accepting the hospitality traditionally offered to strangers of every colour. He or she would be given the best available food and shelter without any hint that recompense was expected. Even nowadays a few hosts – usually Fulanis – are offended by dash from a departing guest. Others consider a gift, but not cash, acceptable; the majority welcome any form of dash that may be received without loss of face. A useful ruse for us, we had been advised, was to pay on departure for 'the horse's food' – which of course costs nothing.

We left the tent flap wide open; at 6,000 feet there were no mosquitoes or other winged undesirables. Rachel was soon asleep, I lay watching a half-moon glimmering behind a frieze of big-leaved branches. Bird chirrupings and distant monkey yells and Egbert's munching wove a pleasing pattern on the deep silence of the bush. It seemed rather a waste to become unconscious when being conscious was so enjoyable.

In fact that night's unconsciousness was productive. In a dream I recalled something that for years had been totally forgotten: the loading technique taught me in 1975 by a Balti trader. Then our luggage also consisted of two sacks and the trader's method of roping them together *before* loading was, once mastered, far simpler than my own convolution of knots.

At sunrise Rachel watched incredulously while I tied complex loops at intervals along the rope, then arranged it on the ground in a meticulously measured esoteric-looking design. 'Seems to me,' she said, 'your brain works *better* when you're asleep!'

By 7.15 a.m. we were viewing The Gate, an anticlimactic arrangement of wooden poles not at all in keeping with that Iron Curtain-type fence. Two small padlocks secured it but anyone keen to get stock through could have done so quite easily. Nor did it even pretend to be human-proof; leaving Egbert grazing and Rachel reading, I wriggled under without difficulty.

That was a magical walk – the early sky pale blue, the cool air faintly herb-scented, the forested slopes vibrant with bird-calls. And then, as I crossed a red-brown meadow, the still hidden sun filled the valley with an ethereal golden haze, an almost unbearably beautiful light.

After a short climb up a new-burnt ridge I found myself amidst some two hundred ear-tagged cattle, the ranch's experimental herd of zebu-Holstein half-breeds. In March all Cameroonian cattle look skinny, but they do not look unhealthy. This lot did. Some were lame, some had suppurating udders, some had oozing sores around their eyes, all were listless with starey coats. I began to understand why the ranch was forbidden to visitors.

Danieli's friend came to greet me, a tall, lithe, elderly man who had evidently been expecting us. He held my hand tightly, smiling down at me and murmuring the Fulani litany of greetings, to which I murmured incoherent responses. His face was sad; to the Fulanis a herd of healthy cattle is the *most* important thing in the world. Strong emotions often transcend language barriers and Rahim must have picked up my own distress; gesturing towards those wretched animals, all overcrowded on their dusty ridge-top, he conveyed that they were starving and looked as though he were about to cry.

In a tiny windowless hut I sat on an unsteady bed covered with a straw mat. The only other furniture was a crudely made wooden cupboard on which stood a row of brightly patterned enamel bowls. Uncovering one, Rahim presented me with a litre of warm, foamy milk. When I hesitated he said, 'Plenty! Plenty!' and pointed through the doorway. His pitiably kyphotic wife had just finished milking three healthy zebu – presumably Rahim's own – and was hobbling across the tree-shaded compound carrying another bowl.

Among the Fulani's many agreeable customs is an eagerness – almost a compulsion – to provide passing strangers with as much milk as they can drink. In theory (the sort of theory that makes total sense as one studies *Hints for Tropical Travellers*, pre-journey) one should politely decline this potentially lethal liquid and go ascetically on one's way. In practice however trekkers see fresh milk not as a health hazard but as the best possible fuel for the day ahead. When I had emptied the bowl Rahim gave me two tiny padlock keys, tied to a grubby, illegible label, and reminded me that my daughter must also have milk.

By 9.30 a.m. Rachel had emptied her bowl and Rahim was showing us the wide track to Ranch Headquarters. Not far from his compound stood a baffling two-storey cattle-trailer of the type associated with intercontinental trucking. Judging by the invading vegetation it had been idle for some time – but how had it got here? Then we realised that this was a motorable track, comparatively recently bulldozed through the bush.

We walked parallel to a long, low, rocky ridge, nearby on our right, with miles of flat stony scrubland stretching away on our left. Even after the rains this would provide poor grazing; now the red earth was naked and cracked between brownish-green bushes.

Where the ridge ended the track swung right and dropped abruptly to well watered green pastureland, amply shaded by tall spreading trees and close cropped by hundreds of sheep and goats – none as yet cross-bred and all in good condition. Very far below lay an immense expanse of cultivated land with Mount Ocu conspicuous beyond.

'We've got our timing badly wrong,' I observed. 'We'll hit that hot spot during the afternoon.'

Soon after the track divided, one branch continuing down, the other climbing towards a jagged escarpment. 'Let's go up!' I urged.

'And eat what?' enquired Rachel. 'More instant stew? How many miles are we supposed to walk on tiny packets of dehydrated vegetables?'

I consulted the USAF and suggested, 'That *up* track could be the right one. We don't *know* we must go down to get to Mount Ocu. The map only says it's 9,879 feet high.'

At that moment we noticed the shepherd, a tall skinny youth lurking nervously behind a tree. In response to my greeting he took refuge in a hut amongst bushes. When I followed and peered through the doorway he joined his hands together, as though in prayer, and whispered something inaudible. It took time to reassure him. Then he emerged and conveyed that the upward track went *nowhere*.

'Good!' said Rachel.

That descent was spectacular: from about 7,000 to 3,000 feet in a few memorable miles. We were still quite high when a Range Rover appeared some fifty yards ahead. It had of necessity been travelling slowly (this track was only *just* motorable) and it went even more slowly when the occupants observed the Murphies on the march. Then it stopped. A small, stout, sallow Frenchman was driving. His companion – also small and stout but very black – wore a fawn lounge suit, an Edwardian solar topi, several gold rings and a pompous angry expression. Neither man spoke English. The driver asked, with a snarl in his voice, how and where we had entered the ranch. The man from Yaoundé (for such he must surely have been) accused us of trespassing on private property.

This seemed a suitable moment to test David's ju-ju. Ritualistically unfolding the Attestation I presented it to Monsieur Topi with the air of someone solving a problem. He looked at it uneasily – very uneasily. Then he passed it to his companion who pointed to one of the seals and muttered something. They looked at each other ... The Frenchman returned the document to me, nodded curtly and drove on.

'Marvellous ju-ju!' I enthused, carefully replacing the fetish in my passport.

Soon after, our descent was broken by a level fertile shelf, a couple of miles wide and several miles long. Here dozens of Fulani brood mares grazed in paddocks with First World fencing; their foals all looked half-bred. In one field, some 200 yards from the track, a mixed-sex work-gang was briskly clearing stones – so briskly that I studied them through my binoculars. All were youngsters, being supervised by a man carrying a long stick. We went quietly on our way, glad not to have been observed.

Ahead lay the unpeopled Ranch Headquarters. Apparently an ambitious 'development' had been abandoned, or at least had had its completion postponed. Four extra-outsize brand-new tractors stood in a spacious yard enclosed on three sides by wire fencing and on the fourth by a high mud wall like the first stage of a medieval fortification. In the centre of this entirely irrelevant obstruction, a tractor-wide corrugated-iron gate stood open. Beyond were a few inexplicable breeze-block buildings (stables? granaries?) and several fancy bunga-lows set in unsuccessful gardens. On either side of the track stood long rows of what can only be described as roofless, mud-brick terrace houses with quasi-Moorish archways instead of doors and quasi-Gothic embrasures instead of windows.

'An embryonic tourist centre?' I speculated. 'With horse-trekking as the centre-piece?'

This suspicion was strengthened when we came upon the weed-infested foundations for some colossal structure – a Holiday Inn?

We were puzzling over the absence of people when a burly shouting man, barefooted and pock-marked, pursued us. Mysteriously, one of his trouser-legs had been cut off at the knee, which gave him a misleadingly clownish air. At first his manner veered oddly from subservience to truculence: then he settled for the latter. He spoke a mixture of Pidgin and broken English but his intentions were clear. We must report to the office – we had caused offence by not greeting anyone – we couldn't leave the ranch without his permission because the road out was blocked and guarded by his friends ...

'He just wants dash,' diagnosed Rachel. 'Give him something and let's get out of here!'

Then the Land Rover reappeared; I waved at it and our companion cowered. The Man from Yaoundé leant out and yelled something as the vehicle turned off towards a bungalow. Our companion discarded truculence, cordially shook hands and wished us '*Bon voyage!*'

Moments later we heard thundering hoofs; eight little boys were galloping after us, riding bareback and shrieking ferociously to urge on their mounts. Hastily I led Egbert into the trackside scrub. As the stallions raced past we glimpsed exultant faces: 'The only cheerfulness around!' noted Rachel.

Volcanic landscapes are magnificently unpredictable. From the ranch shelf our track plunged into an arid red chasm, too irregular to be called a valley, a ravine or a cleft – an eerily unfinished area, as though Nature, like the Men from Yaoundé, had postponed completing this development. The track, gouged out of cliff-faces by people rich enough to acquire bulldozers but ignorant of road-building, had already been so eroded that no truck could possibly use it. 'Now we know,' I remarked, 'why that cattle-trailer has been abandoned.' Here the cruel gradient, combined with sharp loose surface stones and deep cracks, caused poor Egbert some distress.

The noon heat radiated relentlessly from fissured precipices and chaotic rocky gullies. Then, as we slowly climbed from the chasm floor, a watercourse appeared ahead: a dramatically green thin line on the flank of a vast parched mountain. A road-block also appeared, looking more like an international border post than most such do in Africa. My binoculars revealed a heavy pole, stretched between two smartly painted red and white sentry boxes, and three men sitting on camp-chairs.

Where the stream crossed the track, out of sight of the sentries, we watered Egbert, washed, and filled our bottles. As we approached the men I made ready to flourish my fetish but they insolently ignored us. All looked moronic and wore vaguely military tattered tunics. One was abstractedly masturbating and didn't bother to button up when we stood beside him requesting the lifting of the barrier. At last the CO stirred himself and sauntered around Egbert, eyeing the load. He scowled, made a 'No pass!' gesture, and seemed to be insisting, in Pidgin, that we return to Ranch Headquarters. I was about to argue when Rachel moved forward decisively, raised the barrier with one hand and led Egbert through. Quickly I followed, then turned to wave to the CO. He was staring after us, looking comically nonplussed. When I congratulated Rachel she observed, 'It's too hot for palavering!'

It became hotter still as we descended. All around us angular black and red rocks, a few hundred feet high, stuck out of the ground looking oddly like peaks without mountains. Not until 12.30 p.m. did we come to a few warped dwarf trees. Unloading, we left Egbert to make what he could of a straggle of wiry grass and collapsed in sweaty heaps. The trees afforded only minimal shade and were pullulating – every trunk and branch – with giant black ants. These fell upon us in showers –

accidentally, but none the less irritatingly. Minute black flies bit us savagely and incessantly. That was the first of many unrelaxing midday 'rest'-stops.

An hour later we rejoiced to see a fleet of dark rain clouds come sailing over the mountains. We were about to load when another Range Rover appeared, going towards 'Headquarters'. Two of the passengers were German-Swiss cattle experts; the third was a polite but wary-looking Cameroonian in jeans and a facetious T-shirt. When we had introduced ourselves the senior expert, leaving his companions standing by the vehicle, walked with me towards Egbert. He looked more than slightly demented and suddenly turned aside to sit under a tree.

'So you have seen this ranch!' he said. 'So you can believe my frustrations – right? All this, it is what you I think call arseways on – AI to make *big* animals before they have food for them! So the cattle become sick, right? And when calves are born many cows die. Zebu cows are *narrow*, calves with Holstein daddies are *broad* – right? Years ago I come, study everything, tell them, "*First* you spend time and money making new, richer pastures. *Then* you have Holstein semen for some cows, for those who can carry such calves." But no! no! no! At once all cows must have big calves! Then I come back and look again and tell them, "Now you have made half-European cattle, you must give them European feed! In the dry season these animals need brewers' grains, rice bran, cotton seed cake, bone powder, trace minerals." But no! no! no! They want only to *see* big animals, not to spend big money – only to make it ... For them AI is White Man's Magic, never they connect big breeds with scientific feed! When animals go sick or die they say we give bad semen – you see I have frustrations? Why do I come back here wasting time? Never will they listen – not these Big Men. The Fulanis they would work with me, they could learn. These rich men, they are all from areas without cattle, they think this is just one more way of quickly getting richer.' He looked around as his colleague called impatiently. 'Now I go back to my frustrations! Some day maybe we meet again and I can tell you more. Much, much more! But only when I am leaving this country for the last time – you understand? Ha, I see you do! You are an old lady of the world, yes?'

As we continued I felt a twinge of sympathy for the Men from Yaoundé. It is largely our fault that so many Africans are confused about the application of White farming methods to Black countries. For decades agricultural aid advisors have been preaching totally impractical gospels. Our Swiss acquaintance was right to assume that Fulani cattle-men would have co-operated with him; but how many 'experts' from USAID, the FAO or the World Bank appreciate the intelligence, common sense and inherited wisdom of Third World farmers?

In 1985 the World Bank analysed the results of seventeen massive agricultural aid projects in Africa: thirteen were failures. The economic returns on livestock projects averaged *minus 2 per cent,* compared with an 11 per cent gain in Asia and Latin America. Those projects were the idiot brain-children of doctorate-laden academics keen to save Africa's illiterate peasantry from the consequences of their own ignorance. It was assumed that results obtained in high-powered research stations could be duplicated by villagers. Chemical fertilisers were introduced and promptly increased the soil's acidity in humid regions while making almost no difference to yields in dry regions – and thus failing to cover their considerable costs. Monocropping was encouraged at the expense of intercropping. Imported heavy machinery destabilised frail fields. Rainfall variations were ignored. New technologies, seed varieties and crops were introduced, regardless of the disastrous effects they might (and usually did) have on delicately balanced systems. Over the past quarter-century I have heard a lot about – and quite often observed – the crassness of Western aid 'experts' on other continents. But nowhere have they been so destructive as in Africa.

Approaching the big village of Kikfuni, we attracted much amazed/amused attention. No less amazing, to us, was a youngish man wearing a lime-green track suit, expensive runners and a white Panama hat. He welcomed us to his village, introducing himself as George Charles Akuro, home from Hamburg on a two-month holiday. His swaggering progress was attended by several adult 'followers' – male relatives and family connections, all no doubt dependent on the rich exile's largesse – and by half a dozen children clad in garments of German provenance. He had been working in Hamburg as 'an import businessman' for ten years.

'I am home to arrange more business and marry my new wife – we have four children and many others will come!'

I asked how and why he had settled in Germany. Vaguely he replied, 'My missionary friend wanted me to go.' When I provocatively enquired if he would bring his new wife and their four children to Europe he looked quite shocked. 'They would be unhappy and cold! It is very, very cold in Germany. There I have another wife who is used to the weather.'

George stayed with us when we stopped at the first suitable off-licence – suitable because of a lush patch of grass nearby. It was crowded, as village off-licences often are from breakfast-time onwards, and a shiny Nigerian cassette-player rendered conversation impossible. Beer and soft drinks were the same price: 200 CFA (about 44p) per half-litre. Cameroonian soft drinks (brand-named 'Top') are loathsome ersatz 'fruit juices', dyed a sinister orange or green. Cameroonian beer, on the other hand, is of a consistently high standard.

We sat outside the door, on sharply uncomfortable plastic beer crates, and at once George commanded the bar girl to bring a chair. As it appeared I murmured 'Thank you,' being not as yet fully attuned to Cameroon's social mores. I was about to move when George swung the chair around to face us and settled himself comfortably, looking expectant. We had however learned one lesson: never offer a drink to a casual acquaintance. Too many other customers then expected free drinks from the rich White.

George quickly gave up hope and ordered for himself and his followers. 'This is a *bad* country!' he complained. 'A poor bad country where the people are *very* lazy!'

'Why do you say that?' I asked. 'We think it's a *good* rich country where people are kind and mostly have enough to eat and the landscape is beautiful. There are more homeless and hungry people in the USA than there are here!'

'Cameroon is *very* bad,' insisted George. 'All these bush people, they don't know how to live – they are backward stupid people! In Hamburg I have everything – big home, big car, deep freeze, fridge, cine-camera, television, stereo-system, swimming-pool for my kids. See! I show you!'

He drew a thick wallet of photographs from his briefcase and the children crowded eagerly around to marvel yet again at his achievements. There was George, leaning nonchalantly on the roof of a Mercedes by the open driving door – and George removing a silver-foil-wrapped dish from a face-level microwave oven – and George posing by an open refrigerator taller than himself and packed with colourful goodies – and so on. There were dozens of photographs, all of a professionally high standard and looking remarkably like advertisements for the objects illustrated. I wondered ... George somehow lacked the aura of a wealthy import-export merchant.

Watching the children staring with awed incomprehension at these emanations from another world, I remembered those who are working hard and patiently, without publicity or luxury funding, to introduce 'appropriate technologies' to rural Africa. Ease of communication, when it means bright pictures of the enviable unattainable circulating in Cameroonian villages, is not necessarily beneficial. On being shown how well a *jiko* can work, young Africans might understandably ask, 'Why is an ex-tar-barrel oven appropriate for us and a microwave oven appropriate for you?'

Questioned about The Ranch, George was uninformative. 'These are good rich men, making good plans for this area.'

'But *who* are they?' I persisted. 'And *what* are their plans?'

'It is not known,' said George.

Kikfuni is a widespread village of prosperous compounds embedded in greenery; it took ten minutes to walk from that off-licence to the big eight-day-market place in the village centre. The many rows of roughly constructed thatched stalls were empty, but a line of small shops by the side of the track sold a few basic goods. We left loaded with the cheapest Cameroonian foods: bananas at 5 CFA each and giant avocados at 10 CFA each.

The local weather, we were beginning to realise, is Irish-capricious during the little rains. We had been expecting an afternoon downpour but although the sky clouded over and the temperature dropped perceptibly no rain fell.

Here the level land was densely cultivated – an apparently untidy, uncontrolled jungle of crops: kolanut, pawpaw and mango trees, coffee bushes, beans, groundnuts, sugar-cane, bananas, plantains and young maize already a foot high. Such areas give the impression of a land so rich and lush, so smiled upon by Nature, that merely scattering a few seeds around ensures super-abundant food. This false impression has an echo in one of Britain's most offensive racial stereotypes: 'Those lazy Blacks! Trouble is no one has to work where they come from, they just lie around in the sun all day watching things grow!' In fact such 'unruly' regions are agricultural works of art, the result of sophisticated planning based on centuries of precise observations and imaginative experiments. But unfortunately such intensive cultivation is not the rule in Cameroon, being found only in heavily populated areas where the surrounding terrain makes shifting cultivation impossible.

The track was busy as women and children went to and fro from their fields, laughing and gossiping and occasionally quarrelling. The adults greeted us cheerfully, the teenagers giggled shyly, the children seemed half-scared. In maize plots women hacked vigorously at tangles of weeds; where crops flourish, so do their weed competitors and insect foes. One motive for burning fields is to kill weed seeds and insect larvae, another is to reduce soil acidity. The ill-effects of indiscriminate burning are not yet understood.

Some 75 per cent of Cameroonians remain on the land, growing over 90 per cent of the country's food. Moreover, the land is their own. Outside of Zimbabwe and Kenya (for obvious reasons) there are few landless peasants in Black Africa. This may partly explain why rural Cameroonians seem so much more self-confident, relaxed and contented than their fellow peasants in Peru or India. Life is hard, but they are independent. The disadvantages of a rural economy based on subsistence smallholdings are of course considerable, though less acute in Cameroon than in most Black African countries. One snag is the lack of an influential 'farming lobby' organised by large landowners. Many villagers complained to us about the government monopoly on cash crops (notably coffee) which are bought for scarcely half the world market prices. Yet Cameroon has been comparatively lucky; her individual smallholders know that they are people of consequence on whom the national well-being depends. Both President Ahidjo and President Biya have emphasised the importance of agriculture for Black Africa. Neither was lured by outside interests into giving priority to industrial development: hence Cameroon's minute national debt, at a time when most of her neighbours have been ruined by the need to import expensive foodstuffs. Yet red lights are flashing. The population has recently been increasing at about 200,000 a year and, since the mid-1980s, there has been a need to import grain to feed villagers newly settled in the cities. President Biya has stated, 'Agriculture must and will remain the priority sector within the context of the National Development Programme.' But he is ominously silent on the subject of birth-control.

The average Cameroonian holding is less than three hectares (about seven acres) yet throughout our journey we noticed much cultivable land to spare, apart from what was lying fallow. A shortage of labour is one factor limiting Africa's food production; there are no swarms of landless peasants. This situation could be partially remedied if men's working habits became more flexible. Traditionally they confine themselves to clearing new land, turning the soil and growing cash crops: coffee, cocoa, palm oil. The cash is usually kept by the men for their own use. Women are expected to grow enough to feed the family; and what they earn by selling surplus food locally will, with luck, pay for the children's clothing. Meanwhile they also have to bear and rear those children, fetch water and gather firewood (often from considerable distances), prepare and cook meals (a lengthy and tiring process when all the grain has to be pounded), do the laundry, wash-up and clean the compound. Not only ardent feminists condemn this division of labour.

By 6 p.m. we were climbing gradually between hilly fields. Some carried sugar-cane and others – just dug, in readiness for planting – were scattered with high cairns of stones. This was unpromising camping terrain but we rightly guessed there must be a village nearby.

Acha (much smaller and less attractive than Kikfuni) lay at the base of an alluring jumble of mountains: Mount Ocu's foothills. Rectangular tin-roofed mud huts straggled on either side of the track and Mr Nomo Zambo, the only person in sight, hurried from his doorway to invite us to stay. His wife was away in Kumbo, waiting to have her fifth baby at the Mission Hospital, but his nieces were looking after him and could also look after us.

When Mr Zambo and Rachel had led Egbert away, to look for good grazing, a twenty-year-old nephew escorted me to the off-licence. Neuke was small, slight, handsome; he had clear bright eyes, glossy black skin and an open eager expression. The off-licence, furnished only with a few benches and a stack of crates in one corner, was empty of customers.

'Here there are many Muslims who don't drink beer,' explained Neuke. He himself had become a Muslim quite recently, when he married – but he was not, he emphasised, teetotal. The family, we later discovered, were Bamunka; but Mr Zambo wore Fulani dress because ten years ago he had gone over to Islam after quarrelling with Christian relatives about land. To us this seemed something of a *non sequitur*, but that merely reveals our ignorance of local affairs.

Neuke took two '33's from a crate, since there was no one around to serve us. 'I am lucky!' he said. 'Every morning I walk to study carpentry in Kikfuni and come home late. But not today because my teacher has fever. So now I talk to you and it's good to talk English with White people because at school we have bad teachers. Last year two White people came in a Land Rover, to Lake Ocu, but they slept in a big tent in the bush. My uncle was sad and angry. To say "No" when you are invited is bad. We like to look after travellers and share everything we have.'

Neuke deplored the war in Chad. 'It makes me sad – too many dying and starving! But this is a peaceful country – you see how we have plenty, plenty food and no guns and fighting. If we like we become Christian, Muslim, pagan – no one makes trouble about it. No one asks questions about religion or politics. We are lucky, happy people!'

It would be misleading to describe Cameroonian villagers as 'politically aware', yet most seem proud of their country's record since Independence. Neuke was the first of many who expressed to us a genuine appreciation of Cameroon's stability and prosperity.

When I offered Neuke a second beer his response was unnerving – 'I wait for your wife and my uncle, then we all drink together!'

I am used to being misgendered at first glance, when clad and equipped for trekking, but never before had I sat talking to someone for half an hour without their diagnosing my sex. Moreover, it was hard to convince Neuke that Rachel and I are in fact mother and daughter – and even harder to convince Mr Zambo, when he and Rachel joined us.

Throughout Cameroon this confusion persisted, not only in remote villages but in little towns where even government officials, or police and army officers – some from cosmopolitan Yaoundé – invariably assumed me to be male. We decided that the problem was twofold: physical and psychological. My appearance did not conform to the Cameroonian image of elegant, fragile White women, an image derived mainly from magazine illustrations, or glimpses of expatriate wives swanning around the capital. Also, they could not conceive of two *women* wandering through the bush and camping out in the (to them) menacing loneliness of the night.

Mr Zambo evidently took his conversion seriously, whatever its motivation, and though he stood Rachel a beer he would accept only Top from me. 'Now I am Muslim, I don't have strong drink.'

Irish potatoes thrive in Cameroon and are now popular as a 'special dish', often spelt 'Iris' when chalked up on menu-boards in eating houses. So Mr Zambo and Neuke were much perplexed by our Irishness; to them being Irish meant being a potato – not a human being. I was tempted to tell them that Murphies are sometimes known as 'Spuds', which is another name for potatoes, and that potatoes are sometimes known as 'Murphies'. But that would have intolerably confused the issue.

We tried to describe Ireland but soon realised that our friends, like most of the Cameroonians we were to meet, could not visualise the world beyond their own region. They were vague even about Cameroon's neighbours – except Nigeria, which is within walking distance of the Grassfields and not regarded as 'foreign'.

Before supper we were shown into a small yard behind the main hut. The latrine was on the far side, behind a raffia screen – a deep, wide, odourless hole criss-crossed by bamboo poles on which one squatted. On the ground in another corner a deep basin of hot water (four feet in circumference) had been provided for our ablutions, complete with a fresh cake of soap and a giant sponge. Cameroonians – unlike the Murphies when trekking – are almost obsessional about washing their bodies and their clothes. Apart from a few homeless semi-idiots, I cannot recall seeing one unclean individual in three months. Yet we were travelling in areas where tap water is virtually unknown.

In the largest room, measuring some fifteen feet by eighteen, half the floor space was taken up by a four-poster bed – ours for the night. Here Neuke's sister, an attractive fourteen-year-old wearing a BVM medal around her neck, served supper by lamplight. Uncle and nephew sat watching as she struggled to push aside the heavy raffia door-curtain while carrying a laden tray. She was followed by the eldest Zambo boy, a doted-on nine-year-old who stayed by his father for the rest of the evening but didn't eat with us. The fufu was heavier than at Doi's and rather gluey. Instead of jammu-jammu we had a mess of bony dried fish in a sauce not spicy enough to conceal the fact that the fish had decayed before being dried. We sat on home-made wooden chairs, bending over the low table to eat from the communal dishes and piling our bones on a communal saucer.

Discussing our route, we discovered that this village, known as Acha in Kikfuni, was called something quite different by its inhabitants, who in turn called Kikfuni something beginning with 'Mb' – and so it went on, even towns like Kumbo having two or three names. 'But what else can you expect,' remarked Rachel afterwards, 'when villagers living five miles apart don't understand each other's languages?'

As we sipped our post-prandial Ovaltine, I casually enquired about

The Ranch and its development. Neuke asked excitedly, 'How did you get in? Did you see the Big Men?' But Mr Zambo looked sharply at him and said, 'We don't know about these people.' Whereupon Neuke said no more.

By nine o'clock we were comfortably abed, sharing a blanket but each with a little pillow in a freshly laundered blue cotton cover. Overhead was a wickerwork awning, between us and the cobweb-laden rafters. Both inside walls were of cane and through their cracks lamplight shone faintly. Most Cameroonians won't sleep in total darkness and Mr Zambo had been astonished when we assured him that no lamp need be left in our room.

We speculated about our bed's usual occupants. Mr and Mrs Zambo might seem a reasonable assumption – except that Cameroonian husbands do not normally share sleeping-quarters with their wives, merely visiting them briefly (though frequently) in their own huts or rooms. More likely this de luxe bed was shared by our host and his small sons.

4

On and Around Mount Ocu

THE TRACK TO Lake Ocu is motorable but rarely motored; during a glorious five-hour climb, from 3,500 to 8,700 feet, we saw no vehicles and few people.

Resting at one hairpin bend, we watched two tall lean men, armed with gleaming spears even longer than themselves, go bounding up a hillside: monkey-hunters, no doubt. The local small grey white-faced monkey is a favourite source of protein and its numbers are dwindling accordingly.

For hours the track wound around the flanks of golden-grassed mountains, their craggy peaks silver against a cobalt sky. Sometimes tall trees shaded us; sometimes we were crossing wide ledges which supported a few compounds and maize plots; sometimes quick clear streams watered broad green pastures where small boys tended large cattle. Then the mountains became more precipitous, huddled closer and were darkly forested. This track, originally hewn out of the cliff-face by Germans, overhung ravines too sheer for even the boldest hunter. Many monkeys were audible, but wisely remained invisible amidst their refuge of impenetrable vegetation.

By noon we were on the cool top of the local world, walking level around tree-covered summits above profound forested valleys containing one of the few fragments of primeval forest we saw in Cameroon – untouched because protected by the mountains' formation. Nowhere else have I heard birdsong of such variety and beauty: a continuous, complex flow of sweetness, a strangely moving echo from ages past, from a time when there was room on our planet for all Nature's handiwork.

I was walking slowly, my binoculars at the ready, when we were overtaken by three young men and two young women, the latter carrying enormous heaped baskets wrapped in bright blankets. One of the men was armed with a sling made of wood and tyre strips. As we continued together he amused himself by aiming at birds – not for food, just for fun. Even had he wanted to retrieve his prey the density of the forest, right to the edge of the track, would have prevented this. He and his mates could see more with the naked eye than I could with binoculars. Repeatedly he paused to pick up a sharp little stone and have another shot. When he scored his mates grinned admiringly but the women ignored him – though not, I fear, because their ecological consciences were smiting them.

Where we gradually began to descend the forest thinned slightly on our left. By then the track's twistings had addled even Rachel's sense of direction and we might have missed the turn-off but for our companions' guidance. That little path sloped gently upwards through monstrously abused woodland and we braced ourselves to meet the shock for which Mr Zambo had prepared us. 'Beside the lake,' he had said, 'there is a house for tourists – a *mighty* house!'

This hideous cross between a much-magnified log-cabin and a malformed Swiss chalet was an example of government-sponsored vandalism. It squatted on a bulldozed ledge – itself a raw wound on the mountainside – and seemed to have been instantly abandoned on completion. Its untreated boards had weathered to a dingy grey, its doors and windows were rigidly shuttered and bolted and nearby stood a long rusty tin shed. All the surrounding once-magnificent trees were fire-victims and the morbid stench of stale compacted ash and rotting half-burnt vegetation powerfully irritated our nostrils. Apart from two old sardine tins, and an insect-repellent aerosol container (relics of the Whites who wouldn't stay with Uncle?), there was no evidence that this 'tourist house' had ever been approached, never mind occupied, by anyone.

Turning our backs on this tragic squalor, we moved to the crater rim and gazed over the bottle-green lake a hundred feet below. It lay absolutely still, about a mile wide and several miles long, surrounded by virgin forest. Only where we stood had its loveliness been desecrated. Yet 'loveliness' is not the right word: it too much suggests simple, lightsome beauty. And Lake Ocu's atmosphere is unsettling. Without knowing anything of history, one would, I think, sense here a hint of the sinister. Although Cameroonians had warned us that it is lethal even to descend to the water's edge, Whites had recommended it for swimming – and all morning, sweating uphill, we had been looking forward to plunging in. But now it somehow seemed untempting. Besides, in this horribly mauled place there was alarmingly little lunch for Egbert: no grass, only a few stunted bushes with which he was unenthusiastically toying.

At 8,000 feet we were able to enjoy the midday sun while eating sardines and stale bread. Only our own munching broke the silence; Egbert had given up on the bushes and was dozing. No breeze ruffled the lake's surface or stirred the foliage on the crater wall below us. We chanced to be sitting precisely at the centre of this rim and the whole visible world had an uncanny symmetry. Dark green water, lighter green forest, deep blue sky. The forest showed no botanical irregularity, the shoreline no geological irregularity. An eighteenth-century garden could not have seemed more formally ordered.

'It's a bit eerie,' I remarked, 'to be overlooking such an expanse without any sound or movement.' But even as I spoke there was movement: a pair of golden-backed fish-eagles glided from the forest and began slowly to circle below us, their pinions scarcely moving, their grace and power superb.

All Cameroonian lakes are to some degree sacred and Lake Ocu is more so than most. For centuries Ocu was an important chiefdom and at a new Fon's enstoolment he was solemnly bathed in water from the lake. The ritual protection of the chiefdom was among his main responsibilities. (Palace officials looked after the practical details of administration and trade.) Every year, in February, during the guinea-corn harvest, he led his priests, of whom he was the chief, and his councillors, and a representative group of ordinary men and women, to the lake shore. There he conducted the *ntul* rite, to ensure the fertility of crops and women and invoke protection from all misfortunes. A goat was slaughtered and thrown into the water, together with corn and other foodstuffs. Neuke believed that humans as well as goats were sacrificed in pre-colonial times but Mr Zambo indignantly dismissed this as 'a bad story missionaries told us to put us against our chiefs and religions'. However, missionaries did not invent Ocu's ritual slaughtering and burial of slaves, which, together with the planting of trees, were essential components of alliance-building to end inter-chiefdom wars.

Within ten minutes of rejoining the track we came upon a scene that has haunted me ever since. Here the mountains were slightly less steep and for miles ahead, in every direction, the ancient forest had recently been cleared leaving a blackened nightmare of desolation. On every slope the charred corpses of hundreds of mighty trees lay amidst the ashes of their precious jungle undergrowth. I felt physically shocked, as though someone had kicked me in the stomach. I couldn't speak. But the younger generation, brought up in a world being rapidly devastated by human fecundity, have had to grow tougher carapaces.

'You have too many people, you get this,' Rachel noted laconically.

In the day's first village, a steep hour later, Egbert grazed ravenously opposite the off-licence while we sat with a score of beer-relaxed men. Numerous near-naked small children were romping and singing and dancing in the shade of the empty market-stalls. A few had worm-distended bellies; the rest looked vibrantly healthy. Here it was very hot and very lush. On the surrounding slopes many older children were helping mothers and grandmothers as they toiled in fields with punishing gradients.

The locals called Lake Ocu 'Lake Mawes' and were intensely proud of the 'tourist house'. One jaunty young man, home on holidays from 'an office job' in Douala, foretold that many, many tourists would visit Ocu when the funds came through (from Britain) for the new Bamenda ring-road.

Continuing downhill, we crossed a narrow green valley of magical beauty before climbing again, along the flanks of well-wooded mountains, to the broad crest of a densely populated ridge. Having joined a genuinely motorable track, we passed through the elongated village (or little town) of Jakiri. It was 4.30 p.m. and when the sky suddenly darkened I suggested seeking lodgings. But Rachel pointed out that Egbert needed choice grazing, not just – as on the previous night – a skimpy patch of grass left over by the local goats.

In the village centre a large thatched mud building had elaborately carved antique doorposts, featuring stylised naked men and monkeys. When I paused to examine these an unusual current of hostility emanated from three elderly men sitting nearby on stools no less elaborately carved – presumably the Chief's clansmen, to whom the privileges of decorated doorposts and carved stools are traditionally restricted. They returned my greeting with un-Cameroonian coldness and I veered away.

Soon a gigantic beer truck slowly jolted past us, its cargo rattling demoniacally. As there was room to take Egbert off the track, he kept his cool; but further on, in the mountains, there might be no manoeuvering space. Realising that this narrow, erosion-fissured track was in fact the main motor-road to the important town of Kumbo, we followed a loaded girl up a steep 'cut-short' across a cultivated ridge.

Half an hour later, as we were about to rejoin the road, a few heavy raindrops fell from a low, charcoal-grey sky. We hesitated, surveying our immediate surroundings through Egbert's eyes. Probably any of the several nearby compounds would have willingly sheltered us: but there was no grazing in sight, only cultivated fields. Foolishly we continued, telling ourselves that storms are brief during the little rains.

This one wasn't. It quickly became the most spectacular meteorological event to which I have ever been exposed – and exposed is the *mot juste*. The landscape looked utterly unlike anywhere else we had seen and there was no vestige of shelter. From about 7,000 feet we were overlooking, on our left, an immense panorama of bare rolling hills and long ridges – all dug ready for planting. On our right a similar ridge of naked earth sloped up from the road. There were no trees, bushes, rocks or compounds. The soil was not red but an unusual (for Cameroon) dark brown. And we were still climbing, fighting now against a gale-force wind that made nonsense of the load's waterproof covering. Our own capes flapped like demented things, further unnerving poor Egbert, so we took them off. Like all horses everywhere, he detested facing into a rainy gale. It astonished me that after each attempt to turn tail (literally) he responded to my coaxing – albeit very reluctantly – and bravely soldiered on.

Within fifteen minutes the road had become a foaming torrent. The icy wind carried sharp hailstones mixed with blinding sheets of rain. On the road's highest point, below a dark escarpment of jagged rock, the gale almost blew us over. Egbert decisively turned tail and this time he meant it. I didn't even attempt more coaxing.

Now the scene far below on our left had a weird violent beauty. All the hills and ridges were hidden beneath miles of racing ragged black cloud, seen as though from an aeroplane; never had I imagined that clouds could move so fast. And above all this speeding vapour were stationary cloud banks through which brilliant explosions of blue and white lightning danced and flared erratically. The thunder's vibrations tingled from the ground up my legs and throughout my whole body – a truly extraordinary sensation. Its roaring and crackling were continuous, the echoes of each shattering crash merging into the next.

Retreating from the crest, we stood shivering in the middle of the road. There was nothing to be said, nothing to be done. Our situation seemed unreal: two humans and a horse become the helpless victims of this elemental mania – scourged by hail, buffeted by the gale, deafened by thunder, dazzled by lightning, unable to proceed and with nowhere to shelter. Egbert was trembling and breathing fast, his ears laid back. I put an arm over his neck, for mutual comfort, and reflected that this must surely be the storm's crescendo: very soon the drama would have moved on. Then my eye was caught by the raffia bags over the pommel and I used bad language. In one lay Egbert's salt *and* our camera, the latter in a dustproof but not waterproof wrapping. There was no possibility that a camera infiltrated by wet salt would ever work again.

When the wind suddenly dropped I looked at my watch and realised that we had been immobilised for only seventeen minutes. It felt like an hour. Slowly we continued, our teeth chattering. We needed a quick warming march but Egbert was clearly feeling the effects of exposure plus malnutrition. The rain had lightened to what would seem a downpour at home but then seemed a mere drizzle. Half a mile below the crest stood a solitary shack and desperately I knocked on the tin door. A young woman cautiously opened it, uttered a piercing scream, slammed it shut and drew a bolt.

We plodded on. It was 6.20 p.m. and would soon be dark. The rain however had almost stopped and we were considering unloading, and sleeping in space-blankets on the road, when we saw a distant tree and deduced more 'normal' terrain. Around that tree was a patch of level ground, supporting a few clumps of coarse grass. Marvelling at our good luck, we hurried to get the tent up while the rain was minimal, a routine that took much longer than usual by torchlight. Leaving our dripping clothes outside, we snuggled into damp flea-bags and had mint-cake for supper. Large immovable stones lay under the tent in all the wrong places, below ribs and hips. And it had been impossible to push the pegs more than half-way down.

'If it rains again,' said Rachel gloomily, 'we've had it!'

'Think positive!' I urged. 'There *can't* be any rain left around here!'

But there was – lots. The next (windless) downpour started at 11.45 p.m. and continued all night. Because the pegs were insecure the fly-sheet touched the inner tent and by 1 a.m. our bags were sodden.

'This is *worse* than Peru!' pronounced Rachel, through teeth again chattering.

'Don't be daft!' I snapped. 'You've just gone soft after six years at boarding-school!'

At dawn it was still raining, lightly. Emerging naked from the tent I was startled to see three women standing two yards away, staring. They too were startled.

'At least,' said Rachel '*they* realise you're not my husband.'

All our possessions, except our books, were saturated. As we helped each other to pull on wet clothes many other hoe-bearing women appeared on little field-paths – vivid daubs of colour in a drab world of low grey cloud and bare brown hills.

By 6.10 a.m. we were on our way: chilled through, unrested, hungry. Egbert had also had a wretched night and was moving accordingly. And then, further to lower morale, we came upon the inexorable sequel to deforestation.

Above the road on our right a steep mountain had recently been cleared, though not so recently as the previous day's arboreal graveyard. Already the new season's maize had been planted, but the rain-storm had ravaged that entire mountainside. Tons and tons and tons of soil covered the road – statistics come horribly to life. Under forest, such a slope loses almost no soil through erosion. Under crops it can lose from 200 to 400 tons *per hectare* (90 to 170 tons per acre) each year. Thus in one year a *century's* soil formation may be washed away. Rain falling at more than 25 mm (one inch) an hour is erosive. Only 5 per cent of a temperate region's rainfall reaches that figure but Africa often experiences *100–150 mm* (4–7 inches) an hour, such as the deluge we had just endured.

Reading about erosion tragedies, the mind is numbed by an anaesthetic of hectares and years and millimetres and tons and centuries. It is another matter to see and smell and struggle through the event as it is happening. Miserably we squelched and skidded across those tons of squandered soil – made still more poignant by the frail maize seedlings, killed in infancy, that occasionally showed through. That storm had brought disaster to a family as well as to a mountain, a family who had worked themselves to exhaustion to clear the land. They had not meant to commit an ecological crime; they only wanted to feed and clothe and educate their children. In Cameroon one cannot feel the rage provoked by the activities of American beef-ranchers in Amazonia or Japanese logging-companies in Borneo. One can only feel despair.

Those two scenes – the newly burnt miles around Lake Ocu and the denuded mountain – could be used in a strip-cartoon for children to illustrate the fragility of our planet: and especially of *Africa,* where geological old age is a problem. The soil is geriatric, African rocks and mountains being some 4,000 million years old. They therefore weather into coarse, large-grained soils, as is apparent even to non-scientific travellers. These are easily eroded, poor at retaining nutrients and water, low in phosphorus and nitrogen and so by far the least fertile in the world. That visually attractive red soil so common in Africa is in fact a menace. Being full of iron oxides it tends to crystallise, forming rock-hard uncultivable wasteland. Stripped of vegetation, Africa will die – both the land and the people.

Newcomers are often puzzled by Africa's lack of irrigation, but Paul Harrison explains it in *The Greening of Africa*:

Africa's transition (from extensive to intensive farming) is more problematical than in any other area. The Asian option of irrigation is much more difficult. The African landscape, outside East Africa, is generally flat, and her rivers are highly variable in their flow. Surface waters are less common, and shallow ground-water is harder to find. The opportunities for cheap and simple irrigation are limited.

Writing of Africa in general, Mr Harrison makes a point that applies to Cameroon with particular force:

There is still enough land for it to be cheaper and easier, in the short term, for farmers to move their plots every two or three years. Population density has not yet reached the level where intensive farming is unavoidable. But it has reached the level where massive ecological damage can occur if traditional methods go on being used.

Another of Africa's natural handicaps is the infamous tsetse fly, which carries trypanosomiasis, a disease fatal to cattle, horses, camels and humans. (Donkeys and goats have some resistance to it but are not entirely immune.) The human version is known as sleeping-sickness, the animal as *nagana*, a Zulu word. There is a theory – I imagine difficult to prove – that the tsetse fly caused the extinction of the dinosaur and all that lot. It has certainly been around since those days and is now, like the mosquito, proving that it can beat modern science. Between 1925 and 1960 some advances were made against it but when the Whites went home, and the tsetse fly improved its adaptability, things deteriorated. By 1960 Nigeria's sleeping-sickness victims had been reduced from 11 per cent to 0.15 per cent of the population and in Zaire, too, the disease had been almost wiped out. Yet in both those countries – as in Zimbabwe, Angola and Zambia – the incidence is now almost back to pre-colonial levels.

In 1849 Dr David Livingstone saw the tsetse fly as 'a barrier to the progress of Africa'. The history and development of no other race can have been so influenced by one insect. All of Black Africa would probably have been converted to Islam, and thus acquired a written language, had the invading Arabs not backed off when their camels and horses died by the hundred. For millennia trade was severely restricted by a lack of pack-animals; there are limits to what even an African can head-carry. The hand-ploughing which looks so backward to anyone accustomed to Asia's oxen-teams is the inevitable consequence of *nagana*. And now it is threatening the very survival of Africa.

Nagana excludes mixed farming, with a steady supply of free manure, from about four million square miles of Middle Africa. This area would otherwise be capable of sustaining more than 100 million cattle, and a similar number of sheep and goats, and so producing meat and milk worth $50 billion a year. In Cameroon about 8,000 square miles had been freed from the fly but are now re-infested. Therefore there are cattle only on high pastures, far from the cultivated fields, which, being unfertilised (or at best insufficiently fertilised), give good yields for only two or three years. Hence extensive rather than intensive farming is practised, with the removal of the only possible protection against the death of the land.

Despite all the local environmental disasters, we were, that morning, in one of the most agriculturally privileged corners of Africa. There was nothing 'representative' about this thickly populated region of healthy, hard-working peasants – so hard-working that they hadn't anywhere left a patch of grass for poor Egbert.

Our cut-shorts to Kumbo may have lengthened rather than short-ened the distance. But there was heavy traffic on the motor-road (a vehicle every half-hour or so) and those quiet paths took us through an agreeable mix of well-wooded hills, fertile valleys, expansive coffee plantations and shady kolanut stands. From one compound an elderly Fulani hurried out to admire Egbert and presented me with a fistful of kolanuts. These are an acquired taste and a mild stimulant. We hadn't yet acquired the taste but we prudently tucked them away against another rainy evening. The indigenous kolanut has been used for millennia in this region and was the main export crop before the introduction of coffee.

We first saw Kumbo from the crest of a high ridge: many roofs gleaming through dense foliage in a long valley. It looked close but was still two hours' walk away. According to oral tradition, Kumbo was founded in about 1820 as the political capital of the powerful Nso chiefs who, by 1900, had brought many scattered clans under their control, including the Do, Ndzendzef, Tang, Sob, Ya, Ki, Mbiim Mbinggiy, Nggamanse, Jem, Mbise, Langkuiy, Nkim, Kgang, Tankum, Menjei, Ka and Faa. All were encouraged to settle near Kumbo during the nineteenth century, hence the present density of population – and the need for Pidgin as a lingua franca.

At the foot of that ridge tender grass grew by the path and poor Egbert strained towards it eagerly. But alas! this Cameroonian long acre was being grazed by many goats, the majority tethered, though a few were running loose, wreaking havoc among the young crops. It is illegal to leave livestock untethered and this is one of the few laws taken seriously by villagers, perhaps because it long antedates colonial rule. Previously, some villages chose to let their goats, pigs and sheep roam free, using salt to lure them back to their compounds at night, and all cultivation was done five or six miles away. This made life even more gruelling for the womenfolk but increased the villages' wealth, livestock forming an important part of bridewealth payments and Secret Society entrance fees. But the general rule was to tether them and a chiefdom's law-enforcing council took a serious view of infringements.

Cameroon's dwarf goats are so enchanting that I often loitered to watch them. The adults are no taller than a week-old Irish kid but broad and plump, with short glossy coats. Some are all black; most have white and/or bright ginger markings and ginger scuts. When near kidding the nannies look quite *square,* their bellies and distended udders almost touching the ground; twins are common. Very young kids are rarely tethered, and bound around as though on springs; they may sometimes be seen standing on inches-long hind-legs illegally reaching for the most succulent shoots on baby banana plants.

Increased goat and sheep breeding is important in the calculations of those planning to avert future African famines. Dr B. T. Kang, an Indonesian soil scientist who has been working since the mid-1970s at the International Institute of Tropical Agriculture in Ibadan, Nigeria, leads a team which has devised a brilliant system of cultivation known as 'alley cropping'. This increases crop yields by at least 35 per cent and meat yields by 55 per cent – goat and sheep meat, that is. Alley cropping is not one more 'Experts' Fantasy', unable to survive transplanting from its institutional nursery. It makes allowances for Africa's social and economic realities and has been proved to work when implemented by villagers. If taken seriously by national Agriculture Departments (which so far it hasn't been) it could solve many production and ecological problems in humid and sub-humid zones.

On the outskirts of Kumbo, in a dreary suburb of semi-derelict ex-colonial houses and newish jerry-built offices, we tethered Egbert to a wobbly electricity pole on a small patch of grass. Then we sat outside an off-licence, worrying about our malnourished friend. To make matters worse, he was refusing his rock-minerals, recommended by Jane and dissolved daily, as per instructions, in a bucket of water – which was then spurned by our hero, however thirsty he might be.

Kumbo (population 10,000) is almost a city by Cameroonian standards and so it harbours policemen. One now appeared, dandering down the middle of the wide street. He was overweight, thuggish-looking and, judging by his grand uniform, quite a senior officer. At a distance of about thirty yards he paused, stared at us, then imperiously beckoned me.

'What a ghastly type!' said Rachel. 'Don't go! If he wants to talk to you let him come here.'

That however is not the way to win friends and influence people among the world's police forces. Beaming delightedly, I hastened to his side with outstretched hand. Ignoring my hand he asked sharply where we were going to and coming from – and *why?* He was a Francophone, which helped. Gesturing lavishly and talking rapidly, I made a comic scene about not understanding *any* French. When I thrust our passports into his hands he stared uncertainly at them, then suddenly began to chuckle and look quite amiable. Returning them unopened he shook my hand warmly, wished us *'Bon voyage!'*, saluted smartly and turned away.

Rachel by then was deep in conversation with a young man called Patrick who found our Irishness exciting. He was a smartly dressed, beautifully mannered and ebullient ex-pupil of St Augustine's College, a boarding-school where six hundred hopeful youngsters, from all over Anglophone Cameroon, study more or less diligently for British O and A Levels. Three of the nuns, he said, were Irish. Sister Eileen was his special friend and would rejoice to meet compatriots. We must spend the night there – two nights, a *week!*

'Is there any grass around St Augustine's?' I asked.

'Grass,' exclaimed Patrick, *'so* much grass! Hectares and hectares of grass!'

In Bamenda I had dismissed the suggestion that we might stay at St Augustine's; in recent years missionaries have been plagued by 'over-

71

landers' and I doubted if there would be a welcome for two vagrants and a horse. But Egbert's parlous state overcame my inhibitions: we could after all make a donation to the school. I hastened to untether Egbert from the electricity pole that had almost keeled over.

Patrick guided us down to a crowded town centre where garbage was piled in the gutters. Numerous trucks, mostly carrying full or empty beer bottles, severely tested Egbert's *sang-froid* with their squealing brakes and blaring horns. But for his desperate hunger I would have lingered long enough to find the Chief's house where, in 1905, Captain Glauning counted 900 heads of Bamum and Nsungli warriors decorating the façade. These were souvenirs of the famous 1880s war between the major chiefdoms of Nso and Bamum; some 3,000 warriors took part and 1,500 or so Bamums lost their heads.

We said goodbye to Patrick at the beginning of a precipitous three-mile cut-short to St Augustine's. As we climbed, through maize-fields and woodland, I pondered on the Evolutionary Stages of Man. To us the notion of, say, Argentinian heads decorating the façade of No. 10 Downing Street seems primitive/barbarous/savage/uncivilised. To those Nso warriors the notion of accumulating weapons designed to kill women and children indiscriminately would seem shocking beyond comprehension. Are modern White governments, who unequivocally condone the slaughtering of innocent non-combatants, more civilised – in the sense of *humane* – than the Nso warriors who fancied their opponents' heads as trophies and fetishes? Even ritual human sacrifices, from which White colonialists recoiled with such horror, seem less morally depraved than those mass-killings of civilians which have taken place in recent White wars and are now being planned, on a far greater scale, for future White wars. What sort of 'civilisation' is it that quotes its own 'defence' as justification for plotting crimes against humanity on a scale unprecedented in any previous age?

Patrick had not exaggerated. Sister Eileen and her colleagues did seem pleased to meet compatriots and by 3 p.m. Egbert was loose amidst several hectares of fenced grass. It had been overcast and humid all day but the sun then came out for long enough to dry our gear, which disposed of worry No. 2. We slept long and soundly that night, in an austere but comfortable little guest room.

Modern missionaries are motorised and our nun friends knew nothing about bush-paths. But next morning they provided an ancient retainer who showed us what he believed to be the cut-short to Ntem. For several miles this undulated gently through an area of few compounds, some scrub and many eucalyptus plantations with saplings planted close together. Crowded trees produce the highest yields; the roots go deeper and the trunks grow straighter and so are more saleable as poles or stakes. Hereabouts eucalyptus form a most valuable crop, growing up to thirty feet a year, and they may be coppiced every other year. But ecologists worry about their side-effects as they are hostile to all local forest species.

Pausing in the village of Ma for elevenses (cokes and avocados), we learned that this was *not* the Kumbo-Ntem cut-short; to get to Ntem from Ma we would have to go via Ndu. An endearing but gloomy twenty-five-year-old guided us onto the appropriate (we hoped) bush-path. He was gloomy because his family had been unable to afford his secondary school fees and were now unable to afford his brideprice.

Shaded by mango and kolanut trees, this cut-short meandered for two hours past a string of large compounds – as many thatched as tin roofed and each surrounded by crop-crowded fields. Back on the motor-track, we passed the raised barrier of an unmanned check-post and entered one of Cameroon's few tea-plantations. Miles of rolling hills were tidily covered with well tended bushes, and the plantation head-quarters – substantial colonial buildings surrounded by shiny trucks – looked as incongruous as the crop itself.

Outside a long row of drearily uniform workers' shacks a grinning young man shouted an invitation to drink maize-beer. Guiltily we tethered poor Egbert on bare ground before being led into a dark, crowded room, unfurnished save for a few home-made chairs and stools. A young woman with baby on back sat beside a giant cauldron in the centre of the floor, busily filling glasses with a gourd and skilfully filtering the beer through her fingers. Our exclamations of appreciation caused immoderate laughter and indeed this was an excellent brew: thickish and whitish, refreshing and sustaining, its flavour not unlike Ethiopian *talla*. Nobody spoke much English but we enjoyed the con-vivial atmosphere, with toddlers wandering around shoving their fists into glasses and babies beaming at us from maternal backs and a group of teenage girls giggling at us from one corner. The most giggly wore a T-shirt inscribed: I'M NOT GETTING OLDER, I'M GETTING BETTER. From all sides people urged us to have refills but as this rest-stop wasn't nourishing Egbert we left after a second round.

At the door, our 'host' stretched out his hand for payment. I didn't object but was momentarily thrown, having assumed we were his guests. As he didn't specify an amount, I gave him 200 CFA (about 44p). Later experiences taught us that resident Whites tend to create an understandable 'soak-the-rich' mentality among many of the locals.

We had been ill-advised to take a cut-short through the tea. At first all went well; then the bushes became so high and the path so narrow that the load was caught repeatedly and a lesser horse than Egbert would have rebelled. After a nerve-wracking half-hour we found our-selves on what could have been either a rudimentary motor-track or a wide bush-path. We realised it was the former when an open truck, with PRESBYTERIAN MISSION inscribed in multicoloured lettering on both sides, came swaying down the steep hill behind us. It contained uproarious dozens of young people standing with their arms around each other's shoulders. Many were waving bottles of palm wine; all were so loudly singing, or chanting, or cheering that they remained within earshot for fifteen minutes while the truck laboriously chugged up the opposite hill. American Presbyterian missionaries arrived in Cameroon in 1879 but we were glad to note that their converts' natural proclivities have survived.

Soon after, my compass in human form began to suspect that this was not the Ndu track. When we checked with a man carrying a machete on his head he said that the track went to Sabongari and he seemed genuinely distressed to have to break this bad news. We begged him not to worry. Sabongari is north of Ntem so we were moving in the right direction by another route – and a very beautiful one, as the track switchbacked through low, round, cultivated hills with glossy palm and banana groves filling the shallow valleys between.

When the sun came out for the first time, soon after 4 p.m., we were again climbing high, into Fulani country. Many horses grazed on wide smooth pastures and in two hours we passed only one compound. Outside it sat a big group of palavering men; they were too far away to greet us but we were conscious of their stares. This was an exhilarating last lap. Behind us to the south stood piles of static white clouds – looking solid, like alabaster sculptures – but overhead the sky was intensely blue. The sun shone golden on the grassland; ahead were towering rough escarpments, glowing red; below them rose a strange grey rock mountain, perfectly oval, standing alone.

Descending towards that solitary bare rock, we met an ancient Fulani who remains vivid in my memory. Many Fulanis are handsome but there was a serenity within this man, shining out, that gave his lean, worn face an extraordinary beauty. He shook my hand firmly and rhythmically recited the traditional Fulani greetings, his voice gentle. Mysteriously, one felt blessed by this encounter.

As we watched him going on his way, tall and thin, still carrying himself proudly, Rachel said, 'What a *noble* face! D'you think he's as wise as he looks?' She noted then that he wasn't in fact very tall. An illusion of height is often created by the Fulanis' flowing robes and slender build, so unlike the compact muscularity of most Cameroonians.

Nthambaw lies at the base of the oval mountain. A bustling, friendly, happy village, its fifty-fifty Christian-Muslim population live in the sort of harmony that makes Irish people feel inferior. As in many such villages, most buildings look alike. Church, mosque, school, health centre, police post, off-licence – all are tin-roofed mud huts with no external indication of their function. And, whatever that function may be, furniture is minimal and usually crudely knocked together from rough-hewn wood – which seems sad, in an area once renowned for the artistry of its wood-carvers.

The sun was still warm when we arrived at 6 p.m., having covered some twenty-two miles. (We calculated our daily distances on the basis of two-and-a-half miles per hour, a conservative estimate as we realised later when timing ourselves on a stretch of motor-road with colonial kilometre stones.) In the long main street a crowd of wildly excited children provided a spontaneous guard-of-honour as we peered into four minute shops in quest of non-existent food. Then two young men beckoned from a maize-beer shebeen. Both were Old Augustinians who spoke fluent English and said of course we could camp on the village green, which was just that: a large grassy triangle in the middle of the street with a towering tree at its apex. But first we must have some beer – *lots* of beer! We promptly did so, then offered payment only to have it indignantly refused.

In the course of conversation it emerged that Nthambaw is the centre of a chiefdom. We had been told that where chiefs dwell it is good manners to seek their consent before spending a night in a village – an afterglow of Mungo Park's day, when strangers had to obtain a chief's permission (a visa equivalent) to travel through his territory. So we asked the way to the palace, as chiefs' compounds, however unpretentious, are always known. Manga and Semmi seemed to think we were being over-punctilious but amiably escorted us down a mile-long track in the fading light, through the Chief's well shaded coffee plantation.

In the modern secular Republic of Cameroon chiefs no longer wield any political power *qua* chiefs, though some hold government posts and live in Bamenda or Yaoundé. Yet most villagers (especially Anglophones) remain in awe of their chief. His quasi-religious, emotional/psychological significance is still considerable, though he may be a Muslim with Christian 'subjects' – as in Nthambaw. This significance of course predates the arrival of both Islam and Christianity and has to do with the hereditary magical powers of pagan chiefs – so often derided by Whites as 'savage superstitions', though they were no more 'superstitious' than the beliefs held by millions of European Christians.

The isolated palace, semi-encircled by tall trees and gloomy in the dusk, was strangely silent. Outside its high mud walls our companions' unease became palpable. Semmi remained with Egbert while Manga led us through a maze of narrow passages between huts rather bigger than average and under archways so low that even I had to duck. It felt odd to be in such a quiet, apparently childless compound. Only one person was visible, an elderly woman (the senior wife) squatting outside the kitchen-hut preparing green leaves for jammu-jammu. Manga mumbled an inquiry, then moved across to another doorway. Here he bent almost double and spoke to the Chief within through cupped hands, in a low voice, never raising his eyes to the chiefly face. This approach astonished us at the time, though we were soon to become accustomed to it. A not very imposing figure then emerged, aged perhaps forty-five with a hooked nose but very dark skin. He wore a round white cap, a sleeveless embroidered knee-length white tunic and jeans so much too long that they must have been second-hand. His manner conveyed neither warmth nor hostility; plainly such unexpected guests left him at a loss. Manga interpreted in the local language and when I formally sought permission to camp the Chief grunted non-committedly, then went out to view our equipage.

Semmi too bent low and greeted him through cupped hands. At the sight of Egbert he became suddenly animated and Manga translated, 'He says you have a very good horse! From where did you get him? How much did you pay?'

Having been told, the Chief exclaimed, 'Wah!' Next he expressed a wish to be photographed and adopted a rigid military pose. Feeling rather duplicitous, I took several shots in the gloaming with our salted camera. He then said something to Manga, nodded curtly to us and departed.

Manga grinned triumphantly. 'You may camp! If he'd known you're both women he'd have kept you in his guest hut!'

'Why didn't you tell him?' I asked.

'He wouldn't have believed me!' chuckled Manga. 'He'd have said I was playing tricks and got angry. *I* didn't believe you at first!'

It was dark as we walked through the village centre. From a Christian off-licence came taped disco music. From the mosque came devout chanting and through the open door we glimpsed by golden lamp-light scenes of kneeling men touching their foreheads to the ground.

Our setting up camp was impeded by many small boys eager to help. I tried to be patient but in the end had to ask them to desist. Getting a tent up at night is tricky enough without a dozen inexpert little hands tugging at guy-ropes and putting pegs in the wrong places. Several precious objects went astray in the dark but were later found and returned by helpful youths.

Then it was supper-time: bananas only, since no bread had been available in any village en route. But beer is almost always available in Cameroon, whatever the 'infrastructure' problems, so Rachel went to fetch some, accompanied by Semmi, to guarantee the bottles' return. Otherwise she would not have been allowed to take them off the premises.

This 'bottle discipline' fascinated us, in a country not notable for its organisational abilities. Under no circumstances is it possible for anyone anywhere to buy a *bottle* of beer, coke or Top; one can only buy the contents. The deposit system is unknown but it seems the entire population has been so dragooned that *every* empty bottle is returned to source. Perhaps the manufacturers have a purely economic motive for this regimentation, or perhaps they responsibly take into account the perils of broken glass in a country where most of the rural population go barefooted. Cameroonian soles are leathery, but not glass-proof. Remarkably, we never saw a single splinter of glass on the ground.

Virtually every Nthambaw male must have been present by this stage, sitting in rows on the grass all around our tent as though at an open-air theatre – which I suppose is what we were, from their point of view. When I asked Semmi why no women were present he replied, 'Here our Christian women keep quiet. The Muslim ways are stronger.'

Three more Old Augustinians now joined us and though the moon had risen – wondrously silvering the nearby oval mountain – we found ourselves repeatedly confusing the five young English speakers' identities. None would share our beer so we soon became even more confused and rather loquacious, giving longer than necessary answers to their many questions about European habits and customs.

Manga, aged twenty-one, was another thwarted student, the youngest of a Christian family's thirty-four children. (Polygamy is now tacitly accepted by many Black churches as an ineradicable part of the African way of life.) His mother, only sixteen years his senior, had been his recently deceased father's third wife. As the three widows were 'good friends' their compound was 'peaceful'. But so many children had meant less education for the latest arrivals. Having got 'five nice O Levels' (I didn't ask how nice), Manga had had to leave St Augustine's. But he still hoped ... His eldest brother, aged forty-nine, was an economist, married to an ex-Peace Corps teacher, and had been lecturing in an American university for the past eleven years. Being now head of the family, 'he must return soon to live in this village and he will have saved many dollars. I am waiting for him, he will see I need more education. And our President Paul Biya tells us: "It is never too late to learn!" He is a good President, he *believes* in education.'

I tried, unsuccessfully, to imagine an academic economist with an American wife readjusting to Nthambaw. Even allowing for the Cameroonians' passionate attachment to family, village and land, it seemed improbable that he would settle in his birthplace, or anywhere near it. And Manga's yearning for more education would be only one of many demands made on his savings. In Cameroon, as elsewhere in Black Africa, financial prosperity often means a much more stressful life than if one had remained unambitiously in the bush. High salaries and 'status' don't always compensate for the worries and conflicts entailed in having numerous dependants desperately competing for assistance.

Of Manga's other thirty-two siblings fifteen, mostly girls, were still on the land. Seventeen had jobs in Bamenda, Douala or Yaoundé. 'That is how I got to St Augustine's and when I make money I will help nephews and nieces as well as my own children. It is harder for educated Christian families. We like girls to learn, Muslim families need only educate boys. And Fulanis in the bush don't bother about education, they only go to Koranic schools.'

We would have been surprised to find five Old Augustinians in remote Nthambaw had the nuns not told us that many poor families will bust themselves to provide what they consider 'the best' education, which in Anglophone Cameroon means GCE-based. Sadly, the expectation that city jobs will follow is not always (or even often) fulfilled in the way parents intended; 'city jobs' may involve no more than sweeping the gutters of Douala or Yaoundé. When children get bad examination results, families are bewildered, hurt, angry and sometimes resentful; *they* have deprived themselves for years to pay fees, so why hasn't the school delivered the goods for which they thought they were paying?

In Bamenda we had met one nun, with half a lifetime's experience of teaching in Africa, who commented, 'There *is* a difference in what Black and White pupils can achieve at O and A Levels. But many of our kids are first-generation school-goers from illiterate homes. And you have to begin somewhere – their children will do better, and their grandchildren better still!'

To me that prediction has a distinct flavour of self-deception. It is hard to see how British or French curricula could ever have any relevance for Cameroonian children. Why should studying Shakespeare and the history of the British empire (White version) be expected to improve their chances as citizens of an independent African republic? The Cameroonian answer is that examination results based on an indigenous curriculum would not impress potential Western employers or Western universities; and the unrealistic hope of many Black students is to get into a Western university, preferably American.

When we said goodnight to our friends the village elders, who had been strolling around all evening in a protective spirit, at once dismissed the crowd and within moments even the most high-spirited youths were meekly moving towards home. Most of our possessions had to be left outside the tent but we felt no anxiety on that score in Nthambaw – or anywhere in rural Cameroon. Drifting off to sleep, I reflected on the benefits of a small, hierarchical, traditional community. I wouldn't care to belong to one myself, but they do have their advantages.

78

5

On the Tenth Day . . .

WE KNEW THE stage beyond Nthambaw would be rough. This was 'the hot plain' and our Old Augustinian friends, bred on the cool heights, were appalled at the idea of anybody – never mind two Whites – crossing it on foot. But there was no cooler route to the Mbabo mountains.

On the outskirts of Nthambaw a dramatic waterfall, hundreds of feet high, flashed whitely down the opposite mountain – a vivid illustration of the perversity of Africa's terrain and climate. The region's severe water-shortage had caused our friends to take much trouble, at dawn, in order to fill Egbert's bucket. (He then refused to drink; we were discovering that he liked liquid refreshment *only* during the midday hours.)

From Nthambaw a neglected colonial 'motorable track' – happily devoid of motors – descended through scrub-covered mountains uninhabited because of their steepness and aridity. Yet several migrating herds, lean but healthy, were gaining sustenance ('grazing' is not the word) on gradients more suited to goats. During the morning two black and gold snakes, scarcely a foot long, crossed the track; and we marvelled at the variety, brilliant colouring and enormous size of the local butterflies. By 11.30 a.m. we were almost down – and it felt like it. When a cut-short appeared we wandered across a gradual, thinly forested slope in search of lunch for Egbert and turned him loose where tall bunches of stiff, yellowish grass grew between the trees. By then we knew he didn't want to leave us; he had been untethered all night on the village green.

Our own banana supply had run out but we were too hot to be hungry. I sensibly ate salt with my water and when Rachel refused to follow suit we bickered peevishly on this issue. Then she discovered a jigger in her left big toe and I dug it out with a safety-pin. The usual tickling mega-ants and biting mini-flies tortured us. Meanwhile Egbert was being plagued by handsome birds with yellow beaks who alighted on him in twos and threes, parasite-hunting. But to our huge relief he approved of the apparently unappetising grass; for a few days nothing better was likely to come on his menu.

At 1 p.m. Rachel suggested moving on and I snarled, 'You must be mad! This bloody sun is *lethal*!' In between being very nasty to insects I was reading Mungo Park's *Travels in Africa* and I pointed out that he always rested in hot regions 'till half-past two o'clock'.

Rachel studied her left big toe and decided that I had failed to remove the jigger.

I snapped, 'Remove it yourself then!'

Rachel wondered, 'What will your temper be like after three days of this heat?'

All morning the sky had been clear but now clouds assembled with astonishing speed: a phenomenon to which we were becoming accustomed. By 2 p.m. the sky was completely overcast and the heat just bearable. We went on our way, criticising the eerie muted quality of the light and assuming it to be yet another disagreeable feature of this ghastly plain. Days later we heard about that afternoon's near-total eclipse of the sun.

Below that slope a line of vigorously green bushes marked a stream and while Egbert drank we poured clear cool water over each other's heads. On the plain, lines of women were turning the thirsty brown soil, hoping for the little rains – here already a fortnight late. They seemed less prosperous and out-going than their sisters on the high land. One woman, digging with a hefty baby on her back – as is usual – straightened up to stare at us and we saw that she was heavily pregnant. This is unusual; perhaps she was caring for somebody else's baby. A powerful West African taboo forbids intercourse while a woman is suckling, which may be for two or three years; it is widely believed that semen mingles with a mother's milk and weakens the baby. Generations of missionaries have raged against this taboo, one of the main reasons for the African reluctance to accept monogamy.

Our cut-short passed through a deserted compound. Three round straw huts seemed to have been deliberately demolished and several worn-out trainers were strewn over the dusty earth, scarred by cooking-fires. Had some tragic event blighted this homestead – a suicide or murder or sudden death attributed to 'bad magic'? Such misfortunes require an elaborate ritual cleansing ceremony which poor families cannot afford. It costs much less to run up three more straw huts on a 'clean' site.

Beyond the dessicated hamlet of Nsop our track crossed miles of monochrome scrubland. Thousands of termite-hills, with conical roofs, formed a bizarre city between the low bushes. Rachel aptly compared them to 'mushroom clouds'; presumably their clever design averts disintegration when the rains come. The only flecks of colour were orchid-like flowers, striped purple and white and some eighteen inches tall, which seemed to eat flies.

Our grazing anxiety-level began to rise at about 5 p.m. and was very high indeed an hour later – when suddenly fertility reappeared, including a green playing-field by a new school. This was Ntem, a small village surrounded by big trees. We tethered Egbert on a grassy patch, while seeking the Chief's permission to sleep in the school; rain seemed probable and we now knew our tent was not big enough for two on a wet night. Outside the off-licence an amiable youth greeted us – conveniently, one of the Chief's twenty-nine children, who offered to show me the palace while Rachel remained beer-swigging amidst a jovial welcoming throng.

This was a more imposing palace than Nthambaw's, with an incongruous modern bungalow in front of the mud fortifications. The Chief, too, was more imposing: a dignified courteous man in his mid-fifties who spoke good English and was warmly and wittily welcoming: 'Are you pretending to live a hundred years ago, when there were no vehicles in Cameroon?' Having escorted me back to the off-licence – a mile-long walk – he ordered food, stood us beers and himself had a Top. He too was Muslim.

Their Chief's unwonted appearance after dark caused some excitement along the village street and much bowing and cupping of hands. One sensed a strong mutual affection; evidently this Chief's benignly paternalistic attitude was appreciated and he exchanged quips with both sexes and all age groups. Ntem is mainly Christian and its women-folk were out in force, enjoying the Murphy road-show. They particularly enjoyed our statutory gender-confusion session. I had introduced Rachel to the Chief as my daughter and a few moments later, addressing her, he referred to 'your father'. When she respectfully but firmly corrected him he leant forward, scrutinised me by lamp-light and exclaimed, 'Impossible! This is a strong man!'

'It's *not*!' said Rachel. 'It's a strong *woman*!'

Our audience was in paroxysms of mirth, a phrase that applies more exactly to Africans than to any other race I know. They shook and heaved with laughter, seized each other by the shoulders, jumped up and down together and literally fell about in the abandon of their hilarity. Finally the Chief was convinced and made a public announcement, in whatever language Ntem people speak, confirming that this odd bod really *was* female. Whereupon several young women rushed to shake my hand and/or embrace me.

A small boy arrived then with our supper. He offered the dish first to the Chief, who removed its lid and took one symbolic morsel, to prove it wasn't poisoned, before signalling that the rest was for us. In darkness we groped through a thick, highly spiced sauce and found little bundles wrapped in bristly hide. These contained bush-meat (beef) which we were hungry enough to relish despite the bristles.

As we ate, the Chief expounded on family life: 'Some foreigners would like to sell birth-controls in this country but it is wrong to think of economics before children. We love our children, we can't have too many. Ntem has two-and-a-half thousand people and more than one thousand are schoolchildren. So we have built a second schoolroom where you will sleep. We built it without help from government but now we hope they will give us more teachers – and *good* teachers! Bad teachers are worse than nothing. But too many good teachers don't like to live in the bush. I have had difficulties, giving education to twenty-nine children – my daughters also have education. See! There is one speaking good English!' He indicated a comely young woman talking to Rachel. 'But these difficulties are not important. I have seventeen sons and twelve daughters and each one is a gift from God. I am grateful.'

Hearing that I have only one child, the Chief was deeply sympathetic. He obviously felt that his question had been a *faux pas* and hastily changed the subject. This awkward topic of my infertility came up almost daily without its ever occurring to anyone that a personal decision might be involved. For most villagers, *choosing* to have only one child is literally unthinkable. And the few who can grasp that idea consider it grossly immoral. (Or at least the men do; some women, significantly, are more ambivalent on this matter.) It would have been futile as well as rude to try to explain to the Chief why, in future, women should have no more than two children each. Many Whites look ahead, most Blacks don't. To us, but not to them, the African birth-rate of 47 per 1,000 is menacing. Nowhere else in the world has ever experienced such a population increase: 3.2 per cent per annum, despite one child in seven dying before its fifth birthday. Even without droughts, food production cannot keep pace with such a breeding-rate; an estimated 99 million Africans were starving *before* the 1982 famine. Throughout the 1970s Africa's total food production rose at an annual rate of 2.1 per cent, as compared to the First World's 1.8 per cent. Yet in 1982 production had fallen, since 1965, by 12 per cent *per person*. During the same period, throughout other developing regions, it rose steadily per person – by as much as 49 per cent in Asia. Nor should cash crops be blamed, as they often are in the West, for Africa's starving millions. The overall acreage under cash crops fell by 9 per cent during the 1970s and the per capita cash crop production has also been falling, even more dramatically than food production.

Only one incident marred that happy interlude with the Chief. A small boy, carrying a heavy saucepan of jammu-jammu into the off-licence, tripped over the rough threshold and fell, spilling his precious burden. As he burst into tears the crowd roared with laughter – and continued to laugh while he threw himself face down on the ground and lay weeping inconsolably.

Ntem's large empty schoolroom had lakes of water on the mud floor, but one corner offered ample dry space for our flea-bags. The heat was still stifling though there were neither doors nor windows – unnecessary trimmings in such a climate. We lay talking on our bags, naked yet dripping sweat, and by torchlight consulted the USAF, trying to work out the distance to Sabongari. But in this area, curiously enough, the USAF had given up; a white blank on their map was marked RELIEF DATA INCOMPLETE. That day we had asked twelve people 'How far to Sabongari?' and got twelve different answers ranging from eight to seventy miles. Miles or kilometres mean nothing to rural Cameroonians – who also tend to give wildly inaccurate estimates of distances in walking-hours.

In fact Sabongari is about fourteen miles from Ntem. We arrived there at 12.30 next afternoon, speechless with heat-exhaustion.

The first two hours, through flat, dull farmland, were cloudy and just tolerable. In the hamlet of Ngu we enjoyed an eccentric breakfast of avocados, salt and beer; to my secret relief, neither Top nor coke was available. But beer for breakfast, when it's 95°F in the shade and there isn't any shade, must be condemned as irresponsible and probably contributed to our sorry noon state. However, at 8 a.m. Ngu's off-licence was already quite crowded with jolly male drinkers who didn't have to exert themselves during the heat of the day.

The usual juvenile swarm gathered to watch us but soon grew bored and resumed their play. As so often, this consisted of impromptu dancing to the music (surprisingly sweet) of instruments ingeniously contrived from old tins, scraps of wood, lengths of string, bits of wire. From the day Cameroonians can toddle, making music and dancing come as naturally as breathing. Why do some British Blacks, and White anti-racists, scream 'Stereotyping!' if one refers to the Africans' inborn sense of rhythm? Pretending that Africans are not exceptionally gifted in this respect is like pretending they have straight hair.

Around Ngu most huts were palm thatched, a less attractive roofing than grass though vastly better than tin. There were many more dogs, of indeterminate breed but well cared, and numerous ungainly short-coated sheep – peculiarly ugly animals, who always look dirty and dishevelled, if not actually mangy.

By ten o'clock the sun was trying to murder us through an odd haze –

our first encounter with the harmattan. By eleven o'clock I was opining that we should rest, that we were stupidly inviting heat-stroke. But Rachel argued that Sabongari must now be close and that lying in the bush, being preyed upon by insects, is not restful. Against my better judgement, we proceeded. Later, when feeling the ill-effects of walking under the noon sun, Rachel conceded that we should indeed have chosen insects as the lesser of two evils.

Sabongari is a large village – torpid, gritty, smelly and scarcely fifteen miles from the Nigerian border. Its 'Africa hotel' consists of two rows of oven-hot rooms behind one of several off-licences. When we booked in the fat friendly proprietor smiled knowingly. 'Hah! You go to Nigeria with your horse – there you get plenty, plenty money for him!' We were too exhausted to put the record straight. It would take time, Mr Ndanga explained, to prepare a room. No rush, we assured him, subsiding in the bar and gulping four 'lemon' Tops each. At a certain stage of dehydration, one's scorn for Top evaporates; it is marginally less unpalatable than chemically purified water.

As we drank, an agitated young man in a 'CAMBRIDGE UNIVERSITY' T-shirt appeared in the doorway, frowning and shouting at us. We had met him thrice during the morning, as he delivered beer at Wannti and Ngu – and also in the middle of the uninhabited bush, where he replaced three cases of empty beer bottles with full ones. (A significant measure, we thought, of local honesty.) At each meeting he had urged us, in limited English, to go to the border police post as soon as we arrived. 'Go to office quick! In Sabongari you see police very quick!' His concern in the matter baffled us and now he seemed ridiculously upset by our having paused to drink before 'going to office'. I said soothingly that soon we would go but five minutes later he was back with a policeman, who seemed only mildly interested in us and readily accepted my assurance that we were *en route* to the office. After he had gone the young man hung about and insisted on leading us to a mud hut with 'POLICE OFFICE' chalked on its rickety door. Then he vanished and we never saw him again. Daily life in Cameroon was peppered with such mystifying incidents.

The Police Office, some ten foot square, was furnished only with a small unsteady table and two chairs. One dog-eared ledger occupied the centre of the table. Behind it sat a stout, blank-faced Francophone gendarme who very slowly went through our passports, page by page, saying nothing – and probably understanding nothing. I sat opposite him in a semi-coma. Rachel sat on the mud floor beside me, slumped against the wall, fast asleep. The room had no ceiling and it seemed the sun's midday rays were being magnified a hundredfold by the low tin roof.

Two other Francophone officers entered. They shrugged when I said,

'Speak English only!' and for ten minutes stood on either side of their colleague, watching him studying our vaccination certificates. (I asked myself what would happen, on a similar occasion, when our visas had expired. With luck nobody would notice.) Then, ignoring us, all three gendarmes disappeared with our passports into the only other room in the hut.

Time passed. The village was silent. Rachel snored gently. I wondered why Francophone officers are posted to Cameroon's border with an English-speaking country. Meanwhile Egbert, tethered to a mango tree, looked increasingly dejected.

Twenty minutes later the stout officer returned, handed back our passports without comment and said, '*Bon voyage!*' I woke Rachel, who asked if we might pasture Egbert on the indifferent grass across the road. Permission was given and we hastened back to the doss-house to unload.

Our little room was ready. 'A hell-hole!' groaned Rachel, falling onto the rectangle of uncovered foam-rubber that served as a double-bed mattress. Soon she was asleep again. A table and two chairs completed the furnishing. I tried to write my diary but soon gave up; leaving the door and two windows open did nothing to counteract the tin roof but gave access to clouds of those tiny biting flies which were rapidly becoming my most hated Cameroonian insect. Then suddenly the sky darkened and a half-hour deluge blissfully lowered the temperature.

When Rachel woke we had acrimony about the local water. As it came from a deep well, between the rows of 'guest rooms', I decided 'Definitely a *double* dose of pills!' Rachel protested that double-dosed water nauseated her and the matter was settled only after my visit to the latrine, a sentry-box-sized tin hut less than four yards from the well. I was at once put to rout, for the first time in twenty-five years' travelling, and went instead to Egbert's field. On my return I told Rachel, 'That water is having a *treble* dose!'

We went shopping and were grotesquely overcharged for Algerian sardines. Here White travellers are taken for granted – and, if possible, taken for a ride – though only a few score use this crossing-point each year. Later, reviewing our trek, we identified Sabongari as the only uncongenial village *en route*; so much for tourism improving international relations. Even our five Francophone fellow guests, all on their way to or from Nigeria, seemed sullen in a non-Cameroonian way. 'I daresay we seem sullen, too,' observed Rachel. 'Something about this place brings out the worst in one.'

We looked for the cut-short to Sonkalong, so that no cool moments need be wasted next morning, and eventually found it beyond the market-place. Near the stalls someone had recently built a large restaurant with pretensions to being *chic*. Unsurprisingly, it was closed. But promising aromas came from a busy eating-house next door, to which we resolved to return for supper. We hadn't had a square meal since leaving St Augustine's, as Rachel more than once reminded me.

At sundown I settled in the empty bar to drink lots of beer while writing my diary by lantern-light, but a variety of winged insects – mostly large and all noisy – seriously impeded me. At one point I counted seven species simultaneously crawling across the page.

Outside the eating-house we met Peter – tall, handsome, articulate, the eldest son of a local Big Man and a law student at Yaoundé. The eating-house was owned by his father and staffed by two of his sisters. The *chic* restaurant was also Pappa's, a memorial to over-optimism about Cameroon's tourist trade. At a very cramped corner table we sat in semi-darkness. 'Here there is no kerosene,' explained Peter apologetically, 'so the lamp must be turned low. Transport is a big problem in Cameroon – you have seen our tracks, not many vehicles like to use them often. Only beer trucks move regularly. Only the *brasseries* can sell enough goods to make it worth while to wreck vehicles.'

Peter gave us a glimpse of the Anglo/Franco tensions that can exist among middle-class Cameroonians. He was fiercely anti-French, denouncing Yaoundé University for discriminating against Anglophone students – a common complaint.

'Even if we have very good A Levels, Francophones with worse marks get preference. The French side is much more corrupt, even in the bush – you will find this tomorrow when you move in there.' (We didn't.) 'And so many French employers living here encourage corruption. They give jobs only if you pay them 10 per cent of your salary for two years. The British are always honest, they hire on merit alone. But they have not stayed on like the French to make money. Now Cameroon has many, many more French settlers than before Independence. Everywhere in French West Africa is the same. They only pretend to let go. Economically they keep their grip and by corruption make it tighter.'

Our tepid fufu and jammu-jammu cost 500 CFA for both (smallish) portions. 'Bad value,' Rachel decided afterwards. 'Think of all the bananas and avocados you could buy for that!'

Peter warned us to secure our room, as best we could, against mosquitoes. 'This is the worst malaria time, at the start of the rains. In one week hundreds of people here will be sick and children will die ...' He declined our invitation to have a beer in the hotel bar. 'I don't like this man!' he whispered vehemently, glaring at poor Mr Ndanga who was dozing behind the bar, cradling a transistor radio, and who seemed to us perfectly inoffensive if a trifle dim-witted. But, as we had already noticed, Big Men and their families are not always on good terms with the hoi polloi.

By 6 a.m. we were on the cut-short; by 6.05 we were removing our boots to cross the first of the day's three rivers: a shallow stream, some twenty yards wide. The sky was overcast, the air fragrant after a night of heavy rain and the abundant birdlife unusually visible, where our path ran level through an unpeopled mixture of thin forest and scrubland. Often I fell far behind the others, revelling in the best ornithological opportunity of the entire trek.

Next came miles of recently settled land, rudimentary cultivation interspersed with stretches of untamed bush – an extraordinary contrast to the intensively farmed country around Kumbo. In the few compounds of small thatched huts most women wore only wrap-around skirts though it is now illegal for Cameroonian women to go topless: a dotty law in a country where every village woman of child-bearing age has a breast almost permanently exposed.

Here we were overtaken by a little girl, carrying a big basket of bananas, and two little boys and three dogs – one a bitch, being led on a leash of plaited vine. Having left us behind the children paused to confer, then waited for us and gravely presented a hand of bananas.

'Dash?' wondered Rachel in an anxious whisper. But I thought not; only kindliness had inspired that gesture. We continued together, the children clearly baffled by our caravan. They were an enchanting trio, their bodies well developed, their big smiles revealing perfect teeth, their few garments ragged but freshly laundered, their dogs happy, their composure complete. And it was well we met them where we did, for soon the path divided.

'Sonkalong?' we asked. The girl pointed to the least likely looking route, semi-obscured by high dense greenery. And there we said goodbye.

The day's second river was wide, thigh deep, strongly flowing. Both banks supported the remains of a substantial colonial bridge, witness to the decline of empires. In times past (German times?) an important road must have run where now there is only a path – and one so faint that several times we almost lost it. Tropical Nature quickly reasserts herself.

The third river, amidst dense forest, was nasty – less a river than a smelly, slimy, stagnant creek approached through an expanse of deep black mud concealing tree-root snares. A humans-only two-pole bridge spanned the creek and Rachel tripped across; it was my turn to lead Egbert. By then we had learned that he would tackle almost any obstacle, if allowed time to think about it, so I gave him his head and when I became entangled in hidden roots he cleverly pulled me through. The still water was full of horrid little creatures – half-swimming, half-crawling.

Soon we were in more broken country, close to the mountainous border with Nigeria. Sonkalong, where we rejoined the motor-track, straggles over a low hill and was our first Francophone village. In the off-licence (here known as a bar) Rachel conversed with two laid-back gendarmes who assumed us to be friends of a young Englishman living in Somie. They didn't know *why* he was living there; he wasn't a missionary, he just sat around talking to people.

'An anthropologist,' diagnosed Rachel.

The gendarmes kindly led us to a nearby hilltop and pointed out the track to Somie via Lingham, a red thread winding through scrub, forest and cane fields. According to them, we would get to Somie by sunset; we knew we wouldn't. ('Why,' puzzled Rachel, 'can't they correlate time and distance?') In fact the sun was near setting as we approached Lingham, having been refreshed *en route* by a brief heavy shower.

Lingham's 'main street' was soap-slippy and poor Egbert fell heavily, provoking shrieks of laughter from the pullulation of children in our wake. Then the Reverend Mr Eyobo introduced himself: 'I am Baptist minister, it is my duty as a Christian to give you every help.' He was lovable at first sight: aged fortyish, slightly myopic, small, slim, energetic, caring. Swiftly he organised our immediate future. We could spend the night at the home of Mr Makia, the quarterchief; Egbert could graze on 'the fat grass' by the Baptist church; Mr Eyobo himself would lead us to the palace to pay our respects to the Muslim Chief. As we unloaded, a passing youth was summoned to lead Egbert to his grazing. Mr Makia, our elderly involuntary host, looked somewhat taken aback when we dumped our dusty/muddy gear in his already overcrowded living-room before being swept off to the palace.

On that long walk, past flat hectares of maize and sugar-cane, Mr Eyobo explained that there are two Linghams, the old mainly Muslim village around the palace and the new Christian village – an overflow from the Nso region – where he ministered. 'In Cameroon when places get too many people there is room to move. So my Christian people came here, cleared the bush, made gardens. It is too hot, but they have food. We are not poor if we work. The Chief is a good man, a Muslim who helps Christians!'

It was dark when we reached the palace. The Chief sat on his ornamental stool in an enormous shadowy reception-hall – thatched, high-ceilinged, dimly lamp-lit and furnished only with a row of tall drums along one wall. Several men were kneeling around him in attitudes of supplication and we sensed that we had interrupted something important. Our audience was brief. Mr Eyobo explained us; the Chief graciously gave us permission to rest in Lingham; we expressed gratitude and withdrew.

It is often alleged that a disproportionate number of chiefs are Muslim because Mr Ahidjo, Cameroon's first President who ruled for twenty-four years, was himself a Muslim. But Mr Eyobo dismissed these allegations. 'For thousands of years many villages have Muslim chiefs, from times when Fulanis came for slaves and beat local warriors and took land and power. This is not modern politics!'

In Mr Makia's neat back-yard water and soap had been provided for our ablutions but around the kitchen-hut there was, alarmingly, no sign of activity. As we settled down to be sociable in the living-room, Mr Eyobo proudly drew our attention to three newish, over-varnished Nigerian wooden wall-plaques depicting violent biblical scenes – to us a source of anthropological speculation rather than aesthetic thrills. But the ancient Yoruba carved wooden chest that served as a sofa was truly a work of art, though not highly regarded by its owner.

When tea and bread were offered, I tentatively suggested beer as a more appropriate refreshment at the end of a long hot day. Moments later no mere bottle but a crate arrived. Lingham's tolerance was pleasing: a Muslim Chief helping Christian settlers, Baptist teetotallers providing crates of beer ... And at bedtime we had to argue strongly before being allowed to pay for the four bottles consumed.

I asked if there were any conversions, either way, between Old and New Lingham. Mr Makia admitted that some Christians become Muslims because they wish to prosper as traders. 'For so long, only Muslims have traded long-distance – they have all contacts, networks, set up. They have their own kinds of handy arrangements about money and credit. For too many years, all over Africa, men have become Muslim to trade big – and their women do not like this change!'

As his friend spoke Mr Eyobo sighed heavily, shook his head and pulled his fingers through his curls. 'Mammon!' he murmured. Then he asked, 'You are Protestant Christians? What is your denomination?' Both he and our host seemed genuinely distressed when we confessed to having no religion, or none that has a label; they felt acutely that as unbelievers we were impoverished people.

Later, when we begged leave to retire, Mr Eyobo asked gently, 'Can you wait for a little prayer?' And taking a bible from the window-ledge behind him he read aloud, 'The Lord is my shepherd ...' Then he looked up at us and improvised his own exquisitely appropriate prayer for our safety, as we trekked. We were quite overcome, moved beyond any possibility of expressing the gratitude we felt.

Now I always recall Mr Eyobo, when Whites assert that Christianity is unsuited to Africa. Perhaps what Whites have made of it doesn't transplant well, but Christianity didn't start in Europe. We adopted it and fashioned it into a many-branched religion to suit our own cultural/intellectual/national inheritances, shedding much blood in the process. And then, characteristically, we pronounced that ours was the *real* Christianity. Africans have for a few generations been in the process of refashioning it to suit *their* inheritance. And what right have we to judge that Black Christianity is less 'real' than the White version?

I often wondered about the beliefs of people we passed in the bush. We noticed many charms in the fields: bones and palm fronds hanging over junctions on the pathways, little archways of saplings erected between fields, bundles of feathers and leaves secured to rocks with lengths of vine, plaits of straw tied to bamboo poles. Undoubtedly, despite much mosque- and church-going, many villagers remain close to their 'traditional religion', known in my youth as 'paganism'. Recently, 'paganism' and 'heathenism' have been excluded from civilised vocabularies not only because they offend Westernised Africans but because their heavy connotations of 'irreligious', 'immoral' and 'unenlightened' are grossly misleading. By instinct Africans are profoundly religious, in the sense of not believing that feeble and fallible mankind can fend for itself. They believe in a Creator, one remote all-powerful God, who may best be worshipped through intermediaries – various spirits (*not* thought of as gods) and the living-dead. Those last are family members so recently dead that they can be remembered by someone still alive. Their importance in the traditional scheme of things is incalculable and they are thought to be very much amongst those present – helping, or if necessary punishing, their descendants.

Hence Mr Eyobo's distressed reaction to our 'irreligious' state, a reaction that was many times duplicated in conversations with Cameroonians of all faiths. In their terms, by refusing to worship a Creator one is denying human feebleness and fallibility and so committing the cardinal sin of Pride. They may never have heard of Lucifer, but if they did make his acquaintance they would regard him as a very bad boy.

We slept restlessly in a hot cubby-hole behind the living-room, sharing a narrow pallet. From within our gear, piled in a corner, came many rat-scufflings and shrill, aggressive squealings, recalling a night spent in a disused coffee-warehouse in Madagascar. Rats everywhere speak the same language.

As we dressed in the dark a vigorous drummer was walking through the village: Mr Eyobo summoning his flock to matins. And successfully summoning them: his large round church (a tin roof on tall tree-trunks) was more than half-full when I fetched Egbert in the grey dawn-light. Women stood on one side, men on the other; everyone swayed, clapped and fervently sang to the music of ten or twelve drummers. And from the Presbyterian church, hardly fifty yards away, came the sound of no less enthusiastic worshipping. The rival congregations were unmistakably competing in the decibel stakes, an endearing manifestation of sectarianism. As I stood listening to those powerful waves of sound, rolling towards each other across the street, a long bank of cloud to the east was suddenly faintly pink. Soon it would be hot – *very* hot.

By 6 a.m. we were on our way, musing over the semantics of money. Our host, looking agonised, had protested that he wanted *no* payment: 'I only want dash!' On being assured that the 2,000 CFA just pressed into his hand was indeed dash, he beamed and pocketed the notes. Perhaps fortunately, Mr Eyobo wasn't around. We felt sure he had intended Mammon to play no part in our relationship with Mr Makia.

Our up-and-down cut-short to Somie ran through thickish jungle, parallel to low, round, densely forested hills from which came many monkey-calls, including blood-curdling sounds that we had learned to identify as baboon quarrels. The morning cloud quickly dispersed and by eight o'clock we were sweating hard. An hour later we reached Somie, a small village near the base of a steep escarpment – our escape route from the hot plain. We planned to seek out the anthropologist (always an interesting species) and relax until three o'clock, leaving ourselves time to reach the cool heights by sunset.

Few of Somie's five hundred inhabitants were visible, both sexes having gone to the fields – even, to our grief, the bar proprietor. (Somewhere along the route we had lost our inhibitions about beer for breakfast: a process known in times past as 'going native'.) A young Fulani pushing a bicycle – cyclists are not uncommon on the plain – spoke fragmentary French but was nonplussed when Rachel asked the way to the Englishman's compound. She should have said 'White man's'; no one in Somie has ever heard of an *Englishman*. But at last the franc dropped and the youth volunteered to fetch Dave, who was also in the fields.

I led Egbert to scanty grazing beyond the village and on my way back Dave on his bicycle overtook me – an emaciated young man, too fair skinned to be tanned, wearing a huge conical straw hat and looking dazed. An Englishman who has been living alone in Somie for two years has much to say to fellow-English-speakers and we soon scrapped our plan to leave that day; luckily there was ample grazing close to Dave's three-roomed hut. The Chief, an ex-teacher and fluent French speaker, was away. But Dave said his wives would be perfectly agreeable to our staying in the palace guest suite, where, he insisted, we must burn one of his mosquito-coils. He seemed sceptical about the value of our prophylactics: 'Nowadays the mosquitoes are on top, they've got the measure of all those pills.' And he was shocked to hear that we were travelling without our own hypodermics: 'Who knows what percentage of Cameroonians have AIDS? What happens if you need an injection? Do you really want to die?'

During that forenoon we drank a lot of tea and learned a lot about spider divination, Dave's particular interest of the moment. He had just achieved a hard-earned breakthrough and been promised that he could attend a local divination ceremony. Modesty forbade him to explain what an honour this was, but I recognised it as the ultimate proof of trust, respect and acceptance. Diviners are as paranoid as the British Government about their Official Secrets.

According to John Mbiti, the Kenyan scholar equally distinguished as philosopher, theologian, linguist, Christian clergyman and pioneer of ecumenism:

> Diviners are the agents of unveiling the mysteries of human life. This is done through the use of mediums, oracles, being possessed, divination objects, common sense, intuitive knowledge and insight, hypnotism and other secret knowledge. They also keep their ears and eyes open to what is happening in their communities so that they have a store of working knowledge which they use in their divination ... The art of divination presents us with puzzling problems which I make no pretence to solve. A certain amount of communication goes on between diviners and non-human powers (whether living or otherwise or both). It is difficult to know exactly what this is: it might involve the diviner's extra-sensory ability, it may involve spiritual agents, it might be telepathy, it might be sharpened human perception, or a combination of these possibilities. Whatever it is, divination is another area which adds to the complexity of African concepts and experiences of the universe. Divination links together, in its own way, the physical and the spiritual worlds, making it a religious activity.

In cases of particular importance, requiring sensitive diplomatic solutions, spider divination has long been the most popular form in many areas of West Africa, including Western Cameroon. The earth spider (*Heteroscodra crassipes*, large, black and hairy) lives in burrows and so is in touch with the sacred underworld where dwell the ancestral – and some other – spirits. Thus he is well placed to serve as interpreter of their will and is among the animal élite, credited with unique wisdom and to be seen in stylised form on door-posts, finger-rings, tobacco pipes, ornamental stools and tattooed around women's navels. In some areas the earth spider was considered so sacred, less than a century ago, that death was the punishment for deliberately killing one; and those who might know the identity of an accidental killer had to conceal it from the rest of the community.

Diviners keep their spiders in burrows in enclosed shrines, to which leaf-cards are taken when a client seeks advice. These are made from the leaves of an African plum tree (*Pachylobus edulis*) and each is marked with a separate symbol. (They may not exceed three hundred to a pack.) Early in the morning some edible (to a spider) green leaves, or freshly killed insects, are placed inside the burrow under the leaf-cards.

An upturned pot or basket ensures that the spider works in darkness until the diviner and his client return, near sunset, to interpret the cards as they have been 'arranged' by the hungry spider. Should the diviner feel that the will of destiny, or the spirits' guidance, has not been made plain, the whole process may be repeated again and again.

As it is not always possible to find earth spiders, land-crabs may be used instead – and are, around Somie. Even now the evidence provided by spider divination is accepted in courts of law – official government courts, not only traditional village courts. Men who could not possibly be convicted on other grounds have been sentenced to life-imprisonment ostensibly on the strength of the spider's arrangement of leaves.

Dave's lunch – fufu and stewed liver – arrived from the palace at noon on a little girl's head; the Chief's wives provided all his meals for a fixed weekly sum. We discussed our emergency rations for the thinly-populated Tchabal Mbabo and Dave suggested an afternoon ground-nut quest. This was the scarce in-between season, but he knew a man . . .

That quest took us around a forested mountain and along the edge of a deep narrow valley where many women – bright little dots from our vantage point – were planting and weeding. We passed two earth spider (or land-crab) burrows, darkened by wickerwork funnels about eighteen inches long. One of Dave's friends accompanied us, a cheerful character wearing a long gown and carrying a long spear with which he hoped to secure a plump bush-rat or monkey for his supper. He paused to bend over the burrows, but didn't touch them: that would have been taboo.

In a spacious compound, surrounded by lush greenery, two wooden chairs were ceremoniously placed outside the main hut for Dave's guests. After a lengthy lead-in, groundnuts were mentioned. Some time later, a shy young woman brought a sackful for my inspection; groundnuts are the women's cash-crop. We bought two large buckets of unshelled nuts for 1,200 CFA (about £2.70), a bulky purchase until we had time to shell them.

This had once been a smithy family, an ancient and honourable profession in Western Cameroon, and we were shown a disused smelting furnace, and the equipment of a primitive forge, in an old hut in the centre of the compound. Archaeologists estimate that iron was first smelted in Africa some 2,000 years ago, by the people of the Grassfields – which was the beginning of the end for the great forests. No one could have cleared them with stone tools; and the development of intensive smelting and smithing industries hastened their clearing by creating a demand for charcoal. During the nineteenth century, in the Banbungo area alone (a small chiefdom near Mount Ocu), approximately one hundred metric tons of pure iron were produced annually. But this ancient industry was killed in the 1920s by imported European iron.

We were back in Somie by sunset, in time to enjoy a booze-up with thirty or so jolly women not long returned from the fields. They formed a circle – some on stools, some squatting on the ground – in one corner of the village square, a sloping dusty expanse below the palace. These vivacious gatherings – regular events during the planting season – are presided over by the Chief's senior wife and one of his sisters, the latter a strong personality who in the complicated hierarchy of the Somie Chiefdom holds a significant position 'at court'. Gourds of potent maize-beer were being filled from a cauldron in the centre of the circle and handed around; we each took a swig before passing the gourd to our neighbour. Wife of course had her personal gourd and sat on a flimsy metal and plastic camp-chair with Sister beside her on a stool. I was given a lower stool, on Wife's left, and twice she toppled over (whether because of her beer intake or wobbly seat was unclear), falling heavily on me to the delight of all present. Meanwhile Rachel had become embroiled in the gender argument with a group of elderly women. To resolve the matter I took Wife's hand and placed it on my bosom, a direct approach that caused much hilarity.

Now the air felt almost cool. Continuous sheet lightning flickered blue over the Nigerian mountains, fireflies darted brightly and a golden sliver of moon was poised above conical roofs. Despite a long day in the fields, many young women danced exuberantly to their own singing and clapping – a performance that recalled Mungo Park's prim comment: 'The dances, however, consisted more in wanton gestures than in muscular exertion or graceful attitudes. The ladies vied with each other in displaying the most voluptuous movements imaginable.'

Later, as we dined with Dave – eating manioc chunks fried in palm oil from a communal bowl – he told us that pre-marital chastity is not *de rigueur* hereabouts, but fidelity in marriage is. He also advised us that beer would be the dash most appreciated by our Somie hostesses.

Then the three little girls who had delivered our meal led us to the palace through a tangle of rough alleyways. A shy, speechless junior wife ushered us into the State Apartments by lantern-light. One large room boasted a dining-table, four chairs and several five-foot-high drums. Leading off it was the bedroom, containing only a double-bed (more sweat-inducing foam rubber) and floored with disconcerting mock-parquet plastic tiles, most of which had come loose. I was conducted across the wide, high hallway-cum-audience chamber to our basin of hot washing water in a bathroom no bigger than a shower-cabinet. This was also the latrine and a flat stone covered the hole in the floor. I was about to move the stone when I saw *Heteroscodra crassipes* low on the wall beside me – or if it wasn't *Heteroscodra crassipes* it was his first cousin, *very* large and black and hairy. Trembling with terror,

I fled. Moments later Egbert's bucket was emptied out of our unglazed bedroom window and we both went unwashed that evening.

At daybreak, returning to the palace with Egbert, I saw through an archway our three little friends crossing the compound in single file, each bearing a tray. For a moment they looked like a scene from an opera – *Aida,* perhaps – their gaily patterned frocks glowing vivid against pale mud walls, their dark slender arms curving upwards, steadying the trays. That was a luxury breakfast: six hot crisp maize-flour buns and three cups of Ovaltine each.

Dave escorted us to the start of what is known locally as 'the German road', a sensationally steep track cut through the forest of the escarpment and described on French maps as *vestiges d'ancienne voie.* When we said goodbye, on the bank of a swift stream, I would have expressed my admiration were he not an embarrassment-prone Englishman.

Nigel Barley's hilarious books on anthropologising in Cameroon have entertained millions (though not the Cameroonian government) and are so funny that one tends to underestimate the heroism such work demanded. Living for years in a mud hut in stifling heat on a pitifully inadequate diet miles from any other European requires awesome professional dedication. And when we met Dave he had been doing it for longer than Nigel Barley – for long enough, indeed, to have produced the first dictionary of the local language. Dr Barley has observed: 'The best one can probably hope for is to be viewed as a harmless idiot who brings certain advantages to the village.' Yet we sensed that Dave had achieved considerably more than this. Not of course 'acceptance', which couldn't happen without impossible feats of imagination on the part of the Somie folk; but unmistakably he was valued in the village *as a person,* not merely as a bringer of 'advantages'.

On a strip of level land, between the stream and the foot of the escarpment, we saw our first column of driver ants hurrying across the path. It was about a foot wide and small 'squaddies' formed the bulk of the troops, with a few rows of much bigger 'guardsmen' on either side. We paused to watch and at first this seemed an unremarkable phenomenon; these looked no different to the ants that swarmed all over us every siesta-time. Then we became aware of their numbers: thousands, tens of thousands – perhaps millions. Leaving Egbert, I walked to the left, where the column was going, and Rachel walked to the right, from whence it was coming. For more than two hundred yards we followed that marching straight line, across flat fields, without seeing its beginning or its ending. Then we understood how these ants can quickly kill a large animal or human being when they unite in a surprise attack.

The German road has not been repaired since 1915 and, after

seventy-two years of erosion, is much harder to walk on than an unpretentious bush-path. Half-way up we had our first clear view of a baboon colony but Rachel, oddly, seemed not very interested. She plodded on, leading Egbert, while I, enthralled, watched eighteen baboons, of all ages, feeding, grooming, playing, scratching, snoozing, flea-hunting and doing rude things with their genitalia. Curiosity is a conspicuous baboon trait; as I stood motionless two hulking males came to within five yards and sat in the grass, their hands on their knees, returning the compliment of my fascination.

I caught up with the others near the top of the escarpment where they were drinking from a cold, clear spring. Here the resin-tinged air felt exhilaratingly cool yet Rachel, most unusually for her, was dripping sweat as we rounded the last hairpin bend and emerged from the forest – to find ourselves looking directly down on Somie, thousands of feet below.

For a mile or so the road followed the ridge-top, winding through pine-woods and a new sort of glossy scrub. High mountains – which were Nigeria – rose some four miles away beyond an immensely deep valley. A few tin-roofed huts were visible on their forested slopes and I reflected that the concepts of 'Nigeria' and 'Cameroon' can mean little to their inhabitants. Since leaving Kumbo, we had been conscious of the locals feeling much closer to the clans across the border than they do to their compatriots in the distant coastal rain-forests or the deserts of the north.

Near the village of Ribao our *ancienne voie* joined a motorable (in dry weather) track linking Mayo Darlé with Nigeria. Here we were to turn right, instead of continuing into Ribao – but at the junction Rachel suddenly sat down and said, 'Would you like to lead Egbert?'

'How do you feel?' I asked sharply.

'Sort of lethargic,' admitted Rachel, 'and my legs are all achey.'

Maternal concern often manifests itself as irritability. 'Hah!' said I. 'Salt deficiency! I *told* you this would happen if you didn't eat your salt!'

'I'll be OK in a minute,' said Rachel pathetically, resting her head on her knees.

My anxiety level soared. Fourteen years of travelling together had taught me that Rachel's middle name is Stoicism; if she gives in there is something dreadfully wrong.

'You are *stupid*!' I ranted. 'It's crazy to trek in this heat and *not* eat salt!' I produced some, which Rachel meekly consumed. Then she sucked a few glucose tablets. Egbert meanwhile was grazing happily. I mooched off into the scrub, pretending to bird-watch.

Fifteen minutes later Rachel said, 'Now I'm OK. Let's push on.'

I led Egbert and tried to persuade myself that all was well. For miles we followed the crest of that glorious ridge, Rachel sucking glucose at intervals and seeming quite cheerful. A frolicking breeze pushed small white round clouds across the sky and tempered the sun's heat. Occasional thatched Fulani compounds were surrounded by high wickerwork fences. Many cattle grazed between low trees but we saw nobody until the day's one vehicle overtook us: a bush-taxi coming from Ribao.

It stopped. Two soldiers emerged – one Francophone, one Anglophone – their uniforms without insignia, their faces without smiles. The fat Anglophone unzipped his fly and pee'd almost onto my boots while asking, 'Where you come from?'

'From Bamenda,' I replied.

'Not true!' exclaimed the soldier, shaking his little willy and tucking it away. 'Bamenda is far, far! You come from Nigeria – give me your passports!'

I gave them. He stared at the green booklets and enquired, 'You are German people?'

'No,' I said, 'we are Irish people – from Ireland.'

'*Ireland?* What is *Ireland?*' He glared angrily at me, slapping his left hand with the passports.

'Our country,' I explained. 'Where we live – where we have our compound.'

Meanwhile the Francophone had been surveying Egbert's load. He said something to his mate who eagerly asked us, 'What happens you go sick in bush?'

'We have medicines,' I foolishly replied.

'Show us your medicines!' demanded the Anglophone, adding frankly, 'These might be useful for us!'

Regretfully I pointed out that we couldn't show them because they were deep inside the load which was very difficult to undo.

'Show us *everything!*' ordered the Anglophone. 'That is normal, you must show! We are border guards and many smuggle from Nigeria – it is normal to show!'

Here Rachel craftily intervened. 'You undo the load,' she suggested. 'We are too tired and the knots are very difficult.'

'Yes,' I echoed, '*you* undo it. But take care! This dangerous horse, he kick plenty!'

We sat down, like people not in a hurry, and repeated that we were too tired to attempt the hazardous task of unloading such an evil-tempered brute. But we had no objection to their unloading and examining *all* our baggage.

Much argument followed, in an increasingly amiable key. Finally the Anglophone admitted, rather disarmingly, 'We fear horses – we go!' And they went.

We found this confrontation less amusing at the time than in retrospect.

Soon a brief downpour refreshed us. Where Mayo Darlé first came deceptively into view, hours before we got there, cultivated fields replaced forest and scrub. The cultivators – both men and women – were truly black skinned (few Africans are) and regarded us with nervous suspicion. Later we learned that these people are Kwondjas, a tribe who remained enslaved by the Fulanis until the 1950s. Around one corner we came face to face with a leggy Mbororo girl; she emitted a weird wail and bolted into the bushes.

When Rachel again needed to rest we sat on a grassy bank and I somewhat belatedly expressed sympathy. But my suggestion that we should spend the night at a Fulani compound was rejected and I was accused of 'fussing'. I warned that Mayo Darlé was further than it looked but Rachel – fortunately – remained resolute. As we began the long, gradual descent another brief downpour made the track treacherous and Egbert, perhaps remembering his Lingham fall, slowed down considerably.

Two hours later there came a repeat performance of our evening on a bare mountain, with the difference that this storm lasted much longer and the sound and lighting effects were not quite so spectacular. When the heavenly damn burst without warning we were about a mile from the town, on a steep hill that within moments became a river.

Gale-driven sheets of water almost blinded us and I could hear poor Egbert thinking, 'Not again!' For his sake we soon took refuge on the wide verandah of a large roadside shuttered house. But he was unnerved by the torrent's tattooing on the tin roof and would only put his forequarters under shelter, which meant that the waterfall from the gutterless roof streamed directly onto the load.

We sat shivering on a narrow bench in the macabre twilight created by these tropical storms. I studied Rachel and shouted, 'How do you feel?'

'Fine!' she shouted back untruthfully. Her eyes seemed to have shrunk and her shivering was much more violent than my own. I put a hand on her forehead and guesstimated that her temperature was not less than 103°F. 'Nonsense!' she snapped. 'Mothers always exaggerate!'

A smiling woman came tripping down the hill – the only person in sight – her shoes on her head, her wrap-around gown clinging to her portly form. She waved cheerfully and I reflected that Mayo Darlé had probably been praying for rain. Yet such deluges are not what the rainmakers try to attract. We could see the water rushing down the steep field opposite, not being absorbed by the earth but sweeping the topsoil into the Mayo Darlé – which was rising rapidly as we watched.

Then our involuntary host – an elderly man – came racing around the corner of his house. On seeing us he stopped as though pole-axed, but quickly recovered himself and beckoned us to follow him inside. Rachel did so. I stayed with Egbert who needed constant soothing, verbal and tactile, as the thunder crackled and boomed – less continuously than on the bare mountain, which for him made it all the more terrifying.

Thirty chilling minutes later the wind dropped and the rain eased, though only very slightly. I found Rachel slumped dopily in an armchair in a big empty half-dark room. Of our host, or anybody else, there was no sign. By then however we were too demoralised to worry about the finer points of *politesse*.

'Let's go!' I said. 'We've got to get you into a bed somewhere – and fast!'

We waded down towards the Mayo Darlé, by now a wildly swirling red-brown torrent. A man was pushing a hand-cart over the bridge and despair engulfed me. This wasn't a real bridge but a few loose sheets of warped scrap iron laid over a few flexible tree trunks – the hand-cart's crossing sounded like a heavy metal band gone berserk. No horse that I have ever known would take on such a contraption. Without altering my pace I looked at Egbert, who was wearing his 'pained resignation' expression. (His range of expressions was truly remarkable.) Then suddenly I knew that he would, as always, oblige. Which he did, following me across those rattling metal sheets without any trace of nervousness. On the far side three women in a doorway were diverted to see me embracing my horse.

When I yelled an inquiry about 'Africa hotel?' the women yelled back, 'No hotel here!' This, we subsequently discovered, was untrue. Mayo Darlé has numerous doss-houses, being on one of Cameroon's main motorways and a staging-post for trans-continental truckers. But no doubt the good ladies deemed those establishments unfit for Whites.

We now joined the international motorway – a wider earth track, also converted to a river. At the junction stood a sodden gendarme, wearing no waterproofs; sensibly, the locals don't even try to defy such storms.

'From Nigeria?' asked the gendarme.

'From Bamenda,' I corrected, without stopping.

'Halt!' cried he. 'This way not from Bamenda! You cannot *walk* from Bamenda – nobody *walk* from Bamenda! You come Customs and Immigration – show passports, show health papers, fill immigration forms, show baggage!'

I paused, glanced over my shoulder and said through clenched teeth, 'You must be joking! *Look* at us! And my daughter has fever – we're going straight to the Mission.'

The gendarme waved his arms in the air. 'This is not your daughter! You tell me lies! This is your *wife*!'

'Get stuffed!' growled Rachel from the background.

I turned and strode purposefully away up the long main street past a row of colossal parked trucks bringing cargoes (and no doubt AIDS) from the Central African Republic to Douala. A hundred yards on we glanced back. The gendarme was still standing at the junction, peering at us through an opacity of rain.

Reluctant as we were to sorn on the Mission, especially when diseased, there seemed to be no alternative. Two little boys volunteered to guide us through a network of steep laneways – now cataracts. The distance was about two miles but it felt like twenty.

Mayo Darlé's solitary missionary (Franz, a Dutch Mill Hill priest) was unsurprised to see us; he had just returned from a visit to St Augustine's. Standing on his wide verandah, he nodded and smiled through the curtain of rain, and shouted something inaudible above the tattoo on the roof, and pointed to the guest room – where Rachel at once collapsed onto the single bed.

Unloading took a long time; my fingers were numb and the knots rain-tightened. Tethering Egbert nearby, I changed into garments that were damp rather than wet and joined our host in his simple but comfortable living-room. He poured me a beer before saying anything. Then we shouted at each other about Rachel's symptoms. Her diary for 2 April records: 'Felt lousy and was diagnosed as having malaria. A sweet black Sister gave me a chloroquin shot in the bum.'

6

Mayo Darlé and Beyond

THE 'SWEET BLACK Sister' had, I was relieved to hear, used a *new* disposable needle. In most parts of Africa basic medical equipment, taken for granted in the West, is so hard to come by that 'disposable' needles are used again and again – and are regarded, by some doctors, as an even greater AIDS hazard than promiscuity.

Rachel's 'shot in the bum' was supplemented by massive doses of chloroquin pills at six-hourly intervals and after a semi-delirious night she was up, though still very weak, on the following afternoon. However, the experts pronounced that she needed at least three days' rest and would be well advised to ride Egbert for another few days. Relapses, they said, are brought about by too much exertion too soon. Mayo Darlé (population approximately 5,000) has no doctor but through personal experience most of its inhabitants have become malaria experts.

From Egbert's point of view this was a lucky break; he had perceptibly lost condition on the hot plain. After the storm Yaya Moctar, a young Fulani *malloum* (religious teacher) and noted local horseman, put him to graze with his own herd beyond the river. Often I turned my binoculars on that grassy hillside, almost opposite the Mission, to enjoy watching him stuffing himself.

Yaya was a friend of the Foxes, a young lay-missionary couple who, after four years in Cameroon, spoke a marvellous multiplicity of languages including Foulfouldé. They lived in a bungalow in the Mission compound and, with Franz, formed Mayo Darlé's White colony. John Fox (from Ireland) was a teacher and photographer; Jacqueline (from Holland) was a Primary Health Care worker, away in the bush when we arrived. At sunset John dragged himself over to the big Mission bungalow and Franz introduced us. The Irishman was then a shocking sight: tall, gaunt, haggard, with sunken eyes and a ghastly pallor. He could eat nothing and drink only water. Frequent and severe attacks of malaria wreck the digestive system, even when the patient is a strong, well-nourished White. Hence it is a main killer-disease in areas where many are ill-nourished.

Franz was a comparative newcomer and after two years in Kenya, working deep in the bush with one large nomadic tribe, he found Cameroon's patchwork of languages and clans somewhat daunting. 'Where do you start?' he wondered plaintively.

My unspoken reaction was, 'Why bother to start?' It is hard to see any possible spiritual benefit accruing to Africans in the 1980s from the presence among them of White missionaries, however sensitive and sympathetic. The dispatching of those men and women 'to save souls' in Black Africa is unrealistic, if only because of the missionaries' past symbiotic relationship with colonialism. Inevitably we contrasted the roles of Franz, the 'formal' though flexible mission priest, and of the Foxes, new-style lay-workers whose practical activities gave shape and meaning to their lives in Cameroon. The demands made on Franz by his flock were minimal: an annual average of ten confessions heard and ten baptisms administered. (Of course he also provided daily Mass: but that was not a *demand*.) Across the compound, the demands made on the Foxes' skills were endless.

On meeting Jacqueline, I at once got the sort of charge that comes from recognising a kindred spirit. The morning after the storm, as Mayo Darlé sweltered on its lowish riverbank under a cloudless sky, she invited me to accompany her to the Health Centre at the local open-cast tin-mine, which we had noticed on the way from Somie. Mayo Darlé's Mission was founded to minister to the mining settlement, when the French forcibly imported hundreds of workers from the Central African Republic in 1935. (Most inconveniently, the terms of their League of Nations Mandate forbade them to subject Cameroonians to the conditions then prevailing at the mine.) In 1974 the Mission moved to its present site because the tin – and miners – were dwindling. A new church was built in 1985, its design incomprehensibly based on a Fulani compound although in Africa, as elsewhere, the Muslim-to-Christian conversion rate is, and always has been, negligible.

By 1987 the miners' community was down to about 250 and many company dwellings – grimly resembling prison-compound huts – lay empty. A recent attempt to revive the mine had failed and closure seemed imminent. In a small shed, shaded by mighty mango trees, the sad, gentle manager showed us minute quantities of tin being processed with the aid of primitive but adequate (he said) technology. Apart from the rows of dwellings, now half-obscured by vegetation, this ecologically benign enterprise has left the beauty of the surrounding mountains unspoiled.

A decrepit primary school, devoid of what we consider basic teaching aids, catered for two score happy children who seemed to have an excellent relationship with their kindly if ineffectual teacher – and with Jacqueline. But what does the future hold for those grandchildren of forcibly displaced persons? Probably many will migrate to a city and compete desperately for the most menial jobs. The wiser ones will remain around Mayo Darlé and clear enough bush to provide meagre sustenance for a family – very meagre, as the local soil is ungenerous to those without cattle.

Jacqueline had won the rare distinction of being accepted as a friend by the area's notoriously aloof Fulani semi-nomads. These clans refused to accept Islam and take part in don Fodio's Jihad and so reaped none of the conqueror's rewards, which didn't in any case appeal to them. Some have now settled with their cattle in otherwise uninhabited and uncultivated bush. But none think of themselves as belonging to any nation-state and the majority remain seasonal nomads, migrating twice annually with their enormous herds and few possessions. Unlike Muslim Fulanis, they never marry out; a girl who became pregnant by a Bantu would probably be killed and her baby certainly would. (Many Fulani warriors took Bantu women into their harems to consolidate alliances, hence the high percentage of dark-skinned upper-class Fulanis in modern Cameroon.)

I was touched when Jacqueline suggested a day-trip to the compound of her closest nomad friends; she is not the sort of person to display friends as 'tourist attractions'. From Mayo Darlé we drove south-east for half an hour, the jeep weaving like a hunted hare to avoid this international highway's numerous fissures. On our right, far below, the Somie plain was a heat-hazed blur. On our left, hilly grey-green scrub and thin jungle, apparently unpeopled, stretched away to the horizon. Parking the jeep under a wayside mango tree, we walked through those steep hills for forty-five minutes on a surprisingly well-defined path. Many of the low trees were unfamiliar and, Jacqueline said, a valuable nomad food-source. They gather an abundance of wild fruits, berries, roots and medicinal leaves and herbs. We glimpsed a few groups of turkey-sized black birds strutting through the bush; I have never seen others like them. This high, silent hill country was yet another of Cameroon's many contrasting 'worlds' – harsh yet tranquil.

Jacqueline talked, with affection, of the nomads. Naturally they keep no record of ages; youngsters marry when physically mature. Babies are named a week after birth and cattle killed to celebrate the event. There are no family names and personal names change at different stages of development – and sometimes for other reasons, to do with unusual events in an individual's life. All of which, added to a lack of fixed addresses, makes Fulani nomads peculiarly difficult to catch in bureaucratic nets; and the Cameroonian government sensibly leaves them to their own devices.

Those very few nomad children who have sampled schooling find it uncongenial. Their academic concentration span is short, like that of their White contemporaries from TV-dominated homes. Yet out in the forest, when hunting, herding or honey-gathering, they can concentrate on detail for hours at a stretch, showing exceptional patience and persistence.

We passed only one compound, at some little distance; the few low huts merged into their surrounding bush and but for Jacqueline I might have missed them. Her friends' compound was altogether grander, occupying a large, dusty, unfenced clearing amidst spindly trees. Their new main hut was, on the local scale of things, a Yuppie residence, made of imported (from beyond Tignère) bamboos, with circular walls of pre-woven straw matting bought at a market. A small boy and slightly larger girl fled at our approach, despite my being escorted by their beloved Jacqueline.

Jacqueline's special friend, Dijja, was sitting in the sun on a frayed raffia mat, bare to the waist, and for a moment her appearance frightened me. No Famine Appeal poster could have been more harrowing. She was, literally, skin and bone; never before had I met anyone at such an advanced stage of emaciation. Obtusely, I assumed her to be very, very old. In fact, according to Jacqueline's calculations, she was scarcely fifty – but had been suffering from untreated tuberculosis for seventeen years. A lesser being would long since have died but these nomads are hardy folk. When she rose to greet us her breasts flapped like strips of dried leather yet she stood erect and moved with agility. Her greeting was gracious and warm and after the initial shock one forgot her appearance. An extraordinary vitality burned within that skeletal frame. Dijja was among the most impressive people I met in Cameroon: brave, witty, vivacious, with strong views and a formidable air of authority – a *grande dame* of the bush.

We had to bend very low to enter the main hut. Inside, close enough to the doorless entrance for smoke to escape easily, a few sticks smouldered between three stones. Dijja at once added twigs and began to blow on them as two daughters and a daughter-in-law hurried in to welcome Jacqueline and her guest. We sat on one of three homemade beds and gratefully received pint mugs brimming with fresh milk. A teenage girl lay close beside us on another bed, completely invisible beneath a goathair blanket and moaning softly at frequent intervals. She had 'stomach ache', whatever that might signify, and throughout our four-hour visit remained immobile but for an occasional convulsive movement when stabbed by pain. Nobody, except Jacqueline, took any notice of her.

The children soon joined us, after a cautious preliminary peeping session. The handsome three-year-old boy was stark naked; the frail girl (Dijja's youngest) looked about eight but must have been twelve, Jacqueline reckoned. All the men were away, tending their many cattle and fewer sheep. The latter are cash-livestock, to be sold whenever money is needed – which isn't very often. Cattle are rarely sold for cash but are in themselves a form of currency, being used to pay debts or clan-imposed fines, and for such ceremonial obligations as brideprices.

The hut was some thirty feet in diameter and the roof rose to quite a high point. Wood in convenient lengths had been stacked near the fire. A stand made of uneven branches held several calabashes and a few of their modern equivalents, bright dishes imported from Nigeria. Previously a woman's calabash collection was her pride and joy; now enamel-ware is 'in'. Flies swarmed and as my eyes became adjusted I observed that the floor was unswept, the food dishes unprotected from flies and the general level of cleanliness (except *bodily* cleanliness) way below normal. This is one reason why other Cameroonians, including Fulanis, despise the nomads as 'backward'. But, Jacqueline explained, they are also feared and grudgingly respected for the efficacy of their magic. Never having 'gone over' to Islam or Christianity, they are believed to be more closely in touch than most with the spirit-world and their magic is proportionately powerful.

All the young women were good looking, graceful, high spirited. But one was a problem. Fatah, aged twenty-five, refused to marry – or at least to marry any man suggested by her family. She should have been a wife for nine or ten years, yet she had remained steadfastly anti-marriage in a way that would have been impossible for a Muslim – and hard to imagine for any other Cameroonian outside the Westernised élite. Jacqueline suspected that the family blamed her for indirectly encouraging, through her own example as a career-woman, Fatah's claims to independence – though the rebel had been twenty-one, and set in her apparently celibate ways, when Jacqueline came on the local scene. Fatah didn't strike me as a natural celibate: rather the reverse. Was she perhaps a nomad drop-out who felt an inexplicable longing for the wider world and hoped somehow to reach it through a self-made marriage? Or was she simply an unconscious pioneer of feminism in the bush, freakishly individualistic and determined not to become any man's property? Did she, I wondered, have a lover in Mayo Darlé? I didn't care to ask Jacqueline who, had she received any such confidence, would not have wished to break it.

The hours passed agreeably. Dijja herself prepared our 'treat' – aromatic fried butter, onion-flavoured and spiced. This was placed on the floor between us in a little bowl, together with a large communal bowl of cold rice left over from breakfast. Chunks of rice dipped in the hot butter sauce tasted surprisingly good and I stuffed myself while a relaxed triangular conversation flowed between Jacqueline, her friends and myself. Meanwhile the little boy – already an apprentice herd, when the cattle are nearer home – was romping desultorily with a half-grown dog of infinite tolerance who lay close beside Dijja when not being required to romp.

This family belonged to a group known as the Aku who speak their own dialect and have their own hair-styles and dances. They still migrate to and fro across the border mountains; Dijja was born in Nigeria. They have no conception of the world beyond their own territories. Douala means no more to them than Dublin. But the local markets are important, socially rather than economically. Twice or even thrice a week someone walks to a market – this may involve a thirty-mile trek – and returns full of entertaining gossip.

The latest gossip concerned an unusual domestic tragedy. Nomad marriages are arranged very early, sometimes during babyhood, though the ceremony never takes place until both partners are fully mature. However, husbands are free to *choose* their second and subsequent wives, which occasionally provokes friction – or worse. In this case an unprepossessing first wife became so jealous of a comely second wife that she bit off two of her rival's fingers at the top joints and thrust her face into a kitchen fire, wedging it between the stones. The young woman was dreadfully scarred and her sight permanently damaged. Having recovered enough to walk, she took refuge in her parents' compound – and stayed there. Which was the object of the exercise. The neighbours' reaction to this drama proved how unusual it was. A self-contained society, operating beyond the laws of the land, also has to be self-regulatory. Therefore strong taboos ensure that such violent urges are usually repressed.

An hour or so after our rice course a huge bowl of delicious creamy curds was placed at our feet – and soon emptied. Some time later we were handed two filthy tin spoons and encouraged to help ourselves from a dish of thick, dark honey, newly gathered in the forest. It was faintly smoke-flavoured; a fire is lit below the hive – hanging from a tree – to disperse the owners. At this stage we restrained ourselves; honey is hard-won and an important nutrient.

Dijja also suffered from asthma and when an attack began Fatah rushed to fetch a large bottle of spray-on scent which she applied lavishly to her mother's back as a 'cure'. Those grotesquely incongruous 'First World' fumes seemed to aggravate the attack but everyone inhaled them appreciatively and the little boy begged for scent on his hands; this was evidently a regular routine.

The maverick Fatah had her own tiny hut which it was *de rigueur* for me to visit before we left. A frame of rough branches supported a tousled grass thatch and there was just room for the three of us to stand beside the hide-covered pallet. On a little shelf above it stood an improbable array of shampoos, deodorants, insecticides, toilet soaps, scents and cosmetics. Plainly Fatah's imagination had been seduced by the Big Bad World where not *only* cattle are important. She now impulsively decided to accompany us to Mayo Darlé and spend the night in the Foxes' bungalow, as she quite often did when the opportunity arose. But first a hen had to be caught; no honoured guest may leave a compound without a gift of a hen – or a cock, should he prove easier to capture. I carried the unfortunate bird back to the jeep.

Later I asked Jacqueline if, in her view, the Cameroonian villagers' connubial sleeping arrangements mean that most couples' sexual relationships are strictly functional, for the physical relief of males and the fertilisation of females.

'Just so,' replied Jacqueline. 'Village women get their emotional satisfaction from mothering. They couldn't even imagine what we mean by love-making – maybe that's why they seem content without sex while suckling. It's fantasy that Africans enjoy gloriously uninhibited, passionate, voluptuous sex-lives!'

Near Mayo Darlé we met a young nomad woman carrying a large basin of milk to the market; having sold it she would buy the supplementary food needed during this in-between season. She sat behind with Fatah, on the spare tyre, and as we jolted down the track it distressed me to see much of her precious liquid sloshing onto the floor. She often drove with Jacqueline: this was not the first time she had lost a significant percentage of her load. Yet the basin was adequately lidded, had the lid been held firmly in place. I felt utterly baffled; she didn't seem stupid and Jacqueline confirmed that in her own world she was shrewd and resourceful. But she couldn't grasp the simple laws of science that prevent liquid from spilling in a jolting jeep.

This must be the sort of incident that prompted generations of White colonialists to scorn 'thick Blacks'. It reminded me of our Bamenda conversation with an anguished and mildly intoxicated English architect who asserted – after working for fifteen years in Africa – that one cannot train a team of Black construction workers and then leave them to get on with the job.

'Unless you're supervising,' he had said, 'something will go radically wrong. Most Blacks are fine builders in their own styles but anything else defeats them. I don't exactly mean intellectually – some of them learn very fast. But then they won't concentrate. And all the basic principles we've taken for granted for centuries are new to them – so they won't take them seriously if you're not watching. I'm not talking *only* about modern technology – looking after machinery and so on. It's more complicated. Seven hundred years ago we were building the great cathedrals of Europe. Seventy years ago, they were building mud so-called palaces – that was the apogee of their architectural ambition and still would be if we hadn't come along. Is it racist to *say* this? Should we only *think* it? Or should we pretend it's not true or doesn't matter? But if you're living and working here it *does* matter, one helluva lot! For your own peace of mind you've got to try to understand why Africa has such problems – otherwise you'd become profession-ally embittered and intolerant and *really* racist. And probably an alcoholic ...'

Like all the (fortunately few) towns on our route, Mayo Darlé seemed to signify a strong African disinclination to come to terms with having been dragged into the Modern Age. These places look like wounds inflicted on the country by some alien force. The contrast with bush villages, away from 'motorable' tracks, could not be more striking; many villages still retain that simple, orderly beauty so much admired by early travellers in West Africa. Nor is this comparison just one more symptom of silly White romanticism. The towns do not provide a more comfortable or convenient way of life than the villages – rather the reverse. If they have an electricity generator (usually they don't) its unreliability means that it is not a mod. con. but a source of dismay and confusion. A post office may occasionally exist but it can take letters a month or two to travel a hundred miles. A health centre may also exist in theory (the French maps are peppered with them), but it will be so under-staffed and ill-equipped that it is better to stick with the medicine-men, as most people do. A water source may be closer to each compound, but it will almost certainly be more polluted than rural supplies. And health is further endangered by a hazard (now a deadly hazard) unknown in the villages – prostitution.

Often prostitution is someone's problem exported from a village to a town, as on every continent. Mayo Darlé has a colony of more than two hundred prostitutes to serve passing truckers and while bar-crawling I met dozens (many bars are also brothels). Once I was invited to the two-roomed hut of an articulate Anglophone quartet; all were barren and had been rejected by their husbands, leaving prostitution as the only alternative to starvation.

This was the dark side to the Ntem Chief's moving love for – *reverence* for – children. According to traditional beliefs, a barren woman is a non-person. Her husband will not necessarily reject her, demanding a refund of the bridewealth, because she may still be useful as a field worker. But the extended family and the local community will make her feel so inadequate – almost *wicked* – that it is often easier to run away. She sees herself as excluded from the tribe/family/clan. When she dies there will be no one to remember her, to maintain contact with her spirit, so she cannot join the living-dead. It will be as though she had never lived. Barrenness has removed her from the river that flows from birth through life to afterlife; it flows on without her. And even while she lives she is non-existent because unfruitful.

All four women in that sad little hut were believing Christians – two Baptists, one Roman Catholic, one Presbyterian – yet none took comfort from their faith. If anything, having been brought up on the ideal of Christian marriage sharpened their grief. Not only had they failed as women, in their traditional role, but they had also failed as Christian partners in a monogamous life-long union. Belonging to 'Mission Christian', as distinct from 'Black Church', families can make rejection even more humiliating; often the barren wife is blamed for leaving her husband with no choice but to sin. These women's reliance on children – especially sons – to confer immortality had remained undiminished by their exposure to the Christian doctrine of individual posthumous rewards or punishments. None could sufficiently comprehend 'the Beatific Vision' to regard it as an adequate consolation prize for childless women. Not myself believing in the Christian afterlife, I shared their gut-reaction to 'Heaven' and became aware of an ironic closing of a circle. We five women were agreed that immortality has more to do with child-bearing than with 'Heaven' but we had travelled to that meeting-point by different – and opposite – roads.

On another level our conversation was one more reminder of the gulf between individualistic Westerners and most of the rest of mankind. In their own estimation these women had no value as individuals; they saw themselves only as part of a community to which, being female, they should contribute young. Instinctively they were concerned with the survival of the species, to an extent and with an intensity that is no longer necessary. The fulfilment of the individual was not on their agenda.

When I asked what they knew about AIDS the women giggled. There was no problem in Cameroon, only in other places ... It would have been pointless to remind them that most of their clients came from the 'other places' in question. There was nothing they could do to protect themselves, even had it been possible to convince them that protection was necessary. Cameroon is not in the main danger zone (yet) but the virus has of course arrived and we heard of several deaths in the Kumbo region.

As we talked in that shadowy little room – becoming increasingly uninhibited on '33' and Guinness (they preferred Guinness) – I wondered what would happen to my unfortunate friends, and their many colleagues, when their bodies are no longer saleable. Like most African countries, Cameroon has no social security system; family members are supposed to care for one another and usually do, at least in rural areas.

All four women were in their mid-forties and their prices had dropped to 100 CFA (about 20p): the price of a hand of bananas. Many teenagers, they said, could charge 500 CFA and even up to 1,000 CFA (just over £2) if they were *very* fat. I asked why teenagers chose this job and was startled to learn that some are earning their brothers' school fees. Prostitution does not of course carry the same stigma in Africa as in Europe. If times are hard – a crop failure, an expensive illness, storm damage to a compound – it may make economic sense to send a daughter out to earn for a few years, before marriage, even if this leads to her husband paying somewhat reduced bridewealth. Being by then on my third '33' I got lost in the maze of clans and groups now mentioned. Some are openly tolerant of pre-marital sex and see prostitution as nothing more; others condone it, but furtively; others condemn it and would consider a daughter on the streets the ultimate family disgrace. Yet even from among that last group many modern girls now defy their families and come to the bright (lamp) lights of Mayo Darlé because they want to find 'educated' husbands and graduate to the brilliant (electric) lights of Douala or Yaoundé.

Thirty-six miles of hilly motor-road link Mayo Darlé to Banyo, a bigger town, with a post office, a hospital and two Missions (Catholic and Protestant). There are no cut-shorts; the French (or was it German?) road-builders took the shortest cut. However, we decided to look for bush-paths, even if they added miles. By Cameroonian standards the traffic is considerable on this comically circuitous but only trans-continental route from Yaoundé to the Central African Republic and Mombasa. Every hour or so a menacing giant container or oil-tanker goes rattling and roaring and hooting over the calamitous surface, creating clouds of blinding, stifling dust.

While drifting around Mayo Darlé I repeatedly enquired about bush-paths going north. Most people said there was no such thing but at last I met Jackson, a worried-looking Anglophone, who showed me the start of a path which would take us through high hills to Yoli, on the motor-road, where we could ask again. This path began near an unused hospital, completed a few years ago but as yet unopened for lack of trained staff willing to work in 'primitive' Mayo Darlé.

Jackson looked worried because his brown and white in-kid nanny had broken her tether and strayed. She and her young represented all his savings: he had been seeking her since dawn. I joined in the search and roamed the sides of a deep wooded glen. Then a distant figure appeared on the skyline – a woman gesticulating and shouting. We hastened to the road; the nanny had been found in someone's depleted maize-field and could be redeemed on payment of compensation. Jackson looked at me expectantly; he had after all gone out of his way to show me that path to Yoli. We set out to retrieve the goat, inspect the not very extensive damage and palaver with an eloquently angry Francophone woman who seemed to detest all Anglophones. After half an hour damages were settled at 1,000 CFA and muggins paid up.

Mayo Darlé had more than its share of predatory folk, no doubt a result of the permanent White presence. Several of my bar companions – eminently respectable men and women, highly regarded in their local community – were delighted to hear that in the middle of June we would again be stopping off at the Mission. Urgently they begged me to bring them gifts from N'gaoundere: a sack of rice, a pair of 'smart shoes', a length of 'cloth with many colours' for a new frock, and so on and on and on. When I protested, 'We're not rich!' they took that to be my little joke. All Whites are rich and as I seemed an amiable drinking partner, willing to dispense beer within reason, was it not natural that our reunion should be celebrated with gifts?

Malaria prophylactics may not work too well nowadays, as preventatives, but they do mean milder attacks when the virus strikes. On 5 April Rachel felt fit enough to accompany Yaya and me to the Sunday market where we hoped to buy two strong holdalls to replace the bulky sacks, thereby leaving room on the saddle for a convalescent.

This weekly market was disappointing, though it draws villagers from near and far. The only foods available were maize-flour, jammu-jammu greenery, manioc, bananas, avocados, mangoes and a tall pyramid of expensive tins of Ovaltine newly smuggled from Nigeria. In the butchers' corner hunks of beef swarmed with flies and were already smelly. The two zebu heads concerned stood on a trestle-table like noisome hairy sculptures and behind them little boys were doing arcane things with piles of offal. (One day we would discover to our cost exactly what they were doing ...) Dogs lurked profitably and a strangely mottled mother cat defied them to make off with an intestine prize longer than herself.

All the little stalls – mostly Fulani and Hausa – are open on Sundays, lining rough narrow laneways, but the local cash scarcity limits their range and quality of goods. Many tall, bearded, commanding figures were striding around in flowing pastel robes and embroidered caps, looking as though they owned the place – which once they did, before the White man came. Yaya knew everyone and because of his *malloum* status was obviously much respected, despite his youth. He saw to it that fair prices were mentioned and after much deliberation – nothing on offer looked very substantial – we paid 5,000 CFA for two large 'airline' holdalls of tawdry plastic and cardboard, with zipped outer pockets. Yaya suggested reinforcing them on his uncle's sewing-machine and for twenty minutes we sat in a minute tailor's cubby-hole watching him deftly at work; he is a man of many parts. When I made a shocking – insulting – mistake by trying to dash him, he forgave me with one of his most charming smiles.

Next day Rachel seemed stronger still and we went for a 'test-run' stroll on the hills above the tin-mine. Although she claimed to feel '95 per cent' – quite fit enough to walk to Banyo – I insisted on her riding and quoted Mungo Park: 'My recovery was very slow; but I embraced every short interval of convalescence to walk out, and make myself acquainted with the products of the country. In one of those excursions, having rambled further than usual in a hot day, I brought on a return of my fever, and on the 10th of September I was again confined to my bed.'

The bush-path to Yoni crossed steep wooded mountains, separated by spectacular ravines from which baboons abused us. Our compact holdalls left ample room for a rider but Egbert at once made it plain that he abhorred his new role. Nor could we blame him. The load was light: your average Cameroonian donkey would think nothing of carrying twice that weight for twenty miles non-stop. Rachel however is not light and, within moments of her mounting, Egbert reminded us that carrying a hefty rider was not part of his contract. He conveyed this message by walking at a steady one m.p.h. and looking reproachfully aggrieved when two m.p.h. were suggested.

Rachel had to dismount for the hazardous descent from those mountains. Soon after, we came upon our first milk-bar: two very small Fulanis milking three very large cows in the middle of nowhere. They were bewildered when I paid them for an enormous gourd brimming with warm frothing milk. Near Yoni we joined the hot, stony, dusty motor-road and at 11.15 a.m. took refuge under a generously shady tree surrounded by lush grass. The convalescent slept deeply while I conversed with two Bamenda truck-drivers whose vehicle had broken down nearby; they expected to have to spend two or three nights in their cab while awaiting 'a piece' from Douala.

A frisky breeze tempered the afternoon heat and Egbert consented to speed up as we turned off the 'international highway' onto another bush-path. But soon Rachel announced that she would have to walk; folded sacks on a wooden saddle don't do much for the bum. (My suggestion that we should camp immediately was derided.) Our path crossed a series of forested hills – unpeopled and bird-rich – before dropping into a broad, serene, cultivated valley. This was Fulani territory and several prosperous compounds glowed golden amidst acres of young maize. By a cool sandy stream we performed our river ritual: water Egbert, fill and pill bottles, wash selves, brush teeth.

At sunset fortune favoured us with a tranquil tree-encircled campsite on a flat high hilltop where Egbert was turned loose to make the most of scant grazing. Then darkness revealed an awesome bush-fire to the north; sheets of crimson flame steadily widening on a hillside, below swirling clouds of orange-tinted smoke. Our inexperienced eyes couldn't judge how far away it might be and momentarily it seemed threatening. We had seen evidence enough that some bush-fires spread and spread, devouring many miles. Would we be safe all night in our tent? This instant of animal fear was absurd yet powerful: one of those atavistic reactions that remind Western (wo)man how very recently s/he became 'civilised'.

As we struck camp at dawn Rachel mutinied. 'Today I'm 100 per cent fit, so there's no need to ride.' By noon she had proved her point, having effortlessly walked twelve miles. We were then in a newish, partly Anglophone village where the friendliness level seemed markedly lower than usual. While Egbert grazed outside the unwelcoming bar – some way from the road, behind empty market-stalls – both sacks were stolen off the saddle. This was our only Cameroonian experience of pilfering.

Back on the shadeless dusty motor-road we prayed for clouds that never came. Then a cattle-track appeared, accompanying the road but some little distance from it, winding through comparatively cool bush – much of it so dense that often we had to hold back saplings to make way for Egbert.

Near a group of Fulani compounds the track and road amalgamated where a still-solid colonial bridge spanned a wide brown river. I had just finished washing when a herd of migrating cattle came pouring over the crest of a high ridge beyond the river. There is something mysteriously exciting about such a sight; the last time we witnessed it was in Madagascar. I moved slightly to get a better view. Some four hundred glossy, lean, wide-horned beasts – including dozens of small calves, to the rear – came swiftly down the slope, eager for water. They were flanked by slim, nimble donkeys carrying household goods: rolled-up hides for sleeping on, gourds of every size, battered and blackened kettles and pots (just like our own), bags of manioc or maize-flour, a storm-lantern, a rusty tin of kerosene – and, topping one load, a pair of yellow and pink plastic sandals. Only four men were herding: lithe, muscular nomads wearing dusty rags, brandishing long sticks and chanting weirdly. This method of giving directions is perfectly understood by cattle but not, it seems, by sheep. Those inferior animals – about fifty of them, including lambs – came far behind in the charge of two small boys. Men and boys alike glanced at us with indifference (or was it contempt?) before returning all their attention to their animals. Fulani nomads on the move – we were to meet many others – have a strong aura of exclusiveness and independence. One senses a people completely absorbed in their own demanding yet fulfilling way of life, as they have been for millennia but may not be for much longer.

We followed the cattle-track up that ridge and into a deep, densely forested valley. When brilliant feathers flashed through the foliage I made to lift my binoculars – but they weren't there. Only their empty case hung around my neck.

Stricken, I turned to Rachel. 'My binocs! I've left them by the river!'

We stared at one another in silence. Then, 'Shall I go back?' I asked. 'You could wait here.'

'What's the point? All those cattle have been across the bank.'

We continued through the cool evening shadows beneath the trees, then crossed the muddy bed of a dried-up stream and climbed a steep, tunnel-like path bizarrely eroded out of a shiny dark red cliff. Our campsite was far from compounds and cultivation so again we turned Egbert loose. Below this high crest another bush-fire leaped and quivered, sending wavelets of flame to lap at the feet of mighty trees; it was so close that we caught occasional whiffs of incense-like smoke. Having developed a local weather sense, we rightly judged it unnecessary to put up the tent and Rachel spread our flea-bags on the saddle-blanket on an open patch of ground. Soon she was asleep, but I lay grieving over my loss and miserably reviewing, as one does, every detail of 'how it happened'. Objectively I recognised this misfortune as just punishment for having broken a basic Travellers' Rule: CHECK EVERYTHING BEFORE MOVING ON. Subjectively, however, I found my punishment hard to take because bird-watching had been contributing so much, every day, to my enjoyment of Cameroon.

A brilliant moon had quenched all but the brightest stars and the deep stillness of the bush was emphasised at intervals by companionable Egbert-noises. Although it had been an exceptionally strenuous day sleep continued to elude me and, when no Egbert-noises had been heard for some time, I pulled on my boots and went to investigate. In fact he was nearby, merely snoozing between courses, but finding myself soothed by the austere black and silver beauty of the moonlit bush I mooched further along the ridge. Would it, I wondered, be worth while returning to the bridge at dawn? If I didn't, would I always feel that I *should* have?

Suddenly there was a precipice ahead and soon after turning back I began to feel doubtful about our camp's position. However, this was only a mini-crisis; at dawn Rachel could rescue me by whistle. The only snag, apart from missing a night's sleep, was that other people might then be around. That, I suppose, is how folk-legends start – when a white female wearing only boots is glimpsed in the bush at sunrise.

Half an hour later I accidentally wandered onto the path, which eventually took me back to where Rachel lay asleep beneath the moon.

By then I had made my decision: I would return to the bridge.

That dawn journey was, in a limited sense, worthwhile. During the whole river-ritual/nomad episode we had been watched by several men in a nearby ailing truck. One had found the binoculars and taken them to the nearest compound on the assumption that we would be back to search for them. But the Fulanis refused, literally, to *touch* them. Possibly they feared this weirdly shaped White man's fetish, possibly they imagined we might accuse them of theft. So the binoculars were taken to Bamenda where, their finder told the Fulanis, they would be deposited at the Catholic Mission. All this I discovered through an odd coincidence: as I reached the bridge two Anglophone soldiers, returning to Bamenda on leave, stopped to wash in the river and volunteered to be my interpreters.

Banyo lies in a sun-trap saucer half-encircled by rugged blue hills. Although bigger than Mayo Darlé, and an administrative centre, it is not very big. We arrived at ten o'clock and sat outside a friendly bar while Egbert grazed nearby amidst the rusting corpses of jeeps. When two passing gendarmes paused to investigate us my assertion of femininity paid off; once my womanhood had been accepted, slight suspicion became astonished cordiality.

On Banyo's colonial-flavoured northern outskirts, we met a young Anglophone woman doctor riding a mo-ped and wearing a leather jacket over a pretty frock. Being a scientist she didn't misgender me but noted, 'The daughter is very like the mother!' – causing the daughter, naturally enough, to scowl. As we went on our way towards Sambolabbo she turned to follow us, looking slightly anxious.

'Where can you sleep tonight?' she asked. 'Do you know you are walking into the bush? There are no towns this way, you will find no hotel – maybe no house, no compound!'

We explained that we had a tent and could sleep out.

'You are not afraid?' marvelled the doctor.

'Afraid of *what*?' I asked.

Her laugh was rich, musical, expressive. 'Wah! You White people! This is why you people conquered all the world! No fear, all confidence! *I* will not sleep in the bush and I am educated, they say "Westernised". But no, something would make me too much afraid ... Not dangerous spirits – I don't believe in them. Not dangerous animals – we have none here, only snakes. But the loneliness I would fear – you are brave, brave people!' She shook hands again and zoomed off, shouting a last '*Wonder-ful!*' over her shoulder.

Fifteen minutes later the brave people collapsed under a crop-guard's shelter of two loose tin sheets laid across four uneven poles. By then a strong wind was blowing – hot, dusty, gusty – and I remember that as our noisiest siesta. From here the Tchabal Mbabo, twenty-five miles ahead, was a faint but massive blur blocking the northern horizon. The Banyo-Sambolabbo motor-track ends at the base of the range and is virtually traffic free, even in the dry season.

Four long, hot hours, climbing gradually through arid, silent, uninhabited bush, brought us to a campsite where the grazing was so poor that Egbert had to be tethered. And the rock-hard ground left no alternative to tree-tethering, which meant my having to move him every hour or so during the night.

Before sunrise we were striding through the blessedly cool blue-grey dawn, breakfasting as we went. By nine o'clock the heat was brutal and all morning the broken scrubby terrain remained desolate, dessicated and, in Rachel's view, dreary. I, being of another temperament, enjoyed it despite the heat. Baboons abounded and our track was littered with their left-overs – deleaved branches and gigantic empty pods. Also, in one of the few remaining patches of forest, we saw five colobus monkeys – compensation enough for any amount of desolate dessication.

Towards noon a turn of the track revealed an improbable *green* hill surmounted by a wide-spreading tree. When we had unloaded in that merciful shade Egbert sniffed disdainfully at the lush clover-type greenery, then perversely headed off into the bleached scrub far below. We struggled to write our diaries but the unparalleled blood-lust of the local flies made concentration impossible. We tried to Scrabble but our minds were too heat-clogged. We drank a lot of water and ate a lot of salt and took off all our clothes which made it much easier to combat the ants. As we were reloading, at two o'clock, the day's only vehicle passed. It was, cheeringly, a small beer-truck with some thirty passengers perched on the swaying load of crates.

Within an hour we were in Mba, a friendly Muslim village, neat and clean. It has no overt bar but a kindly old man wearing a frilly yellow nightgown (bequeathed by a female missionary?) led us far off the track to an isolated thatched hut where full crates of '33' and Top witnessed to the truck's passing. The ex-nomad sisters who entertained us had heavily tattooed faces – elaborate blue patterns on foreheads, noses, cheekbones – and wore many *malloum*'s amulets. All protective devices are appreciated by the eclectic Cameroonians and it is not uncommon to see one person wearing a *malloum*'s amulet, a medicine-man's charm and a Catholic priest's 'Miraculous Medal'.

The grazing was so good and the bar-hut so seductively cool that we lingered until four o'clock. One young woman was trying to remove a large thorn deeply embedded in her muscular forearm. She dug into the flesh first with a broken matchstick, then with the point of a rusty knife taken from a cavity in the wall, finally and successfully with a needle brought by her sister. She seemed indifferent to her self-inflicted agony though merely watching made us feel sore.

Outside, three naked pickins sat on tattered goat-skins in the shade, playing intently with identical-sized stones. Mba has no school and many older children wandered to and fro, pausing to gaze in wonder at Egbert's load. They were clad in rags but looked cheerful, healthy and undeprived. Their futures may be all the more satisfying because they have escaped that personality-fracturing process which passes for education in most Cameroonian rural schools.

North of Mba aridity again prevailed. From a deep forested chasm on our left came bursts of fractious monkey noises and the rugged scrubland on our right was implacably hostile to campers. The sun had almost set when at last we came to smoothness: an expanse of hard red earth amidst scattered, gnarled bushes. Happily an Egbert-delicacy grew here in abundance, a low dark green plant with tiny white flowers. Knowing this to be his asparagus-equivalent, we turned him loose with an easy mind. Then, going to pee, I startled a two-foot-long black and green snake which slid swiftly under a rock.

There had been no food for sale in Mba and our own supper was meagre: a soup cube and stale Banyo bread for Rachel, mint-cake for me, nuts for both. We Scrabbled by moonlight, then unrolled our bags. The snake had prompted me to consider 'sleeping in' but Rachel protested that in such heat our cramped tent would be intolerable. As I lay scratching my fly-bites a few high wispy clouds drifted gently past the moon, seeming not like clouds but elegant silver ghosts.

Asparagus is more palatable than sustaining so Egbert was to have a day off in Sambolabbo, before our ascent to 7,000 feet. A non-stop three-and-a-half hour march got us there before brutal heat time.

Sambolabbo, a large Fulani village, stands above the wide Mayo Mbamti and directly below the Tchabal Mbabo. We came first to a terraced row of newish houses and shops, with wide verandahs, where we consulted a youth about lodgings and grazing. He was an excellent sign-linguist who at once led us to his father's nearby house. There we were graciously welcomed and shown straight into a disconcertingly affluent guest room. Our disgusting boots had been removed on the verandah; then, seeing a brand-new wall-to-wall nylon carpet, we hastily removed our no less disgusting socks. A double bed, with ironed cotton pillow-cases and an intricately woven counterpane, took up half the floor space. A low, plastic-topped table stood between two easy-chairs. The mud walls were white-washed and the wooden shutters of the unglazed window fitted perfectly. Our elderly host, Ibrahim Ali, was obviously a man of substance. Yet he spoke not a word of French, which puzzled us, given his man-of-the-world air. Later we heard that he speaks five African languages, apart from his native Foulfouldé, and

117

it was hinted that his not learning French had been an anti-colonial gesture.

Ibrahim Ali was tall, slim, dignified, quiet-spoken. When our smelly dusty gear had been stacked in a corner of his guest room (where it looked very lower class) he handed me the door key. Impulsively I handed it back and to my relief he accepted the compliment. One never quite knows how to react on such occasions; he might have preferred not to be responsible for our possessions. But usually acting on impulse seems to work. And his never bothering to lock the door during our absence suggested that theft from a guest is unthinkable in Sambolabbo.

By ten o'clock Egbert was enjoying the riverside grass and we were thirsty. A small boy led us to the only bar, along a narrow path between compounds of various sizes, comprising two to six huts – mostly thatched, some tin-roofed. All were neat and clean, many had decorative shrubs or saplings. Some were enclosed by mud walls, others by high fences of woven grass or bamboo. Each had its prayer-space – raised circles of pebbles, six to eight feet across. In the more prosperous compounds these were edged with upturned bottles embedded in the ground, or with empty tomato purée tins, or whitened stones. Everywhere cocks strutted and crowed and hens and chicks scratched and clucked and cheeped. Outsize ducks waddled and quacked and we worried about their water supply. Invisible lambs bleated. Several elaborately caparisoned horses stood in the shade of mango or avocado trees while their riders did business in the market. 'Not tethered,' noted Rachel. Most Fulani horses, though whole, are extraordinarily docile and dependable. It was already very hot and few adults were about. Numerous small children stared at us, mesmerised, before rushing into their huts. Here, for the first time, we noticed significant numbers of unhealthy-looking youngsters: malnourished, with trachoma, jungle-sores and severely worm-distended bellies.

Sambolabbo's only sink of iniquity was run by Andrew, a fat exuberant Bamenda man who had many other irons in the Banyo-Sambolabbo fire – and needed them, for the local bar trade is sluggish. He greeted us rapturously, rejoicing to meet two Irish topers with whom he – an urbane Bamenda Christian – could deplore the savagery of bush life in general and Fulani society in particular. (Most of the village's few White visitors are teetotal missionaries.) He repeatedly emphasised his Christianity, and also his wealth of wives: a senior wife in Bamenda, a middle wife in Banyo, a junior wife in Sambolabbo. When he took Rachel to be my junior wife I explained, 'Pickin for me' and to short-circuit the gender argument unbuttoned my shirt.

'*Won-der-ful!*' exclaimed Andrew, crashing his fist on the counter. 'Hah! You White people! The women as strong as men!' He glanced at Rachel, sitting in a corner pointedly dissociating herself from this scene of indecent exposure. 'Pickin for you? But she is *bigger* than you! *Won-der-ful!* Where is your husband?' He looked expectantly towards the door.

'We're travelling on our own,' I explained. 'I have no husband.'

Andrew wrinkled his face sympathetically. 'Gone to God?' he whispered.

'I've never been married,' I said.

'*Why?*' shouted Andrew, again crashing his fist on the counter. 'Why no husband? Now you are old, worn out, grey and finished. But when you are young you must be like this fine pickin – you must have husband paying *so much* brideprice!' He paused and narrowed his eyes. 'Your family ask *too much* brideprice?'

'It's not like that,' I said, 'in Europe. Lots of women don't marry. And a few who have no husband do have pickin.'

'How many pickins you have?' asked Andrew.

'Only one,' I admitted.

'*One?*' yelled Andrew, 'Only *one?* Why only *one?* You have no son? *Why* no son?'

I began to wilt. Another short-circuit was indicated. 'After this pickin,' I said, 'I am barren.'

'*Barren?*' Andrew whispered hoarsely. 'Wah!' As he covered his face with his hands I seized my beer and retreated.

Andrew stocked no Top so Rachel decided that the teetotal phase of her convalescence was over, which caused a sharp rise in our cost-of-living. Given a calculator and the inclination, it would be easy to outdo the USAF and produce a reliable map of Cameroon based on the price of beer. In Bamenda 100 CFA (about 22p) per half-litre, in Sambolabbo 275 CFA (about 60p) – and all along our route gradations that precisely indicated 'distance from nearest city' and 'state of local roads'. When I exclaimed at the Sambolabbo price Andrew retorted huffily, 'You have walked on this terrible way from Banyo, you should understand!' Then we did; considering the wear and tear on the beer-truck, Sambolabbo's '33' was cheap at the price.

Andrew, having business elsewhere, soon left us alone but took the precaution of locking the counter opening. We wondered why; a thief could easily have surmounted that four-foot barrier. Perhaps because Sambolabbo is almost entirely Muslim, all beer crates lay under the counter and no bottles were displayed. The bar consisted of a semi-detached mud shack enlivened by a catholic selection of technicoloured posters, printed in Nigeria. From left to right as one entered these were:

1 SUPER FOREIGNMAN: a gross, grinning giant of indeterminate race whose daily menus for all meals were given in nauseating detail:

'20 Fried Eggs, 6 Litres of Soup, 10 Loaves of Bread, 5 Kilos of Steak, 4 Litres of Coffee, 6 Kilos of Rice', and so on.

2   GOD SEES ALL: a snowy-bearded patriarch gazes sternly down at mankind going about its daily tasks, with insets of the Virgin and Child, the Little Flower, St Joseph, St Anthony of Padua, St Rose of Lima and a dove, shaped like a jet-fighter, presumably representing the Holy Ghost.

3   STRIP AN' SQUEEZE!: reproductions of hyper-erotic *Playboy* photographs which an old-fashioned upbringing inhibits me from describing.

4   SUPER MAMMA: a Black giantess with bosoms like barrage-balloons, biceps like rugger balls and a necklace of gold medals won at international weight-lifting contests.

5   OUR HOLY FATHER!: Pope John Paul XXIII blessing a crowd at Bamenda, with quotes from Papal homilies against birth-control and insets of His Holiness at various other African blessing-spots.

6   WE ARE FREE!: All Black Africa's post-Independence political leaders (many looking as though badly wanted by Scotland Yard) arranged around a large central photograph of Nkrumah.

We had already seen most of these posters singly in other bars but the cumulative effect was particularly memorable – and, somehow, sad.

Andrew was now hammering tin sheets onto the roof beams of a new hut opposite the bar. When I proposed calling him to serve a second round Rachel said, 'Isn't it lunch-time? D'you realise we haven't had a square meal since leaving Mayo Darlé?'

'What,' I speculated, 'do *round* meals taste like?'

'Soup cubes and nuts!' replied Rachel.

Sambolabbo's shopping-precinct – a rough-surfaced open space, overlooked by short rows of merchants' stalls – has the atmosphere though not the shape of a town square. By far the biggest mud hut is a whitewashed mosque with an embryonic dome – a slight swelling on the roof. Opposite the mosque, appetising things were happening on a raised platform, under a tin roof. Charcoal glowed beneath half a tar-barrel, on top was a grid and on the grid were bits of what might loosely be termed 'meat'. Sniffing like Bisto kids (an advertising allusion that dates me) we advanced on this gastronomically promising scene, ordered in sign-language and were invited to sit on greasy logs of wood. We realised then that we had queue-jumped; several hungry men were standing around nearby and very properly we had to await our turn. The log-stools were a concession to the visitors, but White queue-jumping isn't on in Cameroon.

Fraternisation would have prospered had we been able to speak

Foulfouldé. There were no women in sight but most men looked friendly, curious, amused – though a few closed, hard faces among the older generation suggested some anti-White (or anti-Christian?) bias. We did of course achieve a certain amount of communication: '*From* Bamenda – *with* horse – *to* N'gaoundere.'

No merchants operate in the Mbabo mountains and as we peered into a succession of shadowy shops, seeking supplies, the gender issue surfaced yet again. Sign-language was· then taken to its (bio)logical conclusion. After much unproductive argument I stood in the middle of the shopping-precinct and bared my bosom to the sceptical crowd, causing a hurricane of hilarity. This ploy would be worse than tasteless among Asian Muslims, but by then I had got the very different flavour of Cameroonian Islam.

Little food is sold in small towns or villages, where most families are self-sufficient. At last our increasing desperation was noticed by a kind young man – small, wiry, vivacious, with a few phrases of French. He led us to a tiny shop where three rock-hard loaves of bread, transported in times past from Banyo, lay on the counter under a strip of sacking. Gleefully we bought them. Elsewhere we collected two rusty tins of sardines, one expensive onion (25 CFA, about 5p) and five small bananas for the exorbitant sum of 50 CFA – bananas don't thrive around Sambolabbo. Without our Somie supply of nuts the nutritional outlook would have been alarming.

While Rachel slept off her injudicious intake of beer, I relocated Egbert in his riverside field. Annoyingly, he seemed less interested in grazing than in a nearby herd of donkeys, including a pretty mare with a gladsome eye. We had already noticed that a donkey mare excited him like nothing else.

Several teenage boys, on their way home from school, greeted me, 'Good mor-en-ing Sir!'

I was beginning to feel the strain of being habitually misgendered, an error only funny when occasional. Having talked to somebody (male or female) for half an hour, it is confusing suddenly to realise that the conversation might have developed entirely differently had the other party known the gender score. Given the low status of village women, this error may sometimes have been to my advantage, yet I always felt an impulse to correct it. Most White women of the late twentieth century don't 'think sexist'. One is simply an individual who happens to be female; not until one's femininity is repeatedly questioned, and frequently disbelieved, does it become important. By the time we reached Sambolabbo I had decided that human relationships, everywhere, are quite complex enough without the Orlando factor.

Outside the school, its headmaster stopped me with a peremptory gesture – 'You are missionary?' I tried to explain. He looked baffled.

For ten minutes we failed to communicate; I gathered only that he was also the *English* teacher, though incapable of expressing himself in that language. (The calibre of most of the many teachers we met was scandalous.) There are scarcely 250 pupils at Sambolabbo's government school; Muslims tend to opt for Koranic schools, despite their curriculla being less conducive to success in the modern world. Most Fulanis remain impervious to urban magnets; they do very nicely as cattle-breeders and/or merchants.

This area is goatless, but many shabby sheep were tethered on arid wasteland opposite our lodgings. I was watching lambs gambolling in the dust when an extrovert young Nigerian introduced himself: 'I am Garvey, an illegal immigrant.' He came from a village four hours walk away and was working locally as a carpenter to earn money to finish his BA course at Ibadan University. 'The CFA is so strong at home, my wages mean a lot. In Nigeria money has become very scarce, if you are not a Big Man. We're supposed to be rich but Cameroon is better off. It always has good sensible rulers, we have not. And we have too many people – nearly one hundred million! Here are not even ten million, so it's easier to rule well.'

Garvey's English was excellent; in rural Cameroon, the most fluent English speakers are usually Nigerian migrant workers. Whatever that country's problems, its educational standards are evidently higher than Cameroon's. Yet the Cameroonian government has always proclaimed that a well-schooled population is the surest guarantee of future prosperity and teachers are among the best-paid officials in the country. Sadly, however, this policy isn't working: one can guess why.

When Rachel woke we drifted back to Andrew, stopping on the way for a kebab each. In the bar a Bamileke woman with baby at breast and beer bottle in hand was (with the other hand) vaguely de-lousing a toddler. 'My young wife!' beamed Andrew, nodding in her direction.

Suddenly it rained torrentially. 'Wah!' yelled Andrew. '*Won-der-ful! Won-der-ful!*' He slapped himself on the buttocks and jumped up and down. 'Forever we have no rain, now plenty, plenty!'

Two non-Fulanis who had been working on the new hut rushed in and demanded beer. One asked how much money our government paid us to walk in the bush, a not unusual question. Andrew however was familiar with the quaint White habit of trekking for fun. 'These people from Europe,' he informed the brick-layers, 'very much like to *see* places! They like to move around and camp the way nomads do. They are never afraid of the bush.'

To most Cameroonians we were inexplicable in a way White travellers would not have been during colonial times. Then they were comparatively numerous and everyone had to ride or walk; our arrival would have surprised villagers only because we lacked servants –

we might have been traders, missionaries, soldiers, government officials. Sometimes, if persistently questioned about our purpose, I explained that my *job* is writing books about countries far from Europe. (A statement which always rings false in my own ears; it seems hypocritical to describe what one most enjoys doing as 'a job', even if by great good fortune that happens to be how one earns a living.) But this attempt to clarify merely thickened the mystery of our presence. 'Writing a book' is an activity as incomprehensible to most Cameroonians as 'programming a computer' is to me; neither reading nor writing is part of their culture. Mungo Park had the same problem in a much more acute form. When granted an interview with Tiggity Sego, Chief of Teesee, 'The old man viewed me with great earnestness . . . I related to him, in answer to his inquiries, the motives that induced me to explore the country. But he seemed to doubt the truth of what I asserted, thinking, I believe, that I secretly meditated some project which I was afraid to avow.'

At sunset, as we again relocated Egbert, the humidity, after that brief downpour, felt like a threat to life. An hour later supper was brought to our room: fufu and jammu-jammu plus two big hunks of delicious mutton.

'Those shabby sheep are ok stewed,' Rachel commented appreciatively.

Four raw eggs were also provided but alas! Rachel has not yet learned to relish this form of protein. I ate the lot and she had extra mutton.

Settled on our comfortable bed, we observed the insect night-life swinging into action. I have seen slightly bigger cockroaches, in Ecuador and Madagascar, but nowhere have I seen more lively cockroaches. Their frenzied activities on the white walls were like some entomological Olympiad.

'And to think they're only limbering up,' said Rachel, 'for when the light goes off!'

7

The Tchabal Mbabo

ANDREW HAD ADVISED us to take the cut-short to Mayo Kelele, also known as Makelele. That, he said bossily, must be our first stop – 'The Chief will give you bed.' The alternative, a track negotiable by motor-bicycles in dry weather, goes round and round and round the mountains for miles and miles and miles. The cut-short simply goes over them – up-down, up-down, up-down – until the final up, at about 6,500 feet. (The altitude we gleaned from the USAF, not from Andrew.)

Egbert was loaded by lamp-light, to the accompaniment of Ibrahim Ali and his sons chanting their morning prayers in the compound. The transfer of 2,000 CFA 'for horse-food' went smoothly though our host had obviously not expected dash.

We moved off under a cloudy dawn sky. Beyond the fast shallow Mayo Mbambi cane-fields were replaced by level bush, merging into uninhabited woodland where we looked in vain for the cut-short. Then, on the far side of a swift bouldery stream, we saw our wide track beginning to climb. A faint narrow path seemed to continue up the valley floor, going more directly towards Makelele. It was the sort described as '*Tracé incertain*' on large-scale French maps but for lack of any other I assumed it to be the cut-short. Rachel disagreed, but pandered to me.

Soon a flood of early golden light was pouring into that green and silent valley – silent but for a myriad bird-calls from amidst a variety of magnificent trees. Densely forested mountains rose almost sheer on three sides and I thought about Africa's distinctive beauty. As I reacted to it, this beauty had as much to do with atmosphere as with the visual impact of the terrain; somehow I was getting elusive yet important messages about the link between land and people. It seems odd to think (and even odder to write or speak) of a place *feeling* as well as looking beautiful. But that was how much of Cameroon affected me; even those harsh hot miles between Banyo and Sambolabbo had their own subtle charm. On trek one tends to let one's imagination off the leash, to give in to all sorts of irrational fancies – which partly explains why trekking is so therapeutic. In that wondrously lovely valley, I toyed with the notion that Africa feels so unlike anywhere else because it is so *old* – the cradle of mankind, they say . . . But soon I had something more practical to think about.

Where the ground began to rise the jungle thickened and soon our path had disappeared, conclusively. 'This can't be the cut-short!' said Rachel.

'No,' I agreed meekly. 'You were right.'

A gigantic baboon loped past a few yards away, scowling at us. He was so big that for an instant, before registering his species, we were slightly startled.

'Shall we go back to the track?' I suggested, well knowing what the response would be.

'Of course not!' said Rachel. 'There has to be some way out of here – let's push on.'

We pushed on, literally – forcing our way through jungle, bending saplings to make way for Egbert. He, as always, became increasingly co-operative as the going got rougher. And it got very rough indeed before we arrived at the edge of a ravine lined with what appeared to be impenetrable vegetation. '*Now* where?' said Rachel.

'*Maybe* there's a way across,' said I. 'You two have a rest while I scout around.'

For twenty minutes I scouted, climbing over some weird botanical obstacles, crawling under others, snake-scaring as I went. There was indeed a way across, for humans prepared to emulate baboons, but even at his most co-operative Egbert could not have made it.

We considered the surrounding mountains and Rachel indicated the northern crest. 'If we could get up *there*,' she said, 'we'd probably find the main track.'

A jumble of spurs lay between us and the slope in question. 'Rest again,' I said, 'while I scout again.'

Not long after I yelled from a hilltop, 'Come! This may be a way!' And it was.

We zig-zagged as best we could, yet the gradient required poor Egbert to pause often to regain his breath. 'We're being cruel!' declaimed Rachel. 'He's only a horse, he's not a bloody baboon – he's not *built* for going up a thing like this!'

Thirty minutes later we were on level grassy ground, close to the track. I congratulated Rachel and we sat under a tree eating nuts. The wretched Egbert was too exhausted to eat; he moved to stand close beside us and hung his head. 'If we were at home,' said Rachel grimly, 'we'd be gaoled for treating a horse so badly. He seems to love us, but I can't think why!'

I gazed down at the valley, very far below, and wondered where the real cut-short could be. Three weeks and many dramas later, we were to find out.

Our extreme cut-short had abruptly taken us above 5,000 feet and as we continued, under a deep 'mountain-blue' sky, the 11 a.m. sun felt pleasantly warm. Inhaling the cool, pure air, I wanted to run and jump. Only then, feeling a normal flow of physical energy, did I realise how enervating the heat had been on that gruelling stretch from Banyo.

During the rest of the day joy was unconfined. For miles we traversed a bewilderment of topographical contortions; never able to guess what might be around the next corner. As the track dodged through this tangle of spurs and ridges it sometimes overlooked melodramatic ravines, or shallow, enclosed 'secret-looking' valleys lined with golden grass, or long, darkly-forested slopes, or strange smooth grey rocks, like domed windowless skyscrapers, suddenly thrusting out of scrubby hills. Swarming baboons made this a noisy and animated region. Each high point was higher than the last and often we glimpsed the whole heat-blurred undulating landscape between us and Banyo.

On the far side of the *most* melodramatic ravine a theatrical-looking escarpment, draped with dark green vegetation, rose for at least a thousand feet and stretched for over a mile before merging into a massive, grassy mountain. Two small compounds shared the saddle where our track crossed from mountain to mountain at the head of the ravine. Patches of young maize grew nearby – and tempted Egbert – but we saw only a distant whisk of vivid garments as women or children hid from us.

Ahead stretched an immensity of golden-green slopes, strewn with odd protuberances of smooth grey rock, characteristic of the area. At once I was taken twenty years back, to the gentler corners of the Ethiopian highlands. Here the vegetation was different, and the distant peaks looked lower, but the light and *feeling* were similar and the path problem was identical. Our track diversified when, offering a wide choice of cattle-lanes visible for miles in three directions, there was nothing to indicate which path might lead to Makelele.

Proceeding in the direction Rachel thought most likely, we met our first fellow-travellers of the day – a Fulani father and son. The little boy was leading a sheep and stared at us with apprehensive fascination. 'Makelele?' we inquired, after the statutory greetings. The young man smiled kindly, beckoned us to follow and himself led Egbert to a high point. There he indicated our path, providing detailed directions in Foulfouldé. We thanked him effusively. It wasn't his fault that we remained quite unable to discern the right track. Luckily it didn't matter when – or even if – we reached Makelele. To be *up* was enough.

Below the brow of a rounded hill Egbert enjoyed a long lunch-break on rich grazing. A siesta without flies or ants, or any need for shade, felt like the ultimate luxury. Lying in the sun, we ate stale bread and onion and watched an elderly man, very small and black skinned, coming over the hill. He was carrying a colossal roll of bamboo matting, six feet long and surely as heavy as himself. Suddenly he noticed us and looked pathetically alarmed. He speeded up, to get past us as quickly as possible, and kept his eyes averted; his gait was an odd shuffling trot. We stared after him, marvelling at his knotted neck and leg muscles. Seen loadless in a village street, he would have seemed old and frail. No doubt he was a servant/serf of one of the area's bovine plutocrats. Not many Fulanis carry loads; that, in their view, is what the Bantu tribes are for.

During the afternoon several chestnut-coloured dwarf antelope bounded across nearby slopes and we saw our first warthogs, two families noisily rooting in a patch of jungle. The boars – almost as big as lions – had formidable tusks. The sows were much smaller and the piglets so minute that as they scampered through the short grass only the tips of their tufted tails (always held aloft as they run) were visible. We had been warned that the boars, if accidentally cornered – a most unlikely happening – can be lethal. Having seen their size and tusks, we could believe it. This combination of antelope, baboons and warthogs sharing territory was common, with baboons and warthogs seeming particularly good neighbours. On this occasion, when the latter fled from us they went towards a large baboon colony, sitting staring not far from the track, and once surrounded by their friends they again began to root, as though feeling quite secure.

At about 5 p.m. we saw far below us – rather to our surprise – the compact village of Makelele, its maize-fields sloping down to the narrow Mayo Kelele. When we arrived only a few men were around. On our long descent they had had time to observe and speculate about us and their welcome was conveyed with a touching mix of warmth and bemusement. As no one spoke French or English, we could do nothing about the bemusement.

The Chief, a gracious old gentleman in a shapeless white gown, decreed that we should be billeted on his much younger half-brother, whose shrub-surrounded compound we had already passed on the edge of the village. An excited small boy guided us to the guest hut, outside the women's inner compound, and then led Egbert to lush grazing beyond the river where many fine horses roamed free. We were now in the Cameroonian equivalent of County Meath.

Our windowless mud hut was ready for occupation: spotlessly clean, with goat-skins spread on the earth floor and blankets and cushions on the grass mattresses of two home-made wooden beds. There was no other furniture, though this was a wealthy family. Our host (Abdoulaye, aged fiftyish) owned the enormous herd we had stopped to admire before seeing Makelele. The dark chocolate-brown bulls – a cattle colour I have never seen in Europe – had prodigious wide-curving five-foot horns and were among the finest we met in Cameroon.

Abdoulaye's two beautiful junior wives wore both bead and gold necklaces and seemed on excellent terms with each other. We didn't meet his senior wife but heard that she had chosen her juniors, as often happens. Children abounded; we never sorted out who was mother to which because, when extended families work well, all adults share responsibility for all children. The Chief had credited my womanhood, after many exclamations of wonder and much chuckling and hand-clapping, but Abdoulaye's womenfolk remained unconvinced; they welcomed us warmly, yet hesitated to shake my hand. Nor were we invited to enter the inner compound of six huts – two oblong and tin-roofed, the rest round and thatched. By sunset four fires were burning in that compound; it takes a lot of wood to cook for such a family and heat their washing water.

The boy who brought our bucket of washing water conveyed that we could also drink it. Later we regretted having used it, as we watched three girls ascending the long slope from the river with buckets on their heads. Moreover, we erred by throwing the dirty water away instead of keeping it for the compound's ornamental shrubs. I suspected at the time that we were doing the wrong thing but it would have seemed disgustingly impolite to leave the family to dispose of our scummy water. Such are the minor culture-clash *faux pas* that litter the way of the traveller.

We were flummoxed when two giggling girls, aged elevenish, presented me with a bowl containing raw maize-flour and nine eggs in their shells. As they stood watching, we deduced that they expected us to produce some hi-tech cooking stove. This was confirmed when a junior wife pushed through the many juvenile spectators around the doorway, handed me an agitated cock and also stood back to observe developments. I cradled the cock – a substantial bird – and stroked its head, whereupon it quietened down.

'Sign language!' urged Rachel. 'Ask her to kill it and cook it – I'm *weak* with hunger – don't just stand there cuddling it! You'll get *fond* of it! And if we don't eat it someone else will!' This was manifestly true. When I mimed killing and plucking and cooking the juveniles' mirth knew no bounds.

Then Jacques arrived, a non-Fulani from Banyo who spoke French. At first we mistook him for a gendarme; he wore a peaked cap and an immaculate bottle-green uniform with many badges. In fact he was an officer of the Meteorological Service, based in Makelele for a few months while compiling statistics. He looked about Rachel's age and was a charmer. But his professional interest in figures made him no more accurate than anyone else about times and distances; he assured us that Sambolabbo was seventy kilometres from Makelele.

As Jacques and Rachel were exercising their French, two beaming girls delivered a big bowl of crisp fried manioc (quite like potato chips) mixed with cubes of tasty though tough fried beef. We devoured this delicacy so fast that Jacques looked alarmed, as though fearing he had fallen among savages. Then Rachel despairingly exclaimed, 'Suppose that's *all*! Suppose they think we don't *like* chicken – or cock . . .'

I soothed her, 'That was just to keep us going.' And sure enough, a giant dish of fufu arrived an hour later, plus lots more (stewed) beef in the jammu-jammu.

Another hour later the cock reappeared, pot-roasted to tenderness, skilfully herb-flavoured and accompanied by more fufu. At the end of that course, even Rachel was replete.

Yawning and content, we undressed, put out the lantern and slid under our blankets: it was chilly enough to need them. I was more than half asleep when gales of girlish giggling were followed by tentative knockings on our ill-fitting door.

'*You* get up!' I pleaded. So Rachel wrapped herself in her blanket and opened the door – to receive a nine-egg omelette. We expressed profound gratitude and tried to eat it. But the maize-flour had been added, and delicate spices, so it closely resembled an outsize Yorkshire pudding. We kept it for breakfast and it tasted just as good cold.

The Tchabal Mbabo is a tiny paradise, created aeons ago by some volcanic aberration. If one knew exactly which paths to follow, it could be crossed from south to north in two days, and from east to west in four. The quality of its beauty is, in my experience, unique. Beyond sloping grasslands, isolated stele-like pinnacles of naked rock soar above narrow green river valleys. Mighty basalt walls, curiously fluted, extend for miles along the crests of scrubby ridges in which house-sized boulders are firmly embedded. Gigantic grassy bowls, hundreds of feet deep, appear unexpectedly under one's boots. In deep clefts, between the rounded flanks of pasture mountains, fragments of ancient forest survive along inaccessible watercourses. And sometimes our path consisted of strange slabs of orange-tinted rock imprinted with white whirly designs looking uncannily like hieroglyphics.

Even for someone as non-scientific as myself, it was fascinating to contrast this region with the volatile Karakoram landscape. The Tchabal Mbabo seems settled, smooth, stable, secure. Instead of the Himalayas' frenziedly jagged and friable summits, its peaks have a serene, gentle grandeur, and must surely be unclimbable, except by the most manic stegophilist. One knows the ten-ton boulders above the track won't come rolling down at the least provocation, nor could the vibrations of one's voice set off a landslide. There are none of the loose, sharp, multicoloured stones and pebbles and rock-slabs that brighten the Karakoram; all such evidences of geological cataclysms have long since been entombed in the soil or washed away. And many thousands of years ago, when someone first discovered the bliss of living in a temperate climate, the region's deforestation and massive erosion were completed – which adds to its mature appearance.

Jacques had recommended the village of Mbabo for our next stop and pointed us in the right direction. We were of course lost within a few hours, but contentedly so; there seemed to be no particular reason for going to Mbabo rather than anywhere else.

Taking our nine o'clock nuts-and-grazing break by a stream, we saw a jackal sauntering up a nearby ridge. Then Egbert registered slight unease: a well-tusked boar, his mud-bath just finished, was standing some twenty yards away. He closely considered us, before joining his wives and children who were trotting along the skyline with manes and tails erect.

We were about to move on when the day's first human appeared, a Bamenda-based Fulani wearing fawn nylon socks and fatally new red plastic shoes. He complained that his feet were killing him. He hated the Tchabal Mbabo because it lacked motor transport. He thought we were mad. Under his arm he carried an umbrella and over his shoulders were slung a thermos-flask and a short Fulani sword in an antique embossed leather shield. No self-respecting Fulani, however urbanised, will travel without his sword – a memento of the good old conquering days.

The day's second human was a terrified little boy who made a wide detour to avoid us. Then for hours we met nobody and wondered why this region is so sparsely populated; it could certainly support many more humans and livestock. We passed only one small village, about an hour's walk from Makelele, where a young man ran after us to present two new-laid eggs. There were also a few solitary compounds, and occasionally in the distance we glimpsed groups of two to four compounds, which hereabouts qualify as 'villages' and have their own quarterchiefs. Possibly these mountains were more densely populated, by Bantus, before the infamous razzias of the eighteenth and early nineteenth century; then Fulani raiders captured thousands of slaves, both for their own use and for export. In the 1780s Cameroon and the Niger delta were the main slave sources; during that decade an average of 22,000 men and women were sold *every year* to White traders.

Throughout the day we saw several more antelope, warthog families, baboon and capuchin colonies – and a lone aristocratic colobus, pacing the length of an outstretched branch in a grove of huge dead trees. Given a coronet, he might have been on his way to the State Opening of Parliament. Usually these are timid monkeys, yet this splendid creature didn't at once leap away but stared down at us with calm disdain.

By then we had lost not only the main path but *any* path and were merely wandering across country. We had almost reached a cul-de-sac when Rachel noticed a cow-herds' shelter on a ridge high above us, apparently at the base of an escarpment. Ascending, we saw a deep grassy chasm between ridge and escarpment – a classic trick of this visually deceptive landscape.

The shelter was a work of art, a conical hut most skilfully woven of coarse golden grass. Three ragged boys emerged and the little ones clutched each other in fear. When I asked, 'Mbabo?' the eldest, aged perhaps fourteen, silently pointed into the chasm and up to the escarpment. There was no path, apart from horizontal cattle grooves, and on the near-perpendicular slope below the rock-wall we went astray. Then the boy, who all the time had been watching us, yelled to catch our attention and indicated the correct route.

'They *are* kind!' panted Rachel. 'Why should he care whether or not we get lost?'

I silently nodded agreement; my lungs felt as though they were bursting.

On the far side of the escarpment we found a wide path and soon after met a migrating herd, including many calves, being kept on the move by five yodelling nomads who ignored us. Behind them, one man stood leaning against a boulder, waiting on a new-dropped suckling calf. Efforts are made not to move with such tinies, since suckling stops have to be frequent, but mistakes will happen. Later we were to see a few tinies being carried – of course on a head, tied to a board.

We lunched above an exhilarating panorama of slender pinnacles and broad valleys. Scores of black and white birds – cormorant-sized, long-necked, ungainly – were feeding on the grassy summit. They had flapped awkwardly into the air at our approach, then settled again only fifty yards away. We saw many such flocks in the Tchabal Mbabo, but nowhere else. While we crunched our nuts thunder rumbled in the distance and clouds briefly gathered to the south, then vanished.

As the terrain became ever wilder two superb red-brown eagles slowly floated down towards the deep valley on our right, passing so close that I didn't miss my binoculars. Then we met a nomad family on the move, probably following the herd. Egbert seemed to glance with horrified sympathy at their donkey's bulging load, topped by four striped umbrellas. The husband responded warily to my greeting; unusually, he was carrying the baby. The four walking children, even the toddler, were loaded in proportion to their size. Mother gracefully carried an enormous, unwieldy cloth-wrapped bundle. I turned to watch as, without apparent effort, she swiftly ascended a precipice that would have reduced us – carrying nothing – to breathlessness.

In the next valley, near a rudimentary two-hut compound, four little boys were pollarding trees on the bank of a stream. Seeing us, they dropped their machetes and raced home, shrieking in panic. That was the day's thirteenth stream or river; long since we had rashly given up removing our boots before fording. On the banks of the fourteenth – the river Djem – we found a campsite as perfect as the day's trek had been.

This hidden, oval valley was dominated by a symmetrical rounded rock-mountain, towering mightily half a mile away to the south. To east and west rose high grassy cliffs which almost converged at the base of the mountain, leaving only space enough for the sparkling Djem to race through. Unfortunately the grazing was poor; this whole region badly needed rain. Firewood too was scarce, though adequate. After supper we sat long by the embers, discussing the ethics of genetic engineering and watching the full moon rise above the branches of a wild fig tree. We also discussed a more immediate problem: should Egbert be tethered? Having that afternoon passed many stallions, mares and foals, we reluctantly decided that he should. As there were no trees near the one grassy patch I tied him to a tough-looking bush growing out of the cliff – having first tested its roots, as best a human could.

Rain seemed possible so we slept in. But we did not sleep soundly; this was by far our noisiest campsite. In a mini-creek only yards away multitudinous frogs croaked incessantly, monotonously. Some nightbird with a peculiarly disagreeable call – a harsh unrhythmic cackle – lived on the cliff just above us and was frequently vocal. Even more disagreeable insect noises – raucous whirrings and hoarse chirrupings – competed with the frogs. Something else (we couldn't imagine what genus) squeaked piercingly at irregular intervals.

'The peace of the wilderness!' muttered Rachel, wakening some time around midnight. 'It's like sleeping beside the M4 with the window open!'

The dawn revealed that Egbert had gone AWOL, taking the bush with him. We were only mildly distraught; he could not have gone far, for I had seen him by moonlight at fourish. Searching the obvious places, we discovered a wealthy compound on the eastern clifftop and reported our loss in sign language to Mohamadou Ali, a quarterchief. At once little boys were dispatched in all directions; one of a bush child's main functions is finding lost animals. Rachel then returned to

Girl with sister. From the Kwondja tribe, in 'the hot plain'.

Ngah Bouba, traditional doctor. The claim to re-establish 'competence' in 'unproductive' women illustrates a woman's main role in African society.

DOCTOR-NGAH BOUBA
TREAT - STOMACH DISCOMFORT, FAINTING
REMOVE POISON, SIDE PAIN, CHEST PAIN
FELERIA, UN PRODUCTIVE WOMEN MADE TO BE
COMPETENT, WIZARD AND WITCHES, GONORIHEA
BACK-ACHE, SLEEPING-SICKNESS, MALERIA-
FEVER UN PRODOCTIVE MEN EYE TROUBLE
GENERAL COUGH, WAIST PAIN, DIERIA AND
YELLOW FEVER

Village chief with wives, Ngybe, near Mayo Darlé. The people of this tribe, the Kwondja, were not so long ago (1950s) slaves of the Muslim tribes who surrounded them.

Hairdressing session. Many Cameroonian women find their chief relaxation in conversation and dressing each other's hair.

Koranic school, N'gaoundere. Fulani children reciting verses from the Koran, inscribed on their tablets.

Yamba women working their ground-nut fields. Ground-nuts are a important subsistence food as well as a cash crop.

Mbororo girls returning from the river, near Mayo Darlé. Mbororos ar Fulanis who still lead a nomadic or semi-nomadic life.

Yamba man trimming palm-tree. This man is dislodging nests of palm nuts, which contain the oil widely used in local cooking.

Yamba woman and child harvesting sweet potatoes.

Jacqueline's friend Dijja, with her youngest child.

Below left: Dijja's daughter, Fatah.

Below right: Yaya Moctar, who 'adopted' Egbert, with his son Ibrahim to whom he is teaching the Koran.

Left: Egbert and his new owner.

Below: Rachel's one day in the saddle.

strike camp, while I checked the nearest of the horse herds we had passed on the previous afternoon.

From the western clifftop, as I got back to base at 7.30 a.m., I rejoiced to see the randy runaway, looking chastened, standing amidst a group of youths who were animatedly discussing his injuries with Rachel, quite undeterred by her ignorance of Foulfouldé. Stallions resent harem encroachments and are fierce fighters. Egbert had been lucky to get away with a deep bite on his right shoulder, just below the spine, and a ten-inch diagonal kick wound – mercifully superficial – along his right ribs. Both injuries were still bleeding and I washed them by the river before applying Karadol, brought all the way from Ireland for some such occasion. Ten minutes later Egbert rolled vigorously and got rid of the powder; but throughout the day I reapplied it regularly and sometimes it remained in place for an hour or so before the next roll. It helped that there were no flies.

Mohamadou Ali was one of those Fulanis with what can only be described as 'a presence'. I felt we should stand up and bow whenever he appeared – as he often did that day, to attend to the needs of his awkward guests. He was deeply upset by our having slept out – and on the ground! – in *his* 'village'. But luckily an Anglophone interpreter soon appeared: 'Our Man from Bamenda', quipped Rachel, and so he was. Moses soothed the Chief by explaining that we hadn't known of his compound's existence until that morning – that we wanted for nothing – that we would gratefully spend the night in his guest hut but would like to spend the day by the river, washing clothes. Our host looked mollified though still somewhat concerned – should he send down chairs? Emphatically *not*, we said. One of the more harmless after-effects of colonialism is a deep conviction that physiologically Europeans *need* chairs.

Upstream, out of sight of the camp, I found a cold, clear pool deep enough to lie in and wide enough to swim two strokes. In my absence a little girl presented Rachel with six cassavas: quite palatable eaten raw, if one is hungry enough. But Mohamadou Ali saw to it that we had no need of emergency rations that day. On my way back from the pool I saw two of his 'followers' carefully carrying tin trays down the cliff. Looking anxious (would we like Fulani fare?), they presented a huge thermos of herbal tea sweetened with wild honey (hereabouts many long black hives hang from trees), dainty pyrex cups and saucers, a big bowl of crisp golden maize-flour buns, elegantly quartered, and a small bowl of clear honey in which to dip them. Seldom have I enjoyed food so much. Those dainty cups were not quite congruous but the herbal tea and wild honey harmonised deliciously with our surroundings.

As we ate, Mohamadou Ali arrived to ensure that we had all we needed and were feeling in no way neglected. An hour later he was back, personally bearing a dish containing a whole roast chicken, subtly seasoned and tender. And over his shoulder was another thermos of honey tea.

From Djem's four scattered compounds an excited group of young men then visited us and settled down, cross-legged under the fig tree, to hold converse with Moses as interpreter.

Moses was elderly, cheerful, loquacious and shifty-looking. By evening I had hatched an uncharitable theory that he was evading the law, and where better to do so? He defined himself as 'A Bamenda good Christian of the Ngemba tribe. I am builder, weaver, smith – I serve this Chief plenty ways, I live here now one year, maybe two year. I forget.'

Having slept by the river, we were of more than ordinary interest. Our campsite was a notoriously haunted spot, so haunted that after sunset no local would even look into that oval valley. Had we heard or seen the devils? Every night they play music and sing and if you hear or see them you soon die in much pain. Regretfully we replied that we had not seen them; to us they sounded like rather jolly congenial fellows. Perhaps, someone suggested, we had used magic strong enough to keep them away. Then someone else recalled that Europeans never see devils, that devils are *afraid* of Europeans. When a youth mentioned the devils' white skins, which could be seen shining in the dark, we realised that this legend must be based on a colonialists' camp-fire sing-song.

In mid-afternoon the Muslims glanced at the sun, trooped off to the river to wash ritually and turned towards where they (wrongly) supposed Mecca to be. With open contempt, Moses watched them praying. Then he turned to us and said, 'These people, they live like wild animals! They are savages born in the bush – they have never seen a film or a school, they learn the Koran only. They don't want to live good, they think only of cattle. Cattle, cattle, cattle! They see animals more important than women and children – they only want families to have help with cattle. They are like stupid cattle themselves – if they would sell animals they can live good in Bamenda!'

'I wonder,' said Rachel afterwards, 'how Fulanis describe their Bantu neighbours!'

Mohamadou Ali was a well-known bovine tycoon; not only did he have a herd of 'many, many hundred' but his two teenage sons, now praying, had already built up herds of more than one hundred each – and even his small daughters personally owned ten or fifteen cattle.

At 5.30 p.m. – well before devil time – two little boys arrived to transport our gear to the guest hut. Each sped up the cliff with various bits of luggage on head, while Moses showed us an easier route. Although we were heavily laden he didn't offer to share our burdens.

134

Mohamadou Ali's compound was a hamlet in itself: seven large round huts and a three-roomed 'bungalow' with a deep verandah. Our room was also a store; sacks of salt, rice and fertiliser were stacked in one corner. A talented wife had decorated the smooth, reddish mud walls with an intricate pattern of black and white whorls. Surprisingly, there was only a single iron bed.

Mohamadou Ali soon bustled in with three brightly coloured Nigerian nylon mats (all the rage along our route) which he arranged precisely to cover the whole floor. Then a camp-chair was brought and he ceremoniously opened it and bowed me towards it. A bucket of hot water followed, standing in a huge basin, and finally came the offer of a transistor radio, which we declined with thanks. All evening we could hear it in the distance, broadcasting programmes in English from Nigeria.

Our host's eldest unmarried daughter and his two junior wives – all beautiful women, looking about the same age – came together to greet us, bowing with folded hands and murmuring inaudibly. They seemed much more timid that the Makelele womenfolk. Moses told us that the senior wife had been in Banyo hospital for several weeks past, 'with a devil in her stomach'. To get there she had had to ride to Sambolabbo, where she got a seat on Andrew's empty beer-crates. ('The less romantic side of living in lovely Djem,' noted Rachel.) Years ago there had been another wife – the immediate successor to the first – but she and First quarrelled so incessantly that Mohamadou Ali divorced her and sent her back to her family. She didn't want to go, because she couldn't take her two children. 'But,' said Moses, 'a man must throw away troublesome women.'

Mohamadou Ali was an autocrat; one sensed his unquestioned authority permeating that populous compound: directing, controlling, subduing. As we ate our fufu and mutton stew (there would be no jammu-jammu until the rains came) we heard him reprimanding one son for playing a reed pipe. Later we could see him kneeling on the lamp-lit floor of his hut across the compound, ironing a pale blue robe. Early next day he was going to Banyo market and none of his womenfolk could be trusted to turn him out well enough. Hot, heavy irons were being carried in relays from the kitchen-hut by girls so small that they found their task an effort.

Being a female Fulani does however have some compensations. Unlike their Bantu sisters they are not, usually, expected to do fieldwork. The Fulanis scorn agricultural labour and, despite having many strapping sons, Mohamadou Ali employed three men at this season – two from the plains and a young Nigerian, Kojo, who joined us after supper.

This was Kojo's fourth year to work in Cameroon during the planting

135

season. 'One month is enough because the work is very hard – all daylight hours seven days a week.' He echoed what other Nigerians had told us; his five-day walk across the border was well rewarded by 3,000 CFA (nearly £7) per day. 'But twice on my journey I must sleep in the bush because there are no compounds. Then I walk all night and sleep in sunlight when I am not so afraid.' Kojo despised all Nigerian politicians. 'They are always, always fighting among themselves – who can have most power to make money! Why not leave one man in control for ten years and see what he could make of our country? We are bitter about taxes – all ordinary people are bitter. We pay taxes on man, wife, huts, gardens – I'm only a poor bush boy but I know it's wrong!'

As we talked countless pickins were peering around corners, eyes wide and fingers in mouths.

Kojo remarked, 'These Fulanis, they live like cattly (sic)!' But his tone was merely condescending, not jeering as that of Moses had been. 'They are honest but foolish people. Here in Adamawa they have so many thousands of cattly, worth millions and millions of francs. If they sold half they could build good schools and hospitals and then their government would help them. But no, they will be sad about selling one or two cattly if they must – it is crazy!'

Before retiring we distributed gaudy postcards of London among the children, who, being unused to seeing pictures, couldn't work out how to look at them. If you live in Djem, Big Ben must seem equally baffling whichever way round you view him. Then, noting adult covetousness, we continued our distribution and these exotic gifts excited Kojo and Moses no less than the pickins. Our host arrived then, to say good-night and goodbye; he would have left for Banyo even before the Murphies swung into action. To dash such a man would be worse than inappropriate; so we dashed some of his sons instead, next morning.

From Djem two sons escorted us for about three miles, the musical boy all the time playing a thin, sweet melody on his reed pipe – a fitting farewell to a place I shall always remember. On the crest of a high ridge, below a pyramidal rock-summit, our guides pointed out the main path without mentioning its destination. 'It's certainly the road to somewhere,' said Rachel. And it did look important: a broad red cattle-track, visible for miles as it crossed the opposite golden-grassed ridge beyond a shallow tree-filled valley. That grass was beautiful but ominous; here the rains were three weeks late.

One of the trek's two serious quarrels marred that forenoon. As we agreed while flying home, two quarrels in three months of twenty-four-hours-a-day proximity was not a bad record. But, being unused to mother-daughter dissension, both clashes at the time felt catastrophic. On this first occasion we were equally to blame and I intuited that an important ingredient was Rachel's post-malarial state. The Tchabal Mbabo, though akin to Paradise, is exceptionally tough going – not at all the sort of terrain Mungo Park would recommend to someone recovering from 'the fever'. So we decided, when we had stopped sulking and were again amiably communicating, to descend sooner than planned and return from the eastern end of the range when Rachel felt stronger.

This momentous decision was taken during siesta-time, by which stage 'the road to somewhere' had long since disintegrated into a selection of equally important-looking tracks. We were close to a dejected, one-hut compound from which two ill-nourished toddlers peeped nervously while we lay in the sun chewing raw cassava. As we were about to move off their mother, clad in rags, returned from the fields, beckoned me to the stake-fence and offered milk by miming cow-horns and the act of milking. She signed us to sit and wait and a moment later we saw smoke and realised that a fire had been lit for our benefit. (Normally fires don't happen until sunset.) The dish of boiled milk must have held at least three pints but our benefactress indignantly refused any payment: her eyes flashed with temper at the very idea.

As we went on our way Rachel said gloomily, 'That's those hungry toddlers' lunch gone down our well-fed gullets!'

'Don't!' I groaned. 'I wouldn't have accepted if I'd known – I was going to give her 500 CFA. Why are the poorest so often the most generous?'

Not long after we saw an extraordinary sight – so extraordinary that we stopped to stare. A tall, slim young man, wearing a natty lounge suit, collar and tie, polished shoes and a grey homburg hat, was emerging from another wretchedly poor compound. His barefooted attendant, wearing a TEXAS IS BIG! T-shirt, carried a black and gold brief-case in one hand and a palpitating cock in the other. Seeing us, the natty character also stopped to stare and we read the label on his lapel: CENSUS OFFICER.

Recovering his poise, the officer advanced on us predatorially. 'You have not been enumerated,' he asserted.

'Oh yes we have,' I said hurriedly, before Rachel could say 'No'. I felt disinclined to sit in the bush for two hours filling out forms in sextuplicate. And I wasn't far wrong; when eventually we were 'enumerated' the process took one hour and fifty minutes. The questions included, 'Where were you on 1 March 1975?' I replied precisely, 'Skardu, Baltistan, Karakorams, Western Himalayas, Northern Territories, Pakistan.' When Cameroon's 1987 Census is published in 1995 –

the earliest date mentioned – I look forward to seeing a special column devoted to the Murphies.

Thwarted of his prey, the officer lost interest in us and headed for the next miserable compound; this scrubby area seemed to have been taken over fairly recently by nomad Fulanis who have abandoned nomadism.

Our new goal, after consultation with the USAF, was the little town of Galim which, according to the census officer, could be reached before sunset. From there we planned to go by easy bush-paths to the slightly bigger town of Tignère, en route for the Tchabal Gangdaba – a lower mountain range where I supposed the climate would be tolerable and the going easier for Rachel.

By 4 p.m. we were on the edge of the Tchabal Mbabo, overlooking many miles of hilly jungle. A distant glint of tin roofs suggested Galim and sections of an undulating red track were visible far below – but we could see no way down. And when at last we found a way we almost wished we hadn't.

This faint path involved us in – among other difficulties – a 2,000-foot descent, of ladder-like steepness, through coarse, waist-high grass which concealed many rough boulders and made it impossible to judge where next one might safely place one's feet. A lesser horse than Egbert would have taken industrial action and even his sang-froid had been diminished by the time we reached level ground.

The ground did not long remain level. Soon we were entrapped in a maze of gullies and deep ditches full of stagnant water: 'Bilharzia!' thought I. Here grew six-foot-high elephant grass and a thorny bramble-like plant which did grievous bodily harm. Eventually Rachel discerned a way out, Egbert was persuaded to jump a wide ditch and we scrambled up a red cliff onto a new-dug field. Then, without warning, black clouds surged across the tranquil blue evening sky and a wall of rain came rushing towards us. Naïvely, we made for a crop-guard's straw hut and tethered Egbert to a convenient fallen tree before cramming ourselves and the load into that tiny shelter, mere seconds before the rain arrived. During the next ten lightning-brilliant minutes we had to shout above continuous thunder.

Hunger prompted us to unpack, in search of sardines, but the first tin was only half-open when a gale drove the rain through our straw walls as though they were tissue-paper. Simultaneously a wide torrent rushed across the floor, transforming it into a lake of liquid manure; animals also use these huts.

As the sky cleared we decided to try to reach Galim, our gear and the countryside being equally sodden. But progress was slow across wet ploughed fields, swollen streams and overgrown irrigation channels. When a narrow track at last appeared the sun had just set and we switched on our torches – only to discover that Rachel's was water-logged and my brand-new battery a dud.

'Things like this,' observed Rachel, 'never happen to people in travel books. Everyone seems better organised than we are.'

Humbly I agreed and slowly we continued by starlight. Soon after came the sound of distant, rapid drumming.

'A compound!' I exclaimed. 'Shelter!'

'And maybe fufu!' gloated Rachel, audibly salivating.

But alas! the drums were approaching and now we could also hear singing and see dim lights bobbing through the bush. When we met four loaded men, returning from market, they hastily scrambled off the narrow path and their nervous anti-spirit drumming and singing became much louder. It would have been futile – even unkind – to ask 'Galim?'

At first this mud-treacherous path ran level through low bush. Then came broken terrain, just as clouds reassembled, leaving us to blunder up and down eroded slopes and grope around baffling corners in total darkness. After a mile or so I suggested, in my boring middle-aged way, that we should admit defeat, before bones were broken, and camp on the path. But eighteen-year-olds are not so easily daunted and Rachel cunningly egged me on with references to the '33' that must surely be available in Galim. Not long after, moonlight began to filter through the long cloud-banks above the horizon and my taut nerves relaxed slightly.

Then came an obstacle not, in my view, negotiable before dawn: a humans-only tree-trunk bridge above a fast river. 'That's it!' I said. 'Here we camp!'

'We can't!' protested Rachel. 'The track's too rocky, there's nowhere to stretch out. And there has to be an animal-ford somewhere, like down *there*' – she pointed to a barely discernible path on our left. 'You stay with Egbert,' she ordered briskly, 'while I investigate.'

Half of me liked this attitude, reckless though it was. But I insisted on going down first – tripping and swearing over tree-roots – to do a recce. That path obviously led to a ford, yet I could find no way through the thick jungle on the far side. With difficulty I scrambled back up the muddy slope and declared, 'It's hopeless! Let's unload right here.'

By then however Rachel was in bulldog mood. 'I'll look,' she said, and disappeared for fifteen minutes, during which I could hear faint splashings and squelchings and the breaking of branches coming from the inky depths.

'I'm an irresponsible mother,' I confided to Egbert, who was philo-sophically grazing as he awaited the Murphies' next unreasonable demand. Then I reflected that eighteen-year-olds are adults, no longer bound to obey parental orders, which soothed my conscience though not my anxiety.

There was an understandable ring of triumph in Rachel's voice when she yelled, 'Come down! I've found it!'

'This is crazy!' I muttered to Egbert, picking up his rope. No doubt he agreed as, still munching, he slithered after me into the blackness where Rachel was awaiting us at the water's edge. We followed her through the racing knee-deep stream and came to a narrow, precipitous, slippery corridor hewn out of the thirty-foot-high bank. Rachel couldn't make it without borrowing my stick. When she had thrown it back I struggled up, wedging my feet in the side-crevices and letting Egbert's rope run to its full length. At the top I turned to encourage him – needlessly, for already he was making heroic efforts to join us. Various bits of extraneous gear were ripped off *en route*: the picket, a water-bottle, both mugs. Having hugged our hero, I retrieved all but one mug.

Tentatively we continued, our way now erratically lit by sheet lightning. Back at the footbridge a loaded man and youth, crossing by torchlight, were so terrified by our appearing that they wavered, clutched each other and for a nightmare moment seemed about to fall.

'We're becoming a public menace,' I said. 'We'd better stop soon.'

All three of us were beginning to wilt when suddenly the path was no longer muddy. Then the moon escaped from the clouds, revealing a flat stubble-field on one side and rough grazing on the other. This time Rachel didn't object when I suggested sleeping in the field, using space-blankets instead of damp bags.

Stubble fields do not make comfortable beds and we slept unsoundly. During the small hours I watched nine loaded donkeys trotting past in the moonlight, going towards the mountains. Their accompanying couple didn't notice us but stared in bewilderment at our gear, strewn over the track.

At dawn we reached a natural bridge across a wide, swift river – one massive sheet of rock, elaborately water-sculpted, extending from bank to bank. As we washed, the fragile morning clouds – covering the sky, but with lines of pale blue between their ridges – caught the rising sun and briefly became a canopy of gold. So lovely was this place that we lingered, sitting with the slanting sun warm on our backs and our legs in the rushing, sparkling water.

The bridge seemed risky for Egbert and we were about to seek a ford when an old man with a machete materialised on the far bank. He had a slight limp, sunken cheeks and only two teeth. Smiling benignly, but making no other attempt to communicate, he led Egbert downstream, through thick bush, to a ford so obscure that we might never have found it.

Those tin roofs we had imagined to be Galim were in fact Wogomdou, which would probably be renamed by Brent Council if within their sphere of influence. At 7.50 a.m. I was shamelessly lusting for beer – it had after all been a hard yesterday and an unrestoring night – but Muslim Wogomdou is barless. However, it is also, like Sambolabbo, at the end of a semi-motorable track. 'Cheer up,' said Rachel. 'In Cameroon beer gets to wherever vehicles get to.'

Soon we were adopted by Ebenki, a slow-witted but sweet-natured Banyo man who laboured for the Chief and said we must meet all the local Big Men. We arrived at the palace just as Wogomdou's school – a small rectangular mud hut – was about to open; but on seeing us the teacher left it closed. Instead his pupils gathered before the palace to broaden their minds by observing White behaviour, which soon became unedifying.

The obese Chief welcomed us amiably and dispatched an aged retainer to fetch beer. Two camp-chairs were unfolded under the palace 'verandah' – several sheets of rusty tin tied to the thatch and looking as though a zephyr might bring them crashing. When a crate of '33' appeared Ebenki stepped forward and quickly opened several bottles with his teeth. (This enviable knack is common in Cameroon.) The Chief couldn't drink alcohol publicly but seemed anxious not to be excluded from any round; at regular intervals bottles slid surreptitiously into the palace. Doing my daily accounts, it shook me to discover that our Wogomdou beer bill came to 7,200 CFA (£16). All the local non-teetotallers had hastened to welcome us – including two gendarmes, wearing crumpled tunics over pyjamas, who while gulping '33' frowningly studied our passports.

Then Nicodemus Ngonba arrived – 'Our Man from Bamenda', a figure we were coming to regard as inevitable whenever the news spread that English-speakers were around. Nicodemus – jovial, overweight, middle-aged – wore a soiled torn shirt and frayed jeans. A World Service addict, he discoursed eloquently on global drug problems, African educational problems, AIDS, Third World debts, the medical pros and cons of various forms of birth-control and what he called the 'philosophy and psychology' of our journey. At no stage did he mistake me for a man and he was the only Cameroonian we met who not only understood what it means to be an author but took an intelligent interest in that career. Naturally we were curious about his own career but he wasn't telling – though a few oblique remarks suggested large-scale cross-border trading on routes without customs' posts.

Meanwhile Rachel was engaged in animated conversation with a poised, courteous nineteen-year-old Fulani who spoke fluent French.

141

Amadou wore a spotless, heavily embroidered cream gown and was so extraordinarily handsome that I found it hard not to stare at him. He lived in N'gaoundere but had 'cattle interests' in the Tchabal Mbabo. Had I been Rachel, I would have felt very tempted to ditch Mamma and hang around with Amadou.

At 9.45 a.m. we were escorted to the edge of the village by Nicodemus. When I remarked that we had seen no Wogomdou women he explained in his mysteriously academic way, 'This is typical of the conquered and converted village. You can notice the people are not Fulani though they are Muslim. This means the women have the worst of both worlds – working in the fields *and* restricted by Islam. You know why tribes all over Adamawa became Muslim? To avoid being enslaved! The Fulani could not enslave fellow-Muslims, so to embrace Islam was to escape the razzias.'

Nicodemus warned us about drought. 'Maize that should have been planted three weeks ago is not yet in the ground. And migrating nomads, expecting full streams, may lose many animals. You too may have problems on the way to N'gaoundere – you must check on this in Tignère.'

For two hours our track undulated through thin jungle, before plunging down baboon-crowded slopes. Here all the long mountain crests are decorated with colossal free-standing boulders, their angles smoothed by aeons of erosion. The variety of shapes seems infinite and often two, three or four boulders are balanced on each other like the playthings of some giant's child. Nowhere else have I seen this phenomenon on such a scale.

Galim is long, narrow, hot, dusty – a town of grey-brown mud dwellings and tight-lipped people. On the outskirts we passed an imposing new mosque, but it was only half built and looked as though construction had been halted for some time. Close by was the massively fortified Chief's palace, a forbidding-looking, blank-walled edifice which did not invite passing infidels to call. At 3.30 p.m. no one was moving in the silent town centre. A few men, squatting in the shade of doorways, stared at us unsmilingly. All but two of the little shops were shuttered and padlocked.

Egbert had as usual refused to drink at breakfast-time and while Rachel gulped Top I took his bucket to Galim's only well, which marks the town centre. It is, we learned later, 180 feet deep – and it feels like it. For fifteen minutes I toiled in the hot sun, watched by those expressionless men. Time after time I dragged the well bucket up, hand over hand, each effort winning only a pint or so of foul, cloudy water. When Egbert's bucket was about two-thirds full I presented it to him. He gulped once, then turned away in disgust.

Seriously worried, we decided to seek advice from the Norwegian

Lutheran Mission. As we approached their shady hilltop compound, on the far side of Galim, many jerry-cans were being unloaded from a Land Rover. The harrassed-looking missionaries directed us to a newly dug well in a field some two miles away; until the rains came it would be Galim's only source of drinkable water. Egbert didn't think much of that bar, either, but drank enough to lower our anxiety level.

As we returned to Galim the sky was suddenly full of low dark clouds and at 5.30 p.m. the town centre seemed no livelier, perhaps because a gusty gale was filling the air with choking gritty dust that stung the eyes and scourged the face. Litter whirled high – an astonishing amount of it, despite most of the shops being shut all the time.

'What a godawful dump!' I muttered.

When Rachel spotted a '33' crate outside a shuttered shop I banged desperately on the door of the adjacent hovel. A young man half-opened it, then dismissed me in English. 'No beer! Beer all finished and no motor – not plenty motor this town!'

Thus Galim achieved a double distinction, as the only Cameroonian town in which we failed to find beer and felt positively unwelcome. Its sullen Islamic heaviness reminded me of Meshed. Nicodemus had attributed this sullenness to the long-established Mission: 'They've set up aggro, they've tried to block funding for the new mosque.' That evening we again met the missionaries, who seemed warm-hearted, well-meaning folk, but rigidly unimaginative. Opposed to an equally narrow Islamic Establishment, they may well have set up aggro. In Cameroon, as in several other countries, we noticed that the modern Roman Catholic Church seems wiser and kinder than most others in its everyday dealings with non-Christians.

It wasn't easy to find lodgings; 'not plenty motor' means no 'Africa hotel'. At last a filthy room – hastily vacated when we appeared – was offered by a tall, thuggish Christian who demanded 5,000 CFA. After a prolonged and unpleasant hassle we beat him down to 2,000, the standard doss-house rate. He then proposed locking Egbert in his empty garage, without fodder, and looked scornfully disbelieving when informed that horses need to eat throughout the night.

When Rachel had taken Egbert to a distant patch of jungle, with alarmingly sparse grazing, we discovered that our own food prospects were no better. Galim doesn't have an eating house, or if it does no one would tell the infidels. The two open shops sold nothing edible. We ended up sitting on the steps outside our room watching a very beautiful pyrotechnic display over the Tchabal Mbabo and faintly hoping our 'host' might send fufu. He didn't.

No rain fell during the night. This was typical of the region's current tantalising weather pattern: much promising cloud every afternoon, but always that promise was broken.

I slept even less than in the stubble-field. Our room was stifling and sweat streamed off me in tickling runnels. The bed reeked of its usual occupant whose dirty garments hung above it. (As Rachel sympathetically remarked, 'Africans are so clean it must be *torture* not having washing water!') Hyperactive cockroaches made quite a din, thudding off the walls when they fought and audibly rummaging through our gear. Mosquitoes whined and bit incessantly. Rachel was evidently having nightmares; she talked loudly in her sleep, using bad language, and kicked me frequently. (Possibly this is what she often longed to do when awake but didn't dare.) My stomach was hideously distended and I vaguely wanted to vomit: the result of no food, and pints of Top instead of water and '33'. In the light of dawn we made an interesting scientific observation. Our smaller plastic water-bottle had been filled with Top and during the night it too became distended. Ever since it has been *round* instead of *square*. 'That,' said Rachel, 'tells us all we need to know about Top!'

At 4.30 a.m. we fetched Egbert by moonlight. He was, predictably, in poor form and as we left Galim Rachel had angst about the ethics of travelling with a pack-animal. She sounded just like those letter-writers who for years have been accusing me of cruelty to my 'four-footed slaves'.

First World attitudes towards animals are becoming increasingly neurotic/sentimental, perhaps because human-animal working partnerships are virtually unknown in a mechanised society. Thus travellers who use pack-animals (not too many nowadays) are regularly berated by people sitting in cosy urban homes – the sort of people whose dogs wear overcoats and whose cats wear bells. 'How,' they demand shrilly, 'could So-and-So be so *dreadfully* cruel to his (or her) camel/donkey/pony/yak/mule?' They forget that by cosy standards So-and-So is being equally cruel to him- (or her-)self. And when reminded of this they argue that humans bent enough to *choose* hardship have no right to *impose* it on defenceless dumb creatures. The normal lifestyle of said dumb creatures is never taken into account. What would their working day be like if they were not accompanying White travellers? I put this point to Rachel but she retorted, 'There was nothing wrong with Egbert's lifestyle! Remember how Danieli adored him? And most Fulani horses are ladies and gentlemen of leisure. We've passed hundreds who never work – they're just status symbols!'

Our bush-path to Garbaia climbed gradually through the jungly foothills of the Tchabal Mbabo. We saw only one compound, memorable for its equine status symbols. While two pretty mares looked on admiringly, an aggressive stallion tried all he knew to attack Egbert. He was a splendid creature, in peak condition despite the drought, and he pursued us for thirty minutes, seeing the intruder off his territory. I had to defend Egbert by non-stop stone-throwing, shouting and stick-waving; yet he several times defied me, approaching almost to within kicking distance. Meanwhile his unwitting rival, stoical as ever, was sedately following Rachel, ignoring this unseemly and uncalled for hostility.

We passed through Garbaia without noticing it; only a butcher's unattended wayside stall suggested a *village*. The meat was black, shrivelled, stinking and covered in flies.

At noon we nut-munched on a high ridge overlooking a long cultivated valley some four or five miles wide. An hour later clouds made it possible to walk on and throughout the afternoon we followed that valley. It was infested by large vicious flies exclusively interested in Egbert. He suffered greatly, though uncomplainingly, and Rachel had a revival of the morning's angst.

Our nut supply was being conserved for the Tchabal Gangdaba and we soon felt hungry again. This area offers no *food for sale*. Bananas and avocados are rare and sensible eating habits mean that compounds have no left-overs that might be bought by passers-by. Only enough food is prepared for each meal and apart from the occasional egg, or milk in cattle areas, the average cupboard is bare from sunrise to sunset. Nor are there any tasty titbits for sale, as in Indian villages.

At 5.15 p.m. Rachel remarked, 'We'd better try to stay in a compound – we need more than pseudo-soup.' By then our path was curving around the lower slopes of a long, steep ridge – rocky and jungly towards the crest, grassy below. The wide Garbaia River meandered along the valley floor between high red banks, with miles of level fields on either side. In the mellow evening light this was a tranquil scene – yet worrying, for the fields were bare, not green with young maize.

Around the next corner a lone compound appeared above the track. Nearby grazed a small herd and by the entrance a ragged figure stood under a tree, gazing towards us. As we drew closer he hurried down the slope to offer milk in fluent sign language. He was small, wiry, middle-aged, dark-skinned; broken discoloured teeth detracted nothing from the charm of his smile. We sat under the tree while he fetched a large bowlful of thick liquid. This was whisked briskly for a few moments, with a special wooden implement not unlike a salad fork, before our host filled our mugs. The slightly smoke-flavoured, slightly tangy drink tasted like a mixture of the finest yoghurt and the richest cream. It seemed a food of the gods. We lost all self-control and each had three brimming mugs while Kamga Kima beamed with joy.

As we guzzled, his (only) wife was slowly ascending from the distant river, carrying a giant cauldron piled with saucepans, gourds, plates, bowls, ladles. She too was ragged, dark-skinned, warm-hearted. As Kamga Kima shouted excitedly to her Rachel muttered, 'They look *awfully* poor – we can't ask them to feed and shelter us!' But we didn't have to ask; Kamga Kima was already resolved to do just that.

Soon Egbert was grazing with the cattle and we were bending low to enter a thatched hut, some thirty feet in diameter, furnished only by a pallet covered with a nylon mat and a wooden double-bed beneath a wicker canopy on carved posts. From the roof poles hung many little leather pouches holding – among other more mysterious things – beans, dried meat, herbs, salt. An ancient Fulani sword in a wooden scabbard hung opposite the entrance and there was a depression lined with ashes on the floor – by local standards the Garbaia valley nights are cold. Wood smoke pleasantly permeated the whole hut and had varnished the bamboo poles supporting the neat thatch.

Only our electric-blue tin folding-chairs struck a discordant note in that spacious compound. Its outer 'walls' were of golden straw matting, and matting screens created secluded corners between the three huts. Opposite us, on a tall stand, firewood had been tidily stacked. Near the entrance a miniature straw hut, like a doll's house, stood on three high legs – and into it a brilliantly plumaged cock led his six wives at sunset.

Those who live in mud huts have little scope for being house-proud but they can be, and usually are, compound-proud. Kamga Kima's garden contained a baby palm-tree, several dwarf ornamental shrubs and a much taller shrub shaped like a Christmas tree and laden with bell-like dark blue blossoms. A pink-blossomed tree was rooted in a pile of round stones and beneath it herbs flourished in an enormous earthenware cauldron, glazed grey and black and pink. The fence was lined with slim, elegant trees, their feathery foliage stirring in a faint breeze against gold and plum sunset clouds.

Around the main cooking fire, Mrs Kima and three daughters (married but living close by) were gossiping and giggling while chopping and stirring by a circular kitchen 'table' – a pile of large stones on which everything to do with the meal was laid. Most daytime cooking is done outside, weather permitting, but nothing is put on the dusty ground although most compounds are so well swept that they look a great deal cleaner than my own kitchen.

As the light faded our host beckoned us to the bathroom corner, behind our hut. The two big basins of hot water dreadfully bothered Rachel who was having a day of chronic angst. 'Just think,' she said, 'of dragging all this water up from the river! *And* how long did it take to collect enough wood to make so much water so hot?'

Soap was also provided, and two small towels, threadbare but clean. The latrine was another of those mysteriously smell-less holes on top of a low earth mound, covered with an old enamel dish-lid. Most rural Cameroonians are acutely fly-conscious. Latrines are never left exposed and food and drink are always kept covered – even *during* a meal, should there be flies about.

In our absence Kamga Kima had tactfully rearranged what was obviously his own hut; his few garments had been removed and clean covers put on two little foam-rubber pillows. Leaving our wash-bag in the hut, I was disquieted to notice him rummaging in a pouch on the wall; the aroma from that direction too keenly reminded me of the butcher's stall we had passed at noon.

Our host apologised for not having a good lamp; the family's only lantern was cracked and smoked fiendishly. But we were content to sit in the dark, watching the scene by the fire. Kamga Kima was a domesticated fellow, the only Cameroonian husband we witnessed helping his wife with household chores. When the daughters had gone to feed their own families he set about cooking cassava amidst much merriment, caused by the ingenuity of our sign language. That was a happy compound; parents and children clearly enjoyed each other's company.

Having firmly declined our host's offer to kill and roast a hen, we were much relieved when he served eight hard-boiled eggs, a mountain of boiled cassava (which he taught us how to peel) and a cup of palm oil and salt as 'dressing'. That combination was both palatable and sustaining – a welcome change from fufu.

Then the valley's stillness was desecrated by the snarling roar of a motor-bicycle: the day's first vehicle. Kamga Kima dashed out and could be heard shouting down the slope. He returned with two Nigerians, a migrant worker and Mohamed Mechanic, who had settled a few years previously in the next village, Tourak. Eagerly our host squatted on his goat-skin, close to our chairs, and asked all the questions he had been longing to ask since we appeared. The answers were at once shouted to his wife, still busy around the cooking-fire. By then it had been moved into the kitchen-hut, by the simple expedient of picking up all the burning wood on a broad shovel and putting it down again on the hut floor. Unfortunately the Nigerians were in a hurry (an uncommon West African condition) so we had no opportunity to question Kamga Kima. But Mohamed Mechanic urged us to contact him next day on our way through Tourak.

Our host then fetched his own supper, a great bowl of scalding soup. He sat cross-legged, holding a feeble torch in one hand and cooling the liquid by repeatedly pouring large ladlefuls from a height – spilling not a drop.

Before retiring we took our dishes to Mrs Kima and said goodnight. Moments later, as we were beginning to undress, our host knocked on the door, entered triumphantly and laid a tray on one of the chairs; that mountain of cassava and eggs had been our hors-d'oeuvre.

With a flourish Kamga Kima unlidded a dish holding kilos of fufu, and then a dish of jammu-jammu, and finally a dish that released lethal fumes. Rotten meat cooked makes an even more powerful olfactory impact than rotten meat raw. We prayed he wouldn't stay to enjoy the spectacle of us relishing our supper. As he placed the re-lit smoking lantern on the tray, and seemed about to settle down on the pallet, his wife – most mercifully – called him.

I moved fast; within thirty seconds the stew was under the bed in a Heathrow duty-free bag. I am famously paranoid about not wasting food but every principle meets its Waterloo.

As Rachel observed, 'It's all in the conditioning.' Most Africans *couldn't* eat Danish blue or ripe Stilton, even if they were starving.

Next morning we furtively deposited our stew in a stream. We had got off to a late (7.40 a.m.) start because Kamga Kima insisted on our waiting for breakfast – pints of new milk and a delicious maize-gruel, popular in this area, to which we soon became addicted.

In Tourak – a charming village of many compounds, overlooking the Garbaia River – Mohamed Mechanic was repairing bicycles under a mango tree. All the three shops were shut. 'They open only every eight days, for the weekly market,' Mohamed explained apologetically. (The traditional Cameroonian week was eight days, for reasons we never understood though they were several times explained to us.)'You will pass no compounds,' he continued, 'between here and the motor-road. So you must take chop with you. To walk all day without eating will give you pains in the stomach.' Whereupon he went bounding off on his motor-bike, through steep rough laneways, in search of chop – like a gallant knight on his charger. Returning with two tins of fizzy Nigerian 'orange juice' and half a dozen eggs, he adamantly refused payment. 'You are guests, it is my honour to facilitate you.' He then insisted that the eggs must be hard-boiled and while someone was lighting a fire he deplored the Cameroonians' treatment of their bicycles. 'These people are not used to machinery – they try to mend something, they destroy it forever! This is good to give me work, but for them it is bad because I must charge a lot to help my family pay their taxes in Nigeria.'

Mohamed advised us that Tourak would be a good starting point for our return to the eastern Tchabal Mbabo and promised to provide a guide to show us the beginning of the 'very difficult' path.

For three hours our track to the motor-road switchbacked through rugged, lightly forested hills, their grassy slopes golden brown. A cool breeze tempered the heat, white cloudlets drifted across a deep blue sky, capuchin monkeys were numerous and much of the vegetation was unfamiliar. We met only two men, of the same tribe as Kamga Kima – judging by the incisions on their cheekbones. Each carried a bow in his left hand and several sharp-tipped arrows in a cow-hide quiver slung over his left shoulder. Our siesta-site, where the track reached its highest point, was one of the most beautiful of the entire trek with the Tchabal Mbabo filling the sky beyond the Garbaia valley and the Tchabal Gangdaba ahead, north of Tignère.

By three o'clock we were on the Tignère-Koncha motor-track, another 'international highway' which continues beyond the frontier village of Koncha into Nigeria. The hard red stony surface was tiring to walk on and fiercely reflected the heat; soon we took a second siesta beneath a grove of mango trees. As we lay gazing at the inaccessible fruit a youngish man arrived with a long forked stick. He glanced at us but showed no surprise and ignored our greetings. Then he removed his Fulani gown, revealing a powerful torso and a new pair of thick corduroy trousers. Walking twice around the tree, he noted the position of the few ripe fruits. An instant later he had swung himself into the dense foliage with baboon-like agility and become invisible. It took him some time to knock down all the marked mangoes: about a dozen. He gave us two, still making no effort to communicate, then replaced his gown and strode away.

During the afternoon there was no troublesome flow of traffic – a vehicle every hour or so – but the terrain was dull: mile after dusty mile of undulating grey-green bush. We passed quite a few compounds, singly or in pairs, and were diverted by the activities of another Census Officer – tall and willowy, in knife-creased khaki slacks and silk shirt and cravat. Two attendants, a short burly youth and a little boy, were herding his dash: three cocks, one sheep lunging wildly at the end of a grass rope and two kids hysterically bleating for their mothers.

'Why dash a Census Officer?' mused Rachel. But it is easy to see how census-taking can be abused; such a figure, with his embossed brief-case of formidable documents, could profitably cow most peasants. Compounds are often empty by day and the willowy one wasted no time winkling Cameroon's citizens out of the bush. Firmly he chalked the closed doors and went on his way. So much for Third World statistics.

This area's water shortage was serious. At most wayside compound entrances, covered earthenware cauldrons stood on wooden trestles with a gourd or mug on top, for the benefit of passing strangers unable to find local water sources. One was not expected to leave dash; this was a truly disinterested service to humanity, a symbol of all that is best in African rural traditions.

All afternoon we passed only one small stream, far below the road, and as I was about to scramble down the difficult slope a woman

149

insisted on emptying her own hard-won bucket into Egbert's – thus adding to that mosaic of spontaneous kindnesses which is our most precious souvenir of Cameroon.

At 6.30 p.m. we camped by the remains of the Mayo Wolkossam, a sluggish trickle in a wide bed. The grazing was poor and something odd in the dense growth along the river scared Egbert badly. We heard inexplicable grunting/coughing noises but saw nothing.

Being by now expert enough to load in the dark, we set off at 5.30 a.m., hoping to get to Tignère before brutal heat time. The humidity was extreme and soon we were commenting on the eerily subdued quality of the light. For the next fortnight visibility was down to about a mile; the hammadan was upon us, though we didn't then recognise it as such.

It was market-day in Tignère and a colourful group of jewellery-laden women and optimistic umbrella-toting men overtook us, all carrying massive loads. Their splayed feet moved fast over the hard gritty road; a packed bush-taxi had just passed and nowadays those too poor to afford motor-transport are at a disadvantage, if the demand for their produce is limited.

Soon after, we came to a derelict shed and two thatched huts: the Customs Post and Immigration Office. Tignère, though some sixty miles from the border, is the first town on this international highway. A tree-trunk barrier left ample room for small vehicles and foot traffic to bypass it.

When I banged on the door of the nearest hut a sleep-stupid gendarme stumbled forth in gaudy striped pyjamas. He was cramming his peaked cap on his curls and looked hung-over. 'No wonder!' said Rachel, pointing to a nearby pile of empty beer bottles.

'Passports!' demanded the gendarme, squinting at me with bloodshot eyes and licking parched lips. I handed them over and he pressed them to his heart. 'I keep! You get back at gendarmerie in Tignère.'

Menacingly I moved forward; only the maternal instinct is stronger than the 'keep passport' instinct. 'Give back!' I ordered. '*We* keep! *We* show gendarme in Tignère.'

The officer blinked uncertainly. I seized the passports and told Rachel, 'Move on, pass the barrier!'

As we advanced the officer yelped, 'Your baggage! You come from Nigeria with baggage, you show baggage!'

'We come from Bamenda,' I said. 'Forget our baggage!'

The officer dived into the hut, grabbed a '33', opened it with his teeth, took a long swig and drew a deep breath. 'Bamenda *no!*' he said. 'This is road from Nigeria, you come from Nigeria with baggage, you show baggage!'

'He's only doing his duty,' said Rachel compassionately. 'By now our coming from Bamenda really must sound like a tall story!'

Infected by this tolerance, I stepped forward and patted our adversary on the shoulder.

'We stay in Tignère,' I said. 'You come meet us Tignère and we drink beer, *plenty* beer!'

The gendarme took another swig, patted me on the shoulder and agreed excitedly. 'Yes, yes! We meet again, we drink, we talk, we are good pals! You are good man! White men are good pals, rich men, brave men – why you come from Nigeria with this horse? You are brave, you have beautiful wife, why you take this beautiful wife with horse from Nigeria?'

From the second hut two customs officers emerged, dressing themselves. Both were polite, sober, friendly; one spoke fragments of English. It seemed the gendarme had wished to keep our passports merely because 'the stamp' was inaccessible. For a moment I imagined this to be another of those fiscal stamps beloved of too many governments. But no. A rubber stamp was in question – *the* rubber stamp, Tignère's *only* rubber stamp, the imprint of which should be on our passports before we entered the town. Or so the theory went. Both customs men agreed that since the stamp was inaccessible we would have to proceed unstamped. They then zoomed off towards Tignère on their motor-bicycle.

When the straggling town came into view, below the track on our left, it was evident that marshy ground by the dried-up riverbed precluded a cut-short. Tignère looks smaller than Mayo Darlé but has several new bureaucratic-looking buildings around the edges.

The customs officers now zoomed back with a young woman sandwiched between them. They stopped, the English speaker dismounted, the motor-bicycle continued and we spent twenty minutes sitting on the ditch 'giving all particulars', which our friend transcribed into a school exercise book. The stamp was inaccessible, he confided, because it had been left in a room to which no one could find the key. His taking down 'all particulars' was designed to soothe his superior, should it ever be discovered that we had entered Tignère unstamped. He had a round, innocent, worried young face and we warmed to him. Unsurprisingly, he failed to notice that our visas had expired the day before.

In the Restaurant Bar Faro Hotel the proprietor, Gabriel, was snoring on a plastic-covered bench amidst an ocean of empty bottles and tins and cigarette packets. Greasy bits of paper, which the evening before had wrapped kebabs, were being pushed around the floor by excited cockroaches. The hotel was a row of six breeze-block rooms around the corner. In No. 4 a fairly clean single bed took up most of the space and the window wouldn't open; but a small table and chair

151

brought joy to my literary heart. There was no Faro Restaurant, despite the garish lettering on the façade.

By 8.30 a.m. we had tethered Egbert on reasonably good grazing and were sitting outside the bar having beer for breakfast. The USAF – who don't mark Tignère – told us that the highest point of the long, narrow Tchabal Gangdaba is at 5,060 feet. The area west of the range soon drops to about 2,500 feet; the area to the east seemed more tempting at 4,000 feet.

Fate then caused an elderly Fulani motor-cyclist to approach in a cloud of dust and stop beside us; he wore an apricot gown and looked dignified even on his machine. The USAF chart fascinated him but having discovered our plans he looked anxious. The path from Tignère to Mana was hard to find and little used. He reckoned we needed help and – it was the will of Allah! – he could provide it. On the following morning, two youths were beginning a journey to the northern end of the range and he would ensure that they collected us from the Faro at dawn. It was characteristic of Tignère that we so soon acquired an anonymous guardian-angel.

In the bar four senior government employees, exiled to the 'administrative capital of Tignère', were sitting behind a long row of bottles as they might be in Ireland at 9.0 p.m. They rejoiced to have the Sunday morning monotony broken by foreign company. From behind the bar Gabriel yelled cheerful greetings to everyone above the din of his giant Nigerian cassette-recorder. A youth was raising opaque clouds of dust as he swept garbage onto the street for the next gust of wind to blow it all over Tignère. A very young Anglophone couple with a baby sat in a distant corner sharing a bottle of mild Beaufort and being physically demonstrative – an unusual sight in Cameroon, where intimacy in public is frowned upon. An aggressively drunk man demanded that I buy him a drink and was verbally ejected by Gabriel who then apologised ornately to me, almost beating his breast.

Then Sama arrived – a large, jolly, off-duty gendarme from Yaoundé, wearing a pale blue cotton suit. Without consulting us, he added to our rows of open beers. 'You had problems,' he said, 'on the road at the barrier. I am sorry, that man is stupid – he is born in the bush, without education. In Cameroon we like to treat guests nicely ...'

Another Census Officer, exhausted and distraught, hurried in and beseeched us to be 'enumerated'. He was excruciatingly conscientious – not, we felt, a collector of livestock. He failed to grasp that the Cameroonian government would not want to know whether our home was 'thatched with grass or leaves', whether we got our water from 'a well or a stream', whether we cooked on 'wood, charcoal or sawdust', whether we used 'a private latrine or a common latrine' (i.e., the bush), whether my husband had 'four or more wives' and how many children

152

Rachel had given birth to 'since her twelfth birthday'.

Towards noon Sama announced that we must pay our respects to Tignère's Lamido, a traditional title of Fulani emirs. Allegedly, he had decreed that television must never come to Tignère, believing the aerials to be magic devices which could spy on activities within his compound. We all laughed uproariously at this primitive superstition. Yet I sensed the usual ambivalent uneasy undercurrent about a Chief's powers and status; these are certainly not disregarded by the majority of citizens, whether their background be urban or rural. (Cameroon's national television service was then new-born and all its pictures seemed to be shots of a severe blizzard. But it was arousing intense excitement in towns with electricity.)

That two-mile walk to the palace, through hellish heat, made me aware of our new friends' excessive hospitality. Tignère seemed blurred by more than the harmattan.

'Do you realise,' said Rachel, sounding justifiably censorious, 'that you've had *five* beers and it's only *noon*?'

I did not reply; I was too busy trying to walk in a straight line.

We were escorted by Sama and a charming local youth, named I think Tikela, who was also somewhat the worse for drink. He giggled and hiccupped while telling me, 'This Lamido has four wives, thirty-nine children and many concubines. But eleven children are dead. He wants one hundred children alive. But many of his young followers and some of his children are leaving his compound because he is so strict.'

We were then about half-way down Tignère's main street: hilly, dusty, stony, narrow. Tikela nodded towards Le Metro, a small bar/disco/night-club/brothel with rows of coloured electric light bulbs criss-crossing its verandah. 'Some of the Chief's followers,' he said, 'would like to enjoy themselves there – not drinking alcohol, only dancing. But if he hears he flogs them.'

The palace was an impressive complex of sandy-floored, uncovered corridors winding between high-ceilinged rooms in one of which stood a gaily caparisoned horse. Within those massively fortified walls, all was cool and shadowy. This helped Tikela and me to sober up as we waited, hunkering against a wall, to be summoned to the Presence. (The others had been told to wait outside the main arched entrance.) A few senior court officials in colourful gowns passed through the corridors, eyeing us with some disdain: perhaps they could smell our fumes. Several graceful young women appeared, then rushed away on seeing the White 'man'. Numerous children peeped around corners and were so beautiful one felt the Chief couldn't be blamed for wanting a hundred of them.

When a retainer had brought Rachel to join us we were ushered into the Reception Hall – large and dimly lit, with a scattering of good carpets and many chairs around mud walls brightened by a large poster of Mecca, several posters of Cameroonian wildlife (issued by Cameroonian Airways) and a sprawling, hectic-hued tapestry of the Peacock Throne.

The Chief – middle aged, courteous, soft spoken (in Foulfouldé only) – sat on a high throne-like carved wooden chair, regarding us with a slightly quizzical expression. He invited us to sit and Tikela knelt unsteadily before him with downcast eyes, mumbling reverent greetings through cupped hands. Our boots had been left outside but now the chief ordered Tikela to fetch them and graciously gave us permission to put them on – which was later interpreted as 'a big honour'. After twenty minutes of conversational hard work – answering questions about our trek – Tikela gave the signal to withdraw. Having met this Lamido, it was hard to imagine him flogging anyone. As for television diktats – I could only applaud his campaign to protect his people from that medium, whatever his motives might be.

Tignère's mini-colony of urban exiles has caused a nasty rash of jerry-built 'gentlemen's residences' to break out around the town's edges. But it has also inspired the opening of what looked to us like a supermarket: a new shop, some eight feet by twelve, stocked with vividly packaged consumer goods imported from Nigeria by an enterprising Hausa merchant. These alas! were mainly inedibles: washing-powder, shampoo, face-cream, hardware. However, we bought big tins of Bournvita and Ovaltine, a box of sugar lumps, several packets of noodles, more tins of sardines and a few tubs of excellent chocolate spread (made in Cameroon) for instant consumption with crisp baguettes. (Tignère's French bread, always new-baked and light, was the best we tasted in Cameroon.)

After a large blotting-paper lunch I left Rachel sleeping and hastened off to water Egbert: but all the stand pipes were dry. Wandering around with horse and bucket, I was soon coated in a reddish muck of sweaty dust. When petrol is available – often it isn't – the bureaucrats create frequent sandstorms by racing around in government jeeps. On Egbert's behalf I was beginning to panic when a kind young woman directed us to a deep well on the southern edge of the town. There a kind young man – a born-again Christian from Bamenda – drew us two buckets and asked me if I was saved. Cravenly I said 'Yes', being by then too heat-exhausted to embark on metaphysics with a zealot.

Tignère's status as 'an administrative capital' has given it a strong Alice-in-Wonderland flavour. Among its new buildings are a Department of Industry and Commerce (the nearest factory is hundreds of miles away) and a transparent *all glass* electricity generating station in which Abe could be observed tending the machinery after dark – and producing electricity, too, though not many locals chose to avail of it. This futuristic construction, when first we came upon it amidst a group of thatched huts, gave us quite a turn.

Another incongruity is the vast, high-ceilinged Central Post Office with mock-marble walls and floor. ('Central to what?' Rachel wondered. 'We haven't seen too many peripheral post offices *en route*.') During our three visits to Tignère we never saw anyone using this criminally extravagant building, where the three clerks were united in their conviction that Ireland is part of 'the continent of England'. Its stamp supply was proportionately limited. However, we heard a rumour that some of the 'exiles', and a Peace Corps 'Community Developer', do regularly use it with irregular success.

The Department of Tourism also has its local Headquarters, a phoney thatched hut in the litter-strewn grounds of the colonial Palais de Justice. The Tourist Officer was said to 'have literature' but we couldn't find him. Someone told us he was lion-hunting with Spaniards.

Towards sundown we strolled to a distant 'suburb' to visit a friend of Franz: Father Walter, from the Tyrol, who ran Tignère's Catholic Mission single-handed and had been in Cameroon for twenty-two years. During a future drama, he was to become significant in our lives.

The generator doesn't run to street lighting and we got lost on our way back to the Faro, where Sama and Tikela awaited us. Having absorbed more '33' at their expense, I invited them to sup with us. Not until we were sitting in Tignère's only 'restaurant' – a cramped, lamp-lit shack down an alleyway off the main street – did they explain that they had already supped. It was then 8.45 p.m. and we received the evening's left-overs, meagre portions of soggy luke-warm rice and a few necks and wings of geriatric hens. For this – by far our worst meal in Cameroon – we were charged 1,700 CFA (almost £4).

On our way back we stopped off at a small bar, opposite Le Metro, belonging to a 'special friend' of Tikela – a plump garrulous prostitute wearing a flouncey high-collared blouse of delicate white lace and a billowing ankle-length purple skirt. Her slim colleague – they both worked from Le Metro – favoured skin-tight denim jeans, a scarlet brassière and high-heeled shiny black boots.

'These are very rich women,' said Tikela respectfully. 'They play only with officers and are very clean.'

By this stage I was, it pains me to admit, hopelessly drunk. Oddly enough, given the prevalence of '33' along our route, and the social pressures to consume immoderate quantities of it, Tignère caused my only Cameroonian descent into clinical intoxication. My diary omits our visit to Le Metro, an evidently exciting experience of which I have absolutely no recollection. So I quote from Rachel's diary:

155

In the small bar we met another policeman and a Bamenda truck-driver (truck bust) who took us to Le Metro – a sort of nightclub. We sat outside on the terrace and drank beer glacée. I danced a few times inside where the lighting was psychedelic. Eventually the truck-driver decided, because he was drunk, that he was in love with me. Our very congenial policeman friend got rid of him and all the chairs on the verandah were moved round so that he couldn't reach me. Mummy was drunk too.

8

Spooked in the Tchabal Gangdaba

I WOKE WITH an undeservedly clear head – which says a lot for '33' – and by 6.30 a.m. we were following our guides through Tignère's fissured and attenuated 'suburbs'. Both youths seemed in awe of us. They were well meaning but dim-witted; twice they led us to cut-shorts across chasms not negotiable by a horse. According to Sama they belonged to a Mana tribe 'converted' during the razzias. He had added disparagingly, 'Those are good honest boys, but very tribal.'

We were becoming increasingly confused by the Cameroonian usage of 'tribe' and 'tribal'. The concept of African tribes so obsessed generations of Europeans that they used the word indiscriminately and by now the Africans themselves often misapply it, when it makes little more sense than if Europeans were to refer to people in the next village as members of another tribe. True, many mutually incomprehensible languages are spoken throughout Western Cameroon and one notices several distinct physical types, apart from the Fulanis. Yet a shared culture, reinforced by centuries of intermarriage, makes it ridiculous to describe the Kunabe or Fang or Nyos or Oku as 'tribes'. These and hundreds of other groups have a strong common identity. On many minor and some major points their customs and beliefs differ, but even casual passers-by can see that by now they are more united than divided. The appropriate word for each group would seem to be 'chiefdom' – or perhaps, nowadays, 'clan'.

On the edge of Tignère, in a 'suburb' of neat traditional compounds, we had a long wait for the other members of our party. Those four lean, dark-skinned Fulanis seemed to regard us with some suspicion and ignored our tentative attempts to communicate. Oddly, Mana being far from any town, nobody was loaded with merchandise.

Our faint – sometimes invisible – path twisted illogically through dusty, scrubby hills. At the base of the Tchabal Gangdaba water appeared – a trickle in a rocky stream-bed – and while our companions washed and prayed we nut-munched in preparation for a 1,500-foot climb on an unremittingly severe gradient.

Emerging from dense forest onto a level crest, our harmattan frustration became acute. Views that should have been spectacular were non-existent. To the east a nearby line of slightly lower mountains was dimly visible; to the west a grey haze obliterated everything. For an hour we continued with our guides. Here the path was clear, following the crest through a harsh dry landscape of stony pale brown earth and low scrub – the only colour provided by occasional clusters of red or orange berries. Then came a mild descent to a not-quite-dried-up river with luxuriant green grass on its banks. Unloading, we dashed the youths and signed to all our companions to continue without us. This they seemed reluctant to do – even the hitherto indifferent Fulanis. They too rested by the water for a little time, then went on their way, looking uneasy. Not knowing when we might next find grass, we gave Egbert a ninety-minute meal.

For the rest of the day our rough path rose and fell steeply. Sometimes it consisted of large, loose, thin 'plates' of rock which Egbert found trying; sometimes it was a dried-up watercourse of large, loose, round stones which we all found trying. For a few miles it wound through a strange, weirdly beautiful bamboo forest – strange because one associates bamboo with dampness and this whole region looked like semi-desert. It seemed completely lifeless, not only uninhabited but without birds or animals. And the harmattan, obscuring the rest of the world, reinforced our sense of extreme isolation.

Not until the late afternoon did grassland appear: an expanse of curving green hills, on one of which grazed cattle. 'Fufu!' anticipated Rachel.

Soon we were standing on a summit, overlooking four large compounds spread across a semicircular ledge far below. By local standards this was a metropolis. '*Lots* of fufu!' gloated Rachel. We hastened down.

Our guides must have mentioned us *en passant*; the elderly Fulani Chief (quarterchief?) hurried to welcome us – smiling delightedly, both hands outstretched, eyes twinkling. He was barefooted, wearing a threadbare shift, tall and very thin with two fingers missing on his right hand. Having led us to his guest hut – as usual on the edge of the compound – he rushed off to organise sustenance.

At last we were beyond chair-territory. Sitting on the hut's threshold, we communicated wordlessly but quite effectively with numerous women and children, none of whom would come close but all of whom were riveted by our presence. Then Abdulla, our host, came half-running towards us with four hot hard-boiled eggs and a battered kettle of drinking water. 'We must *look* very hungry!' said Rachel.

I longed to explore the compounds but that would have been impolite. The huts were of a new (to us) design, the top half of the walls being wickerwork – which meant rather untidy thatches. We got the impression that this village consisted of one very extended family. Three of the compounds were unenclosed and almost merged into one another. But the few small fields of alarmingly shrivelled young maize had been securely fenced with rough-hewn stakes, as had the large corral for the cattle.

A little boy approached slowly with a bucket of cold washing water – then his nerve broke, some yards from our hut. Leaving the bucket, he scampered away. That water was kept for Egbert. As we were shown no latrine, we assumed this family used the bush: a sensible habit in such an unpeopled area. Meanwhile the return home of a donkey herd (eight adults and a foal) was distracting Egbert from his grazing and causing him to behave with unseemly skittishness, kicking up his heels and whinnying coyly.

Our second course soon arrived: an enormous dish of perfectly cooked rice (luxury food in these parts), accompanied by the fried breasts (only) of several chickens, tender, juicy and gently spiced. While eating we watched the sunset routine. Small children rounded up scores of hens, ducks and guinea-fowl. Slightly larger children pursued the donkey herd and tethered them. A youth drove the cattle home from the hills and corralled them, separating the calves from their mothers and fondly stroking the two magnificent bulls before he shut the gate. Abdulla lay near our hut on his cow-hide, head propped on elbow, amiably shouting advice to the younger generation whenever they had problems.

Suddenly, as the light was fading, a tumult of excitement swept the ledge; yells of joy, squeals of laughter, cheers of triumph. Bewildered, we watched all the younger generation streaming from each compound and racing across the grass to converge on the steep cliff-path from Tignère. Then, looking up, we saw a tall young woman descending with a little cloth-wrapped bundle on her head. The youngsters surged up the cliff and surrounded her, shrieking and singing, jumping up and down, clapping their hands over their heads, hanging from her arms and legs and generally registering twenty on the Richter scale of happiness.

'Maybe she's been away in hospital,' I speculated. 'They seem to be not only welcoming but celebrating.'

'We're missing Our Man from Bamenda!' said Rachel. 'Or from Nigeria.'

Abdulla did have two Bantu workmen, presumably seasonal, with whom he was now dining on the cow-hide; but neither was Nigerian. In Muslim circles eating with your servants is fine but eating with your womenfolk is *out*; even Mr Kami didn't sup with his obviously much-loved Mrs Kami. At intervals bones were thrown to a large shaggy dog who sat waiting at a respectful distance. The Islamic anti-dog bias seems not to operate in Cameroon.

Our host had been over-zealous in his organisation of sustenance and meals were coming from every angle. The third is hard to describe but was easy to eat: a big bowl of something semi-solid like a cross between porridge and rice pudding, which sounds unpromising but tasted scrumptious. Having finished that we were about to retire when a fourth supper arrived from another compound: the *best* fufu we ate in Cameroon, with top quality jammu-jammu and a memorable sauce of fried clarified butter. Half-way through that *cordon bleu* offering we had to give up. Luckily Abdulla was then absorbed in conversation with his workmen and it was dark, this being a lampless village. Deftly we secreted the left-overs in another Heathrow bag and had them for breakfast, thus discovering the demerits of cold fufu.

Despite the language barrier, that was a particularly happy 'compound evening'. The wide ledge, protected on three sides by high, steep green slopes, had a rare beauty and tranquillity. Also, Abdulla was a perfect host who took us on our own terms and was attentive without fussing – at bedtime he suggested a fire in our hut! But beyond all that there was a special atmosphere of contentment, serenity, timelessness. Apart from Nigerian enamelware, Mungo Park would have found nothing unfamiliar in Abdulla's 'village'.

It is easy, before the journey, to see oneself as a seasoned, prudent, responsible traveller. Patiently one queues for the relevant boosters; diligently one seeks out the appropriate malaria prophylactics for the region in question; extravagantly one buys hundreds of water-purifying tablets, dozens of multivitamin capsules, a few pain-killers and a course of broad-spectrum antibiotics – 'just in case' ... One's rational European persona is then dominant, yet within weeks it can seem to belong to someone else.

Thus I reflected beside a six-inch-deep river, thirty hours after leaving Abdulla's compound. We had just drunk a few litres each, before allowing Egbert to muddy the issue, and it occurred to me that for days we had been neglecting to use Puritabs. 'We must be mad!' I exclaimed, more for Rachel's benefit than because I felt any genuine alarm.

Rachel shrugged, peered into her mug and said, 'It looks fairly clear.' I peered into mine, where only one tiny thing wriggled near the bottom; the other foreign matter seemed to consist of minute and presumably innocuous grains of sand.

'We'd be madder,' observed Rachel, 'to make perfectly good water taste like a swimming-pool. Anyway, we've seen precisely one human being in the past thirty hours – how *could* this river be contaminated?'

I looked at the dense green growth along the banks. Giant vine-swathed trees supported a colourful abundance of bird-life. Over-hanging the water, exposed by erosion, were ancient, interwoven root-systems, their convolutions seeming macabre in the shadows. Beyond this precious shade stretched flat miles of hot, dry, monochrome scrub-land dotted with thousands (millions?) of tall termite dwellings. Already the high mountain on which we had camped the night before was lost in the harmattan haze. At noon this landscape looked deserted, but we knew it wasn't.

'Birds and animals?' I suggested morbidly. 'What about all those baboons? Can't they spread dire diseases?'

'Now you're being neurotic!' said Rachel. And, having successfully escaped from my European persona, I was content to accept this diagnosis.

After that we became increasingly reckless, only sterilising when close to towns. Yet in Cameroon neither of us suffered even a minor intestinal disorder. Although we were to be afflicted by other health problems, our guts flourished on neat river water.

The previous day had been marred by our second quarrel, for which Rachel was entirely to blame. We ended up totally lost, sleeping (or not sleeping) on a sloping sheet of corrugated rock in a dismal drought-stricken forest. That was the only occasion on which we ran out of water, which didn't improve our tempers; since morning we had lost gallons of sweat. When darkness forced us to stop, high on that inhos-pitable mountain, poor Egbert was too exhausted – or perhaps too thirsty – to eat. Having considered what little grazing there was, he returned to our sheet of rock and stood beside us looking pathetic.

By then Rachel and I had been non-speakers for a record four hours. To dispel this emotional harmattan I told her exactly what I thought of her behaviour during the afternoon. Instantly she apologised and we settled down to be companionably miserable throughout that long, dehydrated night.

Later I reproved myself for having over-reacted; Rachel's uncharac-teristic behaviour may have been triggered by her considerable sen-sitivity to atmosphere. We found ourselves, that day, in an area of uniquely bad vibes. Near Sambolabbo, I had been wondering if Africa's people-Nature relationship contributes something to White travellers' deep-down reactions to the landscape. Then I was thinking only of enjoyment, but if that relationship is significant it must work both ways. And in the heart of the Tchabal Gangdaba something had gone very wrong.

A few incinerated compounds proved that the area had been popu-lated before being recently devastated by out-of-control bush-fires. No vegetation had survived. The ashen monotony was broken only by macabre giant tree-corpses, still standing though lacking all but their central branches. The blackened mountains and valleys and tiny fields felt uncannily spiritually oppressive – an odd phrase, but I can think of none other to convey the atmosphere of that abandoned place. Partly as a result of fire-damage, the terrain was even more gruelling than in the Tchabal Mbabo. Its friable charcoal-grey soil afforded hideously insecure footholds on pathless, near-vertical slopes, from which it too often seemed that one or all of us might slip five or six hundred feet into an inaccessible ravine. That morning we had been conscious of *escaping* as we descended the Tchabal Gangdaba's eastern flank to cross the flattest land of the whole trek.

For hours this plain recalled childhood images of Africa; tall clumps of dry red grass, wizened dusty-green scrub and misshapen flat-topped dwarf trees stretched as far as the eye could see – which of course wasn't all that far. The harmattan was the main cause of our being so utterly lost. Our USAF chart was strong on relief but that doesn't help when one can't see the surrounding mountains; we were now relying on Rachel's sense of direction to get us back to Tignère.

By 5 p.m. forested hills, lowish but steep, had replaced the plain. Then suddenly our path joined a puzzlingly wide track that might once have been a colonial *Piste praticable pour les véhicules tout terrain*. Given a built-in compass, one doesn't have to hesitate; Rachel immediately decided that here we should turn right. Personally I would have turned left – and might never have been heard of again.

At sunset we camped *on* this track, surrounded by immense trees, and freed Egbert to make what he could of scattered clumps of tall grass – spiky and juiceless. The soil was bizarre, as it had been for much of the past two days: hard blackish loose lumps about the size of a golf-ball – difficult to walk on and impossible to sleep on. I have seen nothing else like it, in Cameroon or elsewhere. Happily the track, once we had adjusted our bones to avoid embedded stones, was much less uncomfortable than the previous night's corrugated rock. Yet I slept little; scores of Tignère mosquito bites were torturing me. Invariably, a few days after being bitten, I suffer about forty-eight hours of that painful and persistent itching which at night can reduce one almost to tears. There may be some truth in the old wives' tale that people tormented by mosquito itch are immune to malaria. I have never had malaria and Rachel's (equally numerous) bites have never itched.

At 7.45 next morning, after a two-hour descent, Rachel exclaimed, 'Stop! Listen!' A distant cock was crowing. We were unlost – or at least within reach of guidance, though it might be incomprehensible.

Soon we were approaching a few dishevelled grass huts. As the

White Devils advanced out of No-Man's-Land everyone fled, leaving a quiverful of arrows scattered by the path. We stood and questioningly called, 'Tignère?'

Cautiously a man peered from behind a hut. We beamed ingratiatingly and repeated, 'Tignère?' He pointed into the sky and vanished.

'Never mind,' said Rachel cheerfully, 'we can't go wrong on this path.' But round the next corner our track, hitherto so colonial-decisive, ended as abruptly as it had begun.

We stared across miles of semi-desert; on the pale grey earth, baked hard and smooth, the only vegetation was a stunted, leafless, thorny bush. And then (Cameroon is full of surprises) a cyclist overtook us – ebullient, ebony black, with high cheekbones and a high IQ. He dismounted and offered us water, then pointed to his cycle tyres, pointed to the ground, pointed to himself and said, 'Tignère! Tignère!' Watching him pedalling off across that pathless waste, weaving his way between the thorn-bushes, we hoped our gratitude had got through to him.

A very hot hour later we lost the tyre prints on a stony slope which marked the beginning of a tangle of ridges and ravines, valleys and plateaux. In such broken terrain you may know where your destination is, but not even the best sense of direction can tell you which route is feasible.

Two even hotter hours later we collapsed on a gloomy ridge-top where the trees were ugly (trees are not often ugly) and the biting flies came in four varieties. Everywhere in sight seemed to have been rainless since the flood. Baboons stared scornfully at us from the undergrowth. Egbert tried chewing brown leaves, spat them out and looked hard-done-by.

'There must be water quite close,' said I knowingly, 'because of the baboons.'

'Like where?' challenged Rachel. 'A trickle ten miles away at the bottom of some ghastly chasm! Anyway they probably get their liquid from fruit and things.'

'*What* fruit?' I demanded, gazing around at the universal infertile dessication.

'If we're not careful,' said Rachel, 'we'll quarrel again.'

At 12.10 p.m., crazed by flies and angst-ridden about Egbert, we recklessly continued and came to a shrunken river before climbing the next – shadeless – ridge. Half-way up I came over all queer.

'Are you going to fall ill?' asked Rachel accusingly.

'I *am* ill!' I replied, surrendering to a tidal wave of self-pity. 'The sun is splitting my head and I've heatstroke dizziness and I want to lie down and die!'

'You might as well go on and die,' advised Rachel sensibly. 'There's no point in lying down here.' She looked towards the top of the ridge. '*Trees*,' she said. 'Keep going! I wonder why you're so feeble about heat?'

'I'm just made that way,' I said sadly, tottering on. 'But I'm unfeeble about cold – d'you remember those midwinter nights in Baltistan at minus forty degrees?'

'No,' said Rachel, 'I don't remember them. You must have wrapped me up well.'

The trees hid quite a large compound where an authoritative man ordered a minion to guide us to his brother's compound, close to the N'gaoundere-Tignère motor-road. That path zig-zagged so unpredictably that without guidance we might have spent four days, instead of four hours, finding the road. Walking through two bush-fires, we were fascinated by Egbert's indifference to asphyxiating clouds of smoke and little flames licking around his hoofs. Equally fascinating was our barefooted guide's indifference to acres of glowing ash.

We felt somewhat ill-at-ease about sorning on that quarterchief's spacious compound and at first the atmosphere did seem slightly strained; but within an hour everyone had relaxed. This was an unhealthy though apparently rich family. Our host had malaria, his senior wife had TB – rather badly – and several other relatives brought jungle-sores, stomach-pains and toothaches to the guest hut. When we left before dawn no one was around to receive dash but we soothed our consciences by recalling the numbers of 'cures' and placebos (glucose tablets) already dispensed.

An hour later our path joined the N'gaoundere-Tignère road, on which there is no motor traffic during the night and not much during the day. But the nocturnal animal traffic is heavy; in the thick red dust we counted the clear hoof- or pad-marks of eight different species. I relished walking through that still grey morning on a motor-road which is also an animal highway.

Seeing a milk-bar some way off the road, I dusted out Egbert's bucket – not hoping for more than a pint since the drought was drastically lowering yields. But a kind man half-filled the bucket and we had three pints each. Thus sustained we continued non-stop, soon finding a jungly cut-short, lively with warthogs, that got us to Tignère by 11.45 a.m.

Opposite Le Metro, kebabs were sizzling over a tar-barrel; having walked fifteen miles on milk only, we recklessly bought four. Tropical health experts recommend fresh-cooked kebabs as relatively 'safe' but here we learned that Cameroonian kebabs demand scrutiny before purchase. These specimens consisted of offal which our cats would spurn even if starving. Gobbets of lights, tail gristle, rubbery intestines and heart valves were interspersed with chunks of green-black tripe, hairy strips of hide and slivers of ear. We gave three of the four to local dogs who wouldn't eat them.

In the Faro bar Gabriel greeted us rapturously, flinging his arms around my neck, kissing me repeatedly and exclaiming, 'Mamma! Mamma! My White Mamma come back!' During our absence no rain had fallen and Tignère's water shortage had become a crisis. The stench of the hotel latrine suggested some form of biochemical warfare and the heat (day and night) was almost unendurable.

All our friends advised against continuing to N'gaoundere. Apart from the delayed rains, there was that little matter – hitherto unconsidered by us – of lions. The Tourist Officer, with whom we shared a few '33's' at Le Metro, had indeed been lion-hunting with Spaniards in the mountains between Tignère and N'gaoundere. For years, he explained, no permits to shoot lions had been issued. Then in 1986 the rule was changed; a leonine population explosion had provoked angry complaints from villagers who were losing many cattle. So now a foreigner could kill a maximum of two male adult lions per day on payment of 45,000 CFA (£100) – plus of course two scarce 300 CFA fiscal stamps to be affixed to two of the four documents to be tendered with the application form for a licence ... I recollected an amusing sketch, in John Hatt's *The Tropical Traveller*, of a headless corpse protruding from a tent in lion country. The comic element in that sketch dwindled as I listened to the Tourist Officer. One way and another, it seemed rather a good idea to return to the cool Grassfields.

Later, as we lay sweating in our room, Rachel said sardonically, 'You're letting down your fans – they like to imagine you're brave. They'll hate to hear about your scooting away in panic at the first rumour of a possible lion.'

I squeezed more ineffectual mosquito-repellent onto my torso and replied, 'I always like to keep my head.'

We slept restlessly. Our oven could not be ventilated without admitting mosquito reinforcements, yet the closed door and window failed to exclude poison-gas fumes from the latrine and mysterious, incessant lawn-mower noises from the next room. (At dawn I saw our neighbour putting a gigantic mobile electric fan, *circa* 1920, into the back of his pick-up truck.) At intervals women came and went and loud disputes about payment were frequent. The electric light switch was broken and the naked bulb directly above the bed, though only twenty-five-watt, did not promote sleep. I yearned for our silent, sweet-smelling resting place on the stony track, then consoled myself with the thought that we were scarcely two days' march from Paradise.

Our enthusiasm for the Tchabal Mbabo baffled all our Cameroonian friends. None would even consider visiting the range, which they envisaged as a place so high and cold that the water sometimes turned to *glass* ... A lonely place, made perilous by swirling mists, yawning chasms, wild animals and even wilder people. A discordant place, where the spirits were uneasy and not all the dangers *natural* ... Here as elsewhere, powerful spirits inhabit the highest local mountains.

By the following evening we were encamped not far from Tourak; Mohammed Mechanic had invited us to stay with him on our return but we shirked another night under a tin roof. He was surprised, next morning, to see us back so soon. 'Did you have a water problem? Here it is very bad! Now the rains are six weeks late!'

Our guide was summoned then: Jeremiah, an aptly named Man from Bamenda who regularly traded in the Tchabal Mbabo 'curing people because they have no hospitals up there'. His trade no doubt explained why so many mountain dwellers had tried to buy medicines from us.

'Where do you get your stocks?' I asked.

'For me no problem!' said Jeremiah. 'Plenty friends work in hospitals, work in drugstores, work for doctors. Getting the antibiotics, pills, tonics, creams, needles – all is easy! Then I do some blending. I wish to be doctor, but there is no money for study.'

I pictured Jeremiah blending tonics and antibiotics before giving an injection with a dirty needle – by what percentage has his enterprise reduced the population of the Tchabal Mbabo? He was a tiresome young man, yet pathetic. Leading us towards the escarpment he denigrated Cameroon. 'This is a bad, poor, backward country. I would like to be born an American man, Americans are all rich men. When you are rich you can have everything, you can be happy. In this country I can never be rich, never be happy ...'

From the crest of a long cultivated ridge Jeremiah pointed to our path, at the base of the mighty mountain wall. Although he accepted his dash with a delighted grin, it clearly surprised him; for all his mercenary talk, he had helped us out of sheer goodwill.

That climb, much of it on a boulder-stairway, recalled certain Nepalese paths and poor Egbert found it gruelling; for long stretches he had to proceed in a series of jumps. The cool, damp forest was creeper-draped and fern-laden; waterfalls flashed down precipices and several clear streams ran across the path. Yet we were only two days' walk from the parched desolation of the Tchabal Gangdaba.

Half-way up a young Fulani woman joined us – slim, muscular, carrying baby on back and several litres of kerosene on head. Her frail son, aged five or six, looked dejectedly exhausted until I gave him a few glucose tablets. Mother had huge sad eyes and a very lovely face too lined for her age. When suddenly we emerged from the still, twilit

166

forest onto bright, windswept grassland our companions turned right and we stopped, for Egbert's sake.

Now our aesthetic appreciation of these mountains was enhanced by the physical relief of having escaped into 'good Irish weather'. The following days reminded us of Indian Summers at home – brilliantly sunny, with cool breezes and chilly evenings.

That evening's campsite was so beautiful we imagined (wrongly) it could never be surpassed. All day we had been climbing, sometimes steeply, and by sunset we were on a broad saddle at about 7,000 feet, surrounded by irregular green summits and overlooking a narrow valley with sheer sides. It was so deep that the three gold-thatched compounds on its grassy floor, each built on a separate hillock, seemed like a view from an aeroplane. Nearby was a convenient burnt copse where we gathered charcoal, while away to the west, above a long band of clear blue-green, the sky became a softly glowing expanse of apricot cloud.

At dusk two shepherds came to greet us, a youth and an older man. They had been rounding up their flock on a distant slope and made a detour to invite us to their compound. But by then our fire was alight, our noodles were simmering, our bags were spread on the close-cropped grass. Understanding that for us all was well, they smiled and bowed graciously, called on Allah to bless us and turned back to their sheep. The older man had one of those unforgettable Fulani faces, fine boned and austere, which vividly reminded me of the Amharas. 'Handsome' is the usual adjective for such a male face; but 'beautiful' (which we so curiously reserve for females) seems more appropriate.

Eating our noodles and sardines, we discussed faces, features, expressions: would that shepherd, should he be unwise enough to migrate to Douala or Yaoundé, *look* the same after a year's rat-racing? How much of his outward beauty had to do with inner content? We could guess what his compound had to offer – not much, in European terms. But his life was completely under his own control and to that extent unstressful and satisfying. He was not dependent on any Big Man, or on an erratic urban labour market, or on internationally fixed prices for cash-crops. True, he was alarmingly dependent on the machinations of someone like Jeremiah should he or any of his family fall ill. Yet in compensation he was his own man, beyond reach of the countless complications devised by modern states to regulate society. And you don't see too many faces like his in 'regulated societies'.

Despite the sunset clouds there was, alas! no need to sleep in. We lay watching a grass-fire on the opposite mountain, a blaze without any of the scarey pyrotechnics of bush or jungle conflagrations. It never increased in area but moved across the slope like some gigantic sinuous crimson reptile. Then came an extravaganza of silent blue and white sheet lightning, wide and dazzling over the summits to the east. 'It's like a disco!' said Rachel unromantically, dozing off. On me this display had an almost hypnotic effect. It continued for over an hour; then I too slept, very deeply, until dawn.

The Tchabal Mbabo's milk-bars more than make up for the lack of '33'. Every morning, in all but the wildest regions, we passed at least one isolated compound – or herd's hut in a corral, where cows were being milked, or had recently been milked. It was necessary to be circumspect in our approach; both humans and animals were likely to be discombobulated when we appeared. On one remote over-grazed mountain an adolescent boy was in charge of some twenty skinny cattle. He slept in a hut indistinguishable from a small haystack and when he saw me crouching in the entrance his arms instinctively went up to cover his face and he whimpered with fear. But once the shock had worn off he gladly provided milk and would indeed have given us his entire supply had I not firmly restrained him. I placed 100 CFA in the empty gourd and we left him scrutinising the coin, looking bewildered.

Those were joyous mornings – sitting in warm sun on grassy slopes, surrounded by clouds of cattle-flies, gratefully relishing our gourds of foaming milk as no nourishment absorbed in Europe can ever be relished. And admiring, meanwhile, the extraordinary skill and courage with which tiny children assist their parents in the complicated ritual of milking. Calves cause most of the complications. Having spent the night apart from Mamma – otherwise there wouldn't be any morning milk – each is allowed a few pulls to stimulate the flow before the milker takes over. Naturally the hungry young resent this system and sometimes register vigorous protests. Moreover, some cows try not to let their milk down when a calf's avid suckling is replaced by a pair of hands. Thus the human-bovine relationship can become quite fraught and small children are often required to hold frustrated calves in such a position that Mamma cannot be sure *who* is getting at her teats. Both girls and boys are given this sometimes hazardous task.

Older boys are entrusted with the considerable responsibility of de-ticking cattle. It is impressive to witness two youngsters, aged perhaps twelve or thirteen, roping the hind legs of a colossal bull, deftly throwing him on his side and holding him immobile while scores of potentially deadly ticks are picked off and crushed between stones.

Because Cameroonian bulls lead normal lives they are as amiable – and almost as numerous – as their wives, mothers, sisters and daughters. Meeting them face-to-face on narrow mountain paths there is no need to panic. The Fulanis are so close to their cattle that men who own hundreds know them all by name. Therefore even the most macho-looking bull – weighing well over a ton, with sharp five-foot horns – is desperately anxious to please; however awkward the topography, he will make way for human travellers. These Zebu are worth, on average, about 90,000 CFA (£200) each. Many simple compound-dwellers own 18 million CFA (£40,000) on the hoof, though naturally they don't think of their beloved herds in such demeaning terms. As so many non-Fulanis complained to us, they will only occasionally sell a few bulls to a Hausa butcher when cash is needed for some exceptional expenditure – perhaps to pay a hospital bill, or build a new hut.

One midday we approached a rocky summit, intending to lunch there; by then 'siesta' had dropped out of our vocabulary. All morning we had been climbing to reach this highest point in the Tchabal Mbabo. Many cattle were grazing on the wide slope, then faintly we heard sweet music. A solitary youth stood on a rock on the summit, playing his bamboo flute – silhouetted against the sky, his short gown fluttering in the breeze. He was gazing away from us and we paused, enchanted, to listen. Then he turned – saw us – and leaped off the rock to seize his long stick. We waved reassuringly (or so we hoped) before continuing upwards, expecting to see more grassland ahead – and perhaps another series of the region's slightly phallic peaks.

Instead, we found ourselves on the north-west brink of the range, looking straight down on dense forest 3,000 feet below. This was the most astounding visual experience of the entire trek. We soon discovered that the Mbabo escarpment here forms a twenty-five-mile semicircle; and below the rock-wall eleven profound ravines – extending for miles from the base of the escarpment and separated by other, naked chasms – retain their primeval vegetation. This forest is untouched and untouchable, protected by the terrain from all intruders. I felt an overwhelming sense of reverence and privilege as we gazed down into those rare and precious vestiges of the world as it was before man.

We tried to trek close to the escarpment but, though our path repeatedly approached it, to *follow* it was physically impossible. And the harmattan was still thwarting us; to the north, beyond the ravines, grey blurred hills faded rapidly into blankness.

That afternoon we camped early, tempted on Egbert's behalf by lush grazing in a hidden 'bowl-valley' enclosed by steep green slopes. This site had an almost fairytale feel; it was the sort of place small children imagine when they long to escape from the tiresome adult world. A deep cold stream flowed through it but, oddly, none of the local vegetation burnt well. Luckily dried cow-pats were plentiful and after some effort I got a dung-fire going – smoky, acrid and slow. By sunset we were enjoying soup and noodles and several mugs of heavily sugared Bournvita.

The next day was notable for a shortage of people, a superabundance of wildlife and an even more varied than usual terrain. The many climbs were formidable, often on narrow tricky paths above dizzying drops. At this stage we were, we hoped, making our way back to Makelele. We remarked on our fitness; gradients that would have exhausted us when we left Doi's compound now felt like exhilarating challenges. On the morrow we were going to need all that fitness.

At 5.15 p.m. indirect signs of humanity appeared: four donkeys, grazing not far above the path. Two were winsome mares and Egbert greeted them appreciatively, becoming indelicately excited.

'Damn!' I said. 'He'll have to be tethered tonight!'

Soon the path dropped into a cleft where clear water flowed beneath tangled trees that made it seem already dusk. Here we performed our river ritual, observed from a little distance by a Peeping Tom baboon. There were no other signs of humanity as a final tough climb took us onto the most beautiful of all our Cameroonian campsites.

When Egbert had been turned loose (until bedtime) I neglected my Promethean duties, stood by the edge of our site and gave thanks to be alive in such a glorious place. Opposite, to the south, beyond a mile of parched grassland dotted with low trees, towered a massive solitary mountain of sheer grey rock. To the south-east, in the background, rose that mighty wall of blue mountains we had just crossed. And in the foreground, on a long flat-topped ridge, vividly green grass and a collapsed straw hut marked a deserted corral. Behind the camp our ledge merged into a patch of jungle, above which a steep mountain-wall, all rock and scrub, cut off the view to the north. A mile or so to the west this wall joined a complex knot of still higher grassy mountains on which sheets of flame were visible after sunset – suggesting dwellings not too far away. Some twenty yards from our camp a stream was audible, though invisible and inaccessible, in a deep densely forested ravine. From my high vantage point I could see, simultaneously, four separate warthog families going about their supper business, a baboon colony on one ridge and five russet antelope bounding across the grassy plain. Then swishing leaves made me look around, to see three colobus monkeys staring from the nearby trees.

Rachel meanwhile had been collecting firewood. 'When you've quite finished being ecstatic,' she said, 'maybe we could have something to eat?'

While tending our noodles I remarked on the pleasure of being spontaneously *with* wild animals – just happening to meet them, in the course of an ordinary day, rather than going to a game-park and being driven around in a vehicle by a warden.

'I wouldn't,' observed Rachel, 'call *this* an ordinary day. But I suppose you would.'

She did however agree with my main argument. In Cameroon's game-parks one can see lions, elephants, hippos, giraffes; but a warthog or antelope, met as it were socially, is worth ten lions viewed from a Land Rover.

As we ate by starlight Rachel wondered, 'Where do we go from here? We're pretty thoroughly lost – surprise, surprise!'

That was a nasty crack. At one junction, passed during the early afternoon, she had advised, 'We should go down *that* way, to get to Makelele.' Then she tolerantly gave in to my longing for the alternative, upward route; and now it seemed we were very far from any main path. Our ledge was pathless; the faint trail we had been following ended at the stream and we had found our own way up the rough bare slope.

'Who cares about being lost?' I said. 'This site is the perfect end to a perfect day!'

'Except for poor Eggles,' said Rachel. '*Must* we tether him? Those donkeys are miles away!'

'Hardly two miles,' I calculated. 'And donkey mares are permanently in season – the only animals, apart from humans, that are always ready for sex.'

'Don't be crude!' said Rachel. And then she reluctantly tethered 'poor Eggles' to a stout sapling half-way between our camp and the edge of the ledge.

9

Exit Egbert

THUDDING HOOVES WOKE me at 1.30 a.m. Egbert passed so close that his panic-stricken snorting was audible – and infectious. Simultaneously I heard the alarm bark of baboons and the eerie wailing and grunting of a family of warthogs (parents and four young) whom we had noticed bedding down at sunset in the nearby jungle. Scrambling to my feet, I saw tree-tops moving irregularly against the starry sky; the colobus monkeys were also worried.

'Something's wrong!' I said urgently. 'Egbert's loose and panicking!'

When Rachel failed to react I kicked her awake just as Egbert, frightened by the warthogs' aggressive pandemonium, swung around and again galloped past us, going towards his tethering site. Before following him we had to put on our boots: an unbreakable rule, whatever the crisis. During this brief delay the warthogs maintained their hysterical protest and we could hear no Egbert-noises.

As quickly as was prudent by starlight, we scouted the edge of the ledge. Again we were virtually torchless; in Tignère a crafty Hausa merchant had sold us two apparently new but in fact dud batteries. Already one had expired and the other was producing only a faint glimmer. As we shone this inadequate light over the steep slopes it picked out two large eyes some fifteen feet away. 'There he is!' exclaimed Rachel. But at once the eyes vanished, without any of the noises one would expect if a horse were moving away.

We conferred. As the nearest dependable hospital was hundreds of miles away, common sense suggested that we should not risk broken bones; to have left the ledge by starlight would have been to invite an even greater disaster than the loss of our horse.

Returning to camp, we noted that Egbert had bolted with wholly uncharacteristic force, breaking the sapling and taking with him twenty yards of rope. 'Almost certainly,' opined Rachel, 'he was scared by a snake.'

The monkeys and warthogs had quietened down, apart from an occasional bark or snort, and soon Rachel was asleep again. I lay looking up at the stars and hoping – with the sort of desperate intensity that feels like a physical effort – that the dawn would reveal Egbert placidly grazing nearby. Given the nature of our relationship, this was a not unreasonable hope. We had then been trekking together for six weeks and usually he had been left loose at night unless within reach of tempting crops. Even when I led him some distance away, to the best available grazing, his tendency was to move closer and closer to camp.

I was already patrolling the edge of the ledge when the stars began to fade and the blackness to become grey. As the light strengthened my hope ebbed. Egbert was nowhere to be seen. I felt a ridiculous foreboding – ridiculous because he might be hidden close by in any of a hundred corners. Now the chaotic magnificence of this region filled me with despair – its deep forested ravines, its isolated patches of jungle, its wide expanses of grassland, its long, steep, scrubby ridges, its many twisting narrow valleys, its immense irregular slopes where jackals lived amidst a wilderness of massive boulders. Over supper I had said to Rachel, 'This must be the very best campsite in Cameroon!' Now I was saying to myself, 'This must be the very worst place in the world to lose a horse!'

When Rachel joined me we surveyed the scene through equine eyes. Mares apart, it seemed unlikely that of his own volition Egbert would have wandered far. Our ledge offered the best grazing for miles around and at the end of an exceptionally tough day's trekking it was inconceivable that he would have chosen to explore this rugged terrain by starlight: he wasn't that sort of person. So we began our search by returning to the donkey herd – not even thinking of breakfast.

If asked to specify my unhappiest experience, in quarter of a century's travelling, I would have to say 'Egbert's loss'. It was a disaster on two levels, practical and emotional. How were we ever to get back to a village and food without an animal to carry our gear? Would we have to abandon much of it? If so, how were we to survive for the remaining six weeks of our trek? Those were disturbing questions, yet secondary. From the moment of our meeting, Egbert had endeared himself to me in a special way and as time passed I came to love him more than any other equine travelling-companion – which is saying a lot, for on three continents I have been lucky with my pack-animals. Thus it was the loss of Egbert as a friend, rather than as a convenience, that truly devastated me. I knew my reaction was absurd; at the end of the trek we would have to part from him. But I was conditioned to that and he would then be left (one hoped) in comfortable circumstances with a kind owner. *Losing* him was another sort of experience. *If only* I hadn't argued with Rachel about that path to Makelele! And I was haunted by the implications of those twenty yards of rope. If we didn't find him, if the rope had ensnared him ... His Irish head-collar was so strong and well fitting that he could neither break it nor slip out of it. All that day the vision of Egbert slowly dying of thirst gave me superhuman energy.

I needed it during the next twelve hours. From the donkey herd, whose female complement showed no signs of having been wooed by Egbert, we climbed a high grassy mountain in search of a compound where we might be able to enlist helpers – offering a substantial reward – and buy eggs and milk. (During the small hours I had heard cocks crowing somewhere in that direction.) Half-way up our hopes soared when a distant herd of eight horses and foals came into view. Eagerly we turned aside to investigate them but that long, exhausting detour ended in disappointment.

'Maybe he tried to get off with one of those mares,' I said, 'and was attacked again. Perhaps he's quite near, still hoping to ingratiate himself.'

We split up then, to search all the obvious places, but in vain.

When we found the compound – three ramshackle huts near the windswept brink of the spectacular escarpment – no man was around and the two young women and their many children were much too scared even to attempt to communicate in sign language.

As we debated where to look next a bay with a white blaze appeared a hundred yards or so below the compound – then disappeared behind a hillock. 'Egbert!' whooped Rachel joyously. I thought so too, while not allowing myself to believe it.

We hastened down – and this time the disappointment felt like a physical blow. In appearance that horse might have been Egbert's twin, but he was very ill – scarcely able to walk – which explained his being alone. Miserably we returned to the high ground, passed the compound and spent the next half-hour searching a patch of nearby jungle.

On our way back we heard confused shouting and screaming and saw eight children and a dog, followed by a woman with baby on back, racing down the slope from the compound to a group of horses. Rachel at once realised what was happening.

'No!' she cried, gripping my arm. 'No – it's too awful – it can't be! They're *killing* him!'

I stared – then looked away. The bay was lying on the ground, being trampled and kicked by three stallions. Moments later the family reached the scene and the older children drove off the attackers. The woman knelt by the victim and raised his head; he was still alive.

'It's a sound instinct,' I said, trying to be rational. 'He's *very* sick, so Nature suggests euthanasia.'

'I hope they don't blame us,' muttered Rachel. 'Bad ju-ju!'

Again we hurried down that slope. The family seemed in a state of shock; they looked at us apprehensively but had recovered from the panic induced by our first appearance. To show sympathy for what we assumed to be a family misfortune, I knelt by the wretched horse's head and tried to give him a glucose tablet. When he spat it out the woman expertly re-administered it; this was not the first time she had doctored a horse. But my futile gesture of solidarity greatly complicated the situation. Gradually we realised that the sick horse was a stray, that his attackers belonged to the family, that they saw us as his owners (hence our running to him earlier and now giving 'medicine') and so they felt guilty.

'What a muddle!' lamented Rachel.

'What a ghastly coincidence!' said I.

Everyone looked bewildered when we left, apparently abandoning our sick horse. It had been quite impossible to convey that we did *not* own this bay but were desperately searching for an almost identical animal.

We returned to camp by a different route, probing every corner on the way – every horse-accessible thicket, every scattering of large boulders behind one of which our Eggles might be dozing.

'If we're not careful,' said Rachel gloomily, 'we'll accidentally corner a daddy warthog and that'll be the end of a Murphy.'

At noon we rested briefly on our ledge, eating nuts and planning the afternoon's strategy. Then we again split up, to quarter the grassy plain.

Eventually I found the hoof-prints of, unmistakably, a *galloping* horse. When Rachel had rejoined me we followed them down a steep red cliff on a dusty cow-path – one not used at this season, for the prints of a solitary horse remained clear. I had no doubt that these were Egbert's; having walked behind a horse for six weeks, one becomes very familiar with every nuance of his hoof-marks. Around each bend I expected to find him dead with a broken neck – or, still worse, alive with a broken leg. At the foot of the cliff we lost the prints on rock-hard ground, then briefly found them again, then lost them near the brink of a hitherto unseen and unsuspected chasm.

It is a measure of the unpredictability of this terrain that such a chasm – half a mile wide and some 600 feet deep – could suddenly appear at one's feet. In normal circumstances this mighty fissure, its floor covered with virgin forest, would have seemed a thrilling sight. But now, staring over the edge, I shuddered – picturing a terrified

Egbert (unnerved by a python?) galloping through the darkness to his doom.

'Let's be sensible,' said Rachel briskly. 'If he'd fallen over here we'd see a mark on the trees, they're so close together. A horse wouldn't fall through neatly, leaving the branches to close over again. And if he didn't fall through, breaking branches, he'd be supported by them and visible, even from here.'

This blast of scientific logic partially reassured me and we climbed back up the red cliff, to reach a saddle linking the stony northern ridge and the higher grassy mountains to the south-west.

An hour later Rachel was leading around the edge of a jungle-filled cleft. Abruptly she stopped, staring at the dusty path. 'Some puss!' she noted laconically.

Apart from their size, the leopard pug-marks were identical to those muddy prints left by our own cats on clean sheets and important typescripts. We followed them for some twenty yards, then they disappeared. To stiffen my upper lip I recalled that leopards don't attack horses where Fast Food is abundant – monkeys, antelopes, warthog piglets.

'But a horse wouldn't know that,' Rachel pointed out. 'So naturally he'd bolt. I'm pretty sure those eyes we saw weren't Egbert's – he couldn't have disappeared so silently.'

We agreed then that a prowling leopard would adequately explain both Egbert's bolting and the alarm registered by our fellow-sleepers on the ledge.

By 6 p.m. we were physically and emotionally exhausted but not yet despairing; at least we hadn't found a corpse in any of the area's obvious death-traps. Then, as we collected firewood, a solitary horse appeared against the sky on the eastern ridge where we planned to start the morrow's search. All day I had been cursing myself for having lost the binoculars and now my self-reproach reached a crescendo.

'*Could* it be?' I wondered, straining my eyes. 'It's a *dark* horse, it just *might* be!'

Action was indicated so we rolled up our flea-bags. The remaining daylight would see us to the ridge, if we pushed ourselves, but we would have to spend the night there. Yet again we scrambled down and down, then up and up – adrenalin stimulated by hope. The sun set as we reached the crest of the ridge. No horse was visible and we crossed eagerly to the other side. This time the disappointment, though desolating, was more bearable.

'We're getting used to being emotionally tortured,' observed Rachel.

Again it was a sick horse, with the same symptoms as the other: an oddly arched back, stiff movements, starey coat, runny eyes, laboured breathing. We deduced a local epidemic of some dire equine disease and at once I envisaged Egbert picking it up and languishing in misery. 'Pull yourself together!' said Rachel. 'You're worrying more today about Egbert than you *ever* worried about me!'

'But I've never *lost* you,' I pointed out. 'And now let's look for somewhere level to sleep – in minutes it'll be dark.'

Then a flicker of white at the base of the ridge caught our eye; a young man was praying outside a hitherto unobserved herd's hut. As we moved towards him he noticed us and stopped praying. We waved and shouted cheerfully. He grabbed his stick, screamed at us and gesticulated wildly, pointing towards the high eastern mountains.

'Does he know we've lost a horse?' wondered Rachel. 'Is he trying to say Egbert went that way?'

When we quickened our pace – hope spurting again – the herd began to saunter away from us, his stick behind his shoulders. Then suddenly his nerve broke. Drawing his long gown above his knees he fled at Olympic speed: rarely have I seen a human move so fast. Within moments he had disappeared into a scrub-filled hollow.

'Poor fellow!' exclaimed Rachel. 'He thinks we're devils.'

Outside the well-made straw hut we sat in the dusk, sharing a packet of glucose tablets for supper, while a small herd – bulls, cows, calves – efficiently put themselves to bed in an adjacent thorn-fenced corral.

'Poor fellow!' repeated Rachel. 'Where *is* he now? Maybe he'll never recover from this trauma! And what about the calves? They should be separated from their mothers – now there'll be no morning milk – we're wrecking the whole system!'

'He may return with a companion,' I said.

Rachel shook her head. 'Not a hope! Who'd face two white devils after dark?'

By 8 p.m. I was aware of having been awake since 1.30 a.m. 'Let's move into the hut,' suggested Rachel. 'This ground is all bumps and stones and there's nowhere grassy that isn't on a slope.'

Conditioning is an odd thing; one doesn't normally sleep uninvited in other people's dwellings and guilt consumed me as we bent low to enter that hut. Our feeble torch, conserved until then, showed that it was neat and clean with a narrow 'bed' of goat-skins on grass to one side. Our involuntary host had been about to cook his supper; a few sticks smouldered near the entrance, beside a bowl of maize-flour. It seemed he came of an affluent family. On his bed lay a Nigerian mat-roll containing two soft blankets, a smart sweater, a torch that didn't work, a box of matches, a few kolanuts and a box of sugar-lumps – the last a luxury bought only by the wealthiest in the Mbabo area. A few enamel plates were slotted into the wall, between straw and poles, and a sack of maize-flour stood by the bed. A row of clean enamel bowls, ready for the morning's milk, reactivated Rachel's angst.

'Never mind,' I soothed, 'we can leave 1,000 CFA in the sugar.'

'We mustn't use his clean blankets,' decided Rachel, 'we're too filthy and smelly.'

So we laid our flea-bags (scarcely less filthy and smelly) on the goat-skins. But despite my exhaustion and a comfortable bed I woke often. Gazing out at the stars – pulsating and brilliant – I wondered what *exactly* had happened ... Was Egbert still alive? On returning to camp might we find him there? Or was there a possibility that he had been stolen?

We quitted the hut before dawn, leaving all as we had found it (apart from the sugar box) and hoping our host would not feel compelled to burn his contaminated dwelling.

Between us, during the next four hours, we must have covered at least sixteen miles – ascending and descending, peering into jungle patches, following stream beds, scrutinising little valleys from above. We found two more tiny compounds where communication was imposs-ible but milk was offered.

Back at base we ate more nuts – there was nothing else left – and admitted defeat. Surveying as much of the surrounding chaos as was visible from the camp, we realised that our task had in fact been simplified by the nature of the terrain: many places didn't have to be searched because no equine animal could possibly reach them. By now we felt certain that Egbert was not straying within a radius of eight miles or so. Yet it was improbable that he had wandered farther on his own, simply because he could not have done so without tackling gradients that no sane horse, surrounded by good grazing, would even consider.

'Either he's been stolen,' I said, 'or he's dead in one of those ravines. And why should anyone steal a horse when the place is swarming with them? I think he's dead.'

'I don't,' said Rachel. 'I'm *sure* he's been stolen. The local horses are wild, you can tell no one ever goes near them. Egbert's valuable if you need a broken horse.'

'So *who* stole him?' I demanded. 'How many people have we seen since we got here? That timid family and a few men near the other compounds ...'

'I wouldn't trust the two we met this morning,' interrupted Rachel. 'Maybe he's been horsenapped and they're waiting for us to offer a big reward – or hoping we'll buy a donkey instead. If only someone spoke a *few* words of French!'

I looked at my watch; it was 10.40 a.m. 'Somehow we've got to hire a donkey,' I said, 'and it's no good trying to communicate with the locals. Let's go towards where we saw that grass-fire.'

A difficult rocky climb took us onto quite a big path, which we later discovered was a route to Makelele. By one of those happy coincidences which spangled our Cameroonian experience, we reached the path as an elderly man in a sky-blue robe was passing by. He had the air of a man on a long journey but paused to greet us – and proved to be a brilliant sign linguist. Had a hidden television crew been filming our encounter they would certainly have produced a prize-winner: the Year's Funniest Film, with my excellent imitation of a donkey braying as its highlight. In retrospect, one marvels at the complicated communications sometimes possible despite language barriers. It is safe to assume that we were something new in this man's life – two filthy, haggard and more than slightly *distraites* Whites who had inexplicably lost a horse and were in need of a donkey to carry gear to Sambolabbo. Yet after five minutes of intense concentration he had grasped the essentials of the problem. A donkey was available in Hama Aoudi, the village from which he had come. Like our cyclist benefactor, he pointed to the sole of his new plastic shoe, then pointed to its print in the dust. By following his trail, we could hire an 'Eee-aw, Eee-aw'. Wordlessly but powerfully, he conveyed sympathy for our predicament. There were tears in my eyes as I gratefully shook his hand; understandably, I was in an over-wrought state.

That clear path was, at least towards Hama Aoudi, short-lived. Without shoe-prints we would have got hopelessly lost in a steep wilderness of volcanic boulders, leading to miles of undulating grassland criss-crossed by the usual cattle-tracks. There were no compounds in sight. Ahead, some two miles away, a long ridge of grey shale and loose rock stretched across the green plateau like a man-made wall. Crossing it we met a nomad migration, including three bulls carrying household goods. Their herds – an old lean horseman and two youths on foot – glanced at us with a blend of timidity and scorn. Here the shoe-prints were obliterated but from the ridge-top Hama Aoudi could be seen in the distance, a prosperous-looking crescent of compounds at the base of jumbled mountains.

Half an hour later we were hesitating near the first compound – some distance away on our left, below the (now clear) path. Then a young man came towards us from that compound, carrying a small suitcase on his head, a trannie in one hand and a brolly in the other. Here was the answer to Rachel's prayer: someone who spoke a *few* words of French. Babale Mbambo's words were very few, yet he understood Rachel well enough. Frowning and looking worried, he beckoned us to follow him to the compound. There we could borrow or hire a pack-donkey, but the owner was up on the grassland, contemplating his cattle, so we must wait . . .

An oddly unreal quality marks negotiations between people of vastly different cultures who are all the time struggling to overcome a language barrier. The rest of that day required us to abandon our own way of conducting affairs and take things as they came.

While a youth went to fetch the donkey owner we sat on the verandah of a new guest hut, the only tin-roofed building in an attractive, shrub-surrounded compound. Its two empty rooms looked raw, as though the builders had just left. When a boy brought a large basin of boiled milk we emptied it so fast that Babale looked anxious, then led us to the next compound (his uncle's, some 200 yards away) and ordered food.

Uncle lay on his iron bed in a thatched hut listening to a Ramadan prayer-service being broadcast from an N'gaoundere mosque. His handshake was limp and fever-hot; he had been ill for weeks, Babale said. As we relaxed on goat-skins small children peeped – then fled, shrieking with half-real alarm, when we greeted them. Uncle smiled wanly and asked Babale to explain that nowadays village children don't see Whites. Angst struck again when a boy arrived with freshly cooked fufu and a generous bowl of tender mutton in thick gravy – at a time of day when nobody cooks *and* during Ramadan ... But despite our guilt we fell upon the food; we had after all recently expended vast amounts of energy, fuelled only by glucose tablets and nuts. As we ate Babale brewed strong tea in a kettle on a fire in the centre of the floor, then drew a battered holdall from under Uncle's bed and produced four large white 'shop buns'. Even by local standards these were *very* stale, yet to us delicious. And the symbolism was moving; shop buns are Hama Aoudi's equivalent of caviare.

Returning to the donkey compound, we remarked on the pitiable state of Uncle's maize crop. Babale looked doleful and said that even if the rains came now they would be too late. Those parched and stunted shoots would have to be dug up and the fields replanted.

Outside a small hut Babale removed his shoes and respectfully called, 'Salaam Alaikum! Salaam Alaikum!' as he bent to look through the entrance. Two grey-bearded gentlemen emerged – brothers, it seemed – both wearing flowery robes with the star and crescent embroidered on their caps. These donkey owners were *malloums* and Babale showed them the sort of deference normally reserved for chiefs.

Two perilously unsteady chairs – evidently the products of some carpenter's unpromising apprentice – had been placed on the verandah in anticipation of our return. A twenty-minute palaver followed and at one point the elders seemed upset and angry. Later Babale hinted that they believed Egbert to have been stolen; the three families who lived near our camp were not highly regarded locally.

Gradually it emerged that all our hosts' donkeys had gone to Sambolabbo on a trade mission and wouldn't be back for days. (At the time – significantly – it never occurred to me to wonder why we weren't told this on arrival.) Then it transpired that Babale, when we met him, had been setting out for the village of Mbabo, via our camp and the 'timid' compound. The elders suggested that before going on his way he should accompany us to Hama Aoudi's Chief, who might be able to supply a donkey. But now new hope was flickering – though faintly. Just possibly Babale's intervention might bring about a reunion ... So we chose to return to camp with our interpreter. The elders then ceremoniously presented me with six new-laid eggs which I carefully placed in my bush-shirt breast pockets; by then I had brought the transportation of raw eggs to a fine art.

Babale's route – an effective but nightmarish cut-short – bypassed the shale ridge and the conglomeration of boulders. Instead, it wound level around a bulge not far below the summit of the highest grassy mountain. This very narrow path was treacherously strewn with loose pebbles and overhung a 400-foot drop. On the long climb up from Hama Aoudi I had had to slow down for Babale's sake; here he and Rachel had to slow down for mine. 'There are horses for courses,' shouted Rachel, watching me crawling around that ghastly bulge, my eyes averted from the chasm inches away to the right. In middle age one's head for heights deteriorates dramatically.

At the timid compound Father was as usual away with his cattle and Babale resolutely refused to talk to the womenfolk, either because that would have been improper or because he thought females too inferior to do business with – his attitude suggested the latter reason. We then urged him to leave us to fend for ourselves; he had already done far more to help two strangers than might reasonably have been expected. However, having ordered the eldest boy to fetch Father he moved to a nearby herd's hut and lay down to sleep under a thin anti-fly cloak taken from his suitcase.

Rachel looked anguished. 'He's devoting his whole day to us! And we can't give *him* money! What can we give him?'

'The watch,' I said. Our gift-box held one good wrist-watch, purchased for just such an emergency.

We lay outside the herd's hut – envying Babale his fly-deterring cloak – and I remarked that his endeavours on our behalf perfectly illustrated the African attitude to time. When we met he was setting out on a long journey of some importance; he had an appointment with an 'official' (function unspecified) in Mbabo. Yet our difficulty, suddenly interposed between him and his goal, at once deflected him. What *that moment* presented took precedence over the *future* expectations of someone awaiting him in distant Mbabo. Had that someone been a White official they would very likely have reprimanded him for breaking an appointment and would not have been placated by his explanation that he was 'helping people'.

When Father arrived an hour later another long palaver began. He claimed to know nothing about Egbert's disappearance; until then he had believed us to be the owners of the dying horse. The four local donkeys belonged not to him but to Dawa, who lived in one of the other two compounds we had visited during our search. Possibly the stallion might be borrowed, if anyone could catch him.

Dawa's compound lay below this mountain-top and Babale began the day's third palaver from the edge of a sheer 200-foot cliff. The three of us sat on the brink, while Babale and Dawa shouted at each other. Then Dawa and a friend slowly ascended to our level – obviously feeling the effects of their Ramadan fast – and all five of us sauntered off, apparently in search of the donkey herd. We found Dawa unlikeable; he had a disconcertingly cruel mouth and shifty eyes. If anyone had stolen Egbert, it was probably he.

Very gradually, this palaver bore fruit. The stallion could carry our gear as far as Hama Aoudi, but no farther. From there chiefs would organise transport to Sambolabbo via Makelele. On arrival in Hama Aoudi we were to unload the donkey, point him towards home and leave him to return on his own – a distance of some six miles. When we questioned this procedure Babale reassured us, 'He will always hurry back to his wives and children!'

An hour was spent finding the donkey herd and then it took five of us forty minutes to capture the stallion. Few people realise how swiftly donkeys can move, when *they* want to ... We optimistically named him Angelo. (Many years ago, I had an unfulfilling relationship with an Ethiopian donkey named Satan.) At once Angelo's forelegs were hobbled with a length of vine torn from a tree and as strong as nylon rope. Surprisingly, he did not object to this restriction and we then took a crash-course in the management of Cameroonian pack-donkeys. These are driven, not led, and are steered in the right direction by the waving of a very long stick, from behind, in such a way that the donkey glimpses the stick out of the corner of his eye. We practised this technique by driving him to the camp – a difficult uphill route – with Dawa in attendance. Babale had urged us to load up quickly and spend the night in his uncle's compound. He disapproved of our sleeping in the bush and overlooked the fact that beginning the journey at 6 p.m. would mean driving an unknown donkey over a wide plateau by starlight: not a very practical idea.

Dawa left us when we reached the ledge, offering no advice about loading Angelo. We then had a dress-rehearsal, in preparation for a dawn start. Ingeniously Rachel adjusted the girth and crupper – no mean feat – and we loaded up. The effect was comic; Egbert's blanket met under Angelo's belly and he looked like a furry toy beneath the load. But he accepted it philosophically and seemed bemused when it was at once removed.

We were boiling our eggs when Babale, to whom we had already said goodbye, loomed out of the dusk. He had decided to spend the night at the timid compound but then began to worry lest, without an interpreter, we might have problems at Hama Aoudi. So he had undertaken another hour's hard walking, on his Ramadan-empty tummy, to write a letter explaining our requirements. We provided pen and paper and he spent fifteen minutes laboriously requesting the Chief to help us, in Arabic script. Like many pupils of Cameroon's Koranic schools, he was literate only in Arabic. This final thoughtful gesture quite overwhelmed us.

At 5.45 a.m. we left our most beautiful and most ill-starred campsite – forever, as we then mistakenly thought. Dawa had warned us not to unhobble Angelo until we got to our destination, but his pathetic efforts to hop up dangerously rocky paths prompted us to risk freeing him and he behaved impeccably – trotting briskly, with ears pricked, once we reached the plateau.

Hama Aoudi's Chief was as surly as the village's *malloums* had been gracious. Leaving Rachel and Angelo to wait outside his spacious compound, I caused much alarm by inadvertently intruding on the purdah quarter. Eventually I found the fat, grey-haired, scowling Chief sitting cross-legged in the morning sun reading an ancient edition of the Koran, inscribed in soot-ink and blood on yellowed parchment. Bibliomanically, I ached to examine this manuscript. But the Chief treated me with open contempt; appearances can count for a lot in Cameroon and by then I looked like something off a refuse dump. A minion was ordered to read Babale's letter, the Chief declining to receive any document from my filthy paws. Happily the minion was sympathetic. When my entourage had been summoned many small hands unloaded Angelo, our two-litre water-bottle was filled with milk and two of the Chief's thirty-four children (boys aged ten or so) were told to carry our gear to Makelele. To simplify life, I presented the picket and saddle to the Chief – who didn't thank me. Meanwhile Rachel had led Angelo back to the track, where at once he began purposefully to trot towards his wives and children.

An hour's fast walking took us to Makelele, where our old friends provided bowls of milk and the Chief ordered Ibi, a muscular young Bantu, to carry our load to Sambolabbo. We protested that it was much too heavy for one man, however muscular, but our scruples were laughingly dismissed. Not for the first time, we remarked on the medieval quality of Cameroonian rural life. The exquisite courtesy of the Fulani ruling caste seemed not to belong to the twentieth century. And the relationship between the Chief and Ibi was – starkly – master-slave.

Twenty minutes after our arrival we were leaving Makelele; that day was freakishly without delays – everywhere events moved at an un-Cameroonian tempo. Then the Chief came hurrying after us, waving a hen above his head and followed by a youth bearing a tray of gigantic tomatoes and half a stale baguette. The tomatoes and bread were for sustenance *en route*; the hen was for our supper. Appalled, we watched her being tied to the load on Ibi's head. 'This is worse than factory farming!' muttered Rachel hyperbolically.

We were about to continue when a tall, pot-bellied, dark-skinned man hastened down the slope on our right. He spoke fluent French and had an air of authority; he was a vet based in Banyo but with a junior wife and family in Makelele. His work took him all over the Tchabal Mbabo and he was quite sure that Egbert had been horse-napped.

'Please give me your address,' he said. 'To find this horse may take many weeks – you were among bad people – I know them! But if he is found I will write to you.'

We gave him the Parkinsons' address in Bamenda; later we realised that we should have told him about Egbert's hernia as a 'distinguishing mark'.

Four hours later we were in Sambolabbo; the cut-short was so drastic and so perilous that we felt glad to have missed it with Egbert. A double guilt afflicted us as we watched poor Ibi toiling up near-vertical slopes like there would be no tomorrow – for him – while the wretched hen gasped on his head as though about to die of heatstroke. It soon became plain that Ibi was malarial, with a high temperature and severe headache; he made no fuss but his condition was dreadfully evident.

'What must it feel like,' said Rachel, 'to have a malaria headache *under* a horse's load?'

Hoping that Ibi might not be fasting, we offered him food, glucose and pain-killers. But he was strictly observing Ramadan and, though pouring sweat all the way, he drank not even a sip of water. A learned *malloum* could have told him that he was being over-scrupulous, that 'the fever' released him from his fasting obligations.

Seeing the beer-truck outside Andrew's bar, incredulity was our first reaction; we had been prepared to spend days in Sambolabbo, awaiting that truck. Now Andrew told us that within an hour it would be leaving for Banyo and on payment of 1,500 CFA (about £3.40) each we could have seats on the crates.

Having dashed Ibi in proportion to the circumstances we urged him to rest until the following day; he grinned broadly and without even a moment's pause headed back to Makelele.

As we relaxed over '33's, Rachel began to think about the ethics of adaptability. Should we have been assertive in Makelele and *insisted* on two men to carry? Should we have refused to accept the hen, thus sparing her the misery of that journey? When is it right to impose one's own standards on other people? When is it wrong *not* to do so? At home it would be inconceivable for either of us to condone – let alone cause – such cruelty to a man or a hen. Yet had Rachel not raised this question it would never have occurred to me. I had agonised every arduous step of the way over Ibi's palpable misery and at each of three streams I watered the hen through a leaf. But it never entered my mind that *I* could have averted the sufferings of both.

'So,' said Rachel, 'you believe "when in Rome . . ."?'

'I suppose so,' I replied, rather doubtfully. 'And yet, I wouldn't give in to Doi about antibiotics for Egbert – then I did assert myself.'

'But that's different,' said Rachel swiftly. 'That's not the *African* way of doing things – it's Africa messed up by Europe misunderstood.'

On our second '33' we agreed that in practice one can't be selectively adaptable.

'If you're going to live in the bush,' I said, 'you take the rough with the smooth. You don't expect "special treatment" because you're White and you don't expect the locals to treat each other differently because you're around. In theory perhaps we should have maintained White liberal standards in Makelele – which would have upset and bewildered and hurt the chief. *And* deprived Ibi of an obviously welcome fistful of CFA.'

'You'd have been a rotten DC,' said Rachel. 'You'd have left your district as you found it, complete with human sacrifices!'

'Yes,' I said, 'probably I would.'

We then planned our future: next day a bush-taxi from Banyo to Bamenda, where our load would be reduced to what could be carried in one rucksack – the carrying to be shared on alternate days as we trekked north through the high Grassfields.

Viewing the landscape between Sambolabbo and Banyo, from the top of the beer-truck, we had identical thoughts. All the rivers and streams we remembered crossing a few weeks earlier were now dried up. Had we been trekking as planned, just to the west of this area, the drought would almost certainly have defeated us. 'Perhaps,' said Rachel, 'Egbert's loss is a blessing in disguise – for him and for us.'

Subjectively I couldn't agree; objectively I had to agree.

10

Fun Among the Fons

IN BAMENDA JOY and John Parkinson lavishly provided support of every sort: moral, sartorial, alcoholic and cartographic. They advised on our new route and John lent us detailed though rather elderly French maps – Second Impression 1972, the most up-to-date available. He warned that within fifteen years some villages change their names and/or locations. Some mountain paths also change, as the rains sweep them away and replacements are devised. But despite these limitations the Parkinson sheets, at 1:200 000, were a huge improvement on our USAF charts.

From Bafut, fifteen miles east of Bamenda, we planned to go up the Metchum valley, wander through the Aghem highland to Wum, cross a few mountains to Bafmeng (also called Mme), turn north-east and cross many more mountains to the Mbembe Forest Reserve. Five days after leaving Sambolabbo we were driven to Bafut by Ralph, a warm-hearted and keen-witted friend of the Parkinsons who is a native of that town and filled us in on the local Fon scene.

The last Fon had 250 wives (a suspicious number of Big Men are said to have '250' wives) and children beyond reckoning. The present Fon, born in 1955, has been ruling since he was sixteen and is a man of many talents, both traditional and Western. Being 'modern' he has only three wives, one of whom is a senior government official. When in residence he occupies not his inherited palace but a colonial Rest House that might have strayed from Simla and overlooks the palace compound. He is 'very, very rich, owning many miles of fertile land and receiving tribute from dozens of villages'. As Bafut's Fons are chosen from among the *only* sons of mothers, it is every wife's unusual ambition to have no more than one son and, in the past, it was not unknown for surplus male infants to disappear and be reared elsewhere.

Only in Bafut did our path cross Cameroon's tourist trail – not that there were any tourists around. But those few who do the 240-mile Ring-Road Tour ('Leaving Bamenda's Skyline Hotel at 9 a.m.') are shown around the Fon's palace at 1,000 CFA per head and already the place *feels* like a 'tourist attraction', or at least like a place that has lost its meaning. As Ralph sadly observed, 'The Fon and all Bafut's Big Men are now in the Western economic system and have not much time left over for the traditional life.' This was by far the most imposing palace we had seen and gloriously surrounded by tall forest trees laden with dark pink blossoms. There were surprisingly few children in evidence but many elderly unsmiling women, presumably the residue of the last Fon's collection. When our arrival was observed a few brightly dyed raffia bags, woven by the womenfolk for sale to tourists, were hastily displayed outside one hut. Each large square hut had four rooms with separate doors and not so long ago each room was occupied by a wife. In the inner compound we were shown a few rooms once reserved for the incarceration of junior wives who had misbehaved. The most important and interesting looking buildings were of course taboo to us, as they are to all but the chiefdom's élite. Ralph pointed out an ancient boulder on which the Fon still regularly grinds camwood to make an oily paste with which to anoint supplicants. However involved he may be in the modern economic life of Bamenda, he remains religiously important to his followers.

Ralph – a teacher at Bamenda's Catholic boarding-school for boys – escorted us to the beginning of our cut-short while being informative on the wing. In the 1890s Bafut had a population of about 5,000, the nearby Mankon Confederation the same, the Bali chiefdom about 4,000 and most other Grassfields chiefdoms between a few hundred and a thousand. By African standards the area's population density was then extraordinarily high – about ninety per square mile – and probably had been so for centuries because of the local yam/ palm oil agricultural base. This, the oldest and most efficient crop-mix in Africa, led to high population densities wherever it was found. Also, the Grassfields enjoyed a healthy altitude, fertile soil, remoteness from slave-trading harbours and a strong matrilineal tradition among many of the local chiefdoms.

Among the Bantu clans – the majority – in this region women and children rather than cattle have always been the measure of a man's wealth. Much fertile land requires many women and children; in times past, the more they produced for the market, to feed local craftsmen and traders, the richer a chiefdom became. During the second half of the nineteenth century the Metchum valley was drastically depopulated by raids from Bafut; only those who fled into the most rugged mountains escaped capture. Before that the valley people had been otherwise exploited, not only by Bafut and the chiefdom of Kom but, most systematically, by the rich and well-organised federation of Wum or Aghem, in the mountains north of the valley.

The eight independent Metchum clans spoke mutually unintelligible languages (with two exceptions) and did not have chiefs. Each village was run by consensus politics, decisions taken at public moots. This lack of a formal hierarchy and disciplined warriors left these clans particularly vulnerable to the Aghem raiders who often kidnapped young men and women, releasing them only when the Aghem oil-drums had been filled. Nor were the young women always released. Some were sold in Isu market where for some reason (probably an epidemic) there was an acute woman-shortage during the latter part of the nineteenth century. Others were married off to Aghem men – an excellent source of revenue for their kidnappers, who pocketed the brideprice having had no production costs.

By noon we had regretfully said goodbye to Ralph and were climbing cultivated hillsides on a narrow, muddy path. This region was having an adequate though below normal rainfall and after the drought-threatened Adamawa weeks we felt an atavistic relief at the sight of its generous fertility. Intercropping is popular here; acres of maize, groundnuts, beans, yams, cocayams, cassava and coffee are skilfully mingled on rich slopes of dark red earth from which pointed grey rocks protrude like the battlements of buried castles. And far below, in a deep cleft, we saw oil-palms, raffia-palms, bananas and plantains flourishing by a hidden, singing stream.

Here most huts are square, thatched, bigger on average than the round variety and all of red mud; they seem to glow amidst their surrounding groves of glossy greenery. Our track followed the shaded crest of a high ridge, overlooking miles of jungly hills. This is a strongly Presbyterian area and where the descent began a large mud church bore witness to that community's prosperity, as did an even larger school, with three shiny motor-bicycles parked outside.

In a palm-wine shebeen at the junction with the motor-road a surprising typewritten notice on the wall stated the controlled price of mimbu: 175 CFA (about 40p) per litre. An elderly couple – the proprietors – were drinking from a plastic Johnson's Baby Powder container, with the top cut off, and a baby's feeding bottle similarly modified.

Two silent women with shaven heads – one middle-aged, the other youngish – were introduced by a young man as 'my mothers'. His father had recently died, hence their shaven heads (a mark of mourning) and their need for mimbu which 'makes them feel happy again'. A teacher arrived then, parking his machine in the doorway. He was disillusioned to find that we had no views on the comparative virtues of various breeds of motor-bicycle.

Everybody looked at us strangely when we asked about the cut-short to Ndung.

'It is better you people stay on this road,' said the young man. 'Sometimes there is bush-taxi and you can buy seats – you have money for seats?' When we explained that we prefer walking he insisted, 'It is too difficult!' Then, under pressure, he indicated the relevant path.

Soon our new acquisition was tested. In Bamenda we had been presented with an umbrella by the headmaster (Brother John from Scotland) of Ralph's school. It was one of those gaily striped jobs now common all over the world but used with special zeal in Cameroon where, during the rains, nobody will cross their compound without a brolly – if they can afford one. Setting out from Bafut I had felt a bit foolish; umbrellas and rucksacks don't somehow go together. But when we came through that afternoon's downpour unsodden we blessed Brother John.

A long easy climb took us to a recently settled area of tin-roofed mud-brick dwellings and thriving eucalyptus plantations. Here Mr Joseph Ndango invited us to be his guests: 'You will reach my place by sunset.' He was returning on his motor-bicycle from the school twenty miles away where he taught – an impractical arrangement, he admitted, given the price and scarcity of petrol in Cameroon. We wondered why he didn't teach in the local school, a long low building complete with level playing-field. Although playing-fields are officially regarded as essential, terrain permitting, we never saw anyone using them. This may be partly owing to teachers' laziness and partly to the many domestic demands made on rural pupils' physical energy.

On the outskirts of Acu, a hamlet between fertile hills, Mr Ndango's bungalow looked displaced. A large suburban construction, Western-furnished, it had wrought-iron grills protecting glazed windows and a garage which housed not only the motor-bicycle but an electricity generator. Supper (rice and stewed chicken) came in thermos food-flasks, accompanied by knives, forks and spoons. When I absent-mindedly picked up a handful of rice Mr Ndango looked scandalised. Several lively children roved around but none spoke recognisable English, despite having a teacher father.

The generator's gratings, rumblings and whinings woke us often as we lay on the concrete floor of an empty storeroom. Our host had offered us a bed, but somewhat half-heartedly. Although only thirty-three, he had nine children, several resident followers and a second wife. (The first died in childbirth.)

By 6 a.m. Mr Ndango was breakfasting. 'Every morning I must be gone at 6.30. On this bad road it takes me one hour for twenty miles and my school must open at 7. Otherwise pupils won't come – at this season they must get home early to work in the fields.'

We were urged to make our own Ovaltine and Mr Ndango apologised for the lack of bread. 'Here we are too far from shops and at this season no flour is left because Acu's new settlers are bad farmers. They know nothing about storage, they leave animals to eat the grain.' He was enjoying more rice and chicken; a shy small daughter brought the guests a dish of fried yam.

On the previous evening, a young MIDENO woman worker had invited us to her home and given us a giant pineapple, a fruit best carried interiorly. Not far from Acu we paused to eat it and soon juice was running down our forearms. After a night of heavy rain the morning colours were wondrous – royal blue mountains filling the middle distance, with dark green hills nearby and the red line of our track climbing a slope all pale green under young crops.

We startled many barefooted pupils, clad in Cameroon's compulsory blue school uniform: skirts and blouses for the girls, shorts and shirts for the boys. Unless loaded with plantains, they carried writing-boards on their heads. Many were in their mid- or late teens. The older children of a family often start primary school at eleven or twelve, having previously been busy caring for younger siblings.

An hour later we were between two high grass mountains on which only horizontal cattle-grooves were visible. We had met no one since leaving Acu but now a very pregnant young woman, carrying wet laundry, emerged from the bushes lining a nearby stream and beckoned us to follow her. Climbing steeply from groove to groove, we speculated about her load's weight; it plus pregnancy did not slow her ascent as much as the rucksack was slowing mine. In a little compound, half-hidden by mango trees and banana plants, she dumped her basket and we asked, 'Ndung?'

She stared at us as though we were mad. '*Ndung?*' she repeated.

We nodded. She frowned – then laughed, beckoned again and led us upwards for half an hour.

On a wide level ledge stood a new bungalow – an extension to an old Fulani compound – where we were invited to rest in a posh two-windowed living-room with cushioned easy-chairs and Nigerian nylon mats on the white-washed walls. Scores of vividly patterned enamel dishes, of every size and shape, were displayed on three tables; among with-it Fulani women the collecting of enamelware is the thin edge of the consumerist wedge.

Our hostess looked pure Fulani, her husband pure Bantu. Both spoke basic English and their easy personal relationship seemed as modern as their home; our pints of boiled milk were served in sparkling glasses imported from France. Husband was aged twenty-two, wife twenty; they had three sons, all in appearance like their mother, and 115 cattle. They hoped to send all their sons to Brother John's college, 'the best in

Western Cameroon'. It would not be necessary to send daughters to school. In their view the path to Ndung was 'too difficult', but then most Cameroonians considered whatever we might be about to do 'too difficult'.

Soon we were above 7,000 feet (the USAF said) amidst a bright vastness of grassland. From an isolated compound a young woman led us to a clarifying – in her estimation – vantage point. She too, though speaking only Foulfouldé, conveyed some unease about the Ndung path. We were beginning to suspect that when people said 'too difficult' they meant 'too elusive'. Despite all our guide's elaborate gesturing, we remained unclear about where the descent to Ndung *began*.

We lunched under noble trees, by a swift shallow stream, watching scores of dark chestnut cattle being watered – their midday routine. One sociable bull wandered curiously towards us, sniffed at my boots, nuzzled my hair and then began enthusiastically to lick my sweat-salty arm. The sensation was akin to being sandpapered.

A tough climb took us to the highest point of the range where we followed a tenuous path along the edge of the mountain wall, overlooking the Metchum valley 4,000 feet below. Tin roofs glinted among trees near the river: Ndung, we presumed. Another range of bulky blue mountains, as high as our own, filled the western sky – tomorrow's goal.

Soon the path descended slightly to a long forested spur, then expired in leaf mould.

'We're lost again,' I observed. 'There's no way down these mountains for miles in either direction – they're sheer *walls*.'

Rachel however insisted on continuing, through a shadowy tangle of undergrowth, and we came out on level grassland-cum-jungle. Here the spur was perhaps half a mile wide and a mile long, with 3,000-foot drops on either side. Even in bright sunshine those ravines looked dark and three species of monkey were already protesting at our intrusion.

'That path *must* go on,' said Rachel, with what seemed to me a tiresome lack of logic. 'It was clear enough till we got to the forest.'

'Only because Fulanis collect firewood here,' said I in my let's-be-reasonable voice.

Foolishly we split up, to look for that hypothetical continuation, and soon had lost each other. Time passed and I found myself becoming slightly agitated: there were lots of edges to be fallen over ... Our whistle-system had broken down because of the sound-distorting topography. But half an hour later it reunited us – and Rachel announced that she had found the path.

We were then standing on the edge of a precipice. 'Where is it?' I asked, bewildered.

Rachel pointed over the edge of the precipice.

'Don't be so bloody silly!' I snapped. 'That's not a *people* path, it's a *baboon* path!'

'It's the path to Ndung,' said Rachel doggedly. 'There isn't any other.'

I peered over the precipice and felt queasy; it *was* a precipice – I am not using the word loosely. But, surveying the surrounding peaks, ridges, ravines and spurs, I had reluctantly to agree with Rachel. This wasn't, in my view, a path. Yet there couldn't be any other route down. Our advisers had been right. The path to Ndung was much too difficult.

'Looks like we'll have to go back to the motor-track at Acu,' I said. 'That path's more than difficult – it's impossible. Especially with an unbalancing rucksack.'

'I'll take the rucksack,' offered Rachel.

'Oh no you won't!' I said. 'It's better to die at fifty-five than at eighteen.'

'You mean we're not going back?' deduced Rachel.

'Evidently not,' I said. 'Onward non-Christian soldiers!'

It was a three-hour descent, inducing indescribable hypertension; as an ascent it would have been harder on the body but much easier on the nerves. It was even worse than it looked. The rains had made it slippy. Small rocks, hidden by the vegetation, lurked to be stumbled over. Thin, taut vines were stretched like trip-wires within the vegetation. This was only my second day as a porter and I had not yet fully adjusted to the rucksack. (Later, it seemed to become part of my body.) I fell five times, Rachel twice. And that first precipice was not the end of the matter. We then had to climb another ridge, the descent from which was if possible even more gruelling because much wetter and impeded by hostile vegetation. But I learned something that afternoon; when the chips are down vertigo is a controllable condition because not controlling it would be fatal. Afterwards we remarked on the irony that 'tame' Cameroon had presented one challenge more formidable than anything encountered in the Himalayas or the Andes. We became instant-folk-heroines in Ndung when it was realised how we had arrived. Cameroonian villagers are not sissy but very, very few of them use that route.

Our 'brake' thigh muscles were throbbing as we sat gulping '33's in Ndung's one small huxters-cum-off-licence. And our hands were shaking, as Mr Bernard Ngu astutely observed.

'You are too tired,' he said, 'you are shivering. From Bamenda you can get bush-taxi to Ndung. That would be better.' He told us then about his fourteen-year-old daughter who, having had malaria for two weeks, had just developed a *very* high fever.

At once we provided a chloroquin course and Rachel wrote out, in capital letters, how many should be taken and when. We expected Mr Ngu to hurry off to administer the first dose. Instead, he pocketed the pills, ordered himself another beer and settled down to expatiate on St Patrick about whom he knew an inordinate amount. He was the only teacher at the local Catholic Mission school. The local Presbyterian Mission school had two teachers: 'Always in this province there is too much Presbyterians.' We were invited to spend the night in his sister's compound; he had come recently to Ndung and while building his own house was renting two rooms from her.

It was dark as we slithered down a steep muddy slope, beside the off-licence, to a large palm- and banana-surrounded compound. The L-shaped house had eight rooms leading off the verandah and another row of rooms behind. Yet for all its prosperity this was not a happy compound; eddies of ill-feeling swirled and the numerous children looked unusually cowed. Sister's husband worked in Bamenda; the whereabouts of Mr Ngu's wife was not disclosed but she seemed to be elsewhere. He could have only one wife: 'As teacher in a Catholic school it is too much difficult! I lose my job if I take more wives and to get teaching jobs is not easy.'

In the outer of Mr Ngu's two rooms his fevered daughter lay on an iron bed; despite Bamenda's nearness, she seemed pathetically frightened of us. The only other furniture was a long wooden bench where we sat hoping for fufu, having assured Mr Ngu that we had our own bedding and could sleep on the floor. When I reminded him of the chloroquin in his pocket he administered the first dose, gently and kindly. Then he fetched supper from the kitchen-hut on the far side of the compound; Africans deplore our nasty habit of cooking and sleeping under the same roof. Again it was rice and chicken; in this area rice is now popular, especially at the end of the dry season when maize stocks are running low. Sister's rice tended towards sogginess and the stewed chicken had not been a chicken for a very long time. Mr Ngu placed the lantern on the floor by the two dishes; it would have illuminated them more effectively had he left it on the bench.

During the meal our host donned another mantle when an old woman arrived and grovelled on the ground beseeching a cure; Mr Ngu was, it seemed, a medicine-man in his spare time. After much palaver the patient gladly paid 600 CFA and a plump cock for an ounce of ground dried bark enfolded in a page of my notebook. Then she took her leave with respectful – almost worshipful – gestures and murmurings of gratitude.

'My brother' then joined us – an all-purpose kinship term meaning in this case sister's husband's brother. He hopefully asked if we would like some mimbu and was soon back with a gallon of the most powerful palm-wine I have drunk anywhere. It was more than twice the legal controlled price, but worth it. A few other men drifted in and we all became agreeably tiddly and discussed taking snuff instead of smoking (Mr Ngu had switched ten years ago 'for health and money reasons'), and comparative cuisines and African politics.

'South Africa needs Whites to run it,' pronounced Mr Ngu, little guessing what effect his words would have on an anti-apartheid demo in Trafalgar Square. 'It is a big rich modern state, too complicated for Black men to run alone. My father tells how more convenient Cameroon was under White men. Schools better, hospitals better, roads better. And seventy years ago there was fast telegrams where now we have not even slow mail!'

Poor Mr Ngu had a broken night. Twice his daughter needed to be escorted across the dark compound to the latrine and thrice she awoke screaming – expecting us, sleeping at the end of her bed, to kill her before dawn. No doubt the mimbu helped me to sleep well in between those interruptions, despite a moderate number of mosquitoes and a very bumpy floor – which was also, as we saw in the morning, very dirty. For all its many rooms and luxuriant garden, that was a slummy compound.

Achu is the Cameroonian dish most dreaded by expatriates. Joy Parkinson had told me of what and how it is made; the details were so horrendous I deliberately forgot them lest one day we might encounter it. And now it appeared for breakfast, a delicacy triumphantly borne from the kitchen by our host in honour of his White guests. It looks exactly like the sludge workmen dump on the road when clearing blocked sewers and its looks do not belie it. Mr Ngu kindly taught me how to cope with this ultimate gastronomic abomination, which comes on a vast communal dish, forming a semi-solid lake in a crater of whitish slimy dough. One takes a portion of dough in one's fingers, working inwards from the edge of the dish, and having thoroughly mixed it with achu the consequent nauseating ball must be swiftly transferred to the mouth before it slithers through the fingers. On the previous evening, as we discussed international eating habits, I had by a cruel coincidence mentioned that breakfast is my main meal of the day.

'This is sustaining food for your main meal,' beamed Mr Ngu. 'When we have finished all you can have more. In the kitchen is much more – don't be shy!'

I stretched my face in a ghastly grin and mixed and slurped and gulped and felt myself going pale beneath my tan.

Rachel had gone pale as the Achu was unlidded. 'I *never* eat breakfast!' she asserted traitorously.

On our arrival Mr Ngu had assured us that it was not necessary to find the latrine: 'In an African compound you can make water anywhere, the latrine is only necessary for different matters.'

This is untrue of Fulani – and many other Cameroonian – compounds, but it accounted for the ammoniacal pong around Sister's homestead. After breakfast, when different matters took me to the stinking latrine behind the kitchen hut, an adolescent girl was shovelling its contents onto the roots of nearby banana plants. I decided not to share this observation with my more fastidious daughter; bananas were likely to be our staple food during the weeks ahead.

Mr Ngu begged us to visit his school: 'It is good for me if I bring White friends to look at my scholars.' We climbed steeply on slippy red mud paths, between fields of high maize, to a broad ridge-top. The large State school had not yet opened but Mr Ngu's smaller academy, a two-roomed hut, was already full of large industrious pupils, sharing dog-eared text-books at crudely made desks. He coped alone with six classes, three in each room – a total of eighty-four scholars. Simple sums had been chalked on the blackboards and fly-blown alphabet pictures hung crookedly on the walls, interspersed with children's poems – one of them touchingly good, about the rains coming. Mr Ngu's intelligence had underwhelmed us, yet here one sensed more effort being made than in the average State school.

As we said goodbye a ragged young man came panting up the hill and insisted on our seeing the Catholic church. We followed him down to the ring-road and were nonplussed when confronted by an apparently abandoned mud hut with a pile of stones at one end ('The altar,' our guide assured us) and a few tree-trunk pews lying on the floor. A gourd money-box lay by the pile of stones. 'You dash Christ,' urged the young man. I pretended not to hear; my CFA-padded hips were slimming faster than expected.

It was already too hot when we left Ndung at 8.30 a.m. For hours the terrain restricted us to the ring-road but this Metchum valley is so lovely – winding between high grassy or forested mountains, or through placid widths of cultivation – that we were not impatient to leave it. And all morning only three vehicles passed: the omnipresent beer-truck, an expatriate Aid Land Rover and a bush-taxi which paused to invite us on board.

Our bread-and-bananas elevenses were enjoyed by the Metchum Falls, sitting on a cliff-edge beneath a cool canopy of trees with white water crashing and seething very far below our feet. These Falls are among Cameroon's most boasted-of tourist attractions but as yet mercifully 'undeveloped'. Mr Ngu had apologised for this: 'You will pass the Metchum Falls but I'm sorry our government has made nothing nice there for tourists.'

'It's dramatic enough now,' said Rachel, 'so what must it be like after the rains?'

'Let's hope,' said I predictably, 'they never do make anything nice for tourists.'

'You forget,' retorted Rachel, 'that tourists don't *want* to sit on damp red soil in their nice new tropical outfits, being tortured by flies with ants dropping out of the trees into their hair. They *need* shiny little prefab cafés with red and blue plastic chairs.'

I shuddered, too easily able to visualise just that, when Cameroon's 'tourist potential' has been realised.

The Metchum River is only occasionally visible from the road but at noon the heat drove us to seek it; we had been told swimming was safe if one picked one's spot with care. While attempting to follow a dried-up stream-bed, deep in a ravine, we were thwarted by dense jungle. Then we had to climb an exhausting cliff covered with golden grass – tough, dusty, four feet high – and 'fortified' with piles of menacingly sharp pineapple leaves dumped from a nearby field.

Back on the road, I used the umbrella as a sun-shade and we collected ten unripe but delicious mangoes, lying under trees, and bought a papaya from a fruit-stall at a compound entrance. The uninspiring cross-roads village of Befang coincided with a torrential downpour during which we fruit-ate and diary-wrote in a would-be-smart (concrete and plastic) off-licence. Unusually, we were the only drinkers. A few youths begged for cigarettes, a few women sidled past the door to inspect us, a few small boys settled in a corner to watch us writing – and seemed mesmerised by the speed and unhesitancy of our pens. But that place felt rather unwelcoming, until an idiot girl laughingly presented us with kolanuts and softly stroked our arms.

The humidity was extreme when we continued under a cloudy sky. Now we had left the ring-road and our muddy path soon dropped to river level via a spectacular stairway of slippy boulders. In the depths of a tree-darkened gorge an old colonial suspension foot-bridge crossed the Metchum – eighty feet below, loudly surging between sheer rock cliffs. A faded but still legible notice reminded the natives that NOT MORE THAN TEN PEOPLE MAY CROSS THIS BRIDGE AT ONE TIME. Even in the colonial era, did anyone heed that well meant flourish of British paternalism?

Half-way across, I paused above the foaming brown torrent. That solid plank bridge, with firm handrails, was still sound. Time's ravages, though perceptible, were not yet alarming; even such modest constructions have a way of outlasting empires. I gazed up at a mountain with a difference, cloaked in subtropical semi-rain forest. The mighty palms, taller than any seen elsewhere, were mingled with a variety of other, unidentifiable, giants. And the bridge ended as it had begun, with a boulder-stairway that took us straight into a moist, green-tinged twilight.

The next few hours had a magical, almost eerie quality: we seemed to be in a fantasy world. Nothing was familiar – fruits, berries, nuts, ferns, fungi, vines, mosses – even the leaves were strangely shaped and hued. The sounds and smells were also new; muted bird calls, though we saw no birds, and an amorphous rustle peculiar to this place as thousands of palm-fronds imperceptibly swayed all around and far above us.

This area gets more than its fair share of rain. The air was pungent with the odours of permanent damp, piquant fungi and who knows what mysterious, powerful herbs – the raw material of medicine-men. Sometimes the path was an almost sheer slope of skiddy mud and we had to help each other up. Sometimes streams racing to the Metchum formed miniature waterfalls, leaping from ledge to ledge. Occasionally the path wound level around outcrops of rock, from which massive webs of roots and vines hung like man-traps; on those stretches the black liquid mud was inches deep. Once this path must have been a main route, hence the bridge. Now it seems little used; on the southern side of the range a circuitous motor-track links Mukuru with the ring-road. We met only one man – not in a sociable mood – carrying a spear and followed by four hunting dogs wearing belled collars. These hounds – resembling black whippets but lower and with broader heads – had crossed our path several times before, always with hunters. This was the only distinct breed we saw in Cameroon.

Suddenly we came out on a ledge where the forest was no less dense but consisted of fewer palms and many more unidentifiable giants. Then we were surprised by a hamlet in a semi-clearing, a dozen small huts embedded in riotous greenery. This was the most forlorn settlement we came upon in Cameroon. How, why and when had these people been squeezed onto their hidden ledge? Not many were about; both men and women looked dispirited, debilitated and, when we appeared, apprehensive. Only one very old man, with a bad limp, seemed unafraid. Struggling to remember his few words of English, he gave me a military salute. From here a selection of pathlets led into the forest and, having shown us the right one, this veteran persistently demanded dash – the only Cameroonian who sought a reward for guiding us.

A gradual climb took us onto rugged grassland where cattle grazed. Their small herd deserted at speed as we emerged from the trees and watching him vanish over a hilltop I wondered, 'How many Olympic Gold Medallists are blushing unseen in Cameroon's mountains?'

'Poor little chap!' said Rachel. 'Now he'll be beaten . . .'

The sky had cleared and at this altitude the sun felt pleasantly hot. As we ate more bananas, the USAF told us that from the bridge we had climbed almost 3,500 feet. Yet all day our pace had been slower than usual; leg muscles take time to recover from an Ndung descent. Some two miles ahead, beyond gullies and spurs, we could see a long, low forested ridge, which didn't *feel* low when the time came to climb it. On this severe gradient the forty pounds in our rucksack seemed like eighty. Here a square mile or so had recently been burnt; maize and groundnuts grew between prone tree carcasses. But over the top the forest was untouched and Mukuru remained invisible until we were there – on the outskirts of a widespread village, its neat substantial square huts glowing orange-red in the slanting light. When we asked a puzzled but smiling young woman the way to the Fon's palace she called her little son and told him to guide us.

The compound of Chief Foto, Fon of Mukuru, lacks Bafut's grandeur but retains all that Bafut has lost. It is a village in itself, complex, crowded and purposeful. Long irregular rows of mud-brick rooms occupy three sides of the sloping square. (Everything in Mukuru slopes.) A newish bungalow-type hut stands on the highest ground, overlooking all. There the Fon has his Reception Hall-cum-office, an austere little room furnished only with the chiefly bamboo stool (actually a chair) opposite the doorway, and a small desk-table and chair by the unglazed window. He was busy with paperwork when we arrived, being among those Fons who have been incorporated into the Republic's bureaucracy.

Chairs were at once unfolded on the narrow verandah. Before greeting the Fon we had removed our noisome boots and socks – exuding a deadly miasma of sweat and black mud – and discreetly left them around a corner. Now motor-tyre flip-flops were provided by a young woman too shy to do more than giggle when addressed. Then a thirteen-year-old son, who spoke fluent English, brought a dish of juicy mangoes – whereupon a plump nanny-goat, tethered nearby and clearly a spoiled pet, demanded the skins by placing her forefeet in my lap and thrusting her nose into my face. Consternation! – followed by relief when my predilection for goats was revealed by the simple expedient of hugging this cheeky creature and scratching her between the horns. As she hoovered mango skins from the verandah, less favoured relatives looked on enviously from beneath the eaves of thatched huts.

Soon our page was back: 'Do you need hot water?' He looked relieved when we said no and led us to a pile of large, round stones, reeking of urine and semi-encircled by a scrap of old tin roof. This high ground at the edge of the compound allowed an unimpeded view of our most memorable Cameroonian sunset. Above a corrugation of dark forested crests, masses of many-layered clouds became a celebration of bronze, green, gold, rose, saffron, plum. And against that pandemonium of shifting colours were silhouetted a lone giant palm and the pointed golden roofs of many huts.

Back on the Fon's verandah, Rachel counted twenty-eight small children simultaneously in view, the seniors wearing school uniform. Many women were returning from the fields with hoes on heads. Others squatted outside huts, preparing stacks of greenery for jammu-jammu; like spinach, it reduces radically in the pot. On one long verandah a young woman was grinding maize in a hand-mill – a rusty, cumbersome machine, yet a liberation. Pounding corn is among the African woman's most strenuous tasks. This was the first family hand-mill we had seen, though communal machines are quite usual in large villages and towns. As children scuttled to and fro, fetching water and firewood, the smoke of a dozen fires began to rise from various corners. Just below our verandah, one woman was endeavouring to split a long knotted branch against the grain. With baby on back, she hacked and hacked – her axe identical to those used 1,200 years ago by the people of the Grassfields. I was being tempted to intervene when the Fon, having cleared his desk, invited us inside.

At first Chief Foto had seemed a little distant – even brusque – probably because of gender confusion. But now (a woman having observed me stripped to the waist while washing) he was graciously attentive. A well-built man in his mid-fifties, authoritative yet not domineering, he had served for 'many years' in the Nigerian army before being selected as Fon in 1975. He emphasised that he had only nine children all from the same mother despite 250 (again!) wives. We took this to mean that though many females were dependent on him he was a one-woman man. Later his brother confirmed this: 'Our Fon loves only one wife.'

We sat at the table while Chief Foto, now formally enstooled, received a succession of supplicants with worries. The Aku (people of Mukuru) clap their hands three times to greet their Fon and address him when seated on the floor near the entrance. They don't speak through cupped hands with bowed heads, though I noticed none actually meeting his gaze. He was assisted by a young man, introduced only as 'my sub-chief', who afterwards explained, 'In daylight our Fon solves "official" problems, after sunset he listens to "traditional" problems.' When I asked how often the two categories overlap the sub-chief looked so perplexed that it seemed kind to change the subject.

During these palavers our page reappeared with the drinks tray: three brands of beer, two versions of Top. He came first to us: 'What is your choice?' Then, having served the others, he noticed us absent-mindedly drinking from our bottles, off-licence style, and hurried forward to fill our glasses.

When the last of the supplicants had departed backwards, bowing gratefully, it was fufu and jammu-jammu time; this fufu's lightness suggested that grinding produces a finer flour than pounding. We ate at the table, by the light of the only lamp, while our host dined on his

199

throne in the shadows. Only when he had finished did the sub-chief begin.

After the hand-washing ritual a young woman showed us to our hot windowless room, one of a tin-roofed row. The door was ill fitting and the mosquitoes were energetic though not numerous. Garments hanging around the walls indicated that we had displaced a female – or more likely two, though the bed was single with a lumpy mattress of grass stuffed into nylon sacking. We slept soundly until the crowing of a cock – roosting in the rafters but hitherto unobserved – woke us at 4.20 a.m.

The Fon wished us to breakfast before departing but that would have involved at least an hour's delay. At sunrise women were only beginning to beat batter for puff-puffs (crisp buns made of maize-flour and deep-fried). And the USAF had warned that Benikuma, unavoidable *en route* to the Aghem highland, is at a hellish 1,000 feet, our lowest point since leaving Douala. When the situation had been explained Chief Foto understood and we left him waving and smiling benignly, standing outside his office in his nightgown.

For a few hours we were gradually descending through a brilliant rain-washed world of greens and reds. Near the scattered tree-rich village of Modele (also known as Ide) an ancient woman, shaven-headed and naked to the waist, was quite overcome when she met us. Falling to her knees in the mud, she beamed toothlessly but joyously and, saying nothing, clapped her hands three times as though we were Fons. It seemed she had happy memories of the colonial era.

Scores of pupils, each bearing a hoe and a bouquet of wild flowers, were converging on a school that looked older and better built than most. They greeted us unshyly – indeed, everyone in Modele radiated friendliness. But remembering the ordeal ahead, we prudently declined a 7.45 a.m. invitation to 'Drink with us some native liquor!'

Beyond Modele, amidst densely forested hills, we were agitated by evidence that some ruthless, bulldozing logging company had recently been at work. These are the forests which once inspired good relations between the Ide (Modele's people) and the clans of the Aghem Federation (centred on Wum), whose men were generously entertained when they came down to hunt. This was soon after the Aku and Ide clans settled here (*circa* 1840), to become rival exploiters of the Metchum valley's resources. Then, as the Ide became stronger, through killing or absorbing earlier settlers, Aghem grew envious and uneasy – especially about the Ide establishment of complex trading links with the Benue lands. When it began to look as though they might take control of the Metchum valley trade Aghem declared war, towards the end of the nineteenth century, and reduced Modele to tributary status.

Relations were never good between Modele and Essimbi (also known as Age). Their frequent forest ambushes and slaughterings of each other must have done a lot to control population growth throughout the area. Yet the Ide traded with the Age, in the intervals between killing them. The former were unusually dependent on fish and the latter were the most skilled net-weavers around. So the Ide captured Ndo women and exchanged them for Age nets.

The forenoon's two vehicles were pick-up trucks, delivering for rival breweries and doubling (like Andrew's) as bush-taxis. At brutal heat time we reached hell – a flat unshaded stony track, running for miles between cultivated fields. Soon I was showing symptoms that reminded Rachel of our hen, *en route* from Sambolabbo. Ingeniously she attached the umbrella to the rucksack, enabling me to walk in the shade of my own mobile verandah with both hands free to collect mango windfalls.

An hour later we were in Benikuma, where the sword of Damocles fell at last. In this cul-de-sac village the motor-track ends, some twelve miles from the Nigerian border. Yet it boasts another of those Customs and Immigration posts that dotted our route, this one presumably for the control of smuggling pedestrians and illegally bush-bashing vehicles. As we had to pass the little building, and planned to spend the hot midday hours in the village, it would have been foolish to pretend not to notice it.

Boldly I marched into the Immigration Office with passports extended. Then, seeing the officer in charge, I knew our bluff would be called. This was no semi-literate, semi-inebriated buffoon but a very together and articulate gentleman who didn't imagine we came from Germany because we had Irish passports and who wasted no time cogitating over our 1973 vaccination certificates. Within seconds he had found our visa pages and within a few seconds more he was saying, 'I'm sorry, sir, *very* sorry … But you must know your visas are no longer valid. They have not been valid for some time. Why is this?'

I beamed unconcernedly and corrected him. 'Not "*sir*" – "*madam*"!'

Mr Itoe stared at me incredulously, then leant back, chuckling. '*Won-der-ful!* You women who go walking in the bush, carrying big weights, quickly get to look like men!' But he soon stopped chuckling and lent forward again, picking up my passport. '*So,* your visas?'

I came clean, grateful for an immigration officer who spoke English as well as I do. Starting in the Holland Park Embassy, I ended in the Bamenda Immigration Office.

Mr Itoe listened attentively, then nodded sympathetically. 'This fellow in Bamenda, I know him – a good man but new to his job. *So,* for me you are now a problem! You should return to Bamenda for extensions, but this you have tried … It is very irregular, but I must let you continue. You have done your best. I hope you meet no others who take advantage of your difficulty. And your daughter? She is well?'

I nodded towards the window and Mr Itoe peered through the mosquito-screen at Rachel, sitting on the verandah devouring unripe mangoes. 'But she is beautiful! Why do you drag her through the bush? And I think she is too hungry – green mangoes will give her colic! You must take her quickly to the market and feed her!'

Benikuma's weekly market was a busy yet unexciting affair smelling strongly of rotten fish. Despite being surrounded by rampantly fertile land, this dusty, sun-tormented village seemed one of the poorer places on our route.

Rachel unsuccessfully quested about for baguettes and chocolate spread. I sat outside a crowded, noisy off-licence drinking tepid beer in the grudging shade of tin eaves. The only available alternative was Top. And after the fate suffered by our water-bottle (and myself) in Galim, I had taken a vow of lifelong abstinence from Top.

An overweight Presbyterian minister, exhaling achu fumes and gnawing at a kid's skull, settled beside me. I was, he said, 'plenty lucky to belong to government that pays for travelling to study other religions'. (I wondered by what bizarre deformation of logic he had identified me as a student of religions.) His less enlightened government would not pay for him to study American Presbyterianism. Mopping my face with my shirt-tail I let him burble on and he proudly informed me that there are one million children in the local school: 'Many are good Christians who fight for Christ every day in their hearts.'

I cheered up when Mr Itoe appeared, probably to check that all was well with the dotty Irishwoman. He wouldn't accept a beer because 'I have much work in my office and I must be a good example to these people who drink from breakfast time!' But he got himself a Top and then said, 'It makes me happy that you two can travel so securely in my country. This area is now easy to administer, though too hot for comfortable living. I cannot ask my family to live here so I see them only at weekends. But in times past, before the Germans and the British, there was serious trouble up and down the Metchum. These tribes quarrelled and killed about land, hunting, fishing, trading, women. Life was dangerous then. Now we have peace and prosperity, everyone can move around safely, there is little crime. Some old people say good traditions died in colonial days – and they are right. Now young people can be very confused, going from bush to city. What is good? What is bad? For them nothing is certain – they seem to need our lost traditions. But when the bathwater goes it is not always possible to keep the baby!'

When Mr Itoe had shown us the start of our cut-short to the Aghem highland we said goodbye. Then I looked at the hilly track ahead and groaned and lay under a mango tree and went into a heat coma. Soon after I heard a woman telling Rachel that she, Rachel, was the double of the woman's daughter, Jacqueline, now studying in Mexico. This all seemed so outrageously improbable that I decided I must be asleep and dreaming. But hearing the soulful comparison being made for the third time, I opened one eye. A buxom, very black woman was staring fixedly at Rachel with transferred affection. Had it been less hot I would have pursued the matter of Jacqueline in Mexico. As it was, I quickly shut my eye.

During the next half-hour I listened but didn't look, not wishing to be conversationally embroiled. A kind youth presented Rachel with three ripe mangoes. A gang of rowdy youths verbally molested her – which unpleasantness was unique in our experience of Cameroon. An amiable gendarme conversed with her in French. A less amiable gendarme interrogated her rather aggressively and implied that her husband was in a drunken stupor. Whereupon I opened both eyes, claimed to be a sober *Mamma* and, by way of proving sobriety, heaved on the rucksack and strode off purposefully. It was only two o'clock, but mitigating clouds had gathered.

By 5.50 p.m. we were in impossible camping terrain – precipitous, heavily forested mountains – and beginning to wonder if we would in fact come to a village by sunset, as Mr Itoe had guaranteed. Then, on a steep descent, we overtook three women carrying colossal loads home from the market. In sign language they urged us to follow them and stay with their Fon. Moments later we met him: a handsome young man carrying a fine antique firearm, a type of weapon still much used in this area. He was accompanied by an older man and, having no idea that this was our host-to-be, we offered our hands. Only when these were ignored by the hunter did we realise who he was. Neither man spoke any but local languages, yet it was somehow agreed that we should continue with the women and await the Fon's return outside his palace.

An exhausting half-hour later – the upward path was another of those boulder-stairways so popular hereabouts – we panted onto a small cleared ledge. There our guides smiled goodbye before disappearing into lush greenery. A tiny, tin-roofed, one-window hut, with weather-warped door and shutters, was made to look even tinier by the height of the surrounding palms, mango trees and plantains. Even by local standards it didn't seem palatial.

On the climb up we had been joined by an unusually tall brother of the Fon, returning from school and looking rather absurd in his blue shirt and shorts. At first he viewed us with extreme unease but as he spoke a sort of English we assiduously curried favour. Relaxing slightly, he brought from behind the hut two eighteen-inch-high bamboo stools – the most uncomfortable form of seating ever devised. Then he too vanished into the greenery but was soon back, wearing threadbare jeans and a woman's blouse and accompanied by three elders. One was the Fon's present 'father'. His biological father had died two, three, maybe four years ago – no one could remember exactly when. (Or, more likely, they would not risk misfortune by revealing the date to us.) One of the elders seemed deeply suspicious, almost hostile. But Father was tentatively welcoming, though naturally bemused. He produced a few phrases of German, which at the time bewildered us. Meanwhile the word was spreading and soon thirty-two small, silent, round-eyed children were sitting in a row on a fallen tree-trunk at the far side of the ledge. When I stood up to fetch our malaria pills from the rucksack some of the toddlers shrieked with terror and clung to their minders.

Not until the Fon arrived did we accept that that hut *was* the palace – all of it. We were ushered into a tiny room furnished only with his stool, in this case an ancient, high-backed, elaborately carved chair set on a wooden platform with two steps. The uneven mud floor was filthy. Inside the door stood two iron cauldrons of water with tin jugs and mugs on their lids. On the wall above the stool hung a wooden drinking vessel in the shape of a zebu horn, with a cock's head most realistically carved at its base. This, Brother explained, was used only when the Fon made sacrifices for the protection of his people. Below it, somewhat disconcertingly, hung a large framed photograph of the Fon's elder son (now aged seven) as a baby. This was the Fon's everyday living-room; it had not been opened up specially for us.

As we dumped our rucksack by the cauldrons a storm broke: one of the Big Uns. For twenty minutes the lightning was brighter than the lamp and the thunder – and rain on the roof – made conversation impossible. During this drama, a basin of warm washing-water was provided behind the palace. However unswept floors may be, bodies – always and everywhere – must be scoured at the end of the day. No latrine was indicated; presumably the jungle serves.

Back in the palace beer was flowing, to our delighted astonishment. Getting it to this ledge must tax even Cameroonian muscles and I insisted on paying treble the Benikuma rate. When the storm had passed over the night was very still; this fortunate village seemed to be trannie-free. Then someone in the next hut began softly to play an *ndengi*. Noticing our interest, the Fon summoned the musician, a gentle young man who stood by the door drawing a poignantly sweet melody from his clumsy-looking instrument. Brother translated *ndengi* as 'guitar' but it more closely resembled a zither, made of special wood, velvety to the touch, with the addition of a few bent twigs and strings of fine wire.

This was our most enigmatic stopping place. We never discovered the name of the village, or of our charming host. Next morning, seeing its full extent, we realised that the palace was the meanest dwelling;

most other huts were of the biggish square sort, with pointed thatched roofs. According to the Fon, the population was fifty-six. 'That means,' explained Brother, 'fifty-six tax-payers. We don't count women and children.' From this we calculated a population of about five hundred, assuming nine or so dependents to each male.

The clan language is so peculiar that it was studied 'about ten years ago' by a German who lived in the village for 'about five months'. (Hence Father's German phrases.) Elsewhere we discovered that of the eight main Metchum valley clans, only the Aku and Ide are mutually comprehensible though all eight languages have a common origin. But our nameless village is, linguistically, a place apart. Possibly, hidden in dense forest on a hard-to-reach ledge, its people survived the depredations of the Bafut (and other) raiders and have been *in situ* for longer than the majority now living along the Metchum.

A multiplicity of wives, desired or not, is obligatory for Fons. Yet our rebel host had only one and wanted no more. She was a beautiful young woman, shabbily dressed in a 'Western' frock but slender and poised, with a quietly forceful personality. This marriage reminded us of Mr and Mrs Kami; the Fon and his wife even slept together, with their two daughters, in a double-bed which almost filled the little room that formed the other half of the palace. As we talked before supper, Mrs Fon arrived with a restive baby girl, handed her to Pappa and told him to get her to sleep and put her to bed. One didn't have to understand the unique local language to know exactly what was being said; the scene was startling in its modern-Western familiarity. And the Fon accomplished his task with the skill of one much-practised. Fifteen minutes later a peacefully sleeping infant was being tenderly tucked up. Then Pappa collected the five-year-old daughter, who screamed with terror when she saw us. At once Pappa took her into the bedroom and sang her to sleep. Oddly, we didn't see either of the sons, aged seven and three.

Meanwhile there was the usual to-ing and fro-ing of supplicants; and here, despite the Fon's unorthodoxy and the unpalatial nature of his palace, cupped hands, hoarse whispers and downcast eyes were the order of the evening. One wrong-doer, come to seek forgiveness, crawled on hands and knees from the door to lay his head on the steps of the stool. As this wretched creature was being pardoned and reassured, a drunk stumbled in, like the Fool in Lear, and stood unsteadily before his Fon, loudly mouthing what sounded like abuse. Then he turned to face us, fell over his feet, picked himself up and began to speak English.

'I fought – that's past tense – in World War Two. But you don't know English – that's present tense – so you can't – present tense – understand me. Somebody told me – past tense – that all Europeans know English but that is not – present tense – true.'

This character caused much amusement, not least to the Fon, before the elders removed him; our host was agreeably laid back. Yet we had realised, by the end of an eventful evening, that this young Fon (aged thirty at most) retained more real power than any other chief we had met – even the apparently potent Lamido of Tignère.

Supper consisted of rice and fresh fish, netted a few hours earlier in the stream at the foot of the mountain. A jolly young man with a torch escorted the meal, bearing his own bamboo stool on which he sat close to the Fon; their relationship seemed 'special'. Whenever we obeyed orders to help ourselves – yet again – the torch-bearer kindly illuminated the dishes on the floor. ('Greed highlighted!', Rachel noted in her diary.)

At 9.30 p.m. four supplicants arrived to palaver about the use of land; soon they were followed by two more 'special buddies'. Normally in Cameroon our own sleeping habits and our hosts' coincided; here it seemed things were only hotting up at Murphy bedtime. We unrolled our bags and slid into them without causing comment. The esoteric clan language proved an effective lullaby and we don't know when palavering ended.

Hours later Nature called me and I discovered that the 'lock' on the door consisted of two adjustable nails a few inches long. A lantern had been left alight in our room, turned low; another was alight in the bedroom. Darkness is dreaded.

The Fon and his wife deplored our dawn start. 'You go plenty hungry,' warned Mrs Fon, presenting me with a gigantic hand of bananas. (Everything growing on that ledge seemed gigantic.) Only then did we realise that she spoke some English.

From the palace a narrow path wound through well grown maize – no drought had afflicted this area – to the village proper. We saw then that the Fon's 'ledge' was part of a long valley enclosed on three sides by forested slopes. Many smiles greeted us as we passed between huts where men were standing outside their doors vigorously brushing their teeth with twigs. All those enviable African teeth don't happen by accident.

The path crossed a mile or so of flat land where we were saturated while pushing through coarse, golden-brown, rain-laden grass as tall as ourselves. On the edge of a river-noisy ravine we were about to go astray when a quick-witted young hunter came towards us out of the grass. 'Aghem?' we checked. He pointed away from the path, into the ravine – then up to a series of high forested ridges. He was the only person we met all morning; it was uncanny how often, in unpopulated regions, a guide materialised when most needed.

That climb was long but not unduly severe; usually the path zigzagged sensibly. This was a main route when Aghem men hunted the

Metchum valley and rich traders organised long human caravans to carry the valley's abundant palm oil to Wum, returning with hoes, machetes, spear-heads, tobacco, salt, tree-bark oil-drums, and sometimes goats, sheep and poultry, none of which do well at river level. Now sections of the path are in a mildly perilous state of disrepair and it is much overgrown. But most of the undergrowth is benign, though a barbed thorn on a dead palm frond deeply embedded itself in Rachel's right ear and was not easy to remove.

This forest was no less exciting than Mukuru's though quite different in composition. Many palms grew in deep ravines but all the giants were majestic hardwoods. Often their complicated root-systems provided steps; on other difficult gradients the rock beneath the forest cloak offered footholds. Most of the smooth pale grey trunks were superbly fluted to a height of five or six feet. And some were of a girth that Rachel and I, with hands joined, could not encircle. But even here greedy loggers had been tempted – though their over-ambitious scheme had, not surprisingly, gone phut. Several felled giants had been electric-sawn into planks which were then abandoned. One 200-foot-long victim lay across our path, forcing me to remove the rucksack before surmounting its vast bulk.

Fortunately we were almost out of the trees when driver ants struck. I had unwittingly walked on a column (they were locally numerous) and within seconds my 'attack' provoked theirs. As they invaded under my slacks I fled – to the extent that one can flee, with a rucksack, up an escarpment. Out on the sunny grassland I stripped; by then the enemy were all over me, causing agony. It took time to remove them from every crevice of shirt, slacks, briefs and socks.

Meanwhile Rachel was working her way through the Fon's bananas. 'Let's hope,' she said indistinctly, 'no hunter or herd comes by.'

Clad again, I sat on a boulder and wolfed my share of bananas. Within yards – moments – we had moved from one world to another, from the dim, damp, enclosed forest onto bright, breezy, expansive pasture-cum-jungle. And the Aghem highland stretched ahead for many, many miles.

'D'you realise,' said Rachel, 'that with Egbert we couldn't have used any of these forest paths?'

I had indeed begun to realise that in Cameroon there were advantages to trekking without a horse, though I could not subdue my post-Egbert heartache. Now we could over-exert ourselves, when necessary, without angst about cruelty to Egbert. Also, being able to use foot-bridges, and not being constrained by grazing requirements, greatly enhanced both our freedom of movement and our speed. When we did our statistics in Douala, it emerged that post-Egbert our average daily mileage went from eighteen to twenty-four. But of course the price to be paid for this increased mobility was book-starvation.

'So really,' said Rachel with irritating logic, 'we invested £250 in a pack-horse so that we could have plenty to read!'

11

Wandering Towards Wum

WHY IS THE Aghem highland so sparsely populated? The experts
have no satisfactory answer. Apart from internal dissension and Bafut
'kidnappings', this whole Metchum-Aghem region remained undis-
turbed throughout most of the nineteenth century, protected from
both Chamba and Fulani raiders by the Ocu mountains and its own
ruggedness. Moreover, the Aghem highland is rich in iron ore, firewood,
water, raffia-palms, oil-palms; and, before recent population increases
in the surrounding areas, it was rich in game. The fertile volcanic
soil could support many large villages, yet we found only scattered
compounds and hamlets, and of course cattle beyond reckoning. Since
the turn of the century this has been a Fulani stronghold, an area the
newcomers were able to take over without displacing Bantus.

For days we roamed happily through these unpredictable but always
beautiful mountains, sometimes camping, sometimes staying in compounds, occasionally being drenched by violent afternoon storms but
only once being soaked in our tent. Campsites were not as easy to find
as in the Tchabal Mbabo. This terrain is more broken and jungly, the
ground is stonier, the climbs are often as severe though usually shorter –
and there are none of those immense expanses of pasture so characteristic of the Tchabal Mbabo. Yet we saw many more cattle here –
plump beasts who made their drought-lean Adamawa cousins seem
like poor relations. Once, sitting by a stream in a valley, we counted
seven enormous herds grazing on the slopes all around. Most were
white or dappled grey, the popular local colours; different clans favour
different colours.

Aghem's Fulani compounds are bigger and more sophisticated than
Adamawa's, with lines of attached, though not interconnected, rooms
rather than separate huts. Grandest of all was a milk-bar where we
stopped one noon, a compound the size of a football pitch with rows of

rooms on three sides and a kitchen-hut bigger than our nameless Fon's palace. Open doors allowed glimpses of expansive (and expensive) displays of enamelware. Only women and children were visible, the former all young, elegantly robed and extraordinarily good-looking. They were reclining on verandahs playing with babies or dressing each other's hair in a variety of tortuously complicated styles – a Cameroonian version of young Victorian ladies with nothing much to do and all day to do it.

Bantu servants of both sexes flitted in the background and when we arrived one hurried forward with a Nigerian mat which he unrolled for us on the men's verandah. Ten minutes later another came from the kitchen with a silver-plated tray holding about five pints of hot milk, pyrex cups and saucers, plastic teaspoons and lump sugar in a covered bowl.

We were about to move off, having dashed the boy who served us, when one woman called, 'Wait small time!' – the first intimation that anyone spoke any English. We sat back and attempted unsuccessfully to get a conversation going. Then, after a very small time, the Big Man appeared, aged about thirty-five and as good-looking as his womenfolk. He wore knife-creased khaki slacks and an aquamarine pure silk shirt, heavily embroidered with gold thread – no nasty synthetics for *him*! 'A charming tycoon of Aghem', I noted in my diary. His English was fluent though ungrammatical and when the women's curiosity had been satisfied he escorted us towards the path for Essu.

Leading us along the crest of a sunny, jungly ridge, our companion delivered his potted autobiography. He had never been to school, Koranic or otherwise, and was illiterate in every script. But he spoke English, French, Foulfouldé and six other African languages. (This was not a boast: I had asked.) After fifteen years in Nigeria, training the polo ponies his family exported, he had returned home when his father died. He was the eldest of three sons, all living in the compound, and three of the women and eight of the children were his. ('I won't take my fourth wife until all these are old!') The family herd of more than nine hundred was dispersed for many miles around, only twenty-five milking cows being kept near the compound. Many Grassfields Fulanis, he said, owned as big or bigger herds. These however are always split up into sub-herds of 120 or so, the maximum number that may be conveniently watered in a given area and for which one herdsman can reasonably be held responsible. (So perhaps the seven herds we counted was one dispersed.)

When we parted, our guide pointed into a wooded cleft far below and said, 'Strange people live there – they eat only fish and fruit from the forest. They do not belong to any local tribe, they are on their own.' Later, as we scrambled through that difficult ravine, we saw no one.

But the few small grass huts by the river were peculiar – on high stilts.

Less sophisticated was another Fulani compound to which we were invited by the fourteen-year-old 'adopted' Bantu son of the family. He met us as we were gloomily surveying an unpromising array of rugged mountains, with a view to sleeping on the least rugged. His English was poor but his message clear – and backed up by his 'adoptive' Fulani brother of the same age. This lad was carrying a compound-blaster which he switched on and off at intervals, as though to reassure himself that it was still working. There was something in Nigerian English about a German youth flying into Red Square, which I took to be the Nigerian version of 'Next Week's News'. Both boys worried about us because 'these hills are strong'. They offered to carry the rucksack but Rachel very properly continued to shoulder her White Woman's Burden. The final two hills were indeed 'strong' – almost vertical. On those rocky, scrubby slopes the boys admitted to feeling the effect of Ramadan.

I reached level ground a little ahead of the others and found myself overlooking many miles of ridges and valleys, already shadowed dark blue. Above them stretched a delicate pastel sunset of pinks, greys, yellows – seen through an intricate pattern of palm and plantain fronds. Behind the compound, on lush grassland sloping gently to the summit, there grazed a white milking herd, a dozen fine bay horses and a small flock of less-ugly-than-usual sheep. This compound was built so close to the edge of its ledge that the kitchen-hut overhung the precipice.

Our tall, lean host – Fulani-featured but ebony-skinned – registered extreme astonishment on seeing us. Yet his welcome was warm and his interest in our doings keen. Meanwhile four wives had dived behind the screen of bamboo poles and palm fronds fencing off the kitchen area. In the fading light I approached them, unbuttoning my shirt, as Rachel explained, 'That is *madame*, my Mamma' to our amused host and those of his ten children old enough to take an interest. The wives, peeping through the palm fronds, could not deny the evidence of their eyes and at once emerged to shake my hand. Whereupon our host called, 'Me see too!' His womenfolk fell about when I obliged.

By now the sun, indisputably, had set, so we were temporarily ignored. Cameroon's rural Muslims take Ramadan seriously, to the extent of fasting on afterwards, should they for any reason have broken the fast on one or more days. From the verandah we watched a great rushing about of little boys with bottles and kettles of water. There was much ritual washing, including three rinsings out of the mouth, and then came the bliss of drinking water after a hot fourteen-hour fast. According to the rule-book, prayers should follow, before eating. But if prayers are also taken seriously it makes more sense first to fill distractingly empty bellies and then to pray, when Allah can be given one's full attention. Which is what this family did, and most others observed *en route*. Pap was quickly served, that thick, sour-sweet gruel to which we became so addicted in Adamawa – a soothing food with which to break a long fast. Fufu and jammu-jammu came half an hour later and we ate on the verandah while the family gorged and talked and laughed in a nearby room. During Ramadan there is a festive feeling about every evening meal.

Orthodox Muslims do not 'adopt' – the practice is condemned – but during a post-prandial chat with our host we learned that his three Bantu 'sons' had been acquired, as babies, to strengthen the family's work-force. I wondered what echo was here. Although domestic slavery was part of the West African way of life for centuries, most slaves were not acquired violently through wars or raids. They lost their freedom as a punishment, being enslaved instead of imprisoned, or they were sold as small children by families seriously in debt – a common problem in a society of traders. There was no humiliation associated with slavery as such. Some slaves eventually became important officials of the local chief, many married into their owners' families, many were in due course set free. It was clear that our host's three 'adopted' Bantus were much-loved. Even today, a very poor family might be tempted to sell surplus children to rich Fulanis, thus assuring their future prosperity.

Our large, clean room had three home-made beds of bamboo poles and palm fronds – versatile materials, much used in this area. We explained that we could sleep on the floor, leaving the children in their beds, but the little boys were too frightened of us to share. That evening's lullaby was the fervent chanting of prayers in the next room, partitioned from ours by a matting-screen that didn't reach the ceiling. And by 4 a.m. the lengthy morning prayers had started, while much chattering of wives and clattering of pots signalled the cooking of an enormous pre-dawn banquet. During Ramadan Muslims are encouraged to say many extra prayers and in the towns some Fulani elders spend all day in the mosque, praying incessantly.

At We we again met the ring-road. A motorist might pass the real We, hidden amidst tall trees, and imagine this to be one more unprepossessing shack-sprawl. In fact it is one of the Grassfields' most important and attractive 'pre-motor' trading centres. Approaching from the eastern mountains, we were walking through the village for an hour before coming out on the ring-road. A network of steep, shady, red tracks connects scores of prosperous compounds built in a variety of architectural styles: round, square, oblong, straw-thatched, palm-thatched, tin-roofed – all surrounded by tall mango and kola trees, flowering bushes, graceful palms and groves of bananas and plantains.

Long before reaching the village we realised that someone of consequence had just died. Frequent gunshots reverberated from slope to slope and spasms of drumming were followed by the wailing of pipes and the strumming of *ndengi*. Then we met an elderly man pushing an ancient punctured bicycle with gallons of mimbu on the carrier. He was going to the wake and insisted that we, too, would be warmly welcomed. I longed to accompany him but felt it would be crass for two strangers to intrude on death ceremonies as though these were a tourist entertainment. Later the Fon's eldest son – Bassong – said such diffidence was unnecessary. The arrival of two Whites would have helped the bereaved family by giving them valuable and enduring kudos throughout the chiefdom.

Bassong, aged twenty-five, was warm hearted, good-looking and a fluent English speaker. Meeting us in the off-licence, soon after our early afternoon arrival, he invited us to stay in his father's 'guest house' and we pictured a comfortable hut in the spacious palace compound. Instead, we were eventually led across the ring-road to a hideous quasi-bungalow with concrete floors – much less comfortable to sleep on than earth. The furniture consisted of two battered easy chairs in the sitting-room. The bathroom did have a bath, lavatory and handbasin, all stained dark brown, but after ten years the expected piped water had not yet arrived.

Among our other drinking-companions was a Francophone gendarme, recently posted to Anglophone We and closely studying a Nigerian publication – *Dictionary for Foreigner's English: Colloquial and Offensive Language*. I was tempted to ask whether he wished to avoid or acquire offensive language. Beside him sat a trilingual Francophone teacher, also a newcomer; the children of each linguistic area are, in theory, taught the language of the other. Louis was an interesting character with whom we had an impassioned argument about colonialism. It was one of several that followed similar lines; many of our Cameroonian acquaintances expressed opinions that would enrage British anti-racists.

Louis said, 'It's a big problem in Africa that we want all the Western goodies but we can't make them for ourselves. Then some of us get miserable and angry about depending on Western loans and advisers – and getting into debt so we're trapped by the West. But isn't it our own fault? Now we're supposed to be independent but we're not behaving that way. We're still depending on Western capitalists and letting them exploit us because we're greedy for their goodies. Why don't we have the know-how to get manufacturing organised the way Asian countries do?'

By then we had been joined by a young man working in Douala as an accountant but home in We for a wedding. He held strong views on Africa's rapidly expanding army of Western 'aid' workers. 'We must throw out these parasites,' said he. 'They know nothing about our real needs, or how to use traditional talents and experience. They're on a beautiful gravy-train for themselves but there's nothing in it for us. Now Africa's got to *seem* to go backwards and forget the goodies – that's the only way out of this debt mess. We need some cash aid, but in my job I see the bare minimum is best. Then we must learn how to manage it, *for* ourselves, *by* ourselves.'

'But nobody wants to forget the goodies!' objected Louis.

'And that,' said I, 'is surely the worst colonial legacy – the illusion that to be "civilised" and "successful" you must imitate Whites. Even though there's nothing in your traditions to form a foundation for our sort of consumer society.'

The accountant beamed at me approvingly but Louis argued back. 'Why shouldn't we have goodies, if we can learn to make them for ourselves? Do you think Africans should still be living like savages in the twenty-first century? Being modernised is our reward for being colonised. We had to have colonisers, we couldn't have gone through the past two hundred years without being developed. And nobody was going to do it for love, so we had to be turned into consumers of Western goodies. And we *wanted* them, right from the start, when the first traders arrived on the coast hundreds and hundreds of years ago.'

'OK,' said the accountant, 'you're telling the truth, you're facing the facts. But now we needn't remain consumers, except as much as suits *us.*'

Our debate became untidier, in proportion to our accumulating empties, and it seemed most of those present were finding my antipathy to colonialism irritating. To them the argument that, on balance, Europeans did more harm than good in Africa was, quite simply, unrealistic. Essentially they agreed with Mr Itoe: 'You can't always keep the baby.' I often wondered how different our impressions might have been had we spent three months in Douala and Yaoundé, talking with Cameroonians who read books and newspapers and are aware of a world in which 'colonialism' has become a filthy word.

'We needed Christianity,' said Louis flatly – and nobody disputed this. 'Before the missionaries came we had too much fighting and too many cruel customs.'

I gave up at that point. But was pre-colonial Africa really worse off than modern messed-up Africa, adrift without a cultural rudder on a choppy sea of materialism?

At intervals during the afternoon We's medicine-man wandered in for a beer and a chat, then was off about his arcane business, then was back again. Dr Onambele – tall, portly, affable and clad in a long white gown – seemed rather too aware of being no ordinary village medicine-man. An internationally renowned figure, he is often called on by West African governments for assistance during all sorts of crises. He had just returned from giving advice in Gabon and was soon to leave for a week in Nigeria. Like many Cameroonian medicine-men, he was registered as what we would call a homeopathic doctor and co-operated with Western-trained staff at local hospitals. When he invited us to breakfast Bassong said, 'You must go, this will be good for his reputation when you are seen as his guests. I will lead you, at half an hour after sunrise.'

Before saying goodnight Dr Onambele read our palms, an embarrassingly phoney exercise of his powers. Then he and his apprentice performed a stylised, complicated 'magical' dance for our delectation. Given the amount of beer by then consumed, this was surprisingly graceful. It involved their sharing another '33' and ritualistically grabbing each other's leather pouches, worn round the neck and containing, Bassong said, 'powerful magic herbs'.

Behind the off-licence, in a storeroom-cum-chop-house, we enjoyed excellent fufu and jammu-jammu, with tender goatmeat, for only 300 CFA each. As Bassong escorted us to the lampless guest house he confided that his father hated him, which made him sad, but maybe it was because he so much didn't want to be the next Fon ... Also he was determined not to have more than one wife and five children (he had three already). 'There are jealousy and expense problems in our traditional families. And we Catholic people cannot take Communion with more than one wife.'

We sympathised with Bassong's dread of being selected as Fon. Once selected, most (all?) men, however reluctant, feel compelled to accede. We heard of one reigning Fon whose successful academic career in Germany was abruptly ended when, in defiance of his strongly stated wishes, he received the summons to be 'enstooled'. He was shattered, if not quite as shattered as his German wife. Yet at once he returned to the Grassfields with wife and children, for whom he built a suitably palatial bungalow on the outskirts of Bamenda. He himself felt constrained to settle in the non-palatial palace and acquire more wives.

Some Cameroonians are prone to 'Dutch hospitality' (Rachel's phrase) and at the end of beery evenings issue breakfast invitations not always remembered next morning. So we had a precautionary 6 a.m. meal in the chop-house: a square meal of six golden buns each, with bowls of scalding pap. Already the off-licence was in business. Two teachers were having beer for breakfast, to fortify themselves against eighty-pupil classes. And on the street a jolly character was bouncing up and down, wearing around his neck a drum of nailed-together sardine tins and beating it with an old shoe while talking animatedly to himself between swigs of '33'.

215

'To err is human,' commented one of the teachers, sombrely gazing out at the drummer.

When Bassong arrived we walked beneath spreading mango trees past rich compounds. Sheep were tethered on the wayside grass and Bassong told us that an ancient taboo prevented his family from either keeping sheep or eating mutton. 'These are stupid animals who have no horns. And at night they act like men, standing on back legs and knocking on doors with front legs and casting spells.'

'What kind of spells?' I asked.

Bassong looked embarrassed and giggled. 'Bad spells – *very* bad! Only old men with many children should keep sheep. These animals have so many children they take a man's power.' Then he added, as an unimportant footnote, 'When my grandfather was Fon he often became a sheep at night to discover what was going on all over the village.'

Dr Onambele's compound was unattractive. At the entrance a con-spicuous signboard boasted of his qualifications, prowess and reputation. Outside his quasi-bungalow stood a long, well-polished limousine, the first motor-car we had seen in a compound since leaving Doi's. This morning the doctor was pin-stripe suited and homburg-hatted in preparation for a journey to Bamenda. Although we were enthusiastically welcomed our guide was ignored. Bassong plainly regarded Dr Onambele with a mixture of fear and respect. Equally plain was Dr Onambele's contempt for the Fon's eldest son.

Our host's unmade bed occupied one side of a small, Western-furnished living-room. Hanging low above the statutory oblong coffee-table were two huge gaudy balloons advertising Sprite and Honda. Over the bed hung an enormous curled-up shocking-green inflatable rubber python. From the ceiling hung symmetrically spaced paper frills, foot-long strips of yellowed newspapers. (The only newspapers, incidentally, that we saw anywhere in Cameroon outside of the cities.)

As we struggled to adapt to the décor our host jumped up: 'Come! Before breakfast let me show you my wives!' Pacing pompously, he led us to a row of eight identical grey mud rooms on the far side of the compound. All the doors were open and in each room squatted a smiling wife. Dr Onambele strolled along, naming each and making comments which I didn't take in. Had the wives been told to put themselves on display for the White visitors? The distressing overall effect was of being shown around a private zoo. Yet these women may be as happy as they looked; it must be prestigious to belong to an internationally famous medicine-man.

'I have twenty-eight children,' said Dr Onambele at the end of this tour. 'And much rich land.'

Breakfast happened then, a meal of steamed plantain, six-egg omelettes sodden in palm oil, pint mugs of Ovaltine and what can only be described as a meaty goo. We regretted our precautionary meal.

Having closely questioned me about my work, Dr Onambele foretold, 'When you write your next book you will be swindled. Other people will make much money from it but will give you little – beware! It is easy to swindle you!'

I made no reply, being weak on the social formulae required for such situations.

A few silent moments later our host said abruptly, 'Someone very close to you who is dead returns sometimes in dreams and *is with you* – you are together again. But this does not happen often. This person is dead many years and there are long gaps.'

All this is so true that for a moment I was startled, especially by the emphasis on *is with you*, which is exactly how it feels in those rare dreams. Then I reminded myself that such experiences must be common – and useful to a medicine-man as 'proof' that he can divine people's 'secrets'.

After breakfast Bassong hung back while we were taken to the spirits' shrine, a round wickerwork thatched hut in a secluded corner of the compound. Dr Onambele explained that some of the spirits who come to him in the night feel trapped under a tin roof and others are scared off in the rains by the noise overhead.

'Sensible spirits!' I murmured flippantly to Rachel. But the wider implications of this preference are convoluted.

From the moment of our meeting, Dr Onambele had baffled me. Clearly he was a sharp operator, with an eye to the main chance when Whites appeared. Yet it would be both unfair and obtuse to dismiss him as a cynical charlatan. Sitting with him in that hut, surrounded by the standard implements of his magical trade, it was beyond dispute that he believed in his own powers. And I had an open mind on his dealings with spirits, which in my view may or may not exist.

Our attention was drawn to two crudely carved wooden figures, male and female, some eighteen inches high and very old. Through these the spirits talk to Dr Onambele. A small complete termite-hill, its base wrapped in black plastic, is used to counteract epidemics. One of the three monkey skulls on display ensures that hunters will have success; the uses of the other two were not divulged. Water that has been left overnight in an oddly-shaped bowl – apparently a human skull encased in mud – will cure blindness. A long black antelope horn banishes barrenness, when pointed at the womb, and this is the magic most in demand.

We watched Dr Onambele half-filling a wide tin basin with water from an iron cauldron. Then he asked us to spit on a lump of sugar; we obeyed and it was floated on the water. Next we spat on a match, used to ignite the sugar-lump. It burned steadily while we were being given two powders, one to cure stomach upsets, the other as 'general protection'. (The latter, in the weeks ahead, didn't work too well.) When the sugar had burned out Bassong was summoned and told to fetch an empty bottle which was filled with water from the basin 'to protect you at night in the bush from direct attacks by bad spirits'. (That worked fine.) We were also given a small gourd from which the enspelled water *must* be drunk. Afterwards Rachel looked slightly uneasy when I abandoned our magic bottle at the first opportunity, hiding it in a hollow tree. But we still have the powders and the gourd, our only tangible souvenirs from Cameroon.

As we returned to the bungalow Rachel whispered, 'Dash?'

'No way!' I whispered back.

Our bush-path from We to Wum was a cut-long; the ring-road takes the shortest route – a mere eight miles. On the way, while crossing a high grassy ridge, the ground seemed suddenly to be *moving*. We stopped, staring down, then exclaimed in unison 'A plague of caterpillars!' These however were not fat, black and hairy, like the source of Nigel Barley's frustration further north in Cameroon. They were thin, short haired, black and green – but equally destructive. At a nearby milk-bar we heard that for miles around the mountains had been stripped; soon there would be no grazing left.

The ladies of that compound were engaged in hair-styling their small daughters' curls. We were given mini-stools to sit on, in the shade of a mango tree, while enjoying a large bowl of curds; then I caused great offence by leaving 200 CFA in the empty bowl. It was rejected by a furious young woman with a thin face and a hooked nose. '*Me* dash *you*!' she said witheringly.

The gradual descent to Wum took us through many fields being devastated by caterpillars. One woman, mistaking us from afar for MIDENO anti-pest experts, came sprinting to greet us. Her expression, when disillusioned, would have taken a tear from a stone. She pointed to the surrounding acres of baby maize – a second planting, because the first had been eaten. Now this too was vanishing, even as we watched. And there could be no third planting ...

As Wum and its volcanic lake came into view – still several miles away – we were joined by a young man carrying an outsize oil-stove on his head. He informed us that the local 'rich men' were leaving some fields fallow, seeing no point in wasting seeds on feeding caterpillars.

'But what about the poor men?' I asked. 'What can they do?'

The young man laughed merrily. 'Hah! There is nothing for them to do! This year no chop for poor men!' From which we deduced that he was not a poor man.

Lake Wum, semi-encircled by smooth, low, grassy hills, was easily accessible. The oval of cool jade-green water, immensely deep and about a mile long, is fringed by palms, flowering shrubs and tall graceful trees bearing a strange yellow fruit. There we laundered clothes and swam lengthily and talked with a youth sitting alone under a tree reflecting on his future. He had just finished his seventh grade examinations and was now in a state of high tension, awaiting results. If these were satisfactory he hoped to go to Yaoundé University, after two years at a Yaoundé boarding-school to improve his French, and then to become a teacher. His father was the local quarterchief (a Wum quarterchief is a VIP) and, he said, owned the lake. He apologised for the lack of a tourist hotel, once discussed but not mentioned recently. It was rumoured that a powerful group of elders had opposed this development, arguing that it would dangerously offend the spirits who dwell in Lake Wum.

This youth's curiosity about Europe was unusual. How was our transport, did we have bush-taxis? Did all Big Men have automobiles? How were our houses built? Did everyone have tin roofs? Did we have dwarf cattle or zebu? How many wives did Big Men have? To him the notion of polygamy being *illegal* was not only absurd but threatening, a direct attack on male supremacy. 'Then how,' he asked, 'do Big Men show they are important? And how is their land planted? Who weeds their fields? They must have *so much* servants! Or is it how they can still buy slaves?' Clearly he thought anything possible in countries where polygamy is prohibited. Next he asked, gazing at Rachel's head, bobbing in mid-lake, 'How old is this daughter?' And then, 'You will soon arrange brideprice? If girls don't marry by nineteen latest they run around and become harlots. After marriage it is OK if they have jobs, if they want to work to make money. But first they must have a husband to control them, to keep them living quietly.'

Beyond the lake we climbed through a mature eucalyptus wood, then found ourselves in the quarterchief's spacious compound – witness to the Aghem Federation's pre-colonial wealth. Four imposing thatched mud houses – definitely not huts – had weather-worn, but still sharply detailed carvings on their window-frames and doors. There was no one around, apart from a sow giantess with eight minute piebald bonhams. And of course the chiefly ancestors lay in their communal grave in one corner, covered by a massive slab that could be shifted whenever it seemed expedient to pour libations to (and onto) the great-grandads, whose spirits dwell in Lake Wum.

In the nearest off-licence a local government official said, 'Debts are strangling me!' Five of his seven children were of boarding-school age and if you didn't send them to a good Mission school what chance would they have? For years he had been trying to persuade White priests and nuns to start a day-school in Wum. 'We have now about

219

10,000 people in this town, we need good education.' He despised all government schools.

We were alone in the bar when a stately, well-robed, middle-aged gentleman entered quietly and ordered a Beaufort. By then we had developed a nose for Chiefs, Fons, Lamidos and suchlike. I whispered to Rachel, 'The quarterchief!' And so he proved to be, a most delightful character with whom we talked for the next hour. His main concern was the caterpillar plague. 'For me it doesn't matter, I have many fields in different places. But for my poor people who have only a few small fields it is a sad, sad tragedy!'

This quarterchief had an unusual (in Cameroon) hobby: local history. He told us that when the Germans arrived at the end of the nineteenth century Aghem's population was about 5,000 and most men were part-time traders. In 1904 the notorious Captain Glauning led his German troops into the area, burned Wum and flogged to death a local *Batum* (hereditary ruler of a section of the Aghem Federation). Another *Batum*, our friend's great-grandfather, was arrested with two of his elders and gaoled in Bamenda where all three soon died. The *Batum* of Waindo, wishing to become Paramount Chief, had intrigued to bring about this invasion. Only his people were not attacked and he became, briefly, the Germans' ally and administrator. 'But the Germans also did good things,' concluded the quarterchief. 'They gave us our first roads, schools, medical centres, telegraph service – and scripts for languages we couldn't write before. Colonialism is like the zebra. Some say it is a black animal, some say it is a white animal and those whose sight is good, they know it is a *striped* animal!'

This was Wum's oldest and most attractive quarter, where we spent our first night. An unpleasant entrepreneur tried to over-charge us for a room in a newish shack built on wasteland. It had a loose roof, a dangerous hole in the floor, a grubby mattress and a defective lock. No latrine was indicated and no washing water or lantern provided. Life is much more civilised in the bush.

At midnight the entrepreneur, now very drunk, bashed on our door and yelled frenziedly, 'Are you people asleep! Do you sleep? Have you problem? Let me in! I have no problem!'

I did indeed have a problem, which continued until about 4 a.m. In several nearby huts throngs of men – certainly scores and perhaps hundreds – were drumming, chanting, clapping, semi-hysterically laughing and whooping what sounded like war-cries. I lay thinking positive: at least the disturbance was aurally inoffensive, unlike disco noises or the amplified Hindi film music that so often keeps one awake in India.

Although we hadn't expected to like Wum, an 'administrative capital' on a motor-road, we fell in love with the town at first sight – fortunately, as we were destined to see much more of it than we ever intended.

Here our passports were confiscated and our visa problem ran out of control, becoming inextricably entangled with Rachel's magnetism for the lower ranks of the gendarmerie. The details would be tedious, but we spent many hours persuading the more frankly virile policemen that a) our visas had been cleared by a *senior* Immigration Officer and b) Rachel was not willing to copulate with anyone in exchange for our passports. I felt genuinely sorry for a warm-hearted and undevious Francophone officer who repeatedly begged Rachel to go to bed with him, as the three of us sat beer-swilling in a bar-brothel. He couldn't understand why she wouldn't, since she (and her mother) obviously liked him. When he had resigned himself to his inexplicable fate he continued to be helpful and friendly, with no ulterior motive.

One morning was spent sitting on the verandah of a congenial senior officer named Basil. He had asked us to call to his home on the outskirts of Wum at 8 a.m., to discuss our visa problem – forgetting that the morrow was Sunday, when he always played football with his men from 6 to 10 a.m. His wife was away in Bamenda for the weekend but two of his younger sisters entertained us; one longed to study science at an English university, the other thought an American university would be more fun. Basil's two-and-a-half-year-old daughter sat on my lap reading aloud, unaided, from her Ladybird book – one young Cameroonian who is unlikely to have academic problems.

Remarkably, that Ladybird Reader and the We gendarme's eccentric Nigerian dictionary were the *only* two books we saw in Cameroon, outside of the cities – and this despite our having stayed in several teachers' homes. Nor did we once see, in the possession of a Cameroonian, any newspaper however rudimentary (most Cameroonian newspapers are very rudimentary), or any pamphlet, magazine or even comic. For all practical purposes rural Cameroon remains a pre-literate society, though a percentage of the younger generation is able, after a fashion, to read and write. This must partly explain the frequency with which Mungo Park's comments could be applied to our own experiences and observations, almost two hundred years later. On one level those two centuries have utterly transformed Africa, on another level they have made astonishingly little difference. The continent's veneer of modernity – national airlines and universities, architecturally pretentious capital cities, armed forces equipped with the latest weaponry and jet-fighters – can cause people to forget that many Africans are no better informed, and have no wider a world-view, than their pre-colonial ancestors. Certainly we overestimate the educational potential of the ubiquitous transistor radio. Our young friend under the tree by Lake Wum cherished his trannie but it had manifestly failed to enhance

221

his knowledge of the outside world. For the illiterate (or semi-literate), it is not educational to listen to good news reports on China's changing political scene, or astute analyses of conflicts in Central America or the Middle East, or panel discussions on the expansion of Japanese industry. Many Cameroonians have not the faintest notion where these places are. They cannot visualise or comprehend things or concepts outside their own experience. They cannot distinguish between a republic and a monarchy, democracy and dictatorship, capitalism and communism, an Arab desert and an American wheat prairie. For us it is hard to grasp the intellectual inflexibility and isolation of a society indifferent to the printed word.

In *The Mind of Man in Africa* Dr J. C. Carothers, an ex-colonial medical officer who specialised in psychiatry, considers some of the implications of belonging to a pre-literate culture. And he makes the point that:

> The written word has probably only been invented a few times in this world's history. Yet in other large agricultural populations its impact has been vital for many centuries. It is sometimes argued that its absence from sub-Saharan Africa is to be accounted for by isolation from outside influences ... Yet it *has* been introduced, in its Arabic form, both through the Sudan and from the East Coast, frequently enough. It has even been invented, on two occasions in the nineteenth century, by gifted individuals in Sierra Leone and the Cameroons. Yet it failed to implant itself and grow, and this is the more surprising in view of the high level of organisation and stability achieved by several West African kingdoms in other respects. Nor can this failure be attributed to the disruption of organized life in Africa by the Atlantic slave trade since Arabic literacy in the Western Sudan goes back at least 850 years, about 450 years before the beginning of that trade.

Dr Carothers, having worked for many years in East and West Africa, concluded that because the written word had not brought about the division in people's minds between *verbal thought* and *action*, independent thinking was felt to be extremely dangerous.

Perhaps the most resented colonial criticism of Blacks was: 'They're like children!' Dr Carothers has an interesting theory about the basis for that misjudgement:

> J. Piaget's studies of European children are highly relevant to the problem of the mental development of the child in Africa. About the age of seven or eight years, European children move from a stage in which thinking is essentially egocentric to one of an increasing objectivity ... There is a conscious recognition of the need to ask the

question 'How?' In the conception of causality, the need is seen for continuity and contact, for things to derive from other things, for the birth of new events by reassortment of parts or qualities and, at last, for explanation by spatial and temporal relations and for logical deductions ... It has to be noted that the 'magical' and 'animistic' elements of the first egocentric stage, which gradually disappear from the thinking of the European child after the age of seven or eight years, remain prominent in the thinking of adults in *rural* Africa [my italics].

Dr Carothers then wonders if 'it is mere coincidence that at about the age of seven or eight European children have fully acquired the art of reading ...' My own footnote here is that many illiterate young White adults, in present-day British inner-cities, also suffer from an inability to visualise things or comprehend concepts outside their own experience.

Dr Carothers worked in Africa a generation and more ago. Now his theories are often dismissed as irrelevant because 'things are changing' and Africans are being educated Western-style. Even if this were true, which it isn't, there is something ropey here. The implication is that Africans are 'backward' because under-exposed to post-Renaissance thinking, that the differences between Blacks and Whites – intellectual, physical, emotional, spiritual, temperamental – are entirely a result of Black Africa's culture being pre-literate. But what about millennia of evolution in a different climate, exposed to different diseases, eating different foods, required to exert different skills, holding different religious beliefs? When these differences are not ignored, it seems daft to expect Africans to adapt to Western culture within a few generations and proceed into future millennia with White minds in Black bodies. This of course is what too many Africans seem to want for themselves. But even if a sound Western education really were the answer to Africa's problems, it cannot be provided with the resources at present available. And, as two Kenya sociologists (Diane Kayongo-Male and Philista Onyango) have pointed out, 'The partial education that most Africans receive tends not only to prepare them inadequately but also instils in them unfounded self-confidence. They may ... for a very long time reject any employment that may be available as they consider themselves suitable for superior jobs.'

For decades Whites have avoided openly discussing the 'mind-set' aspects of some African problems. The post-colonial mood was of guilt and repentance and 'taking the blame', but now that taboo is weakening. After quarter of a century of increasingly shambolic Independence it no longer makes sense to pretend that *all* Africa's problems are 'our fault'. And it helps that the emotionally crucial matter of the slave-trade is beginning to be viewed more dispassionately. Britain's 'greatness' was firmly based on its revolting cruelties and enduring miseries, which are associated with still-familiar names. Barclays Bank was founded by David and Alexander Barclay on their profits as 'slavers'; Lloyds first flourished as slave-traders and soon needed bigger premises than a coffee-house; the development of James Watt's steam engine was financed by West Indian slave-owners and traders. Yet Black slave merchants also benefited, as J. D. Fage points out in *A History of West Africa*:

The European slave-traders were *traders,* who bought their slaves from coastal African merchants. In return they provided textiles; all kinds of firearms, gunpowder and shot; knives and cutlasses; ironmongery and hardware; iron, copper, brass and lead in bar form; beads and trinkets; spirits (rum, brandy, gin) and many kinds of provisions. These imports clearly had value to the West Africans, for otherwise they would not have been willing to exchange slaves for them ... In the eighteenth century West Africa's involvement in the slave trade was big business, contributing substantially to the growth of her trade. The slaves had to be fed and cared for while still in African hands, thus providing new markets for local production. The European slave-traders brought considerable new business to African merchants and producers, since they had to buy provisions for the slaves on the voyage across the Atlantic. The slave trade brought increasing numbers of Europeans to the shores of West Africa, so that there was a growing number of buyers for her gold, ivory, gums, woods, palm-oil and many other things besides the slaves and their provisions ... Buying and selling slaves necessitated more professional merchants. These, and the officials who were increasingly needed to regulate trade in each state, and the soldiers in the armies who captured the slaves ... had less time to grow their own food, to make houses or clothing, and so stimulated other people's production for exchange. West Africa indeed became a land renowned for its markets.

Given the viciousness of the slave-trade, good race relations need an admission that both races rode on that gravy-train. Although fuelled by White demand, it could not possibly have rolled without the enthusiastic co-operation of Blacks. From the sixteenth to the nineteenth century, Europeans lacked the military resources and preventive medicines to invade Africa's interior and enslave the estimated eleven million young men and women who were shipped off to the plantations. Nor did African merchants have to be bullied or coerced; they knew a profitable line in trades goods when they saw it. They were of course corrupted – dazzled by goodies – but they never had any scruples about selling fellow-Africans into slavery. Moreover, if those awaiting shipment on the coast, and costing quite a lot to feed, were not bought because of some unexpected drop in demand, they might be used instead as human sacrifices. Human rights were not a big deal, on any continent, during the centuries under consideration.

And what of human rights now? The subject came up when Basil arrived at 11.20 a.m., still in his football togs and accompanied by a follower. He apologised profusely for 'this silly muddle of days' and beer happened and we settled down to discuss everything except passports and visas.

Basil's follower greatly admired Mrs Thatcher because she wants to bring back hanging. 'It is necessary,' he declared, 'and not only for murder. Here we also kill robbers. We execute them by military firing squad if they break into houses. Even if you steal a door-key, or your friend steals it for you, and you enter by door, this is also robbery and you will die if caught. This is a good law. If I work hard and buy nice things no one has a right to steal them and live to enjoy them after prison.'

When I made shocked noises the Thatcher fan protested that priority must be given to a man's right to retain his own property. By depriving someone of property, the criminal forfeits the right to retain his own life. Basil – one of our favourite Cameroonians – obviously disagreed with all this but was cornered. As a senior police officer, responsible for upholding law and order, he could not openly condemn one of his country's laws. But he was subtle enough to convey condemnation without being overtly subversive.

As we stood up to leave Basil exclaimed, 'Your passports! My men are being so stupid! Tomorrow is Monday, you go and collect them in the morning – I will give the order.'

I wondered then if he realised that his men were being not stupid but randy. Their many ingenious stratagems to separate Rachel from Mamma had suggested a high level of enterprising intelligence.

On our way to the town centre I brooded over human rights and White double-think and subconscious or disguised racialism. How would the White liberal world react if the South African government imposed the death penalty on Black robbers? Why does the White liberal world *not* react when a Black government imposes the death penalty on Black robbers? Is this racialism rampant within White liberals? Do we reason, without admitting it, that a death-sentence for robbery is 'only what you'd expect' of a Black government so there's no point in making a fuss? Do we get steamed up about apartheid mainly because *Whites* are the criminals and so are letting 'our side' down? Or do we feel we're not entitled to interfere in Black Africa because 'that's how Blacks want to run their own show and we've meddled enough already'? But that would be racialism gone over the edge – the human rights principle sacrificed to *race* – Blacks killing Blacks is OK, though Whites killing Blacks is wrong ... Surely Blacks under a Black government are no less entitled to human rights than Blacks under a White government?

We had a luncheon appointment with Gussie at a town centre Achu House. (There are chop-houses which specialise in this dire dish.) Gussie – full brother to the Fon of Mukuru – was one of the first people we met in Wum. Now he invited us home to meet his wife, a teacher, and we were arranging a sunset rendezvous when another medicine-man intervened, urging us to stay the night in his compound 'on the edge of the town'. (It was in fact five miles away down a bush-path.) 'You go,' advised Gussie. 'For you people it will be interesting.' I would have preferred to talk to his wife about education but he seemed reluctant to thwart the medicine-man's ambition.

This character, known locally as 'the Doctor', was regarded with mingled derision and unease by most of our Wum acquaintances. He told us to call him Papa, so we did – and never discovered his real name. At first we assumed that our status symbol value had inspired his invitation but it later transpired that he quite fancied Rachel as his sixth wife. He offered her a lift on the back of his motor-bicycle and this was the occasion when I most regretted our camera's salination. I yearned for a pictorial record of Rachel, plus huge rucksack, perched on the pillion clutching the medicine-man's waist as they bounded over Wum's rutted road with a cardboard placard inscribed 'DOCTOR' tied to the back mudguard and wagging like a dog's tail.

One of Papa's twenty-seven children – a barefooted small boy, carrying a big basket of rice – guided me through rough but fertile country. The compound's two long shed-like dwellings were unworthy of their very lovely setting on the brink of a tree-filled valley, but Papa was extremely proud of their sheer size. Not since leaving the Lamidat in Tignère had we seen anything as large as his living-room – some thirty feet by fifteen, with a sofa and four armchairs at one end, a small dining-table at the other and nothing in between. Papa was a Fon's son and sixteen Chief's caps decorated one wall, each with a different feather of 'secret' significance and to be worn on the appropriate occasion *only*. On the opposite wall hung a chief's drum – 'Worth 100,000 CFA (about £225) because these are not made any more and have a lost magic.' Below the drum were a shooting-stick left over from the Raj and a locally made gun, brass-studded, 'for shooting monkeys'. It looked as though it might be equally likely to shoot the shooter. A six-foot python skin nailed to the wall (the snake had been killed in the garden) seemed a great improvement on Dr Onambele's inflatable reptile. By the unglazed window hung a Fatman poster, a Papal Visit poster and an electric cuckoo-clock varnished pale yellow and of decorative value only; Papa's generator worked so irregularly that a supplementary lantern was kept alight all evening.

A dozen juicy mangoes were brought to keep us going and Papa produced a quarter bottle of duty-free Scotch for my benefit, saying that he himself never touched the stuff. After a polite half-finger, I admitted to preferring beer in the tropics. His two youngest, a seven-month-old son and two-year-old daughter, also had their share of '33'. Basil later told us that drunkenness is relatively uncommon in Cameroon, despite beer for breakfast, because heads are made in infancy. And it helps that spirits are virtually unknown outside the cities. Only in Cameroon was I never once offered a home-distilled hooch, though presumably some is occasionally made.

The children's mothers – the two youngest of Papa's five wives – were told to sit down and help themselves to beers. They were good-looking in different styles (fat and thin) and seemed on excellent terms with their husband and each other. The recently-acquired fifth was Rachel's age; Papa was 'about sixty'. He had never been to school and admitted to being illiterate: 'Reading is not necessary for my business.' As the evening progressed I warmed to him. His attitude to his women and children was kindly and he seemed a more genuine *medicine*-man than the celebrated Dr Onambele. Despite his polygamous compound he considered himself a good Catholic and devoutly said grace not only before each meal but even before eating a mango.

When supper arrived – rice, avocados, stewed fresh fish – our host suddenly disappeared, perhaps to soothe the generator which had run out of fuel and seemed about to explode. A well-trained bitch and two pups sat patiently by the table while we ate. Then we discovered that Papa had quit his room for us. We lay feeling oddly regal on a high four-poster with twenty-two chief's cloaks on hangers around the walls, forming a sort of tapestry. Many were very beautiful; Papa's boast that each was worth 50,000 CFA (over £100) seemed plausible. Unfortunately the generator dwelt nearby and continued to growl and rattle all night while giving off near-toxic fumes. Across the flimsy partition the youngest wife and baby were sleeping close beside us; at intervals I could hear the contented snufflings of a suckling infant.

Before breakfast Papa showed us around his estate, some of which was devoted to the growing of medicinal herbs, bushes and trees. Fifteen of his progeny were already toiling in the fields and he acknowledged that he attached little importance to schooling. 'You have much land like I have much land, you no need school for city jobs.'

If I kept a personal Book of Records, that morning's breakfast would have to be entered as 'The Biggest'. Avocados, mangoes, cocoyam, rice, jammu-jammu, fish and Bournvita – all in prodigious quantities. I walked back to Wum rather slowly, when Rachel and the rucksack had bounced off on the pillion. A slim eleven-year-old daughter accompanied me, bearing a huge basket of mangoes. To us it seemed barbarous that Papa on his machine should leave a child to carry such a load for five steep miles. But it would be unthinkable for him to be seen taking goods to the market, even by motor-bicycle. On the way the girl begged for money to buy shoes and I wondered, uncharitably, if she had been instructed to do so. Her manner suggested that this soliciting of funds did not come naturally to her.

Wum offers quite a choice of chop-houses, palm wine shebeens and off-licences. There are also two hotels, using that word in its loosest sense. When we found our passport problem still unresolved – Basil's Monday order must have gone astray – we booked into the Happy Days Hotel at 1,000 CFA per person. This is not the place to go for happy nights. The staff of two young men lay asleep in the bar all day because their disco-cum-brothel operates until dawn seven nights a week. As we lay sweating and awake, hour after hour, the decibel-level became a form of mental torture. Even amplified Hindi film-music is far preferable to those abominations of the electronic age (chiefly Congolese and Nigerian) which made it impossible for even Rachel to sleep. However, the Happy Days lavatory quite often flushed and a tap beside it provided a reasonable supply of water. But unluckily our disintegrating balcony overlooked a gully full of banana plants and town garbage – and it was asphyxiatingly evident, especially after heavy showers, that many of Wum's citizens do not have a lavatory.

The 'Peace, Unity and Hygienic Restaurant' became our favourite chop-house, as much because of its name as its cuisine – though that too pleased. There we met a unique (in our experience) individual, a Cameroonian who took AIDS seriously. He was aged thirty and eloquent: 'Every evening I go home to my wife before dark! After dark is when I get tempted with women – in daylight I am safe. Now I stay always with my wife after dark, only with my wife. Before, I have plenty, plenty women – *too* much women! Now one woman only – I am very afraid!'

All along our route we tried to discuss the AIDS threat with our drinking-companions, male and female, and found many touchy on the subject. Some of the worldly-wise (police and army officers, government officials, secondary school teachers) dismissed the 'AIDS from Africa scare' as an invention of decadent, scapegoat-hunting Whites. The virus, they insisted, had been brought to Africa by American perverts and was not a serious threat because among Africans homosexuality is almost unknown. They refused to believe that African blood banked in Kinshasa in 1959 held HIV antibodies and were sceptical about the role of heterosexual promiscuity. Sometimes I quoted stark statistics: 'A few

228

months ago in one trucking town in eastern Zaire 76 per cent of barmaids were found to be HIV positive and 33 per cent of long-distance drivers passing through. And some of those were on their way to or from *Cameroon.*' But statistics, however ominous, made no impression. As Rachel remarked, 'They won't take it seriously until they *see* their family and friends dying!'

Even if Cameroon's government had the will, money, equipment and trained personnel to confront this crisis, there are formidable 'mind-set' problems. Westerners now see a new disease as a challenge, but to most Africans disease remains something that must be accepted unless the medicine-man can intervene. So they react fatalistically to warnings about a new lethal virus. Also, they tend to live in the present and to become bored or impatient if advised to take precautions *now* to avert disaster several years hence.

The longer we spent in Cameroon the more I appreciated Professor John Mbiti's stress on the importance of the African concept of time. To him an awareness of that concept is crucial to any understanding not only of African traditions but of African behaviour 'in all areas of the modern world'. Africans, he explains, have always regarded time as two-dimensional:

... a long *past,* a present and virtually *no future.* The linear concept of time in Western thought, with an indefinite past, a present and an infinite future, is practically foreign to African thinking. The future is virtually absent because events which lie in it have not taken place, they have not been realized and cannot, therefore, constitute time ... *Actual time* is what is present and what is past. It moves 'backward' rather than 'forward'; and people set their minds not on future things, but chiefly on what has taken place ... Since what is in the future has not been experienced, it does not make sense; it cannot therefore constitute part of time, and people do not know how to think about it – unless, of course, it is something which falls within the rhythm of natural phenomena ... People have little or no active interest in events that lie in the future beyond, at most, two years from now; and many African languages lack words by which such events can be conceived or expressed. This basic concept of time underlies and influences the life and attitudes of African peoples in the villages, and to a great extent those who work or live in the cities as well. Among other things, the economic life of the people is deeply bound to their concept of time.

Our dangerous 'time is money' notion has no meaning in Africa where, as Professor Mbiti points out, apparently lazy people 'are actually *not wasting* time, but either waiting for time or in the process of "producing" time.' These incompatible attitudes to time have probably

229

been at the root of more Black-White misunderstandings than anything else. The Black attitude explains a myriad everyday anomalies and what, in 'the modern situation', look like monumental official blunders. It often reduces to rubble those Five-Year-Plans so beloved of economists. And on the personal level it produces a remarkable number of abandoned, half-built swanky residences on the outskirts of Cameroonian towns. Nor is it unconnected with the (to us) inexplicable delay before our confiscated passports at last reappeared.

12

Trapped by Lake Nyos

BEFORE LEAVING WUM we called on the Catholic Mission and passed its neat camp for 250 of the 4,000 (or so) villagers displaced by the Lake Nyos tragedy and awaiting official decisions about their future. Many of those 'aid' tents were as big as a small hut. Some of the children were playing with the mangled remains of expensive Western toys. Not surprisingly, the camp seemed very quiet. There were none of the frabjous sounds – songs, laughter, cheerful teasing arguments – that normally emanate from groups of Cameroonians. We hesitated on the edge, longing to talk to these victims of one of the twentieth century's most mysterious natural disasters. But we couldn't bring ourselves to intrude on them. During the previous eight months, Wum had had more than its share of eagerly beavering journalists from every continent.

As we landed in Douala, on 18 March, almost one hundred scientists were mid-way through a six-day Yaoundé conference to try to determine why Lake Nyos exploded, on the evening of Thursday, 21 August 1986, releasing within an hour an estimated 1.3 billion cubic yards of toxic gases – mainly carbon dioxide. This gas instantly killed almost everyone in the village of Nyos and the surrounding compounds. About five hundred people were also killed in the neighbouring villages of Cha, Subum and Fang, as the heavy gas filled fifteen miles of river valley. More than 3,000 cattle died on the mountains around the lake – as did birds, snakes, insects. No creature was left alive.

The conferring scientists included vulcanologists, geophysicians, physicians, ethnologists and sociologists from Africa, Asia, Europe, Australasia, North and South America. They debated the nature of the disaster and tried to decide whether or not it was likely to be repeated – either in Lake Nyos or one of the Grassfields' other three dozen volcanic lakes – and also if any warning system could be devised. Subsequently we met a few experts who had stayed on to pursue their investigations from Bamenda's tourist hotel, while they sought to rent a Bamenda house in which to install equipment which would tell them what was happening, at any given moment, on the distant floor of the 680-foot-deep lake. They entertained us with lively accounts of the usual experts' in-fighting at Yaoundé.

A minority faction, mainly Swiss, French and Italian, believed that a volcanic vent cap below the bed of the lake was blown off by the pressure of heavy gases which then, erupting through the water, followed the river course to the valley. They argued that similar disasters could happen elsewhere without warning, including in the dormant volcanic lakes of France, Italy and the United States. The American vulcanologists maintained that the gas had not been violently discharged from the lake floor but had gradually escaped and saturated the water. Felix Tahoun, a Cameroonian scientist, agreed in principle with the Americans, but believed the release had been triggered by a massive rock-fall or some other external agent such as a particularly fierce storm. (August is the *real* rainy season, during which daily storms make those we experienced seem like April showers.) Oddly, no one seems to have asked why the experts, instead of dissenting about the possible role of a rock-fall, had not expended some of their energy, during the previous months, on looking for evidence of such – which would surely be visible to the naked scientific eye, or indeed to any observant eye.

Professor Tchaou of Yaoundé University also supported the American theory and argued that it should be possible to monitor and siphon off accumulated gases from all Cameroon's potentially lethal lakes. He and his Cameroonian colleagues urged the founding of a National Centre for the Study of Natural Risks, which would monitor crater lakes as its first duty. Alas! this is the sort of 'prestige project' which over-excites too many Third World academics and governments – though on such matters the Cameroonian government is more level-headed than most. It would be monstrously expensive to establish and fund. It would offer fat salaries to an élite corps of scientists. Its monitoring, if done efficiently, might possibly, at some future date, save another village from extinction; but the resources thus squandered would be out of all proportion to the good achieved, given the fact that most Cameroonian towns and all villages lack adequate (or any) health care. And in Cameroon's hospitals patients have to provide not only their own food, fuel and bedding, but their own medicines, dressings, hypodermic needles, plaster of paris – you name it, they must buy it. Natural Risks would therefore seem to be a less pressing danger than humdrum diseases.

After the Yaoundé conference (sponsored by UNESCO and other

money-wasting international organisations) various newsagencies naïvely reported 'lengthy on-the-spot investigations by experts from all over the world'. In fact not many scientists spent much time around Lake Nyos, though during the months after the tragedy they enthusi-astically attended Nyos conferences in Hawaii and elsewhere. One American team, neglected by its helicopter, was stranded on the shore for days – of course without camping equipment, as they had expected to be back in Bamenda for sundowners. Apparently it occurred to none of them to go to Bafmeng, scarcely six hours walk away. I'd like to have been a fly on the cliff-face during those days.

The media also announced that 1,746 people had been killed by Lake Nyos, the figure decided upon by the government for global consumption. Local estimates varied from one to two thousand. Given the Cameroonian vagueness about figures, and the circumstances of the burials – most very hurried, under quicklime – there could be no question of anyone compiling accurate statistics. Especially as the military and police gravediggers, and collectors of decomposing bodies, were themselves distressed, unnerved and often terrorised by their task. Several deserted, escaping over the mountains, and have not been heard of since.

The Yaoundé conference was unanimous on only one point: the locals should not be allowed to return to the evacuated area (some forty square miles) until many more scientific observations had been made. Nobody in authority took account of the fact that some of the villagers and Fulani compound dwellers would have preferred to risk another explosion rather than to sit around indefinitely in the demoralising atmosphere of the 'refugee'-camps – in Wum, Nkambe and other points. In the camps rumours were constantly circulating and no one could find out what was likely to happen to them in the future – could they return to their land or would they be resettled elsewhere?

So far as is known, comparable disasters have taken place on only three other occasions this century: in Indonesia in 1979 (seventeen killed), near the Columbian volcano of Turace in 1949 (sixteen killed), and on the Indian Ocean island of Karthala in 1903 (deaths not recorded). It would be interesting to know if any of those areas has similar religious beliefs centred on local lakes. In Cameroon the spirits of Fons and other important religious and military figures dwell in lakes, which also have their own powerful tutelary spirits – how power-ful, Lake Nyos proved.

Oddly enough, those puzzled by the sparse population of the Aghem highland, quite close to Lake Nyos, seem never to have speculated about the strong local tradition of (in Bantu terms) cosmic catastrophe. Yet there are vivid ancient legends of exploding lakes and 'walking' fish – live fish thrown in their thousands onto lake shores. The recently

233

arrived Fulani, who settled happily in Aghem, are not so culturally and emotionally enmeshed with lakes – though already they have been, to some extent, influenced by Bantu feeling.

In hot Benikuma we had eagerly asked the way to the local crater lake, hoping for a swim. But we were advised, begged, persuaded and almost *ordered* to avoid it. Therefore we did so. Given the post-Nyos twitchiness, we might have greatly upset the locals by breaking some taboo and thus angering the lake's spirits. (Or we might have felt, as at Lake Ocu, that we didn't after all feel like swimming ...)

When we left Wum, to find our bush-path way to Bafmeng, Nkambe and the Mbembe Forest Reserve, we knew little about the details of the Nyos disaster – the human details, as distinct from the scientific debate. The unspoken taboo had restricted in-depth conversations to the Bamenda scientists. Otherwise our information was sketchy, picked up at the time of the explosion from vague media reports.

Somehow we mislaid Bafmeng; none of the paths that we had been told about in Wum was marked on our map. After two days' exhilarating trekking – through narrow valleys, some rugged, some lush, and over high Fulani territory – we found ourselves at sunset on the wide summit of a long grassy ridge. (The final stage of that climb had been the steepest yet, an Ndung descent in reverse.) There we spent a psychologically uncomfortable night in a large Bantu compound of tall square dwellings. The many men, women and children seemed unaccountably scared of us and never relaxed, though their hospitality was lavish. No one spoke a syllable of any recognisable language, which was particularly unfortunate because at that stage we were, even by the standards of the Murphys in Cameroon, *very* lost.

We left at dawn – the sky a quiet glory of dove grey and shell pink – and soon reached a puzzling turn of the broad path. It was visible for miles ahead, decisively going *away* from Nkambe. Yet there was no obvious alternative. Near a rich hamlet-sized Fulani compound we sat beside a handsome herd (chocolate or white-and-grey-speckled) and waited for milkers to appear. From this western edge of the ridge we were overlooking a beautiful but baffling world of many other crisscrossing ridges, stretching away to the horizon. Directly below – some 1,500 feet below – was a mile-wide irregular chasm, its jungly sides almost sheer, its floor a confusion of twisting streams, neglected cassava fields and thick scrub. Beyond rose a solitary rock peak – square and grey, a parody of an English Norman church tower based on a steep grassy mountain. Apart from the unsuitable path we had abandoned, none other was visible, anywhere; but we presumed pathlets existed.

Soon two elegantly gowned young Fulanis appeared, accompanied by tiny herd-boys wielding sticks twice as long as themselves. We asked,

'Nkambe?' They spoke some English and by then Rachel spoke scraps of Foulfouldé. It became clear that to get to Nkambe we must first get to Ise, a village not marked on our map. And to get to Ise we must descend into the chasm, cross a river, climb around the base of the churchy peak, turn left along a bouldery saddle and continue up and up to the crest of a high forested ridge where we would find a big track going direct to Ise. Then, before entering the village, we must turn right onto a small path which, after a few days, would join the ring-road near Nkambe.

Four strenuous hours later (the details of negotiating that chasm could themselves fill a chapter) we were on the Nkambe path with Ise about a mile away on our left. Near where we left the track, many military tents on a hillside puzzled us – the only army camp we saw in Cameroon.

Gradually we descended, passing from mountain to mountain, then following cultivated slopes to a one-hut compound where a startled little boy stood alone. Here Rachel was the first to glimpse, through tall eucalyptus and pines, an expanse of blue water far below. She pointed to it and asked, 'What is that?'

For a long moment the little fellow stared up at her in timid silence. Then he gathered his courage and said, 'Lake Nyos.'

Just below the compound we sat in the aromatic shade of a eucalyptus grove, beside two fat tethered goats, and looked at one another. A Bamenda-met scientist had mentioned the bliss of swimming in Lake Nyos; it was now, he said, 99.9 per cent safe. We unfolded the map. Lake Nyos itself, we already knew, was not marked (though several smaller local lakes were) and we later had reason to be grateful for this omission. But there were two villages of that name, Nyos and Nyos-Acha (Lower Nyos) and we reckoned that by following the eastern shore we could avoid both and, with luck, soon rejoin our Nkambe path – though the map, for once being accurate, described it as 'not clearly defined'. Before continuing we ate ten bananas each, tossing the skins to the goats.

The lake had looked quite near when first glimpsed, yet to reach it took another hour and a half. In a few isolated compounds bare-breasted women stared at us fearfully; one, on being asked for the path to Lake Nyos, said, 'Me no hear.' By then the lake was invisible; and it remained so while we climbed steeply on a moist skiddy path through dense pines and eucalyptus. That ridge supported a long, rich village with maize fields flourishing between tall trees and fine compounds built back from the track. Here we were assumed to be scientists; four youngsters, already corrupted by vulcanologists' dash, firmly attached themselves to us insisting that we needed guidance. Two were smallish boys, two adolescent girls – one blind in her left eye. The last thing we wanted was an aggressively predatory escort who would prevent our swimming together. But these adhesive youngsters were extraordinarily difficult to detach; on this one occasion I had to be harshly unpleasant to Cameroonians.

Where we emerged from the trees a very long and sometimes difficult descent began, on a scrubby rocky slope. Now the sky had partially clouded over and Lake Nyos was jade-green. Its extent only gradually became apparent: more and more and more water appeared from behind a promontory of red-brown rock. The flat southern shore, which we were approaching, is thin jungle, or naked devastation, near the water. Uneven grass mountains, unusually green, form the eastern and some of the northern shore. The western shore is of sheer rock cliffs, sloping down to the north. Nyos is among the loveliest lakes I have ever seen – at first the shock of its beauty seems to obliterate its lethal past.

On level ground our path petered out and to find the water (invisible again) we had to force our way through a dense belt of unfamiliar grey-green bush, seven feet high and in places almost impenetrable. Where we reached the shore it still looked battered – strewn for some eighty yards inland with dead vegetation, including palms, that had been uprooted by the violent wave accompanying the explosion. On the nearby promontory cliff a vivid straight line marked the water's lowering; its level sank more than three feet after the expulsion of the gas. Here the 'beach' was of soft, black, volcanic muddy sand – slightly stained with reddish iron compound deposits, spewed from the floor of the lake. What looked like solid black rocks by the water's edge crumbled disconcertingly when one touched them. The experts say Lake Nyos is new-born, not more than a few centuries old.

I was faintly apprehensive lest our swimming might be observed from afar and considered disrespectful to the bereaved or provocative of spirits. But apart from this, and a twinge of guilt about enjoying ourselves in a lake that had behaved so badly, no 'feeling' made us hesitate before plunging in. To us Lake Nyos seemed entirely free of Lake Ocu's negative vibes. Although some water-lilies grew near the shore there was no shallow ledge. I fancied the water tasted faintly of sulphur and that taint seemed to remain on my skin afterwards; but Rachel said I was imagining this. (I don't think I was; and later we heard that scientists' samples drawn from 600 feet down showed the depths then still fizzing.) Otherwise the only 'strangeness' – the ease of swimming in immensely deep water – was not strange to us who all our lives have been bathing in a mini-crater lake, reputed to be 'bottomless', near our Irish home.

And yet, when it came to the crunch we were not really relaxed – only pretending to be so. By mutual wordless consent we stayed within a hundred yards of the shore, instead of swimming far out as in Lake Wum. And when my eye caught a barn-sized boulder, jutting over the water from a grass cliff, I began to think about the 0.1 per cent ... We emerged after about fifteen minutes though the temperature was conducive to an hour-long splash. Afterwards, I wondered why. One would be equally vulnerable to another explosion *in* the water or *on* the shore. But human beings are not always logical.

Finding a route along that southern shore was difficult, especially for Rachel carrying the heavy rucksack. The explosion wave had ravaged the friable ground and we had to climb in and out of five creeks – wet, black, treacherous gullies where the mud was semi-quicksand. If one paused one began to sink. Twice gully sides collapsed and came with us as we slithered down – a nasty feeling. Then at last we were on a firm grassy slope where we soon fell over a large box labelled 'Edinburgh University'. From it, wires ran to the floor of the lake and we presumed it was sending messages to our friends in Bamenda's Skyline Hotel. 'D'you suppose,' said Rachel, 'our kickings in the water have been registered as seismic activity by Edinburgh University?' A *won-der-ful* thought!

As we traversed that long mountain, high above the placid, innocent-looking water, I gazed west and thought of the invisible deserted village on the far shore, over the cliff-top. Now we could see the low dip in the northern shore through which the gas spilled out. A major concern of the scientists was that that flimsy natural dam might collapse, as a result of some mild earth tremor, releasing the lake itself to engulf the valley below.

Progress was easy along that grassy slope – until an impassable, jungle-filled ravine blocked our way.

'We can't get through *that*!' said I decisively. 'We'll have to climb high and see if we can bypass it.'

'You're always so defeatist!' complained Rachel. 'At least we can *try*!'

She then tried, with dire results that became apparent only days later. The jungle she challenged was peculiarly nasty. I half-heartedly advanced a few yards – then retreated. When she, too, saw sense we struggled upwards and eventually found a pathlet, around the top of the ravine, which led us out of sight of the lake. We wondered if it would soon meet our Nkambe path – as it should, according to the map. Then an inexplicable man-made barrier of tree-trunks and branches blocked the way. Laboriously we surmounted it, but no one could have driven cattle past.

Soon another crater lake, shallow and partially weed-overgrown, appeared far below on our right. This was Lake Njupi: also very beautiful, surrounded on three sides by steep grass mountains. On first seeing it I suggested camping by its shore. Then, as we walked on, gazing down at it, we both simultaneously began to find it 'spookier' than Lake Nyos.

So much lush grassland but no herds – not even on the most distant slopes – felt eerie. Far away, high on a mountain, we could see a solitary compound; if there weren't too many intervening ravines, we might get there by fufu-time. 'Let's hurry!' said Rachel – not having found Bafmeng, we had very little food left.

Then we began to descend and came upon the first cattle carcasses. They were still dreadfully decomposing; everything that would have cleaned the bones had also been killed. After that, around every corner, there were more bovine skeletons or bones or skulls – at our feet or in the distance. Some groups of carcasses were half-burned. And, incredibly, eight months later, there were nauseating whiffs of putrefaction. Suddenly I began to react personally, emotionally, to what had previously been – as faraway tragedies always are – an objectively observed event. This was the remains of some Fulani's beloved herd . . .

When we came to the first stricken compound – the one nearest the northern shore – a high washing-up trestle told us it had been Fulani. It was a one-hut compound. For us it should have been a milk-bar, where we sat gratefully sinking pints of milk or curds. Rusting basins, pots and enamelware were scattered outside the hut – and a few plastic shoes. Inside, a Bournvita tin and three mugs lay on the ground by the fireplace, where a blackened dented saucepan stood askew on its stones, above three half-burnt sticks. (Fire-extinguishers use carbon dioxide.) A dog-eared little book lay just inside the door: in Arabic, no doubt an Islamic tract. I thought, 'How strange, to find a book *here*!' I felt an impulse to rescue it but somehow couldn't bring myself to touch anything in that hut.

We hurried away; what had started as a light-hearted detour, to have a swim in Lake Nyos, was becoming an ordeal. No path was visible. Blundering through a terrible desolation of weed-strangled cassava, we came to another compound half a mile farther down the hillside. Only charred roof-poles remained; three huts had been deliberately burned to exorcise evil spirits. Crossing a fast deep stream, we found a distinct but overgrown path which passed two large compounds – their mango, avocado and banana groves laden with unpicked fruit, the jungle already creeping towards the dwellings and covering the graves.

When the path began to climb a scrubby mountain I exclaimed, 'Thank God! This will take us away from the area!'

Now we could hear a roaring river on our left, a semi-waterfall hidden amidst trees rushing down the steep slope from Lake Nyos – the river that carried the gas. 'If it sounds like that now,' said Rachel, 'what must it be like in the rainy season!'

Around the high shoulder of that mountain we could no longer hear the river and were overlooking a narrow valley and a by now familiar sight – many tin roofs, glinting through dense foliage. But there were no people to be seen. And there was no sound – absolutely no sound, of any sort.

'It's Nyos village,' muttered Rachel.

'It can't be!' I said. 'Nyos was on the lakeshore, it's way behind us, up by the water – somewhere over that rocky cliff.' (Thus do the media mislead.)

We walked on – unwillingly, but by that stage like automatons and anyway without much choice. Whichever way we turned, it seemed our only companions that evening would be the dead. As we descended the path widened and was carpeted with rotting fruits. Then we were amongst the houses: many fine substantial dwellings set in fertile gardens with handsome carved doors and shutters. Some were closed, some open – but every compound was a burial plot.

'You must be right,' I whispered. 'This must be Nyos.'

Suddenly the vegetation seemed menacing in its exuberance – almost mocking. Crops growing on – maize, yams, cane, cassava – not knowing they weren't wanted and for eight months being fought by a jungle unopposed. The silence was profound, the only movement our own. And it was 5.30 p.m. Smoke should have been starting to rise, people should have been coming home from the fields, scrubbing themselves in bathroom corners, fetching water, pounding maize, shredding jammu-jammu greens, whisking curds, drinking '33'. We became mourners then – not people reading the newspaper and exclaiming 'How awful!' but people grieving in their hearts for Nyos.

Soon, astonishingly, we were on a rough muddy motor track – the ring-road again, though we were too bemused to realise that.

Nyos was an important village, the hub of an exceptionally prosperous district. Its weekly market drew people from a wide area, hence the deaths of so many visiting outsiders that Thursday evening. Its merchants' stalls served many Fulani compounds on the surrounding mountains and many Bantu compounds up and down the intensively cultivated valley of the fatal river. It had recently been expanding; long rows of newish solid stalls and neat dwellings lined the track. And right beside us, as we stood staring up and down that soundless, motionless 'main street', was an off-licence with its bright frieze of those little beer advertisements which had so often cheered us from afar. The door was open, a 'Papal Visit' poster hung behind the bar, dusty bottles lay overturned on the floor. For us, irrationally yet understandably, that was the ultimate poignancy; there we would first have got to know the people of Nyos. But we said nothing – we had long since ceased to talk, or even to look at one another. There was nothing to say: and each of us had enough to do, keeping a grip on herself.

When I turned to look up the valley a robed figure was standing still in the middle of the road, fifty yards away. My heart lurched with primitive fear – real fear, so real that to recall it can frighten me now. For an instant I truly thought this was a ghost. And, in a sense, he was – a bereft young Fulani from the first compound we passed. He had lost all his family and all his cattle and then had lost his mind and couldn't be persuaded by anyone (we learned later) to leave the area. Slowly we walked towards him and I called out (a measure of my own demoralisation), 'Where is this?'

He replied in clear English, very calmly, 'This was the village of Nyos. But everyone is dead. All my people are dead.' He didn't look mad, just inexpressibly sad. 'Where do you go?' he asked.

'I don't know,' I replied. 'Where does this road go?'

'There is nowhere to go,' he said. 'Everyone is dead. No people are here – nowhere anyone.' He pointed down the ring-road. 'That way is Wum, you go Wum, in Wum are people.'

Suddenly our collective nerve broke; we only wanted to get out of Nyos. I groped in my pocket and pressed a CFA note into the young man's hand – it might have been for one thousand or ten thousand, I never knew. Then I hurried after Rachel who, despite the rucksack, was walking so fast away from Wum, towards Nkambe, that for the next half-hour I couldn't keep pace with her.

The first report of the disaster was written by Father Peter, an elderly Dutch Mill Hill priest, from Bafmeng, in whose parish Nyos and the other affected villages lay. He was the first White person on the scene, arriving in Nyos at noon on the Saturday, the tragedy having occurred on the Thursday evening between nine and ten o'clock. On the Sunday he wrote to his Bishop:

Your Grace, Last night, Saturday night, I came back from Nyos. On Friday rumours reached us that the lake had killed some Fulani and his cows. Then again that the quarterhead of Cha was lying dead in his compound with his two women. On Saturday morning I was so worried that I went with my two catechists, Sylvester and Hortensia, to Ise, which is high on the top, overlooking the Nyos valley. We thought to get information there but all the men had gone down and nobody had yet returned.

The first compound we entered in Nyos we found only 8 dead people. A child and the mammy lying very peacefully outside with the dog and the goat. In one house a big fat pa had tried to crawl to the door; two other young men were lying on the floor. So, too, the next door we opened. We rushed on to Mr Vincent Zong's big compound. He is the government teacher. His wife, Mary, is head of our school in Nyos. Vincent was lying dead with his eldest son, Mary with her baby in the next room. And in the children's room, four girls. Little Jacqueline who attends the school at Ise, was also at home for the holidays. All dead. We rushed on past all the houses in the Nyos market square which were all still locked. We knew that everybody was dead behind these locked doors. We rushed on to the mission. When we opened the door we found Nazarius, our catechist, as if he was saying his prayers with his head on the bed I usually sleep on when I am on trek. Four of his brothers had come from the coast to salute him. All dead. The one had a beautiful watch on, which had stopped at one o'clock in the night. Sylvester stayed behind with Hortensia to bury our catechist. I went as far as the Subum mission, which is about 7 km farther on the ring-road. When I opened the door, I found Lawrence our catechist, lying on the bed, cold as ice. I shouted: Anthony! Anthony! Because I had sent Anthony, one of my seminarians schooling at Fundong, to help the catechist in Subum. Anthony answered. He had survived. He was digging the grave for Lawrence and some other Christians. He and Lawrence were sitting in the half kitchen outside, at ten o'clock on Thursday night. Then something held his breathing. He struggled to get into the house, where he collapsed on the bed. At about 1 in the night, he managed to wake up and look for Lawrence. He had died on the spot. Then, my Anthony, who is perhaps 16 years of age, Form 4, had carried him inside and covered him and gone out to find what had happened. His chest was hurting and he felt very weak, but he started to do the only reasonable thing. He began to dig graves for all the Christians who had died ... The number who had died in Subum was more than one hundred. In Nyos simply all people had died, except one Pa and one boy who had slept a little higher up the mountain. There may have been 500 people sleeping in Nyos that night, because Thursday had been market and people from all sides attend the market. Some went back, others stayed and died. I do not know how many of our Christians of Ise have died because they slept at Nyos, but no one Christian of Nyos itself came to salute me or cry for me. The Church of Nyos has died, with Mattias, the head-Christian, and Nazarius the catechist and Mary the choirmistress ...

This is what I surmise has happened:

Gas under the lake, probably sulphur from the smell of it, had accumulated until it shot out down the slope into the village. The plantains and the high grass were flattened by the blast. It must have penetrated right through every house in Nyos. There was no difference between people outside or inside. Then spreading, it still had power to kill people at Subum, about 7 km away and even at Cha, about 11 km to the other side.

The gas may be building up again. I have heard that the governor wants all people to leave that area.

On Tuesday I shall go with all my parish to make a cry-die Mass at Subum (it is about 5 hours trekking) then in the night we shall proceed to Nyos about 7 km farther and sing for the last time in their church and pray for them. Then in the morning we shall climb back to Ise. We shall carry all the holy books along.

Father James, sixty hours after the event, and before meeting any other White with whom to discuss the situation, wrote a report to his bishop which said almost as much about the causes and consequences of the explosion as any of the scientists' reports after their series of expensive international conferences.

As I panted after my laden but speeding daughter – she must have been attaining five miles per hour – it occurred to me that her speed was futile. Darkness was coming early, under a low, leaden, sullen sky, and we were still passing stricken compounds. According to the map, all Rachel's hurry could achieve would be our arrival at another ghost village before nightfall. (Subum, where Father James found his cherished Anthony burying friends – though we were then unaware of those details.) Beside the track raced the fatal river, narrow and mud-brown and swift even on the valley floor. Rocky mountains rose close by on either side; between them and us were fields of tall coarse olive-green grass mixed with overgrown dying cane. Soon we would have to camp *on* the muddy track, unless we chose to share a compound with the dead.

Here the ring-road (we had sufficiently recovered our wits to identify it) was in ruins; no heavy vehicle could possibly have used it. If the little rains can cause such havoc, what must it be like in August? No wonder news of Nyos was slow to get out and help for survivors slow to get in. Twice we came to vegetation barriers, bushes heaped on the track with shreds of cloth tied to them. I mistook the first for a ju-ju, then realised these must be to warn vehicles that the ground beneath had subsided and was flooded, requiring extraordinary action. But *what* vehicles?

As the light faded I trotted to catch up with Rachel and propose settling down on the track before another compound/burial plot came into view. Then we turned a corner and were astounded to see a bush-taxi jerkily heaving itself towards us through the mud. It stopped. We stopped. For an odd little moment nobody moved. We stood staring, the passengers were evidently doing likewise. Then we advanced – and a gendarme in a strange uniform emerged.

We asked, 'Where is the next village?' – meaning inhabited village.

That gendarme may have been as unnerved by our appearing out of the empty dusk as we had been by the tragic young Fulani's materialisation. He was extremely angry, as some people tend to be in reaction to such scares. Banging his fist on the vehicle's bonnet he said we had broken the law – we were in a Restricted Zone – no vehicle was allowed to pass through without a Special Security Police escort, no pedestrian was allowed without a permit from *Yaoundé*! Did we have a permit from Yaoundé? No? Then where did we think we were going? The way we were heading there *was* no village for forty-four kilometres. There were no compounds, no human beings, everyone was dead or evacuated. We were arrested, he must take us to Wum where we would be punished.

Was ever anyone so happy to be arrested? Not a night in the rain on the track among the dead but *Wum* – Gussie, Papa, Chief Barnabas, the Happy Days Hotel, the Peace, Unity and Hygienic Restaurant and above all our dear Basil who would surely somehow stand between us and punishment ...

The gendarme said we must ride on the roof; there was no space inside. The roof consisted of a few iron struts. My adaptability failed. Criminals we might be; ride on those struts, in the dark, over the chasms of the ring-road, we would *not*. Those rare moments when one becomes a bully seem shameful in retrospect yet feel like common sense at the time. Among the passengers some two youths must be better equipped than we were – physiologically and psychologically – to ride those struts to Wum. It embarrasses me to recall that fracas. Briefly I became autocratic and declared that we would not allow ourselves to be arrested unless we could ride inside, in the back of the vehicle – we weren't demanding extra-special treatment, like front seats. The gendarme then batoned two youths as he ordered them onto the struts; neither had protested, seemingly he struck them as a precautionary measure to ensure that they wouldn't. Everybody was edgy, there in the twilight, with restless spirits – their burials unceremonial and therefore unsoothing – roaming the canefields and the mountainsides.

Later I guiltily asked Rachel, 'Was that "racism", throwing my weight about to get us inside?'

After a moment's thought she replied, 'No, it was what's now known as "classism"!'

'Inside' was no big deal. I don't know what happened to Rachel but I was sitting on a knobbly sack of unripe mangoes behind the driver's seat with a heavy tin trunk on my feet and a sharp object, in the pocket of the fat man beside me, sticking into my left hip. Wedged somewhere above me was an incontinent kid. Spurts of warm urine trickled down my back at frequent intervals. When the dramas of the road surface partly dislodged the creature it was able to establish an even closer relationship and began frantically to suckle my left ear.

'You are not comfortable,' understated the youth on my right, attempting to thwart the kid.

'Don't worry,' I reassured him, 'I like goats.' (Oddly enough, this was still true.) 'But,' I added, 'if you could ask the gentleman on my left to adjust the sharp object in his pocket I'd be much obliged.'

'He can't move,' the youth pointed out. 'There is little room. In this bush-taxi are too many people.' But when we stopped at the next subsidence, where everyone had to disembark and pull on ropes to get the vehicle across, the fat man politely adjusted his sharp object. I had not been neurotically imagining sharpness; it was a new spearhead.

On re-embarking, a replacement hazard appeared before my eyes. One of the youths condemned to ride the struts was now directly above me and his huge bare feet, with rock-hard heels, swung in front of my face, banging my cheeks and forehead as the taxi bucked and slithered. 'Lean forward!' urged the solicitous youth on my right. 'Then you will be more safe.' 'I can't,' I said. 'Someone's cauldron is on my lap.'

This Nyos youth, Martin, had lost all but one of his family. Only he and his sister, both then at school in Wum, had survived. She was sitting in front – with a ludicrous number of other comparatively privileged people – being chatted up by the gendarme. As we passed through Cha, seven miles from Nyos but also stricken, Martin pointed towards a mountain bulking black on our left. Its lower slopes had belonged to his uncle – now, with all his immediate family, dead. Many, many acres of bananas grew on those slopes and Martin thought it cruel of the government not to allow survivors to return briefly to the area, if only on police-escorted day-trips, to harvest all the good food being wasted. 'This would be better for people than sitting idle in camps.'

Our taxi was an ex-limousine, converted to a pick-up. 'Nothing bigger can go on this road,' said Martin. 'It is not a good road.'

Near Cha another subsidence required more extraordinary action. As the vehicle was being hauled across this chasm, we were startled by demented abusive screams. Momentarily the headlights showed an old man, almost naked and with wild hair, running by the edge of the track pointing a stick at us. 'He has gone crazy,' Martin explained. 'He came back from Nkambe to his compound and all were dead and taken and buried – no one knew where. Now he looks and looks, he does not believe they are dead. He lives like a monkey on fruit. If anyone tries to catch him he fights. But he was a very quiet old man.'

Martin and his sister were returning to relatives in Wum ('They are trying to give us a new family') after a visit to friends in the biggest camp, near Nkambe. All our fellow-passengers, he said, had been directly involved in the Nyos tragedy. 'Only such people now have permission to travel through this Restricted Zone, with the Special Security Police to guard them and watch them and not let them go running back to their fields. With time passing more people want to go home, when at first they were too afraid. But I would not like to return – it would make me cry again.'

Soon after, the storm broke; we stopped again and a tarpaulin was spread over the struts. It would in any case have been inadequate: with two passengers up there it was a bad joke. However, those unwittingly brutal feet had now disappeared; the youths were lying full length under the tarpaulin. I began to fret about them as we descended, swerving and skidding on that narrow track above sheer drops too well illuminated by sky-wide sheets of blue lightning. It would be *our* fault, only, if they were pitched into the abyss ... The fat man beside me, squashed against the side-struts, bore the full force of the gale-driven rain and occasionally whimpered softly, like a distressed puppy – a surprising sound from his vast bulk. Martin and I, in the middle, were less exposed but far from protected. It was suddenly very cold and I began to look forward to those warm dribbles from above where the kid was now bleating feebly in sodden misery. Somewhere towards the rear Rachel – also against the struts – was using very bad language *sotto voce*.

Certain interludes, if one hadn't kept a diary and written it all down at the time, would afterwards seem like mere hallucinations – not credible to oneself, never mind anyone else. The few hours after our arrival in Wum come into that category.

As the true rainy season approaches Cameroon's storms lengthen, sometimes continuing all night, and it was still down-pouring when we stopped outside the Happy Days Hotel. (After the Nyos silence, those dire disco decibels sounded almost agreeable.) Moving off the mango sack, I fell into Martin's arms – my feet had been numbed by the tin trunk. Our captor then ordered us to stay put and we assumed everyone else would disembark. Six did, including an enraged young woman who owned the mangoes. She claimed that my weight had rendered them unsaleable and demanded 6,000 CFA (about £13) compensation. The SSP officer shouted to her to get lost but for her the SSP held no terrors. Resolutely she stood outside the vehicle, her sack at her feet, haranguing through the storm and gesticulating like a windmill. I yelled that her mangoes were so hard they couldn't possibly have been damaged. Surprisingly, I seemed to have popular opinion on my side. Then the taxi leaped forward, causing me to fall again – this time onto another kid, hitherto unnoticed, lying on the floor. It shrieked in agony and I felt sick and began wildly to apologise to its unidentifiable owner.

A cheerful voice said, 'No problem, sir! Tomorrow we eat it!'

Our driver proceeded erratically but rapidly, trying to avoid the deeper rain-lakes. Water sprayed up in sheets on either side, as though we were in some sort of aquatic Dodgem Park, and by now 'inside' was awash. I supposed we were going to deliver the remaining eight passengers to their destinations, before we were delivered to our place of punishment. But no. They had become the innocent victims of Murphy criminality and were doomed to spend hours at the mercy of the storm while our captor tried to get rid of us.

Apparently we posed an unprecedented problem. At two official buildings, miles apart, guidance was sought but was not available. Finally the taxi – now coughing and shuddering – forced its way up and up, through a raging torrent, to a ridge top. There stood a sprawling conglomeration of newish buildings. At the entrance the headlights picked out a large notice: DIVISIONAL HEADQUARTERS OF SPECIAL SECURITY POLICE. A much smaller notice had an arrow pointing our way and said, simply, PRISON. We began to feel slightly uneasy. Did the SSP operate quite independently of Basil and his merry men? Already we had tried dropping his name, to no effect. Yet our unease was very slight; one cannot feel seriously threatened among the genial Cameroonians.

The taxi could have been driven into Headquarters and parked under cover; instead, it was left out in the deluge while we and the driver (as witness) raced after our captor across a wide yard to 'Reception'. When we had been handed over to a junior duty-officer, behind a long high counter, the other two vanished. Only one notice was displayed in that cavernous hallway, a list of names headed 'Football Duty for 17/5/87'.

We were drenched and shivering and exhausted; since dawn we had walked some twenty-seven miles on a hand of bananas. Rachel collapsed on a narrow concrete bench, opposite the counter, and fell asleep with her head on the saturated rucksack. I presented passports to the duty-officer, who was polite and amiable but looked like an unkind caricature of a Third World bureaucrat. Slowly he opened an enormous ledger, designed for commercial uses, and picked up a biro which only reluctantly yielded its ink. While 'entering particulars' he frowned, narrowed his eyes and breathed loudly as though carrying a heavy load uphill. Thumbing conscientiously through our health certificates, which have a fatal fascination for semi-literates, he asked if we had ever had leprosy? I controlled an hysterical urge to giggle and gravely assured him that we were not, and had never been, lepers. Finding our visas, he stared silently at them for long moments, then pronounced that their validity depended on their date of issue rather than on our date of arrival in Cameroon.

'That is not so,' I said, quietly but firmly. 'Will you just take my word for it?'

Disarmingly he beamed, 'Yes, sir! I must believe you! You are educated gentleman!'

I let that pass; he was already sufficiently addled; a gender debate might have unseated his reason. Inexplicably, Rachel's passport was now causing him mental torture and our problem became bilingual.

'Your wife is born in city of Eire in country of England – yes?'

'My daughter was born in *London*, in England. "Eire" is the name of our country, Ireland, in the Irish language.'

'Hah! And Sassenach is your place of residence?'

' "Sassenach" is "England" in the Irish language.'

'So why this book say you live in Sassenach when you come from this country of Eire?'

'It doesn't say so, it says my daughter was born in England.'

'But she is only eleven years! So big for eleven years! You marry too young – in Cameroon we do not marry before twelve years, smallest.'

'My daughter is eighteen – you can see the date there – born December 1968.'

'But now we have the year 1987 – this time I think you make mistake!' He drew a scrap of paper from beneath the ledger and began to do sums, holding the tip of a carmine tongue between advertisement-perfect teeth. 'See!' He pushed the scrap of paper triumphantly towards me. 'If she is eighteen she must be born 1948 – it is written there!'

I felt that my own reason was about to be unseated. Abandoning all hope of keeping our encounter on rational lines, I seized his pen and did my own sum while he watched enthralled. 'Hah! You have another way of making figures! Is this way right? Is it good in Europe now?'

Mercifully our mathematical tête-à-tête was interrupted at this point. 'Here is Big Man!' exclaimed the duty-officer, saluting a figure wearing what might have been a Fon's cloak and cap. He was loquaciously drunk and said that I reminded him of his grandfather who always wore khaki bush-shirts. And Rachel reminded him of a Peace Corps girl he wanted to marry and she liked going to bed with him but went back to America and never wrote to him though she promised she would. Then, placing an arm around my shoulder – as much to steady himself as to express affection – he continued affably, 'Let me show you the cells.' As one's host might say, 'Let me show you your room.'

The cells were bare and clean and unoccupied. They recalled Mr Ndango's store-room in Acu – minus the noisy generator – and we felt that we could, if necessary, sleep well in them.

'These are nice cells,' said the senior officer. 'But we have not many to put in them. Wum is too quiet. You are spies from Nyos? Do you have bedding?'

As though on cue our captor reappeared, looking distraught. He was quite likeable despite his proclivity to baton youths for no good reason

247

and leave passengers sitting around in the rain. He had, after all, only been doing his duty when he arrested us. And now, clearly, he did not wish us to be imprisoned. The drunken officer seemed to have no strong views on the subject. Given Wum's limitations as a centre of international espionage, he would have liked to see one of his nice cells occupied by bona fide spies. Yet he too seemed personally well disposed towards us – indeed towards everyone, by that hour of the evening. It was agreed that our passports should be confiscated ('Not again!' groaned Rachel) and we promised to present ourselves to the Chief of Security Police at 8 a.m. for further deliberations about appropriate punishment. Spies, we reckoned, would have an easy ride in Wum.

Back at the taxi we found our fellow-passengers all huddled together using the tarpaulin – inside – as a tent. When they had disentangled themselves we grovelled abjectly but they chuckled cheerfully. There was no problem, it wasn't our fault: 'Life's like that!' said one. Yet they were soaked through; I could hear several sets of teeth chattering.

Our captor offered to drop us off at the innocently named Gay Lodge Hotel: 'This is finest hotel in Wum, only 1,500 CFA for a clean bed.' But it was away on the other side of the town so we booked into Happy Days. Rachel's hunger-pangs were hard to cater for as most chop-houses had closed. I was past hunger. I felt like a football hooligan; I only wanted a bottle of beer in each hand.

At 8 a.m. no one could find the Chief of Security Police. He was, it then transpired, our drunken friend, and 8 a.m. was never his finest hour. It wasn't mine, either, that morning. I had over-drowned my Nyos trauma.

'At some stage,' said Rachel, 'we'll have to contact Basil. We'll never get anywhere with this lot.'

The pyjama'd SSPs who had greeted us seemed to have gone back to bed and there was no one behind the reception desk – no one anywhere in sight. I toyed with the notion of trying surreptitiously to unconfiscate our passports ...

Then Basil walked in; his junior officer escort looked astonished to see me hugging and kissing him like a long-lost son. Our kind captor had told him the Murphies were in trouble again.

'At first,' said Basil, 'I didn't believe him. I thought, these women cannot be like paratroopers, reaching Nyos through the mountains! And now you have a big problem here. This is not my business, but give me your details and I will try to help!'

We unfolded our map, *sans* Lake Nyos. We explained that no one had told us about the Restricted Zone and that garbled media reports had falsely located Nyos village, describing it as 'on the lakeshore' and 'remote and inaccessible' – which it is not, being on the ring-road.

'But,' said Basil dryly, 'the ring-road is almost impassable during the rains. And if you were a journalist, straight in from Paris or New York, inspecting the area by helicopter, you might *imagine* it was remote and inaccessible! But why were you not stopped at Ise? Did you not see the army camp? Many troops are posted there to stop people going near the lake. And did you not come to a big barrier of trees on your path? Did you not think then perhaps you should stop and turn back?'

We admitted that we had noticed the camp but had seen no soldiers. And the barrier on the path had seemed a relatively minor obstacle which we soon got over.

'You get over too many obstacles!' said Basil. 'That is why you have so many problems! Now you wait here for the Chief, tell him your story, then come to my home and we shall see how things develop.'

By then Headquarters was coming to life. We sat in the sun outside reception, overlooking a flooded parade ground. Three friendly ssps in mufti (but with revolvers stuck in their belts) were listening to two elderly villagers being passionately disputatious about goats. One billy (old) had killed another (young). The old billy was free, his victim tethered. As it is illegal to leave goats untethered the victim's owner was claiming the old billy as compensation. But he, being fat, was worth 20,000 CFA (about £45) – whereas his victim, being thin, was worth only 10,000 CFA (about £22.50). Nothing had been decided when another pair of litigants arrived – younger, but also goat-centred. One man's billy had been tethered so close to another's nanny that he killed her by strangulation – a far knottier problem than the first and one to which the elders now applied themselves with as much enthusiasm as though it were their own.

Even in my hung-over state, I perceived an incongruity here. Why were these goat controversies taking place at the Headquarters of the Special Security Police? What did internecine conflict among goats have to do with National Security? A charming ssp with only half a face (the other half had been blown off when his gun went wrong) elucidated. All these litigants were followers of ssp officers and so deemed it expedient to seek justice here rather than at the Gendarmerie. By then we were so Cameroon-attuned that this seemed a perfectly logical explanation.

At 10.20 a.m. the Chief appeared, now grandly uniformed but looking frail. He seemed not to recall that I was his grandfather's double. Realising that for him this was our first meeting, we played it that way.

'Why you were arrested?' he asked.

I told my story, ending with profuse apologies for having unintentionally broken the law.

249

'You should have permit from highest sources of Yaoundé,' said the Chief. He had, we suspected, taken in little or nothing of what I said. He held out a hand: 'Please, give me your passports, to send to Yaoundé. You wait in Wum – is good?'

'But you have our passports!' I protested. 'Your duty-officer kept them last night!'

The Chief wrinkled his brow and looked as if that hurt. 'Here are no passports – I do not have – give me!'

'*Someone* here has them,' I insisted, beginning for the first time to feel genuine alarm. It seemed hideously possible – even probable – that that duty-officer had allowed our passports to be eaten by goats or termites.

'Come back tomorrow,' ordered the Chief. 'Your passports may be found – maybe not ...'

'At what time tomorrow?' I asked, being obstinately White.

'At any time,' said the Chief. 'I am always here, at your service. I am a public servant. It is my duty to help people.'

Thus began another Wum passport saga.

From Wum, the town nearest Lake Nyos, the mass-burials were organised and to Wum came many survivors for medical care and 'rehabilitation'. Now, emboldened by our new feeling of personal involvement, we initiated discussions of the tragedy and discovered an unravellable accretion of rumours, allegations, contradictory statements of 'fact' and fresh Nyos-myths. Perhaps this turmoil of gossip, accusation and fantasy was being used as an anaesthetic to dull the local awareness of what actually *had* happened. In Wum even the most dogged investigative journalists had been forced to abandon their quest for hard facts – details of who had done wrong, and why and how and where. And I had no stomach, after walking through the village of Nyos, for probing scandals. No one could be blamed for the explosion. It was a natural disaster, or an act of God, if one chooses to believe in a God given to such actions. In my then mood it didn't matter *who* was making away with emergency relief supplies, or if the government said more or less people died than was the case. *Everyone* in Nyos village died. And statistics become supremely unimportant when everyone is dead. (In fact everyone didn't die, as we were soon – and shatteringly – to discover.)

We were told of a European scientist – some said English, others German – who in the mid-1970s warned the locals that Lake Nyos was likely to give trouble. We were also told of a quarterchief from the area who in 1982, after Mount Cameroon's latest eruption, foretold a disaster and urged everyone to move away. His prophesy was based not on traditional magic but on personal observations of 'strange things floating in the water and bad smells around the shore'. But his advice was misinterpreted as a ploy to clear good land for occupation by friends of his from 'outside'.

In a shebeen a youngish Bantu man was bitterly eloquent. He had lost fifteen of his family and denounced the mass burials as 'shameful and not necessary'. He and his friends had buried their dead in their compound, where people should be buried, because they could afford to bribe police jeeps to take them to Nyos. Almost every family, he said, had survivors who should have been helped by the authorities to hurry to Nyos to bury their dead 'with respect'. 'For us this is more important than you people realise. We stay close to our dead, they are not gone – forgotten – finish! They stay with us still, in the compound. They have a part to play in the family, helping the living. Even if scientists say the lake is safe again, government has made it hard for many people to go back to Nyos. Too many dead have been treated badly and will be unhappy and angry. For the Fulani it will be easier – they have different feelings.'

Basil, who organised the mass burials, told us later that given the delay in discovering the tragedy, the state of the ring-road and the need for quick burial in a tropical climate, it would have been impossible to organise family burial parties – and dangerous to try, because of the risk of epidemic disease.

A Fulani evacuee was also embittered. The government had promised financial compensation to surviving Fulanis who could show vets' certificates proving cattle losses, yet after eight months no one had received a franc. Like everyone else, he derided the '1,746' official death toll. Many had been buried before the security forces arrived with their shovels and quicklime – many others, in isolated compounds, after they left. 'But the government wanted to seem in control, that way more aid would be sent from other countries. They are trying to get big money from Israel to build a new modern town for all people now in camps! But this is dishonest. We don't want to live in a modern town – we are village and cattle people ...' (When news of the Nyos disaster reached Yaoundé, the then Prime Minister of Israel, Shimon Peres, was on an official visit to Cameroon and Israel at once provided most of the medical aid needed – and much of the equipment for the camps.)

Basil's exertions on our behalf *won-der-fully* abbreviated that second passport saga. After a stern interrogation by the *Biggest* Man around – far transcending in importance any Chief of Police – our passports were returned and we left Wum next morning with changed plans. The Mbembe Forest Reserve was out: all of the Restricted Zone lay between us and it. So our new goal was the Bambouto Mountains, to be reached via the hitherto elusive Bafmeng. Basil had seemed understandably anxious that this time we should get out of his jurisdiction in – metaphorically – a straight line, without further unscheduled wanderings.

251

Therefore we attached ourselves, on the outskirts of Wum, to four wood-collecting children who guaranteed to put us on the correct bush-path.

Just beyond the town, as I was bringing up the rear, a handsome, well-built, sad-faced young man emerged from a side path and quietly returned my greeting. He was carrying an axe and was oddly dressed, in a shirt and shorts of grey and black striped material. When I asked if he was going to Bafmeng – hoping we might have a guide all the way – he replied in excellent English. He wished he could go to Bafmeng, but he was a good-conduct prisoner who, having served seven years of his sentence, was now allowed out once a week to collect firewood for the prison kitchen.

This frankness encouraged me to ask 'Why were you imprisoned?' and his reply shook me because one couldn't not believe him; he was that sort of young man. His father, a prosperous We farmer, had set him up as a butcher in Wum market at the age of eighteen. A few months later he bought twenty cattle from a Fulani who had rustled them. In court he claimed not to have known they were stolen and proved that he had paid the full market price. Yet he was sentenced to twenty-five years imprisonment. And the Fulani was executed by firing-squad.

Despite the brevity of that encounter it remains one of my most indelible – and saddest – Cameroonian memories. There was something extraordinarily moving about the dignity with which this young man accepted a gross injustice. We shook hands where he turned off to climb a jungly hillside and I stood for a moment watching him walk away alone through the bush. I felt our short conversation had helped him; that meeting had a curious flavour – almost as though it were designed.

Six energetic hours later our approach to Bafmeng coincided with the sort of storm that goes down in history. At first we imagined it to be a normal manifestation of the real rainy season (now close) but even by Cameroonian standards it was freakish: ripping off roofs, felling mighty trees, destroying several square miles of crops and demolishing five substantial buildings including a Catholic church. When it began without warning we were some four miles from Bafmeng but already under shelter, in an isolated off-licence-cum-huxters. Luckily this little shack stood in a slight hollow; had it been on a ridge-top it might well have been blown away and would certainly have lost its roof. The parents and three children seemed disturbingly ill-nourished and apa-thetic, reminding us how rare poverty is in rural Cameroon. When we arrived a skinny little fellow, aged about six, was amusing himself by rearranging the very few goods displayed on dusty shelves behind the bar: washing soap, torch batteries, small boxes of loaf-sugar. His younger sister lay restlessly asleep on a wooden bench; she looked feverish. Then, as we raised our bottles to our parched lips, the sky was suddenly black – and Father slammed the door as an uncanny howl, not immediately identifiable as *wind,* seemed to fill the world.

The thunder and lightning were not – could not be – any more dramatic than what we had already witnessed. But never have I experienced such darkness at midday. And the rain seemed not rain but falling water – as in a waterfall. Then it was mixed with thick hail, the size of ping-pong balls, that bounced three feet off the ground and might have concussed us had we been exposed to it. Opposite the shack a mature eucalyptus wood became frighteningly beautiful as trees flung themselves this way and that, like mad tormented dancers staging a frantic arboreal ballet. At first the gale had been blowing from behind us, where the ground rose slightly. When it veered abruptly Father rushed to shutter the wide window but was too late to prevent a flooded floor.

Two hours later the hurricane had dwindled to a storm, the torrential rain was hail-free and we continued – though in such a wind neither umbrella nor capes could protect us. We were now on a hilly 'fair weather' motor track which in foul weather becomes a swirling dark brown river. Schoolchildren, wading through the flood, looked scared: what might they find when they got home? Many tin roofs and unrooted eucalyptus lay strewn about; items of colourful enamelware were perched high in mango trees; plantain groves, coffee bushes and almost-ripe maize had been smashed into the ground. This was a heartbreaking scene of industry defeated, the innocent punished, the hard-working deprived.

We splashed into Bafmeng's first off-licence through a wide red-brown lake below the track. A dozen men and a few women were bewailing the hurricane damage, none quite sober at 4.45 p.m. An elderly Big Man sitting in a corner (Commander Emmanuel) commiserated with our sodden shivering and ordered beers for 'these sad people'. His 'son' Barnabas, a follower inherited from his father, was unpleasantly drunk with bloodshot eyes and refused to shake my hand.

'First I salute Madame! I know how to behave with ladies – I know Germany!' He turned to embrace Rachel, at some length, and leeringly informed her, 'I have spent time in Germany, there I was very nicely looked after by girls like you – yes? You love me?' He swung around, seized my bottle of beer and drank deeply before returning it.

I said, loudly and distinctly, '*I* am Madame. This is my *daughter*. Her name is Rachel and I am her *mother*.'

Here gender confusion reached its bizarre apogee. Barnabas came towards me and turned nasty. 'You are lying!' he sneered, thrusting his face into mine. 'You are *man* – why you want to pretend you are woman?'

Wearily I unbuttoned for the breast-baring routine, but with Barnabas it didn't work.

'Artificial things are not good!' said he. 'We don't want that kind of trouble in Cameroon! We don't like this here, we don't have such problem in this country, we don't like it brought from outside ... We have no saints here but we are better than Europe which has many saints. We in this country can't be fooled by you people – you are *man*!' By now he was staring at me quite wildly and swaying as though about to topple forward onto my suspect bosom.

Commander Emmanuel, who had been trying to intervene, at last made himself heard. He shouted something in whatever Bafmeng folk speak and his follower was temporarily silent. The Commander then turned to me, apologetically. 'Madame, this is bad! You come here wet and he talks of Germany – for what? What help for you to talk of all countries he's seen? He is my son but only because I have to take him when my father dies – I do not like him. But we are all God's children, whichever church – or no church – you attend. For us all God had love enough to die – you are Catholic?'

Before I could reply, Barnabas borrowed Rachel's Beaufort, took a swig, then began a loud confused account of his time in Germany, his two-day visit to East Germany and his views on Communism. When it emerged that he had worked as a docker in Hamburg his reaction to my bosom became less baffling.

An hour later the rain stopped and the evening sun slanted across a waterlogged Bafmeng. Opposite the off-licence was the European-orderly Catholic Mission, an unusually large complex of buildings set amidst neat almost-lawns shaded by rows of spreading trees. The Commander (we never discovered why he was generally known as 'Commander') said that we could spend the night either at the Mission or in his younger brother's nearby empty house. Brother was 'a very big army officer', living in Yaoundé, and his new house was unoccupied. At the Mission they had a visiting medical team of three, caring for Nyos refugees, so perhaps we should stay in Brother's villa? Gratefully we agreed and a very small boy led us through knee-deep (for him) water, head-carrying our rucksack apparently effortlessly. In a huge bedroom two posh Dunlopillo double-beds were made up with fresh sheets and warm soft blankets. Each (urbanisation running wild!) had a bedside locker and the glazed window was securely grilled.

We dined in the Commander's own villa, a hundred yards away. In a spacious living-room, sparsely furnished, he invited us to admire a collection of firearms, dating from various eras, on the whitewashed walls. The party consisted of our host, another follower (a local teacher) and Sister-in-law, who divided her time between Yaoundé and Bafmeng because someone had to supervise the cultivation of Brother's many rich acres. This was the only time a woman shared a meal with us – and with men – in rural Cameroon; but of course Sister-in-law was used to Yaoundé ways. By then both Commander Emmanuel and his follower were truculent-drunk. They shouted angry abuse at each other throughout the meal while Sister-in-law looked disapproving but resigned. Perfectly cooked rice and herby mutton stew were served from giant food-thermoses and cutlery was provided for all, though not used by the men. It seemed tactful to retire the moment we had finished, leaving Sister-in-law to pour palm oil on increasingly troubled verbal waters.

We chose the bed by the window and were almost asleep when our host came lurching in, a lantern in one hand and a gun in the other. This was no home-made brass-studded job, nor had it been left behind *circa* 1640 by the Portuguese. It was a gleaming new army rifle and when the Commander had put down his lantern he pointed it at us and said he wanted Rachel on the other bed. A fate worse than death seemed improbable; our host's competence on that score was unlikely to have survived his beer intake. But death itself seemed quite probable, if the rifle were loaded and its owner continued to wave it about while fiddling with the safety-catch. I spoke soothingly, as one does to a toddler who has got hold of something so dangerous he mustn't be startled. Rachel was pretending to be asleep and I protested that she was exhausted – it would be *very* cruel to wake her – but in the morning she would certainly join him in his bed.

The Commander persisted; he wanted my daughter *now*. Suddenly he sat heavily on the edge of the other bed and again targeted me and hiccupped. By this stage my heart was hammering with fear and my palms sweating. Then he changed his demand: if I would join him now he could wait until morning for my daughter. Another flourish of the rifle accompanied this proposal. I tried to sound as though it fired me on all cylinders, then explained that I, too, was *exhausted*. However, after a few hours sleep it would be my privilege and pleasure to enter his bed.

Still he persisted, his speech becoming increasingly slurred. He wanted me *now* – and again he began to fiddle with something on the rifle that went clickety-click. I decided to join him; even should he prove unexpectedly virile, there *is* no fate worse than death. Then abruptly he threw himself back on the bed, clasping the rifle to his chest. A moment later he stretched out a hand and turned off the lantern – a very un-Cameroonian thing to do, yet he seemed far too drunk to be planning anything cunning. I was beginning slightly to relax when he again mumbled 'Madame! Come under me *now*!' Further clickety-clicks followed and seemed even more alarming now that I couldn't see which way the rifle was pointing. Fleetingly I considered snuggling down with our host, then grabbing the gun. But if it were loaded that could be suicidal. Then I heard – sweetest of sounds! – a long snore; and it was followed, rhythmically, by others. Yet that was an unrestful night. Whenever the Commander muttered and tossed, as he frequently did, I became not only alert but hypertense.

From 5 a.m. I was wide awake and twenty minutes later our host sat up, slid off the bed and said in a small meek voice that he was going to his compound where we must join him for breakfast at 7.30. Then he slung his rifle over his shoulder and slunk away into the grey dawn.

I felt a bit sheepish as we dressed; very likely the rifle had been unloaded.

'You really *were* scared,' recalled Rachel, amused by this maternal over-reaction. 'I'm sure that thing wasn't loaded – where would he get ammo, in Bafmeng?'

'From his very big officer brother,' I retorted. 'But you're probably right, I was just being jittery.'

'You look *haggard*!' said Rachel. 'Did you not sleep well? You *are* silly!'

At 6 a.m. the church bell was ringing as we crossed the almost-lawn to salute Father Peter before leaving for Fundong. In Wum we had been told, 'He's been in Cameroon twenty-eight years, he knows us better than we know ourselves! He's doing more than anyone else for Nyos people, he's a perfect Christian!'

A tallish figure in a white surplice was strolling beneath the trees, reading his breviary. When he saw us his smile melted our hearts. He had thick snowy hair, pink cheeks, big bright blue eyes – and disconcertingly I found myself thinking that pink and blue people look *odd* ... His voice was gentle yet he radiated power – spiritual power. After a few moments' conversation he urged us to spend another day in Bafmeng, at the Mission. 'Be with us today and meet my poor people from the Nyos villages – it will help them.'

The English language seems to lack words for describing this sort of person without sounding mawkish. Rachel wrote in her diary: 'Angelic! – or at least saintly.' I wrote in mine: 'Being a perfect Christian has nothing to do with it. The last person I met who at once gave this impression of sheer, pure *goodness* was an agnostic – our beloved Martin Ryle.'

The Bafmeng Mission was injudiciously founded as a convent; European nuns should never have been expected to flourish in the heart of the Grassfields. When that enterprise collapsed Father Peter laboured alone from his little bungalow and for twenty years the rows of cramped cells lay empty. Then the Nyos evacuees moved in: some men and youths, but mostly women and children from Subum, Cha and Fang, whose menfolk had all died.

An Argentinian lay-missionary woman doctor, based in Fontem but seconded to Bafmeng for a fortnight to deal with evacuee health problems, mentioned a theory that more men than women died, and more adults than children, because alcohol leaves the body extra-vulnerable to carbon dioxide. Yet in some compounds more *children* died. And in the huts where children only survived it may have been because at that time of evening they were asleep under thick blankets. (Cameroonians usually sleep with covered heads.)

Here I felt no inhibitions about talking with and questioning Nyos victims. Perhaps absurdly, yet in a way that felt very real, our own reactions to Nyos seemed to have given us the right to sit with them and share their grief. But Rachel soon sensibly retreated to the living-room to write her diary. At eighteen there is a limit to what one can handle and it is a wise youngster who recognises this.

Most harrowing of all were the Nyos village children who survived. A boy, aged four at the time, spoke no word for eight months – never, under any circumstances, to anyone. Then a few days before our arrival he saw an older boy digging a hole to plant a tree and suddenly screamed, 'No, stop! No dig hole!' Having spent thirty-six hours locked in a hut with the dead, he had watched Ise men digging and digging and then burying all his family in the compound.

One little girl, aged twenty-two months at the time, was put on my knee in an ex-cell. Her aunt, a survivor from Cha, told me that she had been tied so tightly to her dead mother's back that she couldn't free herself. She was not found for two days – two days in a room with seven corpses – so 'She have Mama's neck for chop.' This victim, now aged two and a half, sat listlessly on my knee, the very antithesis of a Cameroonian toddler – usually by that age singing and dancing and bubbling and twinkling with *joie de vivre*.

Even more disturbing was the little girl, aged just three at the time, who was found on the Monday morning, three and a half days after the explosion, in a hut with nine fast-decomposing bodies – her parents and all her older siblings. When the gendarmes entered she came crawling out from under a bed; Basil had mentioned her, saying the men who found her were utterly shattered and cannot rid themselves of the memory of her face at that moment. She had reacted to nothing since, though everyone focused extra love and attention on her, attempting to arouse some emotion – fear, anger, hate, *anything* ... Every evening after supper Father Peter holds an informal and very moving prayer service in the living-room for the older evacuees, followed by a sing-song and dancing. This little girl is always brought in, to provide her with as much stimulation as possible. She courteously accepts caresses, sweets, biscuits – but passively, expressionlessly, with dead eyes. I shall never forget that child's eyes.

Afterwards we wondered if, in the cases of the most profoundly shocked small children, adoption by Whites and removal to a totally different Western environment might be a good idea, though normally such well meant interventions are inadvisable. I couldn't help feeling, in the unjustifiable way one does, that it would have been better for those children had they not survived.

One Nyos man, whose wife and five children had died, told me he was found unconscious and flown by helicopter to Wum hospital where he came to after another thirty-six hours. He said, 'When you walked from the lake you passed my fine compound – it is by that path – you have seen it. I don't like to see it again. Why they make me live? For why? Why they not leave me to die with my woman and my pickins? Five pickins, all good, loving God, then God destroy them – *why*?' He was obsessed by the fact that there had been no warning sound, just suddenly an inability to breathe. He seemed to resent this as unfair – sneaky – and to believe that had there been a warning he could somehow have protected his family. (Which of course is not true.) He denied that it was 'a quick easy death', the consolation those attempting 'rehabilitation' had been offering to the survivors. '*Not* quick! Much, much suffering for some, dying ten minutes, tearing their clothes off and all fear – try to breathe but no air – and so frightened, so frightened!'

That victim was aged about thirty-five and restored to full physical health. Yet I had a strong feeling that soon he would die. Throughout that spacious convent-compound, for all Father Peter's sensitive care, the lack of *the will to live* was apparent. The Mission had provided the evacuees with ample good land to cultivate for their own use (work therapy) but they had no heart for it – those once-vigorous young women who had been so proud of their skill as cultivators, so tireless in their to-ings and fro-ings to all the local markets to sell surplus crops to pay school-fees or buy new clothes for the children ...

After lunch, on Father Peter's advice (he may have noticed me looking over-harrowed), we went to pay our respects to the Fon – as we should have done on arrival, but the hurricane was our excuse. Bafmeng, like We, is a traditionally important trading centre, not the creation of a motor-road. In extent a town, it has a village feeling. Long stretches of cultivation separate its various quarters and the Fon's palace is about three miles from the Mission.

On the way we met Norbert, a Douala airport gendarme who insisted on escorting us to the palace. 'The Chief is my good friend and I like to talk English. It helps me in my job if I sound like English person.' Norbert had lost seventeen in Nyos village: 'My parents, two grandparents, the rest brothers and sisters.' Significantly, he seemed not to have been traumatised in the way most Bafmeng evacuees were. One of his wives and most of his children lived in Bafmeng but *his* world, now, was Douala. For him life went on, post-Nyos, as it could never do again for those whose world was their compound or village. He told us that Nyos and Bafmeng people are 'same tribe with same language' and the Fon is chief of the whole area. Then he led us on a detour, up a steep forest path, to meet his Bafmeng (senior) wife. We found an attractive twenty-two-year-old sitting on a low stool outside a big thatched hut in a coffee-surrounded compound. She was suckling her hefty fourth son. 'Is good woman!' said Norbert. 'She have only boy babies!' Eleven of her immediate family died in Nyos and her welcoming smile did not light up her eyes.

Bafmeng's palace is as big – if not quite as grand – as Bafut's. The Fon, an ex-secondary school teacher, was a fubsy character who suddenly became formidable when discussing Nyos. In 1977 and 1978, and again after Lake Manoun's explosion, he wrote to both local and central government departments expressing concern about Lake Nyos's 'moods' and reporting the unprecedented subsidence of huts in nearby compounds. Inevitably, those letters were ignored. But he told us he kept copies which are now of some interest to scientists – and of some embarrassment to the government.

When Rachel sought permission to smoke she was told that nicotine is taboo in the palace. But alcohol is not and an ancient retainer, wearing a long loose gown, soon appeared with a raffia bag that clinked promisingly. Taking four glasses from a corner shelf he polished them on the end of his gown – which, being itself dust-laden, left them markedly less sparkling than before. This large, long, shadowy reception hall was decorated with an eighteen-foot python skin, a selection of ancient firearms, and faded photographs of the Fon's father and grand-father, surrounded by their respective councils.

By the Fon's reckoning, Lake Nyos killed more than 2,000 people. I asked if he approved of the Restricted Zone policy being indefinitely maintained. Yes, he did: Lake Nyos should never again be trusted. He told us about a Peace Corps teacher who had been stationed in Fundong, a few hours' walk away, for the past two years. Steve Tabor (in whose back garden we were soon to camp for two nights) had been one of the first Whites to arrive in Nyos and he helped with the mass-burials. A scientist by training, and considerably older and shrewder than the average PC volunteer, he had been closely studying Lake Nyos since the explosion (more closely than most of the international experts then busily writing papers about it). Four months and nine days after the explosion he observed a long red gash on the jade-green water, the shape and size of a giant submarine. He photographed it from the cliffs on the west shore and later showed us his pictures. At the Yaoundé conference most scientists agreed that this was not evidence of another comparatively minor eruption but had probably been caused by a rock-fall. To this statement my previous comments on rock-falls may be applied with even more force; Steve's photographs show exactly where to look for signs of such an event.

'If a rock-fall can again turn some of the water red,' said the Fon, 'why should my people go back? Cameroon is not over-populated, they can be settled on the high ground beyond We. There they would be within reach of Bafmeng and relatives and the markets they know.'

I aired my theory that the Aghem highland is under-populated because of a previous crater lake disaster lingering on in the folk-memory.

'That is likely,' replied the Fon. 'But now we know the gas can't move *up*. Heaviness is its characteristic. So there is no reason for my people to avoid that area.'

But, as Norbert observed afterwards, the Fon of We might not agree ...

On our way back to the Mission Norbert told us that the Fon had been deserted by his wife (his *only* wife) who was also a teacher and had refused to leave Bamenda and her good job when he was selected. He longed for her to join him in Bafmeng though she was – according to local gossip – tight-fisted, spiteful and ill-tempered. No one could understand why he didn't just forget her and have lots more wives, as was in any case a Fon's duty. Unless – could it be that what she said about him was *true*?

That night, lying on the concrete floor of a new Mission schoolroom, I slept much more soundly than on Brother's Dunlopillo mattress.

13

Re-enter Egbert

TEN COINCIDENCE-PACKED days later we were in Yaoundé railway station, buying single tickets to N'gaoundere.

In Fundong we had camped in Steve Tabor's compound for two nights and riotously celebrated Cameroon's Day of National Unity. Then, continuing towards the Bambouto Mountains, two misfortunes simultaneously befell us in a Babanki doss-house: severe toothache (mine) and nemesis (Rachel's). At first I thought, 'Toothache – hell! – ignore it and it'll go away.' Rachel had similar dismissive thoughts about a crop of tiresome little sores on her legs, to which I also paid no attention, being then too ignorant to recognise incipient tropical ulcers. (These were the fruits of her rash incursion, with bare legs, into that thorny cleft by Lake Nyos.) However, our upper lips were unstiffening by the time we had almost got back to Bafut, via gruelling bush-paths over precipitous, uninhabited mountains.

Then, on the edge of the town, Rachel's malaria flared again, as malaria will when the body's defences are down – and a dozen tropical ulcers, even when incipient, quickly lower defences. We spent that night where she collapsed with a raging fever at 4 p.m. Our room, behind a sleazy shebeen-cum-chop-house, reeked of achu and was shared with numerous restless small children. By sunset my right jaw was swelling fast and I suspected, correctly, that this was no mere toothache (an affliction to which I am not prone) but an abscess. A double dose of pain-killers did not kill – or even diminish – the searing shafts of pain now affecting my whole head.

Next morning Rachel's fever was down though she remained groggy. I then noticed her much-enlarged leg sores and she conceded that they were 'quite painful'. At 6 a.m. we walked slowly into the town centre; it was market-day and the tracks were thronged. Soon we met Omo, the Fon's 'Tourist Manager', who confirmed that Bafut's only doctors are medicine-men. A kind youth, he proposed that we should stay in his tiny shack at 1,000 CFA per night, while recovering.

Omo lived on the far side of the town, beyond the palace, and when he had swept the floor – raising dense clouds of dust – Rachel collapsed on his frail pallet. Then, noticing two books in a wall-niche, she eagerly asked to see them and I handed her a bilingual (Farsi and French) *History of Iran* and an English *Methodist Hymnal*. She was by then so print-starved that she read the latter. We each began a course of our broad-spectrum antibiotics and I took lots more pain-killers before unrolling my flea-bag and collapsing on the floor. Illogically, I believed that soon we would both feel better.

By 3 p.m. we both felt much worse. I was being driven crazy by pain; Rachel's sores were violently inflamed and swollen and beginning to ooze ounces of pus. The Parkinsons were only fifteen miles away, in Bamenda. Clutching my throbbing jaw, and looking at the appalling happenings on Rachel's legs, I reckoned we needed the Parkinsons, very badly.

'But we can't!' groaned Rachel. 'They're so *kind* – we can't go sponging again!'

Remembering the quality of the Parkinson welcome, on our arriving unexpectedly post-Egbert loss, I didn't share her inhibition. On that unforgettable evening I realised that the Parkinson-Murphy friendship was not just one more of those agreeable but superficial relationships formed as one wanders the world. In temporal terms we were as yet mere acquaintances, but friendship is not to be measured temporally. I had no doubt that Joy and John are the sort of people who, if they knew we were in dire trouble in Bafut, would not have wanted us to be inhibited. We dashed Omo and took a shared taxi to Bamenda, arriving at the Parkinsons just in time for tea.

There was much to be discussed and not until after dinner did John remember that a letter awaited us; it had come the day before. A *letter?* Puzzled, I looked down at the envelope. It was post-marked Banyo and my heart – perhaps disordered by too many pain-killers – seemed to stop beating.

Rachel translated the Francophone vet's hard-to-decipher scrawl, written fifteen days previously. No details were supplied, merely the bare facts that Egbert had been found and was being looked after by the vet. His finder would return him to us in exchange for 20,000 CFA (about £45). It was unclear whether or not the finder and the vet were separate people.

Joy and John – old Africa hands – chuckled. Rachel gasped, 'He must be joking! That's bare-faced holding Egbert to ransom!'

My elation left no room for negative feelings. 'Who cares?' I said. 'When we go back we just take him. We have Doi's fiscal-stamped receipt. No one can stop us walking away with our own horse!'

'Don't get too excited,' cautioned Rachel. 'It may be the vet trying to flog someone else's horse. And anyway does it make sense for us to bush-taxi back to Makelele? We'll have to spend more on fares than we're likely to get when we sell him.'

'Don't be sordid!' I snapped. 'I don't care about *selling* him, I only want to be sure it's Egbert and he's OK. If we haven't time to find a buyer we can leave him with the Foxes in Mayo Darlé.'

'You can argue later,' said Joy, 'when you're fit again. Right now neither of you can go anywhere.'

I happily endured my second sleepless night; but for the abscess and the ulcers, we would not have returned to Bamenda in time to act on the vet's letter.

Joy began her ambulance delivery round early next (Monday) morning. By 7.40 a.m. I had been dropped off at the Bamenda General Hospital where a Paris-trained Francophone dentist holds a daily clinic starting, in theory, at 8 a.m. I was too pain-obsessed to snoop around the hospital, but to get to the dental clinic one has to walk between all the wards and I took in enough – through eyes, nose and ears – to rejoice at not being an in-patient.

By 9.45 there was a long queue, including several unfortunates in – apparently – even more agony than myself. The dentist arrived at 9.50 and saw me half an hour later. He was tall, elegant, gentle, kind. He x-rayed my jaw and told me to come back early next morning for the result; he would have to develop the plates at his home that evening. He mentioned that a tooth-abscess of such magnitude, if it infects the brain, can be fatal. Then, dismissing our broad-spectrum antibiotics as worse than useless, he wrote a prescription for something more appropriate which I must begin to take *at once*. And he added a prescription for powerful pain-killers, imported from France and specifically aimed at tooth-abscesses.

Meanwhile Joy had driven the hideously suppurating Rachel to another clinic, miles away in the opposite direction, where she was given a prescription for Ampicillan – not, alas! available in Bamenda. (My capsules were available.) As a second-best, she started a course of Tetracycline.

Early next morning, after a third sleepless night, I was back in the dentist's queue. He appeared at 9.20 a.m. and looked very taken aback on seeing me; he had forgotten my x-ray. When he at once returned to his home, in some distant salubrious suburb, my fellow-sufferers might have been expected to complain but didn't. (Do Africans *ever* complain about delays? Presumably not, for the reasons suggested by Professor Mbiti.)

That x-ray was not a pretty picture. It showed a treble abscess, afflicting three molar roots, and it had to be cured before its cause could be investigated. All now depended on the antibiotics, which were as yet having no effect.

For four days neither of us wrote up our diaries and my recollection of events is somewhat confused; by that Tuesday I was almost delirious with pain. Yet the Egbert news had induced a euphoria that on one level transcended the abscess – so strangely does mind dominate matter.

Rachel's ulcers were not responding to the Tetracycline and seemed to be worsening hourly. I found them much more worrying than my own condition and was reprimanded for this – 'I'm grown up! You must control your maternal instinct!' Yet the reverse syndrome was also operating. That evening Joy put Rachel in a separate bedroom, since I, plainly, was not going to be a soothing companion during the stilly watches. But within an hour she came limping back: 'I'd prefer to be here to keep an eye on you.'

By then I did look alarming – rather as though I had had a stroke. My face was twisted, with one eye half-closed, and even had I wished to eat I could not have swallowed. The new pain-killers were no more effective than the old. All night I sat up in bed, rocking to and fro non-stop and reading P. D. James's *Death of an Expert Witness*. Few authors could have delivered me from madness that night; P. D. James did. I have ever since felt grateful to her for writing that book. Meanwhile Rachel was sleeping – but restlessly. Could our Wum SSP friend have seen her legs, he would certainly have diagnosed leprosy.

That night was the abscess's climax. At about 7 a.m. the pain began to ease slightly; my antibiotics were winning. But Rachel's were not. There remained only one thing to do: take a bush-taxi to Yaoundé on the morrow (Thursday).

Efficiently the Parkinsons got us organised – exit visas secured, taxi seats booked. In Yaoundé we were to stay a night with friends of theirs, then get the train to N'gaoundere, arriving in time for the famous Fulani celebrations of the first day of Id – marking the end of Ramadan. From N'gaoundere we could, we supposed, get bush-taxis to Galim and walk on – presuming our antibiotics had by then done their jobs – to Makelele and Egbert.

It seems unfair to comment on a city in which one has spent only thirty-six hours. Yet I cannot resist commenting that thirty-six hours in Yaoundé seemed enough; the capital of Cameroon does not tempt one to linger.

We arrived at 2.30 p.m. after a six-hour journey on a velvet-smooth road, recently completed. The hilly green landscape was pleasant but not exciting; we didn't wish we were trekking.

Antibiotic addiction in urban Cameroon ensures that there are many pharmacies; but unfortunately Ascension Thursday is a Christian public holiday so all Yaoundé's pharmacies were closed. Moreover, they would probably remain closed until the following Monday. For what reason? For because on Sundays pharmacies are, naturally, closed. And this Saturday was a Muslim public holiday (Id). And so this Friday was likely to be a 'bridging public holiday'. But nobody was sure about that; it would not be decided until the morning. Decided by whom? The government, of course. And could the government not decide today? No, because today was a public holiday and the government wasn't functioning ... Well then, could the government not have decided *yesterday*? Baffled silence from the young man to whom we were talking.

Possibly a letter from my publisher awaited me in the British Embassy. We asked the young man if all embassies observe all Cameroonian public holidays. Some do, he said, and some don't ...

We soon found the embassy; Yaoundé at least has the advantage of being a mini-capital. The front door was shut but the back door was open. The Cameroonian staff were off enjoying their public holiday, the British staff were so busy trying to decide whether they were or were not on duty that they couldn't find the mail. Thus does Cameroon undermine British phlegm. Subsequently that letter turned up in the British Consulate in Douala, with a kind covering note from the Ambassador.

In Cameroon it is not possible to telephone your friends in the next city to tell them that two diseased Irish vagrants are on the way. But the Farmers gallantly made us feel that diseased vagrants are their favourite sort of overnighters. And in their opulent guest room history was made at 5.50 p.m. when my abscess burst – the physiological equivalent of a hurricane. Suddenly, wondrously, I was free of pain. (Not of course free of soreness, but soreness and pain are two quite different sensations.)

The next day *was* a bridging public holiday. But Bill, our host – moved to terror and pity by Rachel's legs – swore there must be an open pharmacy somewhere and spent hours driving us around the city. At noon we found one and on the spot Rachel began her Ampicillan course. We then bought tickets for the 7 p.m. night train to N'gaoundere and were advised by the girl in the booking-office to be back in the railway station by 5.30, if we wanted to be sure of seats.

It is a Cameroonian idiosyncrasy that no road connects the capital to the important town of N'gaoundere. Everything goes by rail, including cars, jeeps, trucks, motor-bicycles, tractors and bulldozers. Apparently this rail-roading of vehicles is worthwhile because a velvet-surfaced highway runs north from N'gaoundere to the big towns of Garoua and Maroua.

Having paid for our train tickets, it seemed that my CFA-padded hips were ominously slim. Sitting in the comfortable ex-Italian (why Italian?) railway carriage, I counted our remaining notes and realised that we were broke. Seriously broke. Almost destitute. Without money for transport to Galim, without money for even the meanest doss-houses, with scarcely enough money for the next fortnight's food. Suddenly Egbert became financially as well as emotionally important. If the horse awaiting us were not Egbert, or if we couldn't sell him in Mayo Darlé, we would have to borrow from the Foxes.

'Why are we broke?' demanded Rachel.

I did sums on the back of my diary. During the past week we had spent more than 50,000 CFA (about £110) on antibiotics, pain-killers, dental expenses, transport and exit visas – all, except the last, unexpected expenses. (In Cameroon antibiotics are sold at criminally inflated prices.) And those 50,000 CFA made all the difference between having more than enough to get back to Heathrow and not having enough to eat.

'This is a challenge!' I said brightly. 'We're spoiled First Worlders – it won't do us any harm to be destitute for a fortnight.'

Rachel grunted unenthusiastically, looking as though she'd recently had enough challenges, and swallowed her second dose of Ampicillan.

Cameroonian rail travel is orderly and dull, compared to its Indian equivalent, but in our debilitated condition that suited us; we needed rest more than local colour. The carriages were clean and without visible livestock, though towards dawn sounds of muffled crowing came from under one seat. When the train pulled out, only half an hour late, it was full but not overcrowded. After so long in the bush, hearing only Pidgin, Foulfouldé and local languages, it seemed odd to hear our fellow-passengers conversing animatedly in French. (The Francophones speak French much more fluently than the Anglophones speak English.) But for once we didn't become socially involved: soon we were sound asleep.

I awoke at dawn feeling *won-der-ful* – not only pain-free but unsore. ('It's the saliva,' said Rachel scientifically. 'Mouth sores always heal quickly.')

That was a cool, cloudy dawn and through a haze of light rain I gazed across miles of green scrubby hills. The few compounds of small thatched huts looked impoverished and there was little cultivation. Yet the locals seemed sturdy and cheerful. Perhaps they eat a lot of fish; for the rest of the way the track ran close beside the broad brown Vina river.

At 7 a.m. we stopped for an hour at a small station where no one got on or off but much trading took place between hungry travellers and enterprising locals. One of the main items was delicious thick dark honey, sold in large whiskey, gin or vodka bottles at 500 CFA (just over £1) each. As honey is good for convalescents, we invested. The young man beside Rachel was such an addict that he at once ate half his bottle out of the palm of his hand. In between lickings he told us that N'gaoundere's population is '30,000 – or maybe 50,000'.

Whatever its population, the Fulani capital is very much our sort of place. A straggling, friendly pre-colonial town, its old imposing Lamidat and its new less imposing mosque seem far more important than the extensive but decaying colonial district. To have arrived on the first day of Id was the sort of good fortune scatty travellers like the Murphies do not deserve. As we walked the mile or so from the station to the town centre, many groups of children and young people were already out showing off their colourful new Id outfits and exchanging Id gifts. And the streets were dominated by horsemen on extravagantly caparisoned steeds – some of the horsemen, aged eight or ten, having trouble because their steeds were too fiery.

Our food ration for that day consisted of honey on two warm crisp baguettes. We breakfasted near the mosque, an otherwise handsome building spoiled – as is the enormous new Catholic church at Fundong – by peculiarly virulent stained glass windows.

Suddenly the equestrian excitement all around reached a crescendo. Then eight-foot-long copper trumpets were blown by 'slaves' in knee-length tunics as the Lamido emerged from his palace at the head of a medieval procession – mounted on a charger and brandishing a spear. Beside him walked an improbably tall retainer, gorgeously robed and twirling a colossal blue and white umbrella above his master's turbaned head. The horses' manes were tightly plaited and their bridles lavishly decorated with coloured beads and woollen bobbles. Their warrior riders wore fine old brocade gowns, immensely long cummerbunds (to be taken off later and waved during mock battles) and ancient embossed leather knee-boots. Small boys riding small ponies carried small spears. Everyone chanted vigorously to the sound of war-drums, cymbals and trumpets.

Enthralled, we accompanied this exercise in nostalgia through the town centre to a sandy parade-ground. There a huge crowd had assembled to watch daring feats of horsemanship, processions of 'slaves' (old men who may well have been born into slavery), processions of solemnly dancing women singing songs to inspire the warriors, and processions of riderless horses being led by 'slaves'. After several ritualistic mock battles, the Lamido was fanned with ostrich feathers while holding a Council of War. Then without warning he galloped off, spear poised, leading all his warriors in a charge that raised so much dust we soon lost sight of them. But ten minutes later they were back to report 'victory', before twice repeating the performance. Finally, at sunset, there was a public concert of martial music in the Lamidat – to which even we were admitted, on condition we left our boots outside.

Since we could afford neither supper nor '33', we retired early and hungry to a sleeping-place chosen earlier, a small colonial covered grandstand overlooking the parade-ground. The Gendarmerie was nearby and lest vagrants might be unwelcome to sleep on their territory we didn't switch on our torch while spreading space-blankets as insulation against the chill of concrete. Again we both slept deeply, despite empty bellies.

The dawn revealed a bag of mangoes lying a few yards away: relief supplies delivered by Fate. Slavering, I seized it. Scores of cockroaches rushed out but had left fourteen fat ripe mangoes unscathed. Beside the nearest standpipe, we enjoyed a filling if unbalanced breakfast.

Although Rachel's sores were improving fast, it seemed advisable to spend that day lazing around in N'gaoundere. Since we couldn't afford bush-taxis, and hitch-hiking is not on in the Third World, getting to Makelele might involve a lot of leg-work.

The ulcers had to be regularly stuped and squeezed, then painted with mercurachrome and securely plastered against the dust. While scrounging boiling water at the Catholic Mission we heard a rumour that the Norwegian Lutheran Mission jeep just might be going to Galim next day ... But our three-mile walk to that Mission (a suburb in itself) was energy wasted. Even had the rumour been true – it wasn't – we intuited that the jeep's owners would much prefer *not* to have us aboard. They were very clean young Americans and Scandinavians.

Beside the road a nausea-inducing municipal dump – stinking hillocks of rotting refuse – extended for a mile or so. People live opposite, scarcely twenty yards away, in dreary slummy shacks. We returned to the town centre by another route, through a hilly district of attractive Fulani compounds – urban compounds, with high blank mud walls as in old Persian villages. Outside an enormous enclosed market, near the Lamidat, we sat watching the afternoon world go by and enviously sniffing kebabs while trying to concentrate on the millions who endure hunger not merely for a few days but for *life* ... Then suddenly it was dark and all the street stall-holders frantically packed up and vanished. This was a Big Un. For two hours we Scrabbled on the wide concrete verandah of an abandoned colonial-type shop while the street in front of us became a river.

The charcoal-grey sky was almost touching the roof tops as we wandered on, feeling chilled and hungry-gloomy. We were not surprised when the storm resumed, driving us onto the balcony of a beat-up chop-house-cum-bar where we were tortured by the sight and smell of two men eating pasta and mince. When a smiling youth came to take our order my self-control snapped. 'Let's share a "33"!' I suggested – and was not opposed. Never have the Murphies drunk a beer so slowly.

This odd establishment, at a road junction on a hilltop, was open on three sides to the elements. As these became ever more ferocious, we huddled in sagging, brown plastic-covered armchairs in the balcony's one sheltered corner, while an icy gale drove sheets of rain across the few little tables and flooded the floor.

Then Belo appeared, racing up the steps from the street: tall, slim, handsome, kindly. A young Fulani aristocrat, he had just bought this chop-house; he apologised for its beat-up state; soon he would improve it. For eight years he had been working as an interpreter with the Peace Corps and similar organisations: his English, French and German were equally fluent. Moreover, he thought he knew of a jeep, bound for Tignère next day, in which we could travel free. Obviously, though not brashly, he was a rich man. And by this stage of malnutrition even Rachel was without hang-ups about accepting an invitation from someone for whom we had no dash.

This was our only experience of an urban Fulani home. Belo's 'town-house', one of many large though jerry-built bungalows in a tree-rich suburb, also accommodated four non-rent paying village students who otherwise could not have afforded to live in the city. He had no servant and himself cooked our supper of noodles and scrambled eggs: an unhappy-sounding combination, but to us, that evening, a food of the gods. It seems Fulani frugality survives city life. Although adequately comfortable, Belo's bungalow was free (apart from a compound-blaster) of those non-essentials which most rich non-Fulanis find irresistible. Belo vacated his own bedroom for us; he was in any case going to a late-night Id party which we convalescents deemed it prudent to eschew. By 9 p.m. we were asleep on a Dunlopillo double-mattress on the floor. As our host sensibly observed, 'Soft mattresses don't need legs.'

Next morning Rachel's ulcers were no longer painfully inflamed; no wonder Cameroonians see antibiotics as White Man's magic. While Belo prepared breakfast – clove tea and fresh baguettes – we conversed with four pet rabbits who lived, apparently happily, in a huge raised cage opposite the kitchen window. He had bought them as a novel source of food, then fallen hopelessly in love with them. They had been bred, he told us, in Bamenda – by the Parkinsons.

News came then of the Tignère-bound jeep's indisposition; it was awaiting a 'piece' from Yaoundé and would not be travelling for a few days – 'or it could be a few weeks,' Belo admitted cheerfully. He urged us to wait for it: 'I would like you to meet all my friends in N'gaoundere and to stay with my family in our village.' Sadly we declined this invitation, explaining that our allotted span in Cameroon was running out. At 7.45 a.m. we set off to walk, if necessary, to Tignère, on a virtually traffic-free earth-track. The distance is only eighty miles: at worst, without lifts, a three-day marathon.

This was a new and pleasing landscape: lowish mountains, thick green scrub, thin jungle, poor land populated only by a few gaunt cattle and Bantu converts to Islam. For four hours the sky remained overcast and the temperature comfortable. Then the noon sun emerged, but just as we were beginning to wilt a pick-up truck, laden with Fulanis returning from the Id celebrations, gave us a free thirty-mile lift.

During the next ten hot miles I kept Rachel under close though unobtrusive observation, watching for signs of over-fatigue. But she seemed astonishingly fit – an impressive advertisement for Ampicillan.

That was one of our lucky days. In a tiny village an antique Tignère-bound lorry was already packed with people, poultry, goats, sacks and sheep; but somehow room can always be found for a few more bodies and after some haggling the driver agreed to take us cut-price – for 500 CFA.

Half an hour later a violent storm broke. Everyone had seen the black clouds speeding towards us from the north, across a flattish expanse of bush, yet the driver's assistant waited until we were being drenched before beginning to untie the unwieldy tarpaulin. This had to be held down by all the passengers, including me, along the sides of the lorry, as the gale tried to tear it from our hands. The man beside me was wearing over his shoulder a quiverful of arrows – which threatened, in the dark confusion below the tarpaulin, to pierce my right breast.

Remembering the drought-stricken Tignère we had left, it was a relief to see the town flooded – the river impassable to motor vehicles. Regretfully we passed the Faro, unable to afford even a shared '33', and as the sun set we hastened to the Mission and confessed to Father Walter that we were destitute. He already had another guest, a young priest recently arrived from London and touring the various Mill Hill Missions before settling down on his own patch. Rachel went early to bed (walking twenty-two miles on ulcerated legs eventually takes its toll) and the rest of us made merry on the newcomer's Duty-free. I learned a lot that evening, listening to an exchange of illusions and disillusionments between an enthusiastic fledgling and a wise old owl who had spent more than quarter of a century in Cameroon. On one point Father Walter was emphatic. 'Europeans and Africans never have understood each other and never will. You'll meet many Europeans who'll claim to know what makes the African tick, but either they're fooling themselves or trying to fool you. Most Africans are more realistic. They don't even *pretend* to understand the whiteman . . .'

As the sun rose, we were following that familiar motor track towards the Customs Post. I had considered using the Garbaia valley bush-paths, but if again lucky with lifts we would get to Makelele much more quickly by returning to Galim and ascending from Wogomdou. We therefore turned left, just before coming to the Customs Post, and stayed with the 'fair weather' motor track.

This was a sparsely populated and ruggedly beautiful region of jungly green mountains, deep red gullies and long, wide, scrubby slopes. We were climbing steadily, under a blessedly grey sky, and soon the air felt cool. Recent storms had reduced the track to chaos and after twelve miles Rachel wondered, 'Is this still "*fair* weather"?' But moments later we were extraordinarily lucky. The first and only vehicle to appear – an almost empty pick-up truck – gave us a free ride to the far side of Galim, where the climb to Wogomdou begins.

A mini-meal of one baguette and four bananas felt like inadequate fuel for our long ascent below all those curiously decorated mountains. But we consoled each other with thoughts of fufu and jammu-jammu in the Chief's compound. This track had by now been so rain-ravaged that in places it was almost impossible to keep upright; and in mid-afternoon a hailstorm further lowered morale. Yet we arrived outside the Chief's palace at 5.15 p.m. Having carried the rucksack for twenty-seven miles I experienced a weird sensation of weightlessness when free of it and could empathise with astronauts on the moon. Walking into the Chief's compound, I imagined I was about to lose contact with the ground.

Poverty brings out the worst in one; furtively I had been fantasising about free beers, this being the village where we so lavishly entertained the populace on our previous visit. But word soon got around that now we were destitute and our matutinal drinking-companions never reappeared. Instead, we were entertained until sunset by half a dozen youths – the Chief's sons – who brought two more than usually uncomfortable folding-chairs and a giant basin of cold washing water. They apologised for its being unheated; following the late arrival of the rains, all women were away in distant fields doing emergency planting and not returning home in the evenings. As a half-moon rose, the youths said goodnight and vanished, leaving us sitting outside the thatched guest hut in a strangely silent compound.

The entire village, we then realised, was smokeless; it seemed Wogomdou's sexist men were going to retire empty-bellied.

We looked at each other, despairingly, by moonlight. 'Surely,' said Rachel, 'someone must feed the *Chief*?'

Moments later he appeared, for the first time that evening, and welcomed us warmly, laying a faintly flickering lantern at our feet. Then he too said goodnight and withdrew to his nearby sleeping hut with his youngest son, aged about eight.

We had one tin of sardines left, and two small stale shop buns.

'Let's eat them now,' I said, 'or we'll be too hungry to sleep.'

'Let's wait till 8.00,' said Rachel. 'Fufu *may* come.' But it didn't.

We supped sitting on the edge of our hut's only furniture, a single unblanketed pallet covered with stiff goat-skins. As we ate, Rachel drew a nice distinction between *hospitality* (obligatory when strangers of any type or colour arrive in a village) and *generosity*, which here would have involved an individual decision to stand us a beer or two now we were down on our luck. Tradition does not encourage individual decisions and so does not prompt generosity.

At dawn, to avoid a 4,000-foot climb on empty bellies, we asked our host if bananas were available. Earlier, they had been cheap and plentiful in Wogamdou; now they were very scarce indeed. The Chief himself anxiously banana-hunted and twenty minutes later presented us with twelve chubby specimens which we ate on the spot.

Luckily it had been a rainless night; twenty-four hours previously no one could have crossed the 'rock-bridge' river. As it was, we needed advice and physical support from a young man guiding a donkey whose load was saturated. We also had difficulty fording another wide river, furiously flooded and waist deep, with high steep banks of soft black mud. This obstacle didn't bother three heavily laden donkeys whose owner crossed dryly by hitching up his skirt and vaulting onto the hindquarters of the last animal.

It was market-day in Wogamdou and on the crest of a long ridge three laughing women, surrounded by pickins, were selling hot chunks of roast manioc for 50 CFA (about 10p) each. We sat indulging ourselves on a sun-warmed boulder, rejoicing to have found this cheap but effective fuel for the final, near-vertical ascent. Several colourful groups were descending from the heights, appearing and disappearing on the gold-green slopes ahead. When eventually we met them, most knew of Egbert's loss and our present quest and we were greeted like old friends.

By 9.30 a.m. we were *up* and an hour later came to a milk-bar. There a courteous Nigerian worker requested a small boy to provide us with pints and pints and pints of what is, when the chips are down, the best drink in the world.

This direct (we hoped) Wogamdou-Makelele route crossed unfamiliar territory, though several distant peaks and towering escarpments were usefully recognisable. From the milk-bar a testing pathlet led us around a succession of ever-higher mountains. In the rain-cleared air, immense expanses of forested foothills were visible on our right with every detail distinct – like the three mighty waterfalls gleaming white on blue-green slopes many miles away.

At noon we reached wide green pastureland where the wind was strong and singing, and diaphanous scarves of cloud streaked a cobalt sky. Rachel suddenly exclaimed, 'You're right! This place *is* special!' And we agreed that the beauty of the Tchabal Mbabo will be with us forever.

Towards sunset it seemed we would have to camp on the only available flat ground, the crest of a high ridge. A storm was imminent but the area appeared to be uninhabited; we had seen nobody for two hours. Then a Fulani came into view, carrying a load of long branches from a nearby wooded cleft. He paused, laid down his burden (an umbrella was tied on top) and waited for us. After the statutory greetings he pointed into a narrow valley, at the base of a colossal fluted rock-wall, and smilingly beckoned us to follow him. On the way down a fearsome gradient, we saw smoke beginning to rise from Mahounde's hidden compound. He was, it later transpired, a quarterchief; but the rest of that scattered quarter remained invisible.

Soon the storm broke with menacing violence and continued all night; in our tent we would have endured eleven hours of hungry misery. As it was, we had two suppers. Mahounde permanently employed a Bantu couple, Mr and Mrs Asa-Ah, who occupied two square thatched huts (an unusual shape here) outside the wickerwork 'wall' of this otherwise tin-roofed compound. Mr Asa-Ah hurried to greet us on arrival. Then much later, when we had just finished a mountainous meal of rice and herby mutton stew, Mrs Asa-Ah hastened through the downpour, beaming and chuckling, to place before us a huge dish of mildly curried mutton and four giant puff-puffs.

Once the gender-confusion had been sorted out, our gentle and charming host brought his wives and adolescent daughters to sit with us. By this stage the language barrier was rather lower than it had been and we remember that compound-evening as one of our happiest.

Mahounde looked worried when we sped away, unfed, at dawn. The storm had just abated and for an hour our pace was slowed by a dense resting cloud which reduced visibility to some fifty yards. Our faint path was sporadic and, where it faded completely, one couldn't see it reappearing ahead. But here my human compass covered herself in glory; she now knew *exactly* where Makelele was.

Mercifully the cloud had dispersed when we came to an Ndung-type gradient. The path, scarcely a foot wide, was interrupted by three long outcrops of sloping rock, smooth and damp and overhanging a sheer 400-foot drop. I sweated with fear as I crossed these. 'You really do love Egbert, don't you?' commented Rachel.

Each of the region's many streams was now a challenging tumultuous torrent and we were frequently saturated from the waist down – occasionally from the arm-pits down. 'We'll need luck,' I remarked, 'to get Egbert across those two rivers near Sambolabbo.'

'I thought,' said Rachel dryly, 'our plan was to try to sell him in Makelele?'

'We should get a *much* better price in Mayo Darlé,' I said tendentiously.

At midday we were walking for an hour above that most beautiful of all our campsites, where Egbert disappeared – the corner of Cameroon we know most intimately. Here Rachel became solicitous for my mental/emotional balance and warned, 'Be prepared for this horse to be *not* Egbert!'

In Hama Aoudi many greeted us, and revived us with milk, and knew we had returned to be united with our lost horse.

'It *must* be Egbert!' I exclaimed, as we set off on the last lap.

'It *may* be Egbert,' said Rachel firmly.

By 4.30 p.m. we were in Makelele, where the beaming Chief himself conducted us back to his brother's guest hut. At once all our old (young) friends joyfully swarmed around but the Chief left immediately and we expected 'the horse' to appear at any moment.

Milk was provided, followed by fried manioc. Time passed ... More time passed ... And yet more time passed ...

'We really have gone native,' observed Rachel. 'For days we've been busting ourselves to get here and *see* this horse. But now somehow we're able to wait *genuinely* patiently. Funny how Africa gets to one!'

She was right. I felt completely relaxed: but perhaps only because I had no doubt that 'the horse' *was* Egbert.

At 5.50 he arrived, cantering up the slope from the track with a grinning small boy on his back. Self-respect compels me to draw a veil over our reunion; intrepid travellers are supposed to be made of sterner stuff ... The family fell about. They understand people loving horses but they do not understand demonstrations of that emotion.

Predictably, our hero looked somewhat the worse for wear. Clearly he had been ridden hard and often; his coat was sticky and spiky with dried sweat. Also, he had several potentially lethal, vividly coloured ticks embedded near the root of his tail and around his genitals. When I had removed these I groomed him vigorously and within fifteen minutes he was looking much more like 'our Eggles'. (His Irish head-collar had of course 'got lost'.)

But what was the story? Where and when and how and by whom had Egbert been found? The vet was in Banyo and no one knew when next he might visit Makelele. His engaging fourteen-year-old son, Pierre – eldest of the Makelele family – spoke adequate French but was uninformative. We dashed him 2,000 CFA (about £4.50), set aside for that purpose (one-tenth of the specified ransom!) and Rachel wrote Papa an effusive thank-you letter in French. To this day we don't know the story.

As we devoured our unadorned fufu (the jammu-jammu contained rotten meat), Pierre confirmed that it would make economic sense to sell Egbert in Mayo Darlé. Horses abound in Makelele, and Egbert, being docile, was held in low esteem. Fulani horsemen favour fiery steeds, whom only the brave dare mount. And fieriness was not among Egbert's many virtues; a toddler could have ridden him down a precipice. His market-value in Makelele was zero.

'You do look pleased!' said Rachel. 'Are you really going to enjoy trekking for days on an empty belly?'

'We won't have to,' I retorted. 'Now we *know* we've got Egbert we can spend all we've left. We'll surely be able to sell him for at least £50.'

Two Whites and a laden horse send Cameroonians' eyebrows into their curls. Two Whites – one carrying a huge load – and an *unladen* horse confirm a widely held view that all Whites are nutty. But, ironically, our forced march to Mayo Darlé (eighty-seven miles in three days) would not have been possible with a laden Egbert. Unladen, he often trotted of his own volition and I suspected him of wickedly relishing this ludicrous role reversal.

A forced march was essential because so little time remained before our unalterable date of departure from Cameroon. As it was, we could spend only two days in Mayo Darlé: not long enough to find a suitably kind buyer, though Egbert looked glossily handsome after a prolonged soapy scrub-down in the river. So we left him with the Foxes, who lent us 35,000 CFA (about £80). The arrangement was that they would sell him to the sort of person who *deserved* to own him and keep the profit – if any.

As we left the Mission compound, soon after sunrise, Egbert was grazing fifty yards away by the 'parish hall'. I glanced at him, but chose not to say goodbye.

'I'll bet,' said Rachel, 'he reckons he's well rid of those crazy Whites!'

Two months later John Fox wrote to us: 'You are daily in our thoughts because of the continuing presence at Mayo Darlé of Egbert, who is back in fine form after some horse complaint that required injections. Yaya takes care of him with a zeal and a devotion worthy of a Derby winner and has already initiated him into the repertoire of Islamic warhorse for the occasional parades which occur at the Lamido's Banyo palace.'

Four months later the most significant of our Christmas cards – the one that really made our festive season joyous – was a large photograph of Egbert taken in mid-November. A beaming Yaya and his two-year-old son Ibrahim were in the saddle and Jacqueline's letter reported:

'As you can see, Egbert is still part of the family! Not so long after you left, Yaya fell in love with him and was praising his qualities and good-natured character every minute. So, guessing you would agree with me, I decided not to sell him but to leave him in Yaya's possession.'

Index

TRANSYLVANIA AND BEYOND

Dervla Murphy

After the fall of the Ceausescu dictatorship in 1990, Dervla Murphy spent eight important months of her life in Transylvania, immersing herself in the Rumanians' every day lives and culture.

Her travels by bicycle and on foot, led her through the remotest areas of the Carpathians, where she was to meet people who were still both bewildered and exhilarated by the news of the revolution, a revolution they never thought would happen. . .

On her second visit in 1991, she discovered a profound change in the national mood. She also experienced overwhelming hospitality, making friends from all walks of life. Through her friends' eyes she has gained a profound insight into the hopes and fears they have for their country, a country that could be considered the least European of all.

Transylvania and Beyond is a thought-provoking and moving account of one country's fight to recover from the oppression of communism and one woman's fight to understand it.

'**This book of travels opens in a style which no novelist could better.**'
Country Life

FULL TILT

Dervla Murphy

Dervla Murphy, on her trusty bicycle, Roz — short for Rozinante — pedalled some three thousand miles across Europe, through Persia and Afghanistan, over the Himalayas to Pakistan, and on into India.

The epic six-month journey began during the worst winter in living memory and even when the weather improved, there were enough difficulties and dangers to satisfy the most dedicated traveller.

But although the solitary cyclist was grateful for the revolver packed in her saddle-bag, she found, in spite of vanishing tracks and political chaos, a world full of unexpected kindnesses.

'Captivating . . . a curious fascination, and enchantment that holds the reader so engrossed as would an exciting thriller'
Irish Independent

WHERE THE INDUS IS YOUNG

Dervla Murphy

Dervla Murphy and her six-year-old daughter Rachel were very thankful for the warm clothes — and the local diet of dried apricots — when they spent three months in Baltistan, a desolate but beautiful region of Kashmir.

Their journey took mother and child into the Karakorum mountains in the heart of the western Himalayas and along the perilous Indus Gorge.

Accompanied only by a gallant polo pony, they endured conditions that tested their limits of ingenuity, fortitude and courage and, remarkably, with little loss of good humour.

'Distinguished by qualities of heart and endurance . . . engaging, brave and humorous'
Sunday Telegraph

IN ETHIOPIA WITH A MULE

Dervla Murphy

Dervla Murphy and her amiable pack-mule, Jock, set out on a hazardous trek through Ethiopia's remote and hostile regions — against official advice.

During the gruelling journey, she was robbed three times, yet the Ethiopian highlanders were usually hospitable and her dependence on them and increasing familiarity with their way of life broke down the barriers. Reaching Addis Ababa, she concluded that this growth of affection for another race 'Is the real achievement and richest reward of such a journey'.

'Puts her among the select travel writers of the last two decades'
Observer

EIGHT FEET IN THE ANDES·

Dervla Murphy

The eight feet belong to Dervla Murphy, her nine-year-old daughter Rachel and Juana, an elegant mule, united in an unusual 'Andean frolic'.

Together, they clambered the length of Peru, from Cajamarca on the border with Ecuador, to Cuzco, the ancient Inca capital, over 1,300 miles to the south.

With only the most basic necessities to sustain the intrepid trio, their journey was marked by extreme discomfort, occasional danger and even the temporary loss of Juana over a precipice. Yet mother and daughter alike were unflagging in their sympathetic response to the perilous beauty and the impoverished people of the Andes.

'The best sort of travel book . . . delightful and satisfying'
The Irish Times

ON A SHOESTRING TO COORG

Dervla Murphy

From Bombay to the hippy beaches of Goa and on to the tropical tip of India, travelling by boat and bus, staying in fisherman's huts and no-star hotels, Dervla Murphy and her five-year-old daughter Rachel, explored the south.

En route, they fell in love with the tiny mountain paradise of Coorg, whose landscapes and people form the focus of a wonderfully evocative and entertaining travel diary.

'Here is a new vision of the subcontinent'
Times Literary Supplement

'She is the best kind of travel writer; observant, high-spirited, open-minded ... and Rachel is a honey'
Sunday Telegraph

SPANISH PILGRIMAGE

Robin Hanbury-Tenison

For a thousand years, a long, hot, dangerous track over mountains, arid plains and rich countryside has led pilgrims to the great cathedral of St James at Santiago de Compostela. From Roncesvalles in the Pyrenees to rain-washed Galicia, the route covers all the variety of Northern Spain's countryside, with centuries of history and legend.

With his wife Louella and four-year-old Merlin, Robin Hanbury-Tenison travelled this route the traditional way; riding white horses and with the pilgrim's scallop shell emblazoned on their shirts. Their vividly told adventures taught them more about the people and the country than any conventional traveller could learn, and their 'green pilgrimage' reveals a new, ecological vision for tomorrow's world.

MULU

Robin Hanbury-Tenison

The Gunung Mulu National Park in Sarawak, north Borneo, one of the most remote and untouched regions of tropical rain forest left in the world.

In 1977 Robin Hanbury-Tenison and a team of scientists began a study of this beautiful yet hazardous terrain — a dense virgin forest teeming with exotic new species and home to the nomadic Penan tribe. With its breathtaking network of caves, lush hidden valleys, and spectacular mountain range, Mulu proved to be one of the most valuable regions of natural beauty left in the world.

Now, fifteen years on, the Mulu National Park remains virtually intact while the tragic destruction of the surrounding areas stands as yet another example of the senseless exploitation of our planet.

Mulu was the first popular book to bring to the world's attention the significance of the rain forests to our fragile ecosystem. This updated reissue is a timely reminder of our need to preserve them for the future.

IN SEARCH OF GENGHIS KHAN

Tim Severin

In the Month of the Horse, in the Year of the White Horse, Tim Severin along with six Mongol companions and photographer Paul set out on an extraordinary journey. Intent on following the paths trodden by the soldiers of Genghis Khan in the thirteenth century, they ventured to cross some of the most remote and inhospitable territory of Mongolia, the Dead Heart of Asia.

Many surprises awaited them as they found their way through the barren terrain: the August snows, the Black Death that still raged, the ancient lamas and the toothless shaman woman. But perhaps the greatest surprise was that after years of Communist repression, the Mongols are once again free to worship the cult of Genghis Khan without giving offence to the Soviets: the name of their infamous leader and law-giver is now to be found everywhere across Mongolia.

'Written with all the wit and assurance we have come to expect from this remarkable author, *In Search of Genghis Khan* is . . . a delight'
Daily Mail

More best-selling travel books from Arrow

☐ Full Tilt	Dervla Murphy	£5.99
☐ Where the Indus is Young	Dervla Murphy	£5.99
☐ In Ethiopia with a Mule	Dervla Murphy	£5.99
☐ Eight Feet in the Andes	Dervla Murphy	£5.99
☐ On a Shoestring to Coorg	Dervla Murphy	£4.99
☐ Muddling Through in Madagascar	Dervla Murphy	£4.99
☐ Spanish Pilgrimage	Robin Hanbury-Tenison	£5.99
☐ Mulu	Robin Hanbury-Tenison	£6.99
☐ A Ride Along the Great Wall	Robin Hanbury-Tenison	£4.99
☐ In Search of Genghis Khan	Tim Severin	£6.99
☐ The Sinbad Voyage	Tim Severin	£6.99
☐ The Ulysses Voyage	Tim Severin	£3.50
☐ Crusader	Tim Severin	£5.99

Prices and other details are liable to change

ARROW BOOKS, BOOKSERVICE BY POST,
PO BOX 29, DOUGLAS, ISLE OF MAN, BRITISH ISLES

NAME —————————————————————————————

ADDRESS ————————————————————————————

—————————————————————————————————

Please enclose a cheque or postal order made out to Arrow Books Ltd. for the amount due and allow the following for postage and packing.

U.K. CUSTOMERS: Please allow 75p per book to a maximum of £7.50

B.F.P.O. & EIRE: Please allow 75p per book to a maximum of £7.50

OVERSEAS CUSTOMERS: Please allow £1.00 per book.

Whilst every effort is made to keep prices low it is sometimes necessary to increase cover prices at short notice. Arrow Books reserve the right to show new retail prices on covers which may differ from those previously advertised in the text or elsewhere.